1995

The project of this book is to question and rewrite assumptions about the nature of the Augustan era through an exploration of Jacobite ideology. Taking as its starting point the fundamental ambivalence of the Augustan concept the author studies canonical and non-canonical literature and uncovers a new 'four nations' literary history of the period defined in terms of a struggle for control of the language of authority between Jacobite and Hanoverian writers. This struggle is seen to have crystallized Irish and Scottish opposition to the British state. The Jacobite cause generated powerful popular literature and the sources explored include ballads, broadsides and writing in Scots, Irish, Welsh and Gaelic. The author concludes that the literary history we inherit is built on the political outcome of the Revolution of 1688.

CAMBRIDGE STUDIES IN EIGHTEENTH-CENTURY
ENGLISH LITERATURE AND THOUGHT 23

Poetry and Jacobite Politics in Eighteenth-Century Britain and Ireland

# Poetry and Jacobite Politics in Eighteenth-Century Britain and Ireland

MURRAY G. H. PITTOCK

*Department of English Literature,*
*University of Edinburgh*

Published by the Press Syndicate of the University of Cambridge
The Pitt Building, Trumpington Street, Cambridge CB2 1RP
40 West 20th Street, New York, NY 10011–4211, USA
10 Stamford Road, Oakleigh, Melbourne 3166, Australia

First published 1994

Printed in Great Britain at the University Press, Cambridge

*A catalogue record for this book is available from the British Library*

*Library of Congress cataloguing in publication data*
Pittock, Murray.
Poetry and Jacobite politics in eighteenth-century Britain and Ireland /
Murray G.H. Pittock.
p.    cm. – (Cambridge studies in eighteenth-century English literature and thought)
Includes bibliographical references.
ISBN 0 521 41092 4 (hardback)
1. English literature – 18th century – History and criticism – Theory, etc.
2. Politics and literature – Great Britain – History – 18th century.
3. Popular literature – Great Britain – History and criticism.
4. Politics and literature – Ireland – History – 18th century.
5. Great Britain – Politics and government – 18th century.
6. Popular literature – Ireland – History and criticism.
7. Politics and government – 18th century.
8. Celtic literature – History and criticism.
9. Canon (Literature).   10. Jacobites.
I. Title.   II. Series.
PR448.P6P58   1994
820.9'005 – dc20   93–42500   CIP

ISBN 0 521 41092 4 hardback

*For Anne*

To make the wrong appear the right,
And keep our rulers in;
In Walpole's time, 'twas Jacobite,
In Pitt's, 'tis Jacobin!
Edward Coxe (1805)

# Contents

# Acknowledgements

My particular thanks are due to those who spurred this project, in special Howard Erskine-Hill, who sought it out, and has himself helped to make central so much that lay on the margins of discussion of major 'Augustan' writers. Such thanks are also due to Frank McLynn, whose redefinitions of the eighteenth century's events opened new ground for understanding its texts, to Ruth Smith, who let me see a great deal of her work while yet unpublished, to Jane Clark's encouragement, and to Charles Jones's groundbreaking work on language in eighteenth-century Scotland. Jonathan Clark referred me to Richard Sharp, who with Lawrence Smith has provided help with some of the evidence adduced. Roger Crisp and his wife Catherine Paxton provided most homely accommodation while I was researching in England, thanks to a research grant secured for me by R. D. S. Jack and Paul Dukes, while Ross Mackenzie as ever helped to keep me right by argufying from his encyclopaedic store of Scottish history. I am indebted to the work of Eveline Cruickshanks, Paul Monod and William Donaldson in general; more specifically to that of Steven Zwicker, Paul Bywaters and James Winn. In my own university department, I have been rewarded by the stimulating company of Geoffrey Carnall and Colin Nicholson and the course we all teach, Politics, Literature and Society 1700–1830. Cairns Craig has been supportive in new approaches to Scottish literature teaching arising from this research. My last and greatest debt is as ever to my wife, Anne, and our daughter Alexandra, who is learning to be patient. In general, thanks are owed to the staff of the National Library of Scotland and the Public Record Office, as well as to the staff at Aberdeen University Special Collections, on whose MacBean collection much of this research was initially built. The Scottish National Portrait Gallery kindly gave permission for the cover picture of James landing in Scotland to be reproduced from their collection. A research grant from the British Academy enabled work in the Bodleian, Cambridge University Library and the Public Record Office to be completed in record time.

Lastly, I am grateful to have had the blessing of growing up in the North East of Scotland; I hope at not too late a date to catch the echoes of its distinctive civilization in the seventeenth and eighteenth centuries.

Edinburgh, 1993

# Introduction

## Historical aims

The aims of this book are threefold. First, it seeks to liberate eighteenth-century literary history from a historiography which has often itself been imprisoned in the construct of Britain we all inherit, predicated as it is on the social, constitutional and political outcomes of the Revolution of 1688/89. 'Augustanism' and 'Enlightenment' as literary concepts have often been popularly based on a view of a civilized and civilizing, stable and metropolitan society in which historians of whatever colour have ceased to believe in the terms literature has absorbed.[1]

This kind of historicizing, sometimes called 'Whig', I label here by the term 'incremental', intending not to write a revisionist view of metropolitan literary history from a differing partisan viewpoint, but instead to uncover the language in which the metropolis, the centre, the imperial state, makes sense of its achievements. 'Incremental' is chosen to indicate the developmental, progress-oriented minimizing of difference in terms of which such history expresses itself. 'Linear', an alternative term, seems to me to insufficiently identify this aspect.

Within the context of the British state (other contexts are suggested in Chapter 1), incremental history's essential premiss is the Revolution of 1688/89 and the constitutional developments which, flowing from it, established the state itself and consolidated the British Empire. Reliance on this premiss requires a commitment to prioritize certain aspects of British political and intellectual life, to minimize opposition and to exclude marginal or different interests: hence Trevelyan's attack on the Highlanders as 'barbarians', and the barely veiled association of Catholicism with arbitrary brutality in traditional assessments of James VII and II.[2]

This imperial Protestant view, has, like the imperial Protestant map, receded. But sophisticated revisions of it are still found, as, for example,

[1] Cf. David Allan, *Virtue, Learning and the Scottish Enlightenment* (Edinburgh: Edinburgh University Press, 1993), for a questioning of traditional positions.
[2] George Macaulay Trevelyan, *England Under the Stuarts*, 14th edn (London, 1928), p. 455.

Linda Colley's recent *Britons*, a book which argues that Protestantism lies at the core of the building/development/convergence of a common British identity. This explicit view of the centrality of religious faith, neglected by many recent historians, is to be welcomed: but Professor Colley's book nonetheless can be seen as reinforcing the lineaments of a much older kind of incremental history. Nonjurors and dissenters are to her book what lies were to Swift's Houyhnhnms: the thing that is not, which enables her to cover Bishop Ken's stand for 'the Catholic Church, before the disunion of East and West' and Quakerism alike with the blanket term 'Protestant'. Despite the book's many excellences, there is no real acknowledgement of the hostility of Anglicans towards dissenters, or of the variety of religious fragmentation thus compressed by purposive hindsight. Scottish Episco-palians find no place, and nor does Ireland: in fact, it is deliberately excluded, as incremental history must exclude it, for it is an embarrass-ment to 'Britain'. 'It seems history is to blame', as Haines says to Stephen Daedalus.[3]

These margins are relevant. Ireland's population was not far behind England's in the eighteenth century, and the population of the Scottish Highlands was five times what it now is. Thus even purely in terms of demography, the Jacobite threat was greater in the centre's perception than a centralizing history can now make it. This book intends to enter literary history by the margins of eighteenth-century politics: not only the geographical, demographical and confessional margins, but also the *sub rosa* whispers of marginal speech of discontent within the British state.

This book's first aim thus gives rise to two more. It attempts to weaken the border between canonical and non-canonical literature in the eighteenth century in the interests of exposing a shared language of cipher and allusion in response to a changing polity which politicizes the tradi-tional core of Augustan writing in ambivalent terms. Connexions between high cultural writing and other kinds of cultural transmission throughout the British Isles are used both to establish ideas of a 'mediated text' in the circles of Jacobite opposition, and also to show general similarities as well as differences in such practice throughout the four nations.

Thus thirdly, the aim is to catch up with historical thinking by offering, for the first time, 'four nations' literary history. Such a move is intended not only to allow what has been called 'Augustanism' to detach itself from old historiographical positions, but also to give an account of literature's politicizing of and by history in both incremental and typological modes. Typological history, history as recurrence and renewal, spoken of in folk and sacred terms, is the history often chosen by the marginalized and

---

[3] Timothy Ware (Bishop Kallistos), *The Orthodox Church* (Harmondsworth: Penguin, 1982 (1963)), p. 325.

defeated in the account I am offering. It places particular emphasis (of
which more in Chapter 1) on the repetitive or prophetic quality of events.
Such an understanding of history interacts strongly with literature,
because of literature's habit of revisiting compelling images repeatedly.
Dryden and Yeats are only two of the poets who have displayed this at
crucial moments in political history, finding a language of event which
becomes the event itself: 'Did that play of mine send out / Certain men the
English shot?'. Thus what I am aiming to show are meeting-points
between literary and historical understanding of events. Events are the
issue for both kinds of writing, and are what make them one in the field of
typological history. For myths are facts to those who objectify them in
belief, and become part of that nature of things declared by Burke to be a
sturdy adversary.[4]

This book may be accused of overestimating the force of Jacobitism.
Much of the evidence adduced will be, by the nature of things, provisional, codified, uncertain. But there will be a great deal of it, and taken
together I trust it will prevail. It is not intended to show that the vast
majority of English, Scots, Welsh and Irish were Jacobites; only to suggest
that Jacobite and associated nationalist views and beliefs were sometimes
the sympathies of many, and always those of a significant minority.
Edward Gregg, in a recent hostile review of Paul Monod's *Jacobitism and
the English People*, suggests that the Jacobites were like the third party in
British politics, low in bedrock support and good only for a protest vote.
Professor Gregg is psephologically vulnerable here. Not only have the
Liberals / Alliance attracted around 20 per cent of the vote in five of the
last six elections (beside many spectacular by-election victories), but
almost half say they would support them if they had a chance of winning.
This is the core of the matter, and I would claim no more for Jacobitism.
But what should not continue to evade scholarly scrutiny is the assertion
that only those prepared to risk all they owned and a gruesome death can
be counted as interested in supporting the Stuarts.[5]

## Literary evidence

As indicated above, this book looks closely at literature outside the canon.
The corpus of songs and poems we inherit from the Jacobite movement is
of great significance in establishing the ideology and political analyses of
Jacobitism, as well as allowing us to read the Jacobite cause as a contemporary text: relating in literary terms intertextually, in historical terms
evidentially, to its period context.

[4] W. B. Yeats, *The Collected Poems* (London: Macmillan), p. 393.
[5] Edward Gregg, 'Review of Paul Kleber Monod's *Jacobitism and the English People, 1688–1788*, *British Journal for Eighteenth-Century Studies* 16:1 (1993), pp. 71–2.

Unfortunately, anyone approaching the Jacobite lyric with such ideas in mind runs up almost immediately against a scholarly claim which renders this choice research material useless: the view that the Jacobite lyric is usually written subsequently to the events it describes. David Johnson, writing in his *Music and Society in Lowland Scotland in the Eighteenth Century* (1972), argues that

It has been stated that Jacobite songs arose spontaneously out of the Scottish people's deep emotional involvement with the rebellions of 1715 and 1745. I can only say that I have seen no evidence supporting this; most of the recorded Jacobite songs were actually written as an act of self-conscious nationalism, between 1790 and 1820, by such people as James Hogg and Lady Nairne.[6]

This assertion does not receive a footnote, but it is echoed by writers with more specialized interests in the period, such as William Donaldson in *The Jacobite Song* (1988), who calls the 'overwhelming majority' of Jacobite songs 'brilliant fakes': but offers only 'half a dozen titles' of what are, incontrovertibly, late compositions, such as 'The Skye Boat Song' and 'Cam' ye by Athol'. To be fair, the main body of Dr Donaldson's book doesn't quite echo the strength of his introduction's claims : but the scholarly position is plain. Not much faith can be placed in the contemporaneity of the Jacobite song.[7]

Yet I suspect that this widespread view needs to be clarified. What both Johnson and particularly Donaldson may really mean is not that the vast majority of *all* Jacobite song is post-Jacobite, but that the vast majority of *all good* Jacobite song is so. I assume that this is the case because given the vast amount of eighteenth-century printed book and pamphlet Jacobite material any cursory examination of a research library would reveal, it is impossible that it could be otherwise. Indeed, this is the line pursued more explicitly by David Daiches when he argues that it is the aggressive and satirical Jacobite material which is contemporary; the (good?) erotic and sentimental which is later.[8] It is important to make this distinction clear, because if aesthetic quality is all that is at stake, the Jacobite lyric is fully rehabilitated as a historical, if not a literary, document with no further ado.

Quality is a difficult question to tackle academically (if not adminstratively or pedagogically) in the 1990s. It is easier to show that the variety of eighteenth-century Jacobite lyric we inherit is greater than implied above. In 1989, in an annotated edition of a dated Jacobite songbook from the 1740s on contemporary paper, I suggested a threefold categorization of

6  David Johnson, *Music and Society in Lowland Scotland in the Eighteenth Century* (London, 1972), p. 4.
7  William Donaldson, *The Jacobite Song: Political Myth and National Identity* (Aberdeen: Aberdeen University Press, 1988), pp. 3–4.
8  David Daiches, 'Robert Burns and the Jacobite Song', in Donald Low (ed.), *Critical Essays on Robert Burns* (London and Boston: Routledge & Kegan Paul, 1975), pp. 137–56 (138).

the songs we inherit: the aggressive/active song, calling for war or opposition to the Whig state; the erotic song, portraying the absent king as
lover; and the sacred lyric, in defence of Episcopacy or what can only be
called Anglo-Catholicism. That these categories can all be found in the
early eighteenth century was made clear in that edition, and will be made
clearer here. Moreover, I shall argue for a contiguity of Jacobitical interpretation among differing classes and cultures in these islands: that the
erotic ballads of London display a similar iconography of sacred
monarchy to the *aislings* of Munster, and that the 'mediated text' produced through interaction between folk and dispossessed high culture
voiced dissatisfaction in allied terms. That the Jacobite song was crucial
in voicing the ideas and sentiments of the Jacobite cause is clear from its
widespread military use and popularity with the Jacobite leadership,
Charles Edward himself being an afficionado.[9]

But there is yet more to be said than a scouring of archives alone can
reveal. The strong disincentive which existed to writing down Jacobite
songs in the Jacobite period should strongly suggest to us that much of the
lyric corpus is lost, or if not lost, surviving in forms we cannot prove were
contemporary, and yet may well have been. Central to this assertion is the
focal position occupied by Jacobite folk culture, or its propagandistic use
by high culture, during the Jacobite period.

Sometimes the internal evidence of the songs supports this view. The
fine song, 'Lochmaben Gate', first collected by Hogg, has left (apparently) no earlier written trace. But it deals with a particular Jacobite rally
on 27 May 1714, which had been prepared to demonstrate support in that
area of southern Scotland. Such particularity renders a remote date for
composition less likely – many of the Regency or Victorian compositions
are sentimental as much due to their vagueness as anything else. More
important to note is the disproportionate strength of Jacobitism in the
richest folk cultural area of Scotland: the North East. Jean McCann, in
her unjustly neglected thesis 'The Organization of the Jacobite Army,
1745–46' (Edinburgh, 1963), shows how recruitment in the Episcopal
North East was proportionately more than 30 per cent higher than in the
West Highlands. And they took their culture with them. It was a North-
Eastern ballad singer, 'Mussel-Mou'd' Charlie, who was the last survivor
of the 'Fifteen (d. 1782), while the importance of folk and street singers to
the support and spread of Jacobite ideology is recognized by many
writers, beginning with M.G.D. Isaac, in his thesis 'A Study of Popular
Disturbance in Britain 1714–54' (Edinburgh, 1953). Donaldson himself

---

[9] Frank McLynn, *Charles Edward Stuart: A Tragedy in Many Acts* (London: Routledge, 1988),
p. 284.

mentions how limited print runs were used to circulate forbidden propaganda-songs in 'safe' areas.[10]

Also of note is the fact that writers on folklore can find Jacobite songs and attitudes at the heart of the corpus they are studying. Airs such as 'Chevy Chase' seem to have been used to indicate Jacobite support within a ballad tradition entered by explicit Jacobite songs, such as 'Lord Derwentwater's Goodnight' (variants of which even rendered the English earl a Scottish popular hero), while the transmission of that tradition itself could be coloured by political sentiment, as will be evident later. Moreover, the eighteenth century is a period when printed culture is increasingly intruding on and interacting with folk culture. When aided by a nationalist vernacular revival, as in Scotland, or the cross-class outlawry of opposition, favourable historical circumstances were intensified by ideology and opportunity. There was a convergence of high and folk culture in the Jacobite milieu, as those who wished to defend a peculiarly Scottish (or Irish) high culture were forced into alliance with their own folk culture as the only alternative to surrender to the cultural standards of the British state. This is an area of research which strengthens the Jacobite lyric's place in both history and literature, but as yet it has only been touched on: J.G. Simms' chapter on 'Swift and Oral Culture' in Swift's tercentenary tribute volume is one example of this.[11] The process also appears in the adoption of Belhaven's lurid and sententious speech against the Union in the popular broadside, 'Lord Belhaven's Speech in Parliament', one of the early ancestors of the 'bought and sold for English gold' school of Scottish political history:

> While all the world to this day,
> Since Nimrod did a sceptre sway,
> Ensigns for sov'reign power display,
>     Shall it be told,
> We, for a little shining clay,
>     A kingdom sold.[12]

To read this, as so much of early Jacobite poetry, does not dispose one to think of Burns as a faker of Jacobite songs, more a packager, an image-maker, a presenter: those heroes of our age, and the guardians of quality. So perhaps that question is answered too.

[10] James Hogg, *Jacobite Relics*, 2 vols. (Edinburgh, 1819–21), 1: pp. 132, 293n; Alistair and Henrietta Tayler, *Jacobites of Aberdeenshire and Banffshire in the Rising of 1715* (Edinburgh and London: Oliver and Boyd, 1934), p. 146.

[11] Derwentwater is referred to further in Chapter 2; see also Roger McHugh and Philip Edwards (eds.), *Jonathan Swift: A Dublin Tercentenary Tribute* (Dublin: Dolmen Press, 1967), in particular Austin Clarke's essay on 'The Poetry of Swift'.

[12] LORD BELHAVEN'S SPEECH in PARLIAMENT, *The Second Day of November 1706 ... To which is subjoined*, BELHAVEN'S VISION. *A Poem* (Edinburgh: A. Robertson, 1766), p. 35.

The alliance between high and folk cultural perceptions is accompanied by a split between official and unofficial high culture, out of which many historical and typological Jacobite codes were born. Dryden's *Aeneid* was an officially acceptable version of what was unofficially (as Dryden knew when he introduced extensive Jacobite vocabulary into his translation) already a Jacobite document, a statement almost of the Jacobite credo: the exile and restoration of the Trojan Stuart, rightful heir of Brutus, made by James Philp of Almericlose in his *Grameid*, and more explicitly by Maitland in his translation of the central books of the *Aeneid*, dedicated to Mary of Modena in 1691. Throughout the first half of the eighteenth century the *Aeneid* and the plight of the Stuarts was to be linked in the high cultural coda of Jacobitism. Such a typology might suggest to us the inherent political instability of the 'Augustan' concept: the *Aeneid* was after all central to the image of Augustus. The Jacobite lyric, more broadly the Jacobite poem, is itself the key to a literary revisionism of the 1688–1760 period. A Jacobite literature exists for this period at all levels of society, from all points of view, the vanguard in verse for the ideology of the cause, sometimes literally, as when 'The White Cockade' played the Irish Brigades into battle at Fontenoy.[13] It is time to stop demythologizing the documents, either as literature or history. They exist, just as tartan existed before Lord Dacre allows it to.[14]

Variety and quality having been argued for a contemporary Jacobite song, only popularity remains. There are two central points I advance in support of the Jacobite lyric's popularity: the first is its use and adaptation of popular sets and airs, which show an intention to reach an audience familiar with the culturally demotic; the second is its responsibility for maintaining and distributing some of what are now the most widespread songs in our historic culture, such as 'God Save the Queen' and 'Auld Lang Syne' (the first being so strongly Jacobite that a Hanoverian set to it (which we inherit) was one of the government's great propaganda successes in the 1745 Rising). A Jacobite poet like Fergusson's opposition to the invasion of Scots by classical music in the later eighteenth century thus becomes one dimension of Jacobite high culture's affection for a vehicle which presented its aims to a popular audience; a traditionalism also evident in the harpers and bards maintained by Welsh and Irish Jacobite gentry. The folk\orientation of Burns is part of the same pattern: a pattern

---

[13] John Cornelius O'Callaghan, *The Irish Brigades in the Service of France* (Glasgow: Cameron and Ferguson, 1870), p. 355.

[14] Hugh Trevor-Roper, 'The Invention of Tradition: The Highland Tradition of Scotland', in Eric Hobsbawm and Terence Ranger (eds.), *The Invention of Tradition* (Cambridge: Cambridge University Press, 1983), pp. 15–41.

which drew its authority from the conservative reaction against capitalist innovation argued for by both Eric Hobsbawm and E.P. Thompson.[15]

These are the points of departure, and this book allies them both with military attempts to secure the British state for the Stuart cause and with less violent political beliefs which tended to the same end. More Jacobites hoped for another Monck than did for another Montrose, but they are justly termed so for all that. From a language of past events they tried to articulate a restoration of those same events, in speaking history trusting to hear its echo. We speak, or have spoken, a different history, whose echoes do not convict its errors of guilt, as in Stuart drama: it expects to move on. But if we listen for those echoes they are louder than we care to hear, and still resonate in the British state which survives today. So here is offered a reconstruction of the Jacobite voice, without reducing it to the dimensions of war or conspiracy, which those same echoes, at least in fiction, over-throw at last, as that same Stuart drama makes ambivalently plain:

> Integrity of life is man's best friend,
> Which nobly, beyond death, shall crown the end.[16]

---

[15] As in E. P. Thompson, *Customs in Common* (London: Merlin Press, 1991); E. J. Hobsbawm, *Bandits* (London: Weidenfeld & Nicolson, 1969).

[16] Cf. Sandra Clark, *John Webster: The White Devil and The Duchess of Malfi*, Penguin Master-studies (Harmondsworth: Penguin, 1987), p. 122.

# 1

# Invasion and xenophobia

## The breaking image

Thus was Life's Sacred Tree of old
Committed to a Guardian Angel's Care . . .
Thrice happy James, whose First Year's Reign
Hath brought Astraea back to Earth again!

Joshua Barnes

To be sure we may say with Vergilius Maro,
*Fuimus Troes.*[1]

The Baron of Bradwardine

On 5 November 1688, fifty years after the National Covenant had been signed in Edinburgh, William of Orange landed in England. His coming brought full circle Fortune's wheel which had deposed one Stuart through the fanaticism of the northern kingdom, and now evicted another by the fear and apathy of the southern realm.

Like so many patterns of recurrence, this description is too simple to stand as linear history. But to the Stuarts, and to this book which is an explanation of the poetry and ideology of their cause, such a reservation is redundant. For the Stuart cause (and on occasion, the ambition of its kings) was habitually expressed in a language of typology, with metaphors of prophecy and recurrence-salvation history, and not without its messianic force. This offered a profound and rich political analysis of the realms they had lost, won and lost again in the course of half a century. It was also a tongue which, increasingly after 1688, betokened the exclusion it lamented. As this kind of view of history declined in the following century, it was clung to tenaciously by the Stuart cause, and those to whom its interests were allied – and this was to a degree due to the marginalization of the historicity they represented. Typological history, history as recur-

---

[1] G. W. Keaton, *Lord Chancellor Jeffreys and the Stuart Cause* (London: MacDonald, 1965), p. 336; Sir Walter Scott, *Waverley*, ed. Claire Lamont (Oxford: Clarendon Press, 1981), p. 303.

rence, myth, archetype and image is often the history sought by the defeated, whose linearity and incrementality have been exiled into colonialism or absorbed in a greater identity (as 'British' history so often absorbs its peripheries). Incremental, progressive history is on the other hand the language of victory, that of the British state over Scotland, Ireland and the Stuarts being one example famously visible in the broadening from precedent to precedent of classic Whig history; that of Communism over Tsars, White Russians and the Baltic states being another. As is evident from the fate of the latter, incremental history's prophecies of destiny and exclusion of marginal interests (e.g. Scots, Irish or Native Americans in the United States) are not necessarily 'true' any more than is typological history's lamentation, mythogeny and messianic hope. Typological history does not evolve along timescales: it takes a mythic or remote historical era, and glorifies it either to lament its passing or praise its return. The prophets of ancient Israel provide one of the clearest examples of typological history in action, with the nation's past covenant with God always being betrayed and always renewed; others are found in the returning Stuart Aeneas of Dryden, the Cuchulain of Pearse's *Scoil Eanna* and the Rising and the use of Zimbabwe's ruins as a focus for native nationalism in Rhodesia.

These categories are not absolute, but typological and incremental history are habitual opponents along the battle-lines drawn above. Centering, imperial or ideological states usually choose the latter; those whom they usurp the former. The Dalai Lama is renewed from generation to generation as Communist destiny exiles the identity of Tibet. Yeats' 'The Second Coming' is a classic expression of such typological protest against the progressive forward pressure of incremental history. Originally written in outrage at the Bolshevik Revolution and the murder of the Tsar and his family, Yeats' poem denies Communism its claimed historical destiny. It is only a new aberration, a repetition of Cromwell's king-killing (hence the derivation of the 'falcon and falconer' image from Marvell's 'Horatian Ode', itself a wry typological comment on the 'Augustanism' of Cromwell).[2] We are in the era of the 'rough beast', but gyres will narrow again once they have widened, narrow to an era of order (and here the need for typological interpretations of disaster can clearly be seen, since no disaster is irreversible in a history which repeats itself: no gyre will disorderly widen for ever).

This was how the ideology of the Jacobites spoke, particularly in the poetry in which typology's high cultural expressions often display themselves. The Revolution broke the image of kingship restored at the Restoration, but another restoration would come. Appropriately enough, the

---

[2] Murray G. H. Pittock, 'Falcon and Falconer: W. B. Yeats and Marvell's "Horatian *Ode*"', *Irish University Review*, Autumn 1986, pp. 175–9.

man who had sought the role of Vergil to the Stuart Augusti found a
central expression of key metaphors for these events in two great poems:
*Astraea Redux* and the *Aeneid*. In the former poem, Dryden distanced
himself from the Cromwellian era by seeking to herald the return of what
had already been called 'the golden age' of the first Charles: and he did
this by using the classical and Christological typology of Vergil's Fourth
Eclogue, which both reminded its audience of the virgin purity and power
of an earlier Astraea, Elizabeth, and also the martyrdom of the new king's
father. 'Redit et virgo, redeunt Saturnia regna' heads *Astraea Redux*, and is
the keynote to the poem. Though Dryden was not alone in using this
ancient image, most of the other Restoration poems did not do so.[3] And
this was part of his larger design. Thirty-five years after Dryden expressed
a central Vergilian image of Restoration, he found one to express his
outrage at Revolution:

> Arms, and the Man I sing who, forced by Fate
> And haughty *Juno's* unrelenting Hate
> Expell'd and exil'd, left the *Trojan* shoar ...
> His banish'd Gods restor'd to Rites Divine,
> And setl'd sure Succession in his Line ...

The political situation has altered: where *Astraea Redux* is explicit,
Dryden's *Aeneid* deliberately cloaks its politics in translation, a translation
which expresses its typology through hint and allusion in order to speak it
publicly. In this way too, Dryden has fashioned a new metaphor appropriate to changed times: one of form (translation, approximation, code) as
well as content (exile and return).[4]

Yet the translation's message is early apparent, for all its encloaking. As
James Winn observes, where Vergil's hero is forced to fly by fate, 'fato
profugus', Dryden's is 'forced, expell'd and exil'd'. Similarly

Virgil's Aeneas simply brings his household gods into Latium; Dryden *restores*
'His banish'd Gods ... to Rites Divine', a phrase in which some readers surely
read the hopes of the persecuted Catholics.

The idea of 'restoring' of course, links the opening lines of Dryden's
translation with *Astraea Redux*, setting up a recursive link between the
Vergilian texts (as in fact exists) and within history itself, the figures of
Astraea and Aeneas both being cyclical in the sense of their typological
return as just ages or rightful dynastic founders. The shaping force of
Dryden's translation is its intention to reiterate recurrent, as well as
express contemporary history. The restored Augustus of 1660 has become
the wandering Aeneas of 1690, who will, Dryden's Vergil seeks to proph-

---

[3] Howard Erskine-Hill, *The Augustan Idea in English Literature* (London: Edward Arnold, 1983),
pp. 208, 214.
[4] *The Works of John Dryden*, Volume 5, ed. William Frost (Berkeley, CA and London: University
of California Press, 1987), p. 343.

esy, become Augustus once again. 'And settl'd sure Succession in his line'
does not appear in Vergil's text: in Dryden's it tells its own story.[5]

The depth of Dryden's Jacobite language will be discussed more fully in
Chapter 3. But before embarking on a general outline of the language of
Stuart archetypes inherited at the Revolution, it should be said that
Dryden's interpretation of them is at the heart of the matter. This book, in
interpreting Jacobite poetic language in context, seeks to revalue the
Jacobite margins of the incremental account we inherit, robbed as they
are of serious political weight by the politics of hindsight, which have
doomed them to defeat. In doing so, it proposes a new central typological
field to examine these margins and their writers, one less oblique than 'the
gloom of the Tory satirists'. I do not wish to argue that Jacobite ideas had
complete control of a classical and sacred typological critique of the British
state: to say such would be folly, not least because of the ambivalent
expression of the Patriot opposition in the 1730s. But I do wish to suggest a
wider definition of what is Jacobite, at least at the margin, than can be
divined from the number engaged in plotting and warfare. To judge a
modern political party's vote on the number of its activists would be a
gross error; how much more so when to be such an activist was illegally to
risk death? There are perhaps four hundred gunmen in the IRA: the vote
for one of them, Bobby Sands, in one constituency alone was some fifty
times that in 1981, while funds pour into terrorist coffers from respectable
citizens in the United States. In the context of such comparators, to argue
Jacobite strength on the basis of those in arms is unreliable in the extreme.
In 1651 on his march to Worcester, Charles II was hardly more successful
than Charles Edward in attracting English supporters: yet nine years
later, England in large part rejoiced at his restoration. The force mustered
by Henry Tudor in 1485 was smaller than Charles Edward's army: yet we
do not consider that the Tudors governed for over a century on the basis of
coup d'etat alone. Those who accept Jacobitism as a marginal force are
using referents that would not stand the test of comparison. While Dr
Johnson's opinion that a free vote might bring a Stuart restoration is only
opinion, the reader might consider how few in Britain today would give
their lives for a cause, when many would not give a higher marginal rate of
income tax. It is important to demand of those who minimize Jacobitism
an awareness of such comparators, too seldom shown.[6]

'Augustanism' as a traditional category of definition no longer goes
unchallenged, but the very typology inherent in the term has an ambi-

[5] James Anderson Winn, *Dryden and his World* (New Haven and London: Yale University Press,
1987), pp. 487–8.
[6] Cf. Rosalind Mitchison, 'Missing Elements', *London Review of Books*, 14 May 1992, p. 24; Linda
Colley, *Britons: Forging the Nation 1707–1837* (New Haven and London: Yale University Press,
1992), p. 81.

valence unconfessed by the historiography which is its progenitor. The word contains a question all too rarely asked: who *is* Augustus? And from the beginnings of the term in Atterbury's Preface this is a question being framed behind the ambivalent word concealing it. When Atterbury writes, in connexion with Waller's poetry, that 'I question whether in Charles II's reign English did not come to its full perfection; and whether it has not had its Augustan age as well as the Latin', he is writing about a time which, in 1690, has already ended. As Howard Erskine-Hill argues, Atterbury writes 'to bid farewell to Augustan achievement with the end of the Stuart era'.[7] That there are competing uses of this terminology is not in doubt: but what is central is the doubleness of Augustus, not only in topoi such as Astraea or Aeneas, but in the very pattern of a classical inheritance which itself welcomed the new age with ambivalent uncertainty.[8] At the heart of the years following 1688 lay a double vision of absent, typological and metaphysical ideal set against a material reality which usurped this imagery, either through consent or conquest, dependent on the historicizing of the writer. But, as J. R. Jones saw in his 1972 book on the Revolution, this struggle to interpret has had its metaphysics smoothed away by the genesis of a purely incrementalist view of Augustan 'order':

All Liberals and Marxists have a vested interest in seeing the Revolution as one of the stages in the process of historical changes which produced the world in which we live. Only very old-fashioned Catholics now share the values and principles which James II held. Consequently 1688 provides a very clear example of the dictum that 'history is the propaganda of the victors'.[9]

As inheritors of that 'victory', we need to examine its claims: and the fact that James VII and II has recently received more balanced treatment seems a sign of the strain the 1688 constitution is under in its attempt to cope with nationalism, political realignment and the demands of the European Community.

But Jones's statement itself is partially the victim of the incremental assumptions it sets out to qualify. 'Values' and 'principles' which are 'old-fashioned' themselves have been aborted by 'progress'. As I have already argued elsewhere, Stuart ideology, more enduring in its metaphors than its policies, continued as an ideal to be aspired to long beyond its dynastic shelf-life (Pittock, *Invention of Scotland, passim*). I now turn to these metaphors and their growth.

The symbols of the Stuart dynasty, out of which their account of the nature of their own power grew, derived from both Scottish and Tudor

[7] Erskine-Hill, *The Augustan Idea*, pp. 236–7.
[8] As in, for example, Edward Young's Satire IV, *Bell's edition of the poets of Great Britain*, vols. 84–7 (86) (London: John Bell, 1777), p. 108.
[9] J. R. Jones, *The Revolution of 1688 in England* (London, 1972), p. 8.

sources. But whereas the Tudors seldom allowed ideological metaphor to usurp rather than merely represent policy, Stuart monarchs on the English throne habitually mistook means for ends. Charles I's attitude to the Anglican Church was in some respects an iteration, indeed a reification, of Henry VIII's ecclesiastical ideology: [the] 'Brittanic Church was withdrawn from the Roman Patriarchate by the Imperial authority of Henry VIII'.[10] But this essentially Anglo-Catholic position, which in the phrase 'Imperial authority' rejected the Donation of Constantine and argued back to the secular power's right to convene general councils, was carried by Charles and Laud in England beyond the realm of political possibility open to Henry and Cranmer, and in Scotland defied the reality of a Reformation imposed in the teeth of a sovereign's authority, not in confirmation of it. For Charles and Laud, the Henrician ideology of Church control became a reality as an end in itself, not a means to certain political objectives. Yet that ideology was an inheritance from the Tudor dynasty. Charles might not have made such decisive policy errors in Scotland had he not succeeded to an English throne with an ecclesiastical authority constructed by the Tudors and approved by their ideologues. Divine Right itself 'was a derivation from the claims of Roman Emperors to be represented in the Councils of the Church', a position which was in essence Henrician. Constantine was a key figure in such arguments, and his English birth, paralleled with Elizabeth's in Foxe's *Martyrs* (1563), was an engine for the particularist claims of Anglicanism.[11] Elizabeth herself had been portrayed as the English Virgin, not Queen of Heaven but Queen of England, a replacement for the Madonna, and in herself a sign of manifest destiny. Hence the peculiar appropriateness of the imagery of Astraea applied to her, for Vergil's Eclogue, interpreted through Christological eyes, presented Astraea as a type of the Blessed Virgin. She was also *virgo spicifera*, the bringer of fertility to the land, 'our *State's* faire Spring', or as George Peele put it in *Descensus Astraea* (1591), she was the good shepherdess:

> Feed on, my flock among the gladsome green
> Where heavenly nectar flows above the banks . . .

John Dowland pointedly substituted '*Vivat Eliza*! for an *Ave Mari*', while Frances Yates quotes the following passage in confirmation of the power of the Astraea-cult surrounding the queen in her last years:

---

10 Frances Yates, *Astraea* (London: Routledge and Kegan Paul, 1985 (1975)), p. 39; J. Basire, *Ancient Liberty of the Britannic Church* (1661), p. 44.
11 Cf. Roger A. Mason, 'Scotching the Brut: Politics, History and National Myth in Sixteenth-Century Britain', in Mason (ed.), *Scotland and England 1286–1815* (Edinburgh: John Donald, 1987), pp. 60–84 (69); Yates, *Astraea*, p. 42.

This Maiden-Queen Elizabeth came into the world, the Eve of the Nativity of the blessed Virgin Mary; and died on the Eve of the Annunciation, of the Virgin Mary. 1602 ...

She was, she is (what can there more be said?) In earth the first, in heaven the Second Maid.[12]

Certain of the images of Stuart iconography are clearly anticipated in this late sixteenth-century phase: for example, Sir John Davies' image of Elizabeth as alchemist changing the iron age into a (Saturnian) one of gold was later used by Cowley of Charles I. Indeed, so strong was the Stuart inheritance of Astraea that it could usurp the gender of its subject, leading to a feminization in portrayals of some of the family such as Charles I and Charles Edward. Britannia was also part of the feminization of Stuart imagery in response to Astraean typology, and it may be that Joan Kinnaird's observation that 'feminism in its earliest phase' owed so much 'to conservative and Anglican values' is a sign of the attractiveness to women of this Stuart image, which reached its highest ambivalence in Charles Edward's cross-dressing as Betty Burke in 1746.[13]

If the Stuarts inherited the image of Astraea from Elizabeth, they also inherited that of Arthur from Henry VII, who had 'claimed himself as the heir of Cadwallader's vision ... of restored British monarchy', declaring that 'he was restoring the kingdom of Arthur'.[14] Although Henry initially used this idea as a means of reconciling both Wales to England and warring factions within England itself, it had uneasy imperial implications towards Scotland, reflecting as it did claims to a 'British' overlordship. English monarchical foundation-myth had long carried such overtones, claiming suzerainty over lesser kingdoms. King Arthur's realms were held to have included Scotland, and to reach back further: Brutus the Trojan's eldest son, as ruler of England, was *de jure* suzerain of all the British kingdoms by right of primogeniture. Constantine, the ancestor of Henrician claims to ecclesiastical sovereignty, was himself described as 'king of the Britons', while Henry VIII had a list of English claims to Scotland drawn up in 1542, as an *aide-mémoire* to his subsequent 'rough wooing'. Such a list, as had its predecessors back to 1301, made use of the Brut-myth, which had as its source the 'ur-myth of a British people under the great-grandson of Aeneas, Brutus' created by Geoffrey of Monmouth in the twelfth century. Thus the English monarchy's foundation-myth, codified under the Plantagenets and revivified under the Tudors, showed

[12] Yates, *Astraea*, pp. 30–1, 41, 42, 60, 67, 78.
[13] Ibid., p. 66; Joan Kinnaird, 'Mary Astell and the Conservative Contribution to English Feminism', *Journal of British Studies* 19 (1979), pp. 53–73 (54–5).
[14] Roberta Florence Brinkley, *Arthurian Legend in the Seventeenth Century*, Johns Hopkins Monographs in Literary History III (Baltimore: The Johns Hopkins Press, 1932), p. 2; Elizabeth Jenkins, *The Mystery of King Arthur* (London, 1975), p. 167.

the legitimacy of hereditary right as descending from Aeneas. While Astraea symbolized the mystical justice of the monarch's person and polity, Aeneas was the emblem of the political legitimacy which allowed the eternal renewal of that justice.[15]

For the Stuarts, this myth was double-edged. From one perspective, it was especially appropriate for them to use it, since after 1603 they were the first monarchs of a united Britain. William Herbert of Glamorgan, in *A Prophesie of Cadwallader* (1604), calls James 'The Lord's great Stuart . . . our second Brute', who 'shall three in one, and one in three unite', a conflation of political authority and near-blasphemous Trinitarian imagery. Such compliments were commonplace in kind if not degree: 'James was not only *like* Arthur; he was also considered *to be* Arthur returned', even anagrammatically: 'Charles James Steuart / Claims Arthur's Seat'.[16] The Arthurian monarchical myth, linked with that of Brute since the twelfth century, was important as a foundation for Divine Right claims. Throughout the seventeenth century, as Elizabeth Jenkins points out:

... those who supported the Divine Right of Kings upheld the historicity of Arthur; those who asserted the final authority of the English Common Law ... turned ... to the laws and customs of the Anglo-Saxons.

(Noteworthy here is the incipient incrementalism of Common Law precedent set against the legendary once and future typological king.) King was identified as British, Parliament as Saxon in the clashes of sovereignty which followed: a sign that the Arthurian foundation-myth was serious politics. It certainly was to James himself, the Venetian ambassador remarking that

the King's naming the kingdoms 'Britain' was like the decision of 'the famous and ancient King Arthur, to embrace under one name the entire kingdom'.[17]

But if the Arthur–Aeneas myth of English kingship was of advantage to James in the sense that it confirmed his claims to be a *British* king, in another way it compromised and indeed challenged the specifically *Scottish* foundation-myth he inherited in his northern kingdom. Though his descent from Fleance could be woven into the English myth, it was harder to find a place for the overtly Celtic Scottish tradition, itself a rebuttal of the Brutus story's claims, and an essential and defining nationalism for those of its own country: 'for them [the English] it was easier and much more satisfying to identify the new British king with Brutus, Arthur and Constantine than to greet him as the lineal descendant of Fergus Mac-Ferchard'. The nationalist myth of the Scots kings as descendants of

---

[15] Roger A. Mason, 'Scotching the Brut', pp. 61, 62, 69; Yates, *Astraea*, p. 48.

[16] Brinkley, *Arthurian Legend*, pp. 8–10.

[17] Jenkins, *The Mystery of King Arthur*, pp. 168–9; Brinkley, p. viii.

Fergus, Celts rather than British Trojans, was however used by the Covenanters to emphasize the patriotic quality of their aims, and the Stuarts, though sometimes minimizing, never altogether abandoned it, especially in time of larger-scale political crisis. During the 1680s, when an attempt was being made to turn Edinburgh into a distinctively Scottish royal capital, portraits of the Scottish royal line from its foundation were commissioned for Holyrood Palace, where they still hang. More than simply 'overweening pride in a long and largely fabricated pedigree',

... the ancient line of kings supplied a vital counterweight to an English historiographical tradition which insisted that Scotland was and always had been a dependency of England.

In other words, the Stuart dynasty was prepared to run with the hare and hunt with the hounds when it came to defining their political role. As descendants (variously) of a Greek and Egyptian (Gathelius and Scota) on one side, and of Trojan Aeneas on the other, with mutually irreconcilable claims to sovereignty, there was perhaps little else they could do.[18]

But it was the English myths that were initially adopted with great energy, perhaps because they held out (more in theory than reality) the promise of ecclesiastical and political power more absolute than that enjoyed by the Stuart kings hitherto. James's early enthusiasm for Anglo-Scottish union was certainly underlined by a desire to adopt the iconography of English kingship. As the Stuart dream of enforcing the metaphors of such kingship collapsed in tension and eventual war, a more varied symbolic language emerges, which finds increasing space for the peripheral symbolic images of Scotland and Ireland, as well as more marginalized spaces in English society. The royal oak was an icon which, although foreshadowed earlier, owed its centrality to Charles II's escape after Worcester in 1651, when 'Old Pendril, the miller, at the risk of his blood, / Hid the King of our Isle in the king of the wood'. But as the words of this song suggest, the king's escape had iconographic force conferred on it by its association with traditional emblems of pagan fertility, which themselves were linked most strongly with the Celtic areas of his realm. As Marian McNeill writes in *The Silver Bough*, 'the oak, the largest and strongest tree in the North, was venerated by the Celts as the symbol of the supreme Power ...', and was central to Scottish folk ceremony. On the other hand, the oak was also Druidic, and hence Welsh, the last and chief Druid stronghold having been Anglesey: 'to the royalist, Druids added

[18] Mason, 'Scotching the Brut', pp. 60–1, 64, 76; Hugh Ouston, 'York in Edinburgh: James VII and the Patronage of Learning in Scotland, 1679–1688', in John Dwyer, Roger Mason and Alexander Murdoch (eds.), *New Perspectives on the Politics and Culture of Early Modern Scotland* (Edinburgh: John Donald, 1983), pp. 133–55; Revd Robert Baillie, cited in Audrey Cunningham, *The Loyal Clans* (Cambridge: Cambridge University Press, 1932), pp. 270–1.

another strand to the British myth, confirming the magical and priestly role of the king: Druidic oak became identified with royal oak'.[19] Thus pagan symbolism was lent to the Christian authority of Divine Right. Another pagan exemplar of Stuart right was Fionn MacCumhail, a returning monarch like Arthur or Astraea, who will be restored from typology to incrementality in a saving *renovatio* when his country requires: but the emergence of Fionn in Stuart typology, though marked in Ossian and the *aisling* poetry of the eighteenth century, seems subsequent to the Revolution of 1688. Exile and the Irish war emphasized the new-found peripheralism of a dynasty which had lost its throne partly through adhering too closely to the values of Anglocentric monarchical control.

The Stuarts developed these values more markedly than their pre-decessors however, and not just in terms of the length they went to realize them. Although the image of Stuart sovereignty was compromised in the contradictory claims of the English and Scottish foundation-myths, in other areas of imagery the Stuart kings Celticized their English inherit-ance. James, lauded as the new Arthur on his accession in 1603, used the Arthurian image to emphasize Wales and Cornwall – indeed, it appears to have been a Welshman who first suggested to him the title of King of Great Britain.[20] This emphasis perhaps meant that it was eventually easier to use Arthurian foundation-myth as a peripheral metaphor, where the 'theme of Arthur as huntsman', together with the emphasis laid by both Charleses, James VII and II and Anne on hunting and country pursuits was an element in the contemporary growth of the image of rural peri-phery rather than metropolis as representing the seat of true sovereign authority. The monarch's authentic power resided in the country not the city, a political point reinforced by the royal oak episode, and which neatly dovetailed both with the renewed fertility promised by a returning Astraea and the Celtic belief that 'God blesses the reign of good princes by a succession of peaceful and abundant seasons'.[21] Rural renewal and retreat grew into one of the chief metaphors of Stuart political authority in the period 1630–60: Charles's 1632 proclamation to the gentry to return to their estates marks a convenient starting-point in this process, whereby 'the hyperbolic landscape ... embodies the desire to invest the state with

[19] *The Nightingale: A Collection of Ancient and Modern Songs, Scots and English None of Which are in Ramsay*, Epilogue by Mr R. Fergusson (Edinburgh: W. Darling, 1776), p. 160; F. Marian McNeill, *The Silver Bough*, 4 vols. (Glasgow, 1957), 1:77; Douglas Brooks-Davies, *The Mercurian Monarch: Magical Politics from Spenser to Pope* (Manchester: Manchester University Press, 1983), p. 151.

[20] Brinkley, *Arthurian Legend*, p. 23; Yates, *Astraea*, p. 214; Francis Jones, *The Princes and Prin-cipality of Wales* (Cardiff: University of Wales Press, 1969), p. 49.

[21] Richard Barber, *The Figure of Arthur* (Worcester and London, 1972), pp. 109, 122; Isabel Rivers, *The Poetry of Conservatism 1600–1745* (Cambridge, 1973), p. 172; Bruadighe of Thomond on the Irish bardic tradition, cited in John Daly (ed.), *Reliques of Irish Jacobite Poetry* (Dublin, 1844), p. 37n.

the quality of nature'.[22] 'The Book of Sports', which 'sought to confirm this relationship [between Anglican authority and the popular tradition] against Puritan attack', the encouragement of rural folkways and Archbishop Laud's opposition to enclosures were all material political manifestations of a development reflected in literature by the importance of topographical poetry as a subgenre: the divine ordering was best observed in a localized environment, intensely realized. Nor was this, as has been suggested, mere high cultural posturing:

The legend of the revival of 'merry England' after the Restoration is one which historians have perhaps been too impatient to examine. Even if some of the more sensational claims are discounted (Defoe, as a good accountant, assures us that 6325 maypoles were erected in the five years after the Restoration) there is no doubt that there was a general and sometimes exuberant revival of popular sports, wakes, rush bearings and rituals.

The ruralism of Stuart ideology experienced further growth in the Civil War period, when the king was militarily as well as ideologically confined to the peripheries of his authority, while after 1688, the upheaval of exile did much to endorse the retreat and topographical poem as a Stuart-leaning subgenre.[23]

The early stages of such a development can be traced in Denham's *Cooper's Hill* ('Oh happiness of sweet retir'd content! / To be at once secure, and innocent') which brought 'into focus the scattered topographical themes of earlier poetry' in a world where 'political disaster is commonly presented as a Fall, ruining the landscape as the first Fall was supposed to have done' (Isabel Rivers, *The Poetry of Conservatism*, p. 6; James Turner, *The Politics of Landscape*, pp. 5, 91, 169). The ambivalence of Marvell's gardens was found in specifically Royalist form in writers such as Henry Vaughan, with his 'landscapes ... shadowed ... by the dark tension, the stealth of an "underground" religious community ... Vaughan's vocabulary for nature is also often that for war.'[24] The Stuart political landscape, ruling the 'undiminished squirearchy' of nature by the power of 'The proud *Dictator* of the State-like wood: / I meane (the Sovereign of all Plants) the Oke' was contaminated by civil strife. In similar vein, Pope later recalled the rapine of conquest in the context of a renewed oak-like stability:

[22] James Turner, *The Politics of Landscape: Rural Scenery and Society in English Poetry 1630–1660* (Oxford, 1979), pp. 12, 105.

[23] E. P. Thompson, 'Patrician Society, Plebeian Culture', *Journal of Social History* 7 (1973/4), pp. 382–405 (393).

[24] *The Poetical Works of John Denham*, ed. Theodore Howard Banks, Jr (New Haven: Yale University Press, 1928; London: Humphrey Milford: Oxford University Press), p. 65; Chris Fitter, 'Henry Vaughan's Landscapes of Military Occupation', *Essays in Criticism* (1992), pp. 123–42 (123, 134).

Rich Industry sits smiling on the plains,
And Peace and Plenty tell, a STUART reigns.[25]

The 'civil obedience' of the 'calm rivers' of a Stuart nature paradise is
restored, but this is the last phase of its restoration. The ruralism of Stuart
imagery developed from celebration to violation and retreat; it was to end
in the topographical poems of such as Alexander Robertson of Struan,
lamenting for the compulsory retreat, the internal exile of those doomed to
spend their lives evading Hanoverian soldiery.[26]

Despite the belief that the 'emphasis of the restored monarchy [after
1660] on hunting ... gave to poaching ... a self-conscious edge of social
protest', and James Turner's argument that Stuart ruralism cleared the
idealized land of its unpleasant peasant inhabitants, there does seem to
have been a genuine 'bias to the poor' in elements of the ruralist approach.
The ordering links between landlord and tenant that a country ideology
emphasized were those which succoured the growth of crossclass cultural
alliances in the Jacobite period, most notably in the development of a high
culture which defined itself in folk cultural terms, as found in the vernacular revival in Scotland and the Irish *aisling* poems.[27] The 'Book of Sports',
and the permission of 'morris dancing' and 'may games' early emphasized
this feature of Stuart ideology (discussed in Julian Davies, 'The Growth
and Implementation of Laudianism'). Even before the Revolution, a
convergence of high and popular cultural ideas could be seen in the
London street shows, which

tended to draw on two different iconographical and mythological traditions,
learned and popular respectively; the classical tradition, and the 'trades' tradition
of craftsmen in general and the City companies in particular. One might see
Astraea, but also Jack Straw ...[28]

By the eighteenth century, these displays had become sufficiently politicized to attract the disapproval of government, as I will argue in
Chapter 2.

But if Stuart ruralism was a potent force in legitimizing a political order
in accord with the divine governance of Nature, ecclesiastical ideology
emphasized Stuart rights over the spiritual, not merely the physical, land.

---

[25] Turner, *Politics of Landscape*, pp. 95, 97, 105; *The Poems of Alexander Pope*, ed. John Butt, the
one-volume Twickenham Edition (London: Methuen, 1977 (1963)), p. 196.

[26] Turner, *Politics of Landscape*, p. 105; 'Struan's Farewell to the Hermitage' in Alexander
Robertson of Struan, *Poems* (Edinburgh, 1749), pp. 241ff.

[27] Turner, *Politics of Landscape*, pp. 177ff.; Buchanan Sharp, 'Popular Protest in Seventeenth-
Century England' in Barry Reay (ed.), *Popular Culture in Seventeenth-Century England* (London:
Routledge, 1988 (1985)), pp. 271–308 (302).

[28] Julian Davies, 'The growth and implementation of Laudianism', unpublished D.Phil. thesis
(Oxford, 1987); Peter Burke, 'Popular Culture in Seventeenth-Century London', in Reay
(ed.), *Popular Culture*, pp. 31–58 (45).

The King had two bodies after all, and these bodies each possessed an authority separately presented and accounted for by its image-makers, though in essence conjoined. Propagandists for either used heavily typological language to defend the quality of Stuart claims. Just as Constantine, the British monarch of Rome, had been 'Sol Invictus', so to George Chapman James was 'our British Phoebus', heir both to Constantine's political and ecclesiastical inheritance:

The accession of James I brought ... in the eyes of mythographers of the *Ecclesia Anglicana*, the recreation of the Ancient British Church as it had existed in the island when Christianity had first been brought by St Joseph of Arimathea.[29]

It was to be no coincidence that Nonjurors loyal to Stuart ecclesiastical claims described themselves after 1689 as 'the British Catholic Churches'.[30] As mentioned earlier, it was Charles and Laud's attempt to carry out Henrician caesaropapism in a 'Thorough' fashion that led to their downfall. But earthly defeat enriched the language of typological authority:

The Regicide led to an outpouring of typology. Many writers saw Charles I as a postfiguration of the martyred Savior ...

The countering claim of Cromwell's Davidic kingship was never as forceful, and Cowley's *Davideis* (1656) may reclaim such images for Charles himself. He was the Sun King, but now 'a sun hidden in a cloud', the 'Hieroglyphick king' whose followers henceforward might only express his authority in codes and images of power, not power itself: a 'King of Sorrows' whose kingdom truly was 'not of this world'. Charles's prescient words of December 1642 to the Duke of Hamilton, 'I will either be a glorious king or a patient martyr', were decoded as prophetic foresight, while the magnitude of their rhetorical opposition could be seen as identifying the king directly with the double role of Christ. Parallels between the two began as early as 1648, and were in full swing by 1650, even if their 'signs and wonders' sometimes took on a rather bathetic tone:

When our Saviour suffered, there were terrible signs and wonders, and darknesse over all the Land: so during the time of our Soveraigns Martyrdom, there were strange signs seen in the sky, in divers places of the Kingdom: and it was thought very prodigious, the Ducks forsook their pond at Saint *James's*, and came as far as Whitehall, fluttering about the Scaffold.[31]

---

[29] Sir Roy Strong, *Henry Prince of Wales and England's Lost Renaissance* (London: Thames & Hudson, 1986), pp. 138, 182; Ernst H. Kantorowicz, *The King's Two Bodies* (Princeton: Princeton University Press, 1957), fig. 23.

[30] Cf. Henry Broxap, *The Later Non-Jurors* (Cambridge: Cambridge University Press, 1924), pp. 32, 39.

[31] Lois Potter, *Secret Rites and Secret Writing: Royalist Literature 1641–1660* (Cambridge: Cambridge University Press, 1989), pp. 45, 158–9, 173–4, 186; Paul Korshin, *Typologies in England*

Charles's death lent a new aura of sanctity to what had seemed to many a merely political use of his ecclesiastical authority: his execution was not only a gross violation of seventeenth-century political expectation, but also a typological return of the martyrdoms of the early Church. After all, did the claims of the Anglican Church not rest in part on a resistance to Papal pretensions based on doubtful documents? Was not the restoration of royal authority a promise of a return to the age of the Fathers and before that the Apostles? And now it was not the Emperor who martyred but the king who was martyred, thus the keenness of later Jacobite references to the Georges as 'Nero', the Beast, the killer of SS Peter and Paul:

> The *Martyr's blood* was said of old to be
> The *seed* from whence the *Church* did grow.
> The *Royal Blood* which dying *Charles* did sow
> Becomes no less the seed of Royalty.[32]

Thus Cowley praised the reconciling king who had righted the wrongs of Emperors in the apostolic age with his own healing martyrdom, in defence (so typology might have it) of a Catholic Faith subject to a restored and purified caesaropapism. The Pope was Pontifex Maximus, but so was Augustus: and thus was the high priesthood the property of the new Augustus, whose son (like Christ's ancestor) was also the exiled David in flight from his enemies.

The rhetoric of sacrifice which followed Charles's death was thus strongly reinforced by a Christian typology based both on the sovereignty of the king within the Church and his status as God's vicegerent on earth. Charles's wearing of a white robe at his coronation, subsequently reinforced by other images including a fall of snow on his coffin, none falling around it, fed an image of him as the 'white king', a king who in real life echoed the pure aloofness conferred by the carefully crafted court masques. His 'alchemical union of white and red' (Douglas Brooks-Davies, *The Mercurian Monarch*, p. 94), married both the colours of the Stuart banner and the concepts of purity and sacrifice. His 'whiteness' trans-figured the king into Idea, and perhaps recalled the Transfiguration of Christ. The Scots sold Charles to Parliament: so Judas the Messiah. Charles's own words, 'I die a martyr for the people' echoed the unconscious prophecy of Caiaphas, that it is fitting one man should die for the people. The traditional favour, sometimes of clothing, granted to the headsman paralleled the casting of lots for Christ's garments; and in what Lois Potter has identified as 'the royal image: Charles I as text', the king

---

*1650–1720* (Princeton: Princeton University Press, 1982), pp. 59, 79; Joseph A. Mazzeo, 'Cromwell as Davidic King', *Reason and Imagination* (New York: Columbia University Press, 1962), pp. 29–55.

[32] Abraham Cowley, *Poems*, ed. A. R. Waller (Cambridge, 1905), p. 425.

himself becomes textualized in codified and Christlike terms: 'Some writers simply use the abbreviation "Ch ..." for both Christ and Charles, leaving the reader to choose between them.'[33]

This textualizing was a process which Charles seemed to have found important, not only in the Neoplatonic imagery of the 1630s or his portrayal as Sovereign Reason in paintings such as Rubens's *Landscape with St George and the Dragon*, but also more immediately on the brink of death, when his stutter left him and he posed as martyr for the people: perhaps a demo(cra)tic as well as a hieratic pose. It was the development of the 'people' in the ideology of royal text which perhaps acted as an enabling force in the eighteenth-century convergence of high and folk cultural Jacobite aims.[34]

But it was the execution of 1649 which crystallized what can be called the textualization of Stuart imagery. Hitherto, high-seeming iconography had always been compromised by political ambition. For many opponents of the king and his successors, this would continue to be the case: but the king's status as victim was a disturbingly parallel obverse to his earlier pretensions. From Pantocrator to the Suffering Servant, Supreme Governor of the Church to slaughtered traitor: for those Anglicans who were ideologically so, the parallel was unavoidable. The king, gone from authority, became the text justifying that authority: again a Christological parallel. Charles's textualization was accompanied by Charles's text: *Eikon Basilike*, perhaps a genuine, perhaps contrived collage of the king's thoughts. In either case, the belief the king had written it placed it in the vanguard of texts which sought to endorse royal authority, either plainly, or through the hieroglyphs the times required.[35]

For, central to our understanding of the textualization of Stuart imagery, its use as a means of communication, literary celebration and authority, a conversion of political means into artistic ends, must be the knowledge of an inevitable encoding which accompanied it. In many instances it was not safe to write openly in support of the ideology of Stuart authority. Hence a range of codes, secret languages and visual symbols were given a determining priority: and here in the 1650s, lies a great part of the root of later Jacobite expression: the fertility images of Stuart stumpwork prefiguring the ciphered decorations and double-bottomed bowls of a later age, as topography and typology confirmed the status of the absent king in seventeenth and eighteenth centuries alike. At the same time, both Cromwellian and Hanoverian images 'grew out of royal icon-

---

[33] Potter, *Secret Rites*, pp. 156, 186; cf. C. V. Wedgwood, *The Trial of Charles I* (Harmondsworth: Penguin, 1983 (1964)), p. 192– 'I am the Martyr of the people'.

[34] Murray G. H. Pittock, *Religious Politics Under Charles I and James II* (Huntingdon: Royal Stuart Society, 1991), p. 2.

[35] Cf. Edward J. C. Scott (ed.), *eikwv basilike* (London: Elliot Stock, 1880).

ography', but these, particularly the latter, lacked the conviction of their originals, as both Paul Korshin and Linda Colley point out. One of the ways this is evident is in the ambivalent images of the 1650s, themselves made possible by the very richness of royal textualizing: Hobbes's world-monarch in *Leviathan* (1651) or the tragic hero defying the 1642 closure of the theatres at his own closure in Marvell's 'Horatian Ode'. Both philosopher and poet delicately balance *realpolitik* against indefeasible right:

> Though Justice against Fate complain,
> And plead the ancient rights in vain;
> > But those do hold or break,
> > As men are strong or weak.

In this typological poem, Marvell declines to endorse typology, though the Horatian Ode was frequently a Royalist subgenre.[36] But his skill in presenting such multiple readings is partly rooted in the inherited and increasing depth of the Royalist text, whose encodings were perforce rarely explicit. The ambitious iconography of the early Stuart kings was confirming and protecting itself in its own typologies and their ideological expression. This anticipated the Revolution: but it also permitted ambivalent readings of the royal idea since that idea's expressions were themselves often ambivalent, saving explicit productions such as the 1649 medal displaying Charles I and II as Phoenix. Typology was truth, but it was hard to prosecute objectively: and this was to remain its attraction.[37]

Charles's sons seem to have held differing views as to the 'truth' of their father's ambition and death. Charles II was restored with great pomp, presented at his coronation in terms of Roman conqueror, Old Testament figure, Neptune, the sun and Christ: Augustan and Davidic king in terms of secular authority, with imagery of the British Phoebus and Christ Himself to remind an audience of his sacred power. 'SPQL' boasted the arches through the city, and if the Great Fire of 1666 did not quite allow Charles to find London built of brick and leave it marble, it nevertheless made possible significant and striking changes in the city's architecture. Charles was the returned Augustus, though in the very strength of the imagery used some have seen the inception of its disintegration:

Certain of the authors nevertheless see kingship not only as a mystical entity but also as a concept to be manipulated. In other words, one here finds a noumenal view on the threshold of its demythologization: a noumenon, e.g. Charles in procession, is beginning to be only a phenomenon, an entity whose meaning depends on the wishes of the onlookers. Historically, it is only a short step from this to the dethronement of James in 1688 . . .[38]

---

[36] Potter, *Secret Rites*, p. 195; Yates, *Astraea*, p. 9.    [37] Kantorowicz, *Two Bodies*, fig. 23ff.
[38] Gerard Reedy sj, 'Mystical Politics: The Imagery of Charles II's Coronation', in Paul J. Korshin (ed.), *Studies in Change and Revolution: Aspects of English Intellectual History 1640–1800* (Marston, England: Scolar Press, 1972), pp. 19–42 (21, 23, 39).

Such a verdict may more accurately reflect the divisions between Charles II and his father than any profound historical shift, for the new king seemed more Tudor than Stuart in his preference for manipulating iconographies rather than believing in them. In Scotland, Charles used straightforward force to suppress the remaining hardline Covenanters, leaving the imagery of pan-Anglican triumphalism firmly on the shelf in favour of a tough administration which gave out gradual concessions (notably in 1667, after the battle of Rullion Green). Yet he was not opposed to Stuart sacramentalism: merely more cautious in its use, stressing a populist dimension rather than that of Throne and Altar. During his reign the Royal Touch was given for the King's Evil (not only scrofula, but a variety of swellings) to 100,000 people, a substantial proportion of the population. The Touch was a sign of that miraculous kingship denied by Pope Gregory VII in 1081: it may therefore have been an important part of royal sacramentalism in an Anglican state. Although James VI and I had sought to discontinue its use, Charles I had (despite Parliamentary opposition) practised it: as late as 1838 in the Shetland Islands, 'a few crowns and half-crowns bearing the effigy of Charles I were still used, in default of the royal touch, as remedies for the Evil ...'(touchpieces of Henry 'IX' were in use in Ireland this century). Charles II practised the Touch with considerable freedom. Perhaps in rebuttal of what may have been Cromwell's (unsuccessful) attempts to exercise it, Charles, as his nephew and great-nephews did after him, used the Touch in exile as an additional sign of his status as rightful heir. Sir Thomas Browne sent a child to Breda to be touched (a sign of confidence in the Touch among contemporary physicians reflected elsewhere), and in his last five weeks in Belgium, Charles II touched two hundred and sixty. Throughout his reign, the Royal Touch was to be used as a sacramental prop to his authority: in the crisis-ridden year of 1682–3 twice as many were touched as in the average year; in the June of Charles's restoration, six hundred 'were touched at a single healing'. Charles II was careful in his use of Stuart signs, but decisively theatrical in their use when occasion warranted.[39]

James was different. His views were much closer to those of his father: indeed, he seems to have felt that during the Civil War, Charles I had gone too far down the road of compromise with his own status. During his brother's reign, James had suffered the double indignities of the Test Act (1673) and the Exclusion Crisis. During the latter, in exile in Edinburgh, he seems to have attempted to forestall problems such as his father had in Scotland by making the city a Royalist intellectual capital, a focus of art

[39] Sir Raymond Crawfurd, *The King's Evil* (Oxford: Clarendon Press, 1911), pp. 82, 101, 102, 103, 104, 106, 112, 121; Marc Bloch, *The Royal Touch*, tr. J. E. Anderson (London: Routledge and Kegan Paul, 1973; Montreal: McGill, Queen's University Press, 1973), pp. 71, 188.

154, 49#

and learning. Indeed, it has been argued that James's contribution at this time was strongly instrumental in bringing to birth the subsequent fruits of the Scottish Enlightenment.[40] It would be worth noting, however, that some of the images of antiquity he revived had a distinctly pre-Reformation tinge.

On the throne, James attempted to restore the twofold secular and sacred sovereignty his father's images had sought to project. In Scotland, his support for an Episcopalian elite of classicists, lawyers, theologians and senior professionals, coupled with a degree of toleration for all but armed Covenanters and their supporters, rendered his position more secure than his father's had been. Even in 1689, James's supporters might have carried the Estates had the crucial meeting not been mishandled. This was different from the situation fifty years before. But in England, the Declarations of Indulgence of 1687–8 broke the link they were intended to preserve: that between sacred and secular authority. James's attempts to revive his father's sacred authority could not come through his position as governor of the Anglican Church, as he was Roman Catholic. As such, he could not seek the mystic headship of a church of which he was not even a member. Instead, he sought mystic overlordship through the medium of toleration. James probably knew that, even had he wished it, the straightforward imposition of Roman Catholicism was an impossibility. Instead the King would stand for toleration between denominations, showing both his sovereign mercy and his sovereign authority towards and over all his subjects. He thought there were many in the Anglican Church who would see this policy as not dissonant from the comprehensive mystique of royal authority. He was wrong.

Toleration struck at the spiritual roots of the Anglican Church as well as its government. By accepting the beliefs of Roman Catholic and anti-prelatist schismatic alike, it damaged both the autonomy of the middle way, and its special status under the paradigmatically Christ-like authority of the Crown, which was now attempting to force an engulfing ecumenism on the Church that, only a generation before, had been the ultimate symbol of royal ascendancy. James was attempting to preserve his role as father of the Church, but the fatted calf he proposed to slay to feed the prodigal sons of Dissent and Rome was seen as an act of betrayal by his Anglican first-born. Since 1669 at least, James had been 'all against persecution merely for conscience sake', and he acted consistently with this in releasing 1600 Quakers from prison in 1687: they were more grateful in terms of subsequent support than were many of the Nonconformist groups James proposed to favour with toleration. His objection to 'the . . . barbar-

---

[40] Hugh Ouston, 'York in Edinburgh', in Dwyer, Mason and Murdoch, *New Perspectives*, pp. 133–55.

ous cruelties, used in France against the Protestants' was not believed by many among his own subjects, who chose to overlook events such as the granting of asylum to the Huguenots on condition of their religious conformity. Instead, fear of James's Catholicism was played up both as a political gesture and a symptom of contemporary paranoia.[41]

Amid a deteriorating political and ecclesiastical atmosphere James continued to emphasize the sacramental qualities of his kingship, which as with his brother were brought into play at critical moments in his reign: 4422 were touched in the year of Monmouth's rebellion (when Monmouth was also practising it), while some 700–800 received the Royal Touch at Oxford just before the controversy over the Presidency of Magdalen College in 1687. James spent as much money on touchpieces as he did on promoting Catholicism: his own sacramental status (itself partly rooted in the claims of Henrician Anglicanism) being important to him, as were its applications. The Gallicanism of his son, advertised by his supporters, is perhaps witness to a faint echo of this parity of esteem between caesaropapacy and the Bishop of Rome.[42]

Certainly, while James's Anglican opponents registered his reign as a change of ideological direction, his defenders continued to speak of royal power in a language consistent with that used of his predecessors. James was variously 'Mighty Caesar ... The Muses' Glory and Astraea's Pride', 'James the Just', 'God-like James', 'Britain's Royal Tree', 'The Root of Monarchy ... And an adored Oak of Trophies' (the Royal Oak), an image combining the providential salvation of his fleeing brother with a metaphorical justification for his own power.[43] Dryden, whose *The Hind and the Panther* was an attempt to change the parameters of religious debate while defending James's supremacy, continued to give his patron the Vergilian assent and compliment he had offered Charles II. In 'Britannia Rediviva', welcoming the birth of the king's heir, Dryden makes the Vergilian parallel once again explicit:

> Not Great *Aeneas* stood in plainer Day
> When, the dark mantling Mist dissolv'd away,
> He to the *Trojans* shew'd his sudden face,
> Shining with all his Goddess Mother's Grace ...

Here, trembling on the verge of blasphemy, can be seen the status of the young Prince of Wales as Aeneas, in the role of 'a pre-Christian type of Christ': a parallel drawn more clearly in Dryden's translation of *Aeneid* I: 834, where Aeneas' 'descent out of a cloud at Carthage' echoes Christ's

[41] F. C. Turner, *James II* (London, 1948), pp. 307, 311, 313–14; J. R. Jones, *The Revolution of 1688*, p. 112.
[42] Turner, *James II*, p. 333; Yates, *Astraea*, p. 82.
[43] Keaton, *Lord Chancellor Jeffreys*, pp. 334, 336, 337.

identifying Himself as the Messiah. In this typological equation, political
and theological myths are bonding with each other: the 'Goddess Mother'
is Mary of Modena, bearing the name of the Blessed Virgin, Mary Queen
of Heaven; and she is also Venus, mother of Aeneas. Hence she belongs
both to the typology of the *Aeneid* and the Fourth Eclogue, with its
prophecy of the birth of Christ / return of Astraea / coming of Augustus.
As Astraea, Mary of Modena is 'virgo spicifera'; as a type of the Blessed
Virgin, she is 'Porta caeli et stella maris' (Feast of the BVM, 31 May),
'aromatibus myrrhae et thuris' ('aromatic with myrrh and incense', the
symbols of suffering and God's presence – Assumption of the BVM, 15
August). The Feast of the Virgin falls in the Stuart season of May/June ('A
month that owns an Int'rest in your Name: / You and the Flow'rs are its
peculiar Claim', as Dryden puts it in *Astraea Redux*), the dates of Restoration Day and the birth of 'Britannia Rediviva', James VIII and III, on
White Rose Day, 10 June. May is Mary's month, and as 'Stella Maris'
Mary was a name appropriate for the mother of the soon-to-be-exiled
Aeneas, since Venus herself, Aeneas' mythological mother, was both a star
(planet) and born of the sea.[44]

But despite the tensions between claim and compromise in James's
sacramental authority, his deposition must seem a violation without the
permanent hindsight to which we are inevitably heir. For although the
Anglican nature of his claims to ecclesiastical control were being destabi-
lized by his religion, with consequent effects in the political sphere (his
administration trusted him less on several points than his brother), James
had an unequalled claim to legitimacy, senior heir as he was of every
English and Scottish surviving royal line (save only that of Baliol) since
before the Norman Conquest. He was (and not only to Dryden) 'God's
Image, God's Anointed', the manifest inheritor of a millennium of indefeasible hereditary right. Hence it was of the utmost importance to his
opponents that the legitimacy of his successor should fall under suspicion:
the origins of the warming-pan story lie in the rock-solid nature of James's
claims. Previous competitors for the crown had often been able to challenge the claims of its holder; James's were unchallengeable. But in the last
four months of the old-style year 1688/9, he was challenged: and defeated.
Aeneas left his kingdom; Augustus was ousted. The foundation-myth of
England was compromised, and Astraea left the earth, as seemed proven
by the famines of William's reign. Even a century later, the countervailing
images of organicism and fertility adopted by the Jacobite cause could be
heard, though in an altered form:

---

[44] Stephen Zwicker, *Politics and Language in Dryden's Poetry: The Arts of Disguise* (Princeton:
Princeton University Press, 1984), pp. 120, 202, 253; Korshin, *Typologies*, p. 5; Dryden, *Works*,
5: 348; *Office of Our Lady*, 2 vols. (London: Darton, Longman and Todd, 1962).

Plant, plant, the tree, fair freedom's tree,
Midst danger, wounds and slaughter;
Erin's green fields her soil shall be
Her tyrants' blood its water.

Here the blood-sacrifice Stuart metaphor turns to a Republican one, but the collocation of fertility and freedom lingers on from an earlier age, as in Aogan Ó Rathaille's 'The Vision':

A film of enchantment spread, of aspect bright
from the shining boulders of Galway to Cork of the harbours:
clusters of fruit appearing in every treetop,
acorns in woods, pure honey upon the stones . . .
in the name of the faithful king who is soon to come
to rule and defend the triple realm for ever.[45]

Triple realm of Britain, triple crown of the Papacy: Church and State mixed with the ease and potency which gave the imagery of the Stuarts its special mystique, celebrated even in exile through the great typologies found in the verse which spoke of their cause: the Vergilian Augustus, the *renovatio* of Astraea or *redeat* of Charles Edward Stuart. In the end, the Stuart text was to defer closure in perpetuity: and this is a mark of the openness of the myth, and its success.

# Revolution and reaction

I wish that all honest hearts may give the glory of this to God, to whom indeed the praise of this mercy belongs.                                    Cromwell at Drogheda

I am not ashamed to offer this essay to your Majesty ye original was p'sented to Augustus Caesar it is natural to dedicate ye Translation to your Majesty who is not only of ye same Country but descended of ye same family wth Augustus Caesar . . .        Dedication of Lord Maitland's *Aeneid* to Mary of Modena, 1691

When lawless men their neighbours dispossess,
The tenants they extirpate or oppress
And make rude havoc in the fruitful soil
Which the right owners pruned with careful toil.
The same in Kingdoms does proportion hold:
A new Prince breaks the fences of the old . . .
Arthur Mainwaring, 'Suum Cuique' (1689)

---

[45] John Dryden, *The Poems and Fables*, ed. James Kinsley (London, 1962 (1958)), pp. 328, 356, 430; *Popular Songs, Illustrative of the French Invasions of Ireland*. Percy Society Vol. xxi (London: Percy Society, 1840), p. 84; Sean Ó Tuama, *An Duanaire 1600–1900: Poems of the Dispossessed*, tr. Thomas Kinsella (Mountrath, Portlaoise: The Dolmen Press, 1981), p. 155.

Ye warlike Scots of ancient blood, ye martial sons of the mountain, roused from your distant homes, I call you now to battle, and claim your aid against the Batavian general, and the conspiring band of Saxons who have vilely sold their liberty and their King for cursed gold ... O degenerate men ... Rather than that the illustrious James, the son of Fergus, the descendant of mighty ancestral kings should be sold for Dutch gold ... who would not meet the flash of arms ... Wherefore lead on, bright sons of the mighty Fergus ...

James Philp of Almericlose, *The Grameid*[46]

From before the first use of the term 'glorious revolution' (by John Hampden in 1689), literary divisions had arisen in echo of the political battle-lines drawn by the events of the previous year. A similar process took place to that which had occurred in the 1650s: the Stuart cause became increasingly textualized, broadening yet further its range of images of exile, martyrdom and deferred reward. On the Williamite side, as under Cromwell, there was an attempt to usurp Stuart sacred and political imagery to bolster legitimacy: despite the fact that Mary was the best claim to this the new regime had, such usurped images in a majority attached to William. The Dutchman became a new hero of foundation-myth, appearing both as Augustan/Aenean restored monarch and Julian conqueror, as in this poem by Richard Stone:

> The Mighty *Julius* whose illustrious Name
> Till now stood first in the Records of Fame;
> Who by his Courage kept the World in awe,
> Was but a type of the Divine *Nassau*.[47]

But there is a central difference between this and most Stuart use of Roman typology. William is here primary; the typological forerunner(s) are only that. William doesn't confirm their eternal validity so much as he makes them fade into history. Caesar is 'but a type' of William, the king who makes things new because he has usurped the old. Incremental progress is subtly undermining typological celebration even while apparently endorsing it. In its very appearance it is becoming obscured by the glory of a new order. Where this technique was used, the evident reason for it was Williamite lack of typological authority save that based on illegitimate inheritance, an act of betrayal. What Paul Korshin has called

[46] J. G. Simms, *War and Politics in Ireland 1649–1730*, ed. D. W. Hayton and Gerard O'Brien (London and Ronceverte: The Hambledon Press, 1985), p. 9; National Library of Scotland MS Dep. 221/62 5v; William J. Cameron (ed.), *Poems on Affairs of State: Augustan Satirical Verse 1660–1714 Volume 5 (1688–1697)* (New Haven and London: Yale University Press, 1971), p. 117; James Philp of Almericlose, *The Grameid*, ed. Alexander D. Murdoch, Scottish History Society Volume III (Edinburgh: Edinburgh University Press, 1888), pp. 97–9.

[47] Eveline Cruickshanks (ed.), *By Force or by Default? The Revolution of 1688–89* (Edinburgh: John Donald, 1989), p. ii; cited Korshin, *Typologies*, p. 118.

'the enervation of the Stuart myth' is visible in post-Revolutionary com-
plimentary verse, such as this poem from a collection of elegies on Queen
Anne:

> *Vespasian*, whose Imperial Name
> Triumphant rides upon the Wings of Fame
>     That measur'd Time's swift Hand,
>     Not by the Ebb and Flow of Sand,
> But the more reg'lar Motions of his Mind,
> Which ev'ry Beat, struck Blessings to Mankind,
> No more Illustrious Shade shall mention'd be,
>     But as the Type of Thee.

'No more ... But as the Type of Thee'. Such was the elegiac comment
often passed by poetic eulogy of the post-Revolution monarchs on the
typology they had usurped.[48]

But if this planned obsolescence was one of the ways in which the new
regime distanced itself from the ideological baggage it pretended it was
preserving, its poets chose other routes also. *On the Happy Accession of Their
Majesties ... A Pindarique Ode* is a poem which, as Stephen Zwicker points
out, offers 'an irresolute and contradictory mixing of constitutional
idioms' in its attempt to conflate Divine Right and contract theory
portrayals of monarchy:

> No dull Succession sanctifies his Right,
>     Nor conquest gain'd in Fight,
>     But o're the Peoples minds, and there
> Does *Right Divine* triumphantly appear.
>     The mind, impassible and free,
> No pow'r can govern, but the deity,
> Howev'r o're Persons, and o're Fortunes may
>     A bold Intruder sway;
>     The *Right Divine* is by the people given,
> And 'tis their Suffrage speaks the mind of Heav'n.[49]

This poem represents an attempt to withdraw from the embarrassments of
typological language used of a usurper not by hinting at its obsolescence
but through altering its metaphor of authority. The type of God's authority is now not the King, but the will of the people, and therefore the
typology of Divine Right, divorced from its traditional premises, must
find its traditional conclusions altered. Once again incrementality is
masking itself in the language of typology: contract theory shadows an
evolution typological politics would deny. But such (mis)use of ideas of

---

[48] Korshin, *Typologies*, p. 119.
[49] Stephen Zwicker, 'Representing the Revolution: Politics and High Culture in 1688', in
Cruickshanks, *By Force or by Default?*, pp. 109–34 (115).

divine authority which still found strong sympathy among the population (hence the merit in adopting them at all) was less a gesture towards democracy than a high cultural strategy for evading acknowledgement of a betrayal of kingship more profound, because more concealed, than that of Cromwell.

A third strategy was to discard typology altogether, to deconstruct it in fact, by exposing the detached nature of the Stuart 'text', grounded on no reality. This was the attempt to 'build a Williamite myth by satire', using *ad hominem* smears and mockery to discredit the whole typological edifice erected to justify such foolish and despicable figures as the Stuarts were portrayed as being. Perhaps provoked in part by an irritation that 'high culture should have been so firmly attached to the Stuart monarchy', it attempted to produce a popular culture which mocked at typological pretension:

Whig writers attack the Stuart cause with the low humour of the popular tradition, in which the fallen man is always ridiculous, never an 'archangel ruined'. They borrowed the forms of 'low culture' in order, first, to prove that the accession of William and Mary had been accepted by *all* classes of English society, and, second, to discredit Jacobite authors by opposing to their 'wit', the plain common sense of the freedom-loving Englishman.[50]

The deconstruction of Stuart 'wit' was, like much deconstruction, an Emperor's New Clothes phenomenon, its purpose being to divert attention from the nakedness of the Williamite claim by pointing out that the Stuarts were really wearing no clothes:

> The tories wish for James again,
>     The papists for his spouse;
> They say that she alone shall reign
>     Then Hey for wooden shoes!
>
> Perkin ap Dada Prince of Wales
>     Shall be High Admiral,
> And if the Dutch dare hoist their sails,
>     He'll burn and sink them all –
> The only way to prove his right
>     To th'scepter or the hod.
> If he beshit himself by flight,
>     He's Jemmy's son by God.
>
> Then will begin that Golden Age
>     The papists long to see . . .
>             'Mall in Her Majesty' (1689)

---

50 Cameron, *Poems on Affairs of State* 5, p. vii.

The mention of 'Golden Age' is a mocking reference to the Stuart myth of Augustan and Astraean return, while 'Perkin ap Dada' suggests that the Prince of Wales is a pretender (Perkin Warbeck, to whom his ancestor James IV gave aid against Henry VII), the son of Count Dada the Papal Nuncio, and a ridiculous figure from the Celtic fringe ('ap Dada'), not English at all. Similarly, the poem elsewhere mentions 'Teaguelanders': both the Irish and Welsh are being mocked as pro-Stuart backwoodsmen. 'My Welsh blood's up', exclaims 'Perkin' in another poem: the title 'Prince of Wales' is being deliberately confused with Welsh nationality in order to marginalize the Stuart prince.[51]

This satirical Williamite verse is perhaps the most important element in the varieties of critical strategy used against the Stuart 'text'. Not only does it 'use popular ballad forms that suggest a "factory" for anti-Jacobite propaganda' in an attempt to secure popular culture for Williamite views; it also emphasizes the specifically English nature of the Revolution: the way in which it, and the events which followed it, are a kind of English takeover of the British Isles. The penal laws in Ireland, the neglect of the Treaty of Limerick's terms, the propaganda war with Scotland, the Alien Act, the Union: all these and more are foreshadowed in the often riotously pro-English anti-Celtic nature of Williamite satire. And of course the most famous Williamite song of all belongs to this kind: 'Lilliburlero', supposed to have sung James out of his three kingdoms, 'once in the mouths of all the people' as Beauclerk told Johnson, and itself full of anti-Irish and anti-Catholic sentiment:

> Ho, brother Teig, dost hear the decree
> Dat we shall have a new debittie:
> Ho, by my soul, it is a Talbot
> And he will cut all de English throat.

That such sentiments could welcome the appointment of Tyrconnell in Ireland in 1687 hardly boded well for the future of James's regime.[52]

In addition to the manipulation or mockery of existing languages of royal compliment, a typology specific to William himself developed during his reign. As Stephen Baxter puts it:

William ... may not have been a Hercules or a David [both images used of James], and he was certainly not a Christ figure; but he was, at least during his lifetime, the Revolution personified.

William's presentation as the personification of Revolution can be found first in his appearance as republican deliverer in the medallic imagery of 1688/9, as in Smeltzing's 1688 medal with the legend 'ATAVUM PRO

---

[51] Ibid., pp. 25, 28, 29, 34.
[52] Ibid., p. 30; J. G. Simms, *Jacobite Ireland* (London: Routledge and Kegan Paul, 1969), p. 32; T. Crofton Croker (ed.), *The Historical Songs of Ireland* (London, 1841), p. 3.

LIBERTATE FIDEQUE' ('For the Liberty and Faith of our Ancestors') or the
invasion medal depicting the Belgian Lion holding the 'Cap of Liberty'.
Smeltzing's 1689 medal makes clear the overthrow of a central image of
Stuart typology, depicting 'A great Oak tree . . . bent and broken; beside it
a slender Orange tree. The sun is rising . . . ', while the 1689 Coronation
medal carries on this theme. The presence of uprooted or destroyed oak
trees as symbols of Williamite conquest suggest strongly that the oak is not
a neutral patriotic image but remains pro-Stuart in for example, Pope's
*Windsor Forest*.[53]

William is displayed as conqueror in the occasional medal, though he
was sensitive to this appellation. If not Aeneas or Augustus, he was at least
the Laocoon whose warning to the Trojans had been heeded. The 1688
Invasion medal depicts a horse saddled with the Declaration of Indulgence, and the monitory words of the Trojan seer adapted to Stuart
Britain: 'Britain, never trust to the Horse' is the translation. William's
propagandists were hinting that James was not really a British Trojan at
all, but the stalking horse of a foreign power, France (though France too,
in fact, claimed Trojan ancestry). William was the warner, the deliverer,
the restorer, tangentially if at all the conqueror: in short, how the Revolution liked to see itself (Woolf, *The Medallic Record of the Jacobite Movement*.
p. 12).

Although scurrilous and satirical Jacobite verse abounded in the replies
given to Williamite attack, Jacobite propaganda was not, like its rival,
based mainly on the concealment of the weakness of its own position. Its
central ideas rapidly adapted themselves to challenge, establishing in
response to Williamite success both a radicalized Jacobite voice and a
popular one, based on an alliance of high and folk culture which developed markedly over the next half century. Some of the popular voice's
view of the Revolution still survives in popular form:

> William, Mary, George and Anne,
> Four such children had never a man,
> They put their father to flight and shame,
> And called their brother a shocking bad name.

Or to the air of 'Lilliburlero' itself:

> Rock-a-bye baby, on the treetop,
> When the wind blows, the cradle will rock,
> When the bough breaks, the cradle will fall,
> Down will come baby, cradle and all.

[53] Noel Woolf, *The Medallic Record of the Jacobite Movement* (London: Spink, 1988), pp. 10, 22, 28;
Stephen Baxter (ed.), *England's Rise to Greatness 1660–1763* (Berkeley, CA: University of
California Press, 1983).

The oak-bough was broken because of James VIII and III, still in his cradle.[54]

Yet despite new developments in its expression, Jacobite ideology remained very much the product of traditionalist typology, codified and complex on a high cultural level and deeply loyal to the iconic beliefs which had generated it, though these were now textualized not only in high cultural typology, but also in the demotic language of street theatre itself. By the early 1690s:

The Jacobites were beginning to exploit street theatre, and in turn popular theatre was drifting towards Jacobitism. This was further evidenced by an incident at Bartholomew Fair in September, when a Merry Andrew – the English equivalent of the Lord of Misrule – was arrested 'for telling the mobb news that our fleet was come into Torbay, being forced in by some French privateers ...'

Ballad singers were widely used in London to distribute Jacobite propaganda, which could reach levels of 10,000 copies, as Mark Goldie informs us.[55] This move towards populism was emphasized by James's 'Whiggish' declaration of 1693, 'in which he pledged himself to defend the rights and liberties of Englishmen, to relieve the people of burdensome taxes, and to respect Parliament's wishes on religious matters'.[56]

Not only street theatre but the theatre proper showed Jacobite influence. Just as in the last years of Elizabeth, when London stood in danger from Essex's rebellion, certain plays were regarded as having a subversive message. John Dryden's *Cleomenes*, dealing with usurpation, was suppressed in 1692, 'and could only be staged after the offending passages were removed', while his *Don Sebastian* had already been satirized in 1690 for its Jacobite tendencies:

> If e're this Play shou'd have the Grace
> To be beheld by your sweet Face,
> Take heed how you are to it civil,
> For, Sirs! believe me! 'tis the Devil.
> A *Williamitish* Piece all thro',
> With which you nothing have to do.
> *Sebastian* better does the trick,
> With Bobs and Innuendo's thick,
> Which Abdicated Laureate brings
> In praise of Abdicated Kings.

---

[54] Cf. *The Golden Treasury*; Woolf, *Medallic Record*, p. 12.
[55] Paul Monod, 'Pierre's White Hat', in Cruickshanks, *By Force or by Default?*, pp. 159–89 (165); Mark Goldie, 'Tory Political Thought 1689–1714', unpublished Ph.D. thesis (Cambridge, 1977), p. 183.
[56] Monod, 'Pierre's White Hat', p. 165.

Paul Monod has recently argued that Otway's bloody *Venice Preserved* (later feared as a Jacobin and Chartist play) was repeatedly used in a Jacobite context: and this is not a new suggestion. *Richard III* lost its first act, as being too strong a reminder of usurpation (though of course it was the triumphant Henry VII to whom Stuarts linked themselves through the typology of the foundation-myth), while *Richard II* itself, feared by both sides as 'politically explosive', was off the stage between 1681 and 1719.[57] Sometimes the audience took it upon themselves to use otherwise perhaps innocuous plays as a source of moral judgement on the Revolution:

Mary ... inherited her father's love for drama, but she was occasionally embarrassed by it. Soon after her accession, she ordered a performance of Dryden's anti-Catholic play *The Spanish Friar*, which deals with the seizure of a king's throne by his daughter; she was stared at by the audience whenever usurpation was mentioned.[58]

The actors themselves sometimes took up this theme, as in a performance of *The Orphan* around 1717, when the lines from Act II 'It is the birthday of my Royal Master' were used to begin the play on 10 June, White Rose Day, James's birthday. Paul Monod suggests that

It is possible that the founding in 1718 of the High Church and Jacobite newspaper, Elizabeth Powell's *The Orphan Reviv'd: or, Powell's Weekly Journal*, was connected with this incident.[59]

But it was of course not only the Jacobites who could use the theatre, for the new regime was conscious of the importance of display as a means to expressing an iconography of power, even where this was distinct from the old typological issues clung to by the Stuarts. Some of the themes of the new regime found lighthearted treatment in the late comedies of Congreve, and the Nonjuror Jeremy Collier's blast against the stage in the late 1690s can possibly be seen as a protest against its usurpation by certain themes as much as its immorality in general. The Nonjurors (perhaps one in six of the English clergy nonjured) held a high moral ground allied to the material dispossession they had suffered, which can be seen as mocked in the materialist and contractual obsessions of plays like *Love for Love* and *The Way of the World*. Like the Nonjurors in the Church, the Jacobites as a whole became increasingly marginalized into being the consenting audience rather than the controlling dramatists of contemporary theatre, even if they competed to adopt Whig stage heroes such as Cato as their own, successfuly enough to lead one pamphleteer to suppose that Addison's

---

[57] Cf. David Bywaters, *Dryden in Revolutionary England.* (Berkeley and Oxford: University of California Press, 1991), p. 7; Monod, 'Pierre's White Hat', pp. 159–89, 164, 167, 168, 170; *Notes & Queries* cxcii (1947), pp. 90–3; cf. Brinkley, *Arthurian Legend in the Seventeenth Century*, pp. 143–4.

[58] Monod, ibid.      [59] Monod, 'Pierre's White Hat', pp. 164–7, 170–1.

1713 play showed its author a closet Tory.[60] But on the whole Jacobites felt excluded, and that is perhaps why the 'disaffected aristocrats, gentlemen and merchants' of the cause built up links with popular and folk culture, theatres on the margin (a similar process went on in Scotland after 1707, when the vernacular revival was a high cultural strategy to defend a peculiarly Scottish political dimension against the metropolitan encroachment of new 'British' cultural norms). A dispossessed high culture gravitated to the language of rebellion and dissent, and in London an alternative theatre of Jacobite display developed, as in the 10 June 1695 Dog Tavern riot, 'a few feet from the Drury Lane theatre' which can be seen as '... commenting directly on Whig dominance over the official stage, by creating ... theatre of the streets'. The presence there of 'popular singing-men' emphasized in nascent form what was to be a major tactic of underground Jacobite communication in the eighteenth century: the use of balladeers, street-singers, minstrels, fiddlers and other musical journey-men to convey either in code or more obvious form the words and airs of the Stuart cause, through which so much of its ideology at the periphery (of Saint-Germain's concerns as well as Westminster's) was conveyed in the century to come.[61]

High cultural writers like Dryden had foreshadowed something of this approach (for example in the use of popular chapbook culture in *The Hind and the Panther*), while in our own century the effectiveness of such a method in defence of an underground political position can be seen on our own doorstep, as Leslie Shepherd points out in *A History of Street Literature*:

In Northern Ireland, folk songs were recruited by the IRA. Thousands of penny song cards eulogizing the legendary lives of dead IRA gunmen were sold in the Belfast pubs, reinforcing a new mythology of hatred.[62]

Hatred was not the sole Jacobite message: there were also martyrdom, the promise of a golden age, chronic injustice and (till it was too late to believe in such things – indeed, Jacobite historians like Innes had a hand in the demythologizing) the foundation-myths of political and ecclesiastical authority.[63] Sometimes these were reversed to hint at the injustice of the conqueror: as when King Arthur (in Dryden's libretto for Purcell) is shown as having a yellow face. This, expressed in what has been called 'the worst banality in Dryden's libretto' may become a more comprehensible statement when we learn that the term 'Shaun Bui', 'Yellow Jack', was being applied in Ireland to followers of William III. Hence Arthur's

60 *Mr Addison Turn'd Tory; or The Scene Inverted; Wherein it is Made Appear that the Whigs Have Misunderstood That Author in his Tragedy Call'd Cato*, By a Gentleman of Oxford (London, 1713).

61 Monod, 'Pierre's White Hat', pp. 164–7, 170–1.

62 Zwicker, *Politics and Language*, p. .153; Leslie Shepherd, *A History of Street Literature* (Newton Abbot: David and Charles, 1973), p. 144.

63 Roger A. Mason, 'Scotching the Brut', p. 77.

yellowness is a sign of his usurpation, his status as 'false Arthur' hinted at
in the final chorus:

> Our natives not alone appear
> To court his martial prize;
> But foreign kings adopted here,
> Their crowns at home despise.

That despising lighted on Dryden, who was replaced as Poet Laureate by
Nahum Tate. Tate's libretto for *Dido and Aeneas* (1689) contains (un-
surprisingly) little or no discernible reference to the impact of the foundation-myth on contemporary politics.[64] But Jacobite writers were
already on the point of adopting the *Aeneid* as their own: deepening the
Stuart text of Vergilian celebration into a whole code of exile and return
which was to endure well into the next century, as in *Ascanius, or Aeneas and
his Two Sons* (1746) which shows even Whig language yielding at last to a
recognition of the power of Jacobite code.[65]

The forceful image of an exiled Aeneas, a dispossessed Augustus, was
developed rapidly by Jacobite writers: not only Dryden (whose *Aeneid* will
be discussed in detail in Chapter 3) but other writers such as Lord
Maitland, who dedicated a part-translation of the epic to Mary of
Modena in 1691 in these revealing terms:

there are some things in the sixth book which seem to have a particular relation to
the affairs of England, such as Visc. Strafford's murder; Doctor Oates his testi-
mony, the unnatural Usurper & some of his chiefe Agents . . . yet I have kept close
to Virgil's words . . .

Not only does Maitland's preface commit itself to a view of the *Aeneid* as
political allegory, it also suggests to the Queen and its other readers a
vision of the Stuart period as a lost golden age of Augustan value:

when he [Augustus] had for ye last time shut ye temple of Janus, & universall
peace reign'd over ye face of ye earth, about ye time ye King of Kings, ye Prince of
peace, ye Saviour of mankind appear'd in the flesh . . .

The Christian and Augustan overtones of Astraea's *renovatio* are both
implicitly aligned with the Stuart age, an alignment reinforced when Lord
Maitland goes on to say that Mary of Modena is herself of the same family
as Augustus.

The translation of Book vi in particular bears out Maitland's prefatory
claims to political reference, as Aeneas finds in the underworld:

---

[64] Robert Etheridge Moore, *Henry Purcell and the Restoration Theatre*, with a foreword by Sir John
Westrup (London: Heinemann, 1961), pp. 38, 40, 70, 76; cf. John O'Daly, *Irish Jacobite Poems*
(1866), p. 49n.

[65] *AEneas and his two Sons* (London: J. Oldcastle, 1745/6); *Ascanius, or The Young Adventurer*
(London: T. Johnston, 1746).

Here those who brothers for a crown disown,
Turn out their parents, and usurp the throne,
Enslave the people whom they swore to serve,
Receive the punishment their crimes deserve . . .

Here's one his country & his master sold
To lawless tyranny for foreign gold,
Brought in a powerfull Lord to rule the state,
Who spight of oaths & honour would be great . . .

In contrast to the world of *Aeneid* vi (much used by Pope in *The Dunciad*) there is the age of Augustus, who will '. . . bring back Saturnian times / The golden age to blest Italian climes'. The Italian family of Mary of Modena and the loss of her husband's kingdom for his loyalty to Rome made this reference specifically pertinent as well as generally appropriate.[66]

In his dedicatory preface, Maitland apologizes twice for his nationality, hoping that 'your Majesty shall . . . believe that it's possible for a Scotch-man to write tollerable English . . . ', and in view of what Colin Kidd has recently said about Scottish Jacobite Latinity it is interesting that both of the *Aeneid* or *Aeneid*-style Stuart texts of the early 1690s were by Scots.

Although Maitland's piece was (and protested itself to be) a simple translation, not even varnished with code like Dryden's, James Philp of Almericlose's *The Grameid* was an epic of the 1689 Rising itself, modelled on both Lucan's *Pharsalia* and, most obviously, the *Aeneid*. As its only editor, Alexander Murdoch, writes, 'Virgil has evidently been so thoroughly studied and absorbed by our author, that his parodies have often the freedom of spontaneity'.[67]

'We sing the Scottish wars and civil strife', Philp opens, immediately laying the blame for such strife on the anti-Aeneas, William, asking 'Does she [Britain] herself prepare to cut off, in fatal strife, the British race'. The word used is 'Brutigenum', the nation originated by Brute, and hence originally Aeneas. William, the anti-Brute (a real brute) is a usurper whose conduct promises only a nation divided against itself, for the organic identity of Britain depends upon its loyalty to the exiled native king, Brute's heir. At this point, however, Philp shows a tendency to alternate between Anglo-British and Scottish foundation-myths, remarking the gravity of the situation in more native terms: '. . . the martial land and house of Fergus fall, by their own arms'.

The action of the poem focuses on Graham's own native territory, 'the

---

66 National Library of Scotland MS Dep. 221/62, 2rff., 68r–69r.

67 Ibid., 5v; Colin Kidd, 'The Ideological Significance of Scottish Jacobite Latinity' in Jeremy Black and Jeremy Gregory (eds.), *Culture, Politics and Society in Britain 1660–1800* (Manchester and New York: Manchester University Press, 1991), pp. 110–30; Philp, *Grameid*, pp. xxiii, xxxvii.

land of Angus', which in Latin is 'locus Aeneadum', 'Aeneas' being usually Scotticized as 'Angus'. Dundee, the hero, prepares to defend the cause of King James, as does his fellow-Trojan King Louis of France: 'great Louis, in Hectorean arms'. Graham's allies, such as Glengarry, quote the *Aeneid* as they stand ready to defend their cause. Glengarry's own brother bears the name 'Aeneas', while Cameron of Lochiel calls his men to fight for 'the sacred Caesar' in an attempt to restore 'the golden age' of Astraea. Commemorating Restoration Day on 29 May, Dundee observes:

I will perform this annual solemnity in honour of the peace-bringing Charles. He, arms being laid down, put an end to the Civil War, and peace restored, brought round the Golden Age.

'Brought round' is a noteworthy phrase, since on such a cyclical view the validity of typological history and Stuart hopes of a second Restoration depended. More generally, the passage itself has strong Augustan parallels (ending civil war, bringing peace and the golden age of the Fourth Eclogue) and echoes the nostalgia for the Stuart past found in Atterbury's and Maitland's prefaces.[68]

In defiance of claims of a bloodless 'Glorious' Revolution, Philp's work emphasizes Lucanian darkness and violence as a counterbalance to its Vergilian promise of hope and restoration. Instead of the nascent myth of a British state of free and sovereign parliaments with civil and religious toleration, Philp offers us images of horrifically renewed civil war: 'Insane Britain conceives fearful revolution', Alecto stirs up evil. 'Fatal strife' is emphasized, and contrasted with the 'illustrious youth, the splendour of your great ancestors', James Prince of Wales, for whose right the royalist forces fight. Light emanates from the Stuart cause, darkness from its opponents: the 'bright sons of the mighty Fergus', roused by the Fiery Cross, war to dispel the darkness of gold and Dutch corruption.

Philp's mixed use of foundation-myths leads to an attempt to resolve the long-running tensions which had existed between hegemonic English and nationalist Scottish accounts, so that the Stuarts may be seen as leaders of a united patriotic resistance (even though pro-Scot and anti-Saxon comments infest the narrative of the poem). Philp writes of 'the birth of the divine Prince [James] on the same day as that on which Constantine first breathed the air of Heaven'. The allusion appears to be that Constantine who was the forerunner of Henrician claims to royal sovereignty in ecclesiastical matters: but in fact Philp is referring to Constantine II of Scotland. An actual Scottish king is being melded with the language of British foundation-myth in fruitful confusion.

[68] Philp, *Grameid*, pp. 1, 2, 5, 17, 18, 103, 123, 133, 170.

Another method used by Philp to Scotticize the Arthur/Brutus story is to emphasize a strongly local geographical colour, not only in his description of Angus as 'locus Aeneadum', but also in the presentation of 'Ardesier' as 'Arthurshire', while the narrative mixes Scottish and Anglo-British foundation-myth references freely. Yet a distinctively Scottish resistance is emphasized amid these archetypal recollections: Dundee is the 'last Hector' of the British race, but also a new Calgacus (the patriot leader of the Caledonians at Mons Graupius, to whom Tacitus gave the famous line 'solitudinem faciunt, pacem appellant' ('they have made a desolation, and call it peace')). This is curiously relevant, since the whole propaganda of the Revolutioners is that they are bringing peace, but in fact they are laying waste: William and Mary are Tarquin and Tullia, echoing the 1689 anti-Williamite satire of Arthur Mainwaring. Philp seems abreast of recent developments in the argument.[69]

Philp also, perhaps following the patterns of Gaelic poetry in the wars of Montrose, appears to be the first writer in the Lowland tradition to formulate what was later to be a popular Jacobite icon: that of the Highlander as patriot, a Scot true to liberty and history, as opposed to the corrupt Lowlander:

He [Graham] despised the Lowland race, slow to war and ready for a bribe – the cowardly herd of easy-going rustics, the faithless inhabitants of the well-tithed lands.

These are those who would join with the Saxons who have 'vilely sold their liberty and their King for cursed gold . . .'. The 'bought and sold for English gold' view of the Treaty of Union is already here in embryo: and this idea of gold as the principal corrupting force of the new regime is one which also finds its echo in English criticism of the financial revolution. Against such corruption stands the Highlander, fighter for liberty and scorner of pelf:

Hence, too, this great and never-failing Highland contingent appears to uphold the throne, one generation succeeding another, in glorious deeds and uncontaminated fidelity . . .

This is putting it a little strongly, even from an enthusiastic Jacobite. But what is important about Philp's statements of this kind is that they rebut the view that the patriot Highlander image is a creation of the sham Celtification of nineteenth-century Scotland (a view still perhaps that of the scholarly majority), by presenting an image of the true patriotic Scotland as essentially Highland: and it was this image of the Highlander as patriot, struggler through history to liberty, heir to the Celtic Fergus, as was his lord the Stuart Caesar, which originated some of the most potent

[69] Ibid., pp. 2, 3, 13, 15, 20, 34, 37, 46, 54, 99, 111; Cameron, *Poems on Affairs of State* 5, pp. 46ff.

images of a Celticized Scotland. For only the 'Scots of ancient race ...
tartaned bands of ancient Albion', as Philp puts it (in despite of Lord
Dacre) were prepared to fight for Scotland and its 'exiled Caesar' (and
this held good for Lowland and even English Jacobites, who tartaned
themselves out as psychological Highlanders, like Graham himself in the
poem). Dundee, the 'last Hector', as he was to be 'last and best of Scots' in
Dryden's translation of Pitcairne's Latin elegy, majestically throughout
the text defends Brutus' people, the Trojans, and Fergus' people, the
Scots, against 'the Dutch Prince' and his 'Belgic general' (Major-General
Hugh Mackay of Scourie – but psychological nationhood is all). The
'illustrious James ... son of Fergus' is 'sold for Dutch gold' amid a
xenophobic atmosphere of resistance which unites Anglo-British and
Scottish foundation myths against a foreign enemy and his foreign supporters, whether these be Dutch or Scots.[70]

The concerns of *The Grameid* may seem remote, though they are the
record of a combatant's view, but as I hope to have already begun to show,
such concerns are reflected throughout contemporary Jacobite literature.
Answers to Williamite satire are quite ready to see in the new king an
anti-Aeneas:

> To make the parallel hold tack,
> Methinks there's little lacking;
> One took his father pick-a-pack,
> And t'other sent his packing ...

runs one comparison of William to Aeneas, while Arthur Mainwaring
writes in 'The King of Hearts' (1689), of William's allies (in this case Lord
Delamer) as anti-Aeneases: 'I sing the man that raised a shirtless band / Of
northern rabble, when the Prince did land'.[71]

This kind of sentiment, so skilfully incorporated in Dryden's rendition of
the epic, was already commonplace by the mid-1690s, so commonplace
perhaps that apologists like Sir Richard Blackmore attempted to answer it
directly by adopting both Arthur and Aeneas for Williamite use: 'sing the
*Briton* and his righteous arms' Blackmore wrote, attempting to counter
charges of foreignness as well as usurpation. But such use of legitimist
typology could often sound uncomfortable and contrived, leading to the
need to emphasize William at the expense of his archetypes, a method
which (as suggested above) rendered the typology redundant in favour of

---

[70] Philp, *Grameid*, pp. 30, 43, 47, 89, 90, 97, 99, 104, 107; Hugh Trevor-Roper, 'The Invention of
Tradition: The Highland Tradition of Scotland', in Eric Hobsbawm and Terence Ranger
(eds.), *The Invention of Tradition* (Cambridge: Cambridge University Press, 1983), pp. 15–41;
See Murray G. H. Pittock, *The Invention of Scotland: The Stuart Myth and the Scottish Identity 1638
to the Present* (London and New York: Routledge, 1991), p. 35 for a discussion of Pitcairne's
elegy.

[71] Cameron, *Poems on Affairs of State*, pp. 83–4; Zwicker, *Politics and Language*, p. 234n.

its latest exemplar. Williamite inability consistently to sustain Vergilian categories can be seen in the verse of Matthew Prior:

> If Namur be compared to Troy;
>> Then Britain's boys excelled the Greeks:
> Their siege did ten long years employ;
>> We've done our business in ten weeks.

Here, not only do the Williamites excel the ancients, they reverse the foundation-myth roles, being themselves Greeks rather than Trojans.[72]

Even where Trojan-ness was sustained, it was ahistorical in terms of the typological legitimations of Britain and France, emphasizing successful conquest far more than past example:

> Arms, and the Man, they sing, no *French* finess,
> But hearty blows and *Brandenburg* address.

'An Epistle to Mr Dryden' (published in the aptly named *The Muses Farewel to Popery & Slavery* (1689/90)), continues with a typically William-ite mixture of inherited and current ideology: 'Give us a King, Divine, by Law and Sense'. The uneasy dependency of non-satirical Williamite verse on a typology at odds with its claims was already laying the foundations for 'the enervation' which led to the blandness of early Hanoverian patriotic verse, 'lacking in the tumid enthusiasm of the seventeenth-century paean'.[73]

One argument of the Stuart text which developed in the 1690s was the xenophobic element in renderings of the foundation-myth. Before address-ing this development in context, it is useful to examine those who were victims of internal Williamite as opposed to external Jacobite xenophobia: the Irish, whose experience of the early years of the Revolution was even more traumatic than that of the opposition in mainland Britain. The new xenophobia of the 1690s cut two ways.

The position of the Stuarts in relation to Irish feeling was bound to be different from that which they occupied in the opinion of their English and Scottish supporters. Unlike British Jacobites, the Irish could not think of James's dynasty as native, whether in terms of its foundation-myth or claims to ecclesiastical or political authority. Ireland was a conquered state, partially colonized by the Stuarts themselves. But the later Stuarts had had some sympathy with the Catholic Irish and had been in turn defended by them, though not to the extent portrayed by racist propa-ganda in the Civil War period. As a result, the association of the Stuarts

---

[72] Brinkley, *Arthurian Legend*, pp. 150ff.; *The Poetical Works of Matthew Prior*, with a Memoir and Critical Dissertation by the Revd George Gilfillan (Edinburgh: James Nichol, p. 51.

[73] *The Muses Farewel to Popery & Slavery*, 2nd and revised edn (London, 1690), pp. 103–4; Korshin, *Typologies*, p. 119.

with the native hero Fionn, set to flower in the eighteenth century, had perhaps been made possible. The exilic experience of the Stuarts after 1649 and 1688 could also be aligned with the long absence of Oisin, a point obliquely referred to by Macpherson's Ossian epic.

During Charles II's reign, Ireland was under the tolerant viceroy Ormonde for sixteen years, and Catholic landownership more than doubled, rising another ten per cent under James, before falling by almost forty per cent under William, and a further two-thirds under the Georges. This process was fuelled by Anne's 1704 Act, which prohibited a Catholic leaving his estate to a Catholic eldest son, enabled that son's conversion to render his father a tenant for life and prohibited Catholics from buying land or leasing it for more than thirty-one years. The change of emphasis in the so-called tolerant Revolution regime is quite marked: indeed, a famous Irish historian sums up a study of Ireland in the Jacobite period by observing that:

It was to be many years before Catholics regained the status and opportunities that they had briefly enjoyed under a Jacobite administration.[74]

When James attempted to regain his throne via Ireland, he agreed that the English Parliament had 'no right to pass laws for Ireland' (an occurrence not entirely irrelevant to Swift's *Drapier's Letters* only thirty years later). The king was compelled by his need of support to listen to Irish Catholic grievances more closely than any of his predecessors. Although James was subsequently criticized for his desertion of Ireland after the Williamites had turned the tide, the country had invested so much life and hope in the Stuart cause, and the alternative proved to be so very much worse, that continuing Jacobite links were almost inevitable. It was in Ireland that the 'bloodless' Revolution proved the biggest lie, not only in terms of the thousands of Wild Geese that left to fight for France and the hundreds of thousands that followed them, but also in simple casualty figures, Aughrim (1691) being quite possibly the bloodiest battle ever fought in the British Isles. As Seamas Dall MacCuart put it in 'Elegy for Sorley MacDonnell':

> In Aughrim of the slaughter they rest;
> Their skeletons lying there, uncoffined,
> Have caused the women of Ireland to beat their hands,
> The children to be neglected, and the fugitives to wail.

Again, as in Philp, the images of desolation are balanced with the light and fruitfulness which flows from the Stuart king:

> Bring ye flowers – bring ye flowers,
> The fresh flowers of spring,

[74] Simms, *Jacobite Ireland*, pp. 3, 4, 262, 267.

Invasion and xenophobia

> To strew on the pathway
> Of James our true king.
>
> 'King James's welcome to Ireland' (1689)

Since traditional Stuart typology was not so readily accessible in Ireland, the Stuart cause and its leader are typically seen in general terms of fertility and renewal, the good kings bringing light and life to a starving land.[75] This vision, consonant with the view of royalty held by Irish bards such as Tiag MacDiarc Mac Bruadighe of Thomond (that fertility and good kingship go together), survived well into the eighteenth century in Irish patriotism:

> O! the French and Spanish
> Soon our foes will banish;
> Then at once will vanish
>     All our grief and dread;
> City, town, and village,
> Shall no more know pillage,
> Music, feasting, tillage
>     Shall abound instead;
> Poetry, romances,
> Races, and long dances,
> Shouts, and songs, and glances,
>     From eyes bright with smiles!–
> *Our* King's feasts shall Fame hymn
> *Though I may not name him*
> Victory will proclaim him
>     *Monarch of the Isles!*[76]

Meanwhile James, like so many of his Irish followers, was in exile, and that moreover on account of his religion:

*Righ Shemus*, King James, represented the faith of Erin, and so became her comrade in martyrdom.[77]

This comradeship was realized in song in material and immediate terms as well as remote and symbolic ones:

> Here's a health to *your* and *my* king,
> The Sovereign of our liking,
> And to Sarsfield, underneath whose flag
> We'll cast once more a chance;
> For the morning's dawn will bring us
> Across the seas and sing us

---

[75] Ibid., pp. 8off., 229; Crofton-Croker, *Historical Songs*, p. 29.
[76] J. C. O'Callaghan, *History of the Irish Brigades in the Service of France* (Glasgow: Cameron and Ferguson, 1870), p. 164.
[77] Anon, 'Irish Jacobite Songs', *The Royalist* VII:3 (1896), pp. 41–6 (45). Feeling towards James in Ireland was more mixed than this might suggest.

> To take our sword and wield a brand
> Among the sons of France.
>
>              'After Aughrim's Great Disaster'[78]

Here, in the aftermath of Aughrim, king, general and exiles are seen as sharing an air of optimism and defiant adventure rather than defeat and martyrdom. And this was no fantasy: James VII and II, his son and grandson all fought alongside the soldiers who made up the Irish Brigades: and in the first instance, these soldiers formed James VII and II's personal army in France. Only one third of his British forces served under the new regime.[79]

If the prejudice shown against Ireland (and increasingly, as the 1690s progressed, Scotland) was evidence of xenophobia directed against the peripheries of the emerging state of Britain, the xenophobia shown by the marginalized Jacobites against the occupants of power was its protesting counterpart. John Tutchin's 'The Foreigners', which appeared in 1700, was a good example of the kind of material that was circulating, berating as it did the influx of foreign influences represented by William, and mocking the passivity of the natives:

> Long time had *Israel* been disus'd from Rest,
> Long had they been by Tyrants sore opprest;
> Kings of all sorts they ignorantly crav'd,
> And grew more stupid as they were enslav'd . . .

This picture of the English Israel is a much more enervated one than that of Dryden's *Absalom and Achitophel*, on which it is partly modelled.[80]

Rising xenophobia was also reflected in images of betrayal by elements in the indigenous dynasty. If William was the foreign king with no claim to the throne, then Mary was the treacherous native daughter, as in 'The Female Parricide':

> Oft have we heard of impious sons before,
> Rebelled for crowns their royal parents wore;
> But of unnatural daughters rarely hear
> 'Till those of hapless James and old King Lear.
> But worse than cruel lustful Goneril, thou!

This 'lustful Goneril' (a typology of Mary which survives in Catholic circles into this century) had helped the 'alien' to 'buy a foreign army to deface / The feared and hated remnant of their race' in Britain.[81]

---

78 Patrick Gakin, *Irish Songs of Resistance* (London: The Workers' Music Association, 1955/6), p. 18.

79 For continued service of James's soldiers under William, see John Childs, *The Army, James II and the Glorious Revolution* (Manchester: Manchester Press, 1980), p. 206; Paul Monod, 'For the King to Enjoy his own Again', unpublished Ph.D. thesis (Yale, 1985), p. 112.

80 Frank H. Ellis (ed.), *Poems on Affairs of State* Volume 6 (New Haven and London: Yale University Press, 1970), pp. 224, 230.

81 Cameron, *Poems on Affairs of State* Volume 5: pp. 118, 156, 157.

The idea that the crown was foreign and served foreign interests made the uses of revenue from taxation suspect. Thus it is that in William's reign a central Jacobite criticism of the new regime takes shape, which was to last until at least the accession of George III:

> The trade was sunk, the fleet and army spent,
> Devouring taxes swallowed lesser rent . . .

Not only is the new monarch corrupt and profligate: he is a warmonger, having only taken the British thrones so that he might perpetuate conflict with France. This complaint was felt especially keenly in Scotland.[82]

In such circumstances, there was growing sympathy for James as a patriotic figure, which did not seem markedly affected by the Assassination Plot of 1696, in which the plotters called James their 'father'. This sympathy was noted by visitors from abroad, 'Andre Bonet, the London resident of the king of Prussia' being 'surprised that . . . Jacobite literature could circulate so freely'.[83] Often, of course, it circulated in encoded form: the beast-fable in particular being a popular subgenre in the 1690s, useful because it could reinforce xenophobic distaste of the Williamite regime by presenting it in terms of unpleasant or non-native animals, though it also condemned the complicity of the 'free-Born English Brute', a pun on the foundation-myth. From this period comes one of the fabular comparisons about the change of regime which was to prove most popular during the next fifty years:

> Thus *Jove* was blest by every grateful *Frog*,
> When o're the *Fens* King *Stork* succeeds King *Log* . . .
>
> *The Anti-Weesils: A Poem* (1691)

This comparison, used here against James VII and II, could be applied to William and the Hanoverians in the years to come, culminating in Pope's use of it in *The Dunciad*, an adoption into high culture of a popular political code: one of the ways in which *The Dunciad* echoes *The Hind and the Panther*, showing how the world has changed in the interim.[84]

'The vicious tide of xenophobia' feared by Defoe brought many elegies to James VII and II when he died in 1701. James was the exiled patriot monarch, not the foreign incomer, and his quality of nativity exiled helped to focus a conflation of popular and high cultural readings of loss. By 1694,

[82] Ibid., p. 118; *A Second Book of Scots Pasquils* (Edinburgh, 1827), p. 96 ('Epitaph on King James VII').

[83] *The Secret History of the Calves=Head Club*, 7th edn (London, 1709), p. 42; Paul Monod, *Jacobitism and the English People* (Cambridge: Cambridge University Press, 1989), p. 100; this may be the event referred to in John Doran, *London in the Jacobite Times*, 2 vols. (London: Richard Bentley & Son, 1877), 1: p. 71.

[84] Frank H. Ellis (ed.), *Affairs of State* 6: pp. 353–4; *The Weesils: A Satyrical Fable* (London, 1691), By Thomas Brown on Dr Sherlock; *The Anti-Weesils* (London, 1691), pp. 8, 10. James is presented here as a panther.

long before the age of sentimental Jacobitism, James was being addressed in terms of the love song. Erotic loss coined a new metaphor of Stuart support to sustain the image of an exiled native Aeneas among a wider audience, and this was often merged with beast-fable to present the love-song as the song of a native bird, or the king himself as such a bird: the blackbird in the case of James VIII and III, the moorhen in that of Charles Edward Stuart. 'The Blackbird' itself, apparently Irish in origin, is one of the finest examples of this kind, with its wonderful ability to slide over the whole range of registers from king to bird, in expressing lightly disguised Jacobite code to a wide audience:

> Once on a morning of sweet recreation,
>     I heard a young maiden a-making her moan,
> With such sighing and sobbing and sad lamentation,
>     Crying, 'My blackbird most royal has flown!
>
> In England my blackbird and I were together,
>     Where he was still gentle and generous of heart,
> O woe to the time that they sent him thither,
>     And now they have forced him to dwell far apart.
>
> In Scotland, he's deemed and highly esteemed,
>     In England he's known as a stranger to be;
> But his fame shall remain in France and in Spain,
>     Good luck to my blackbird, wherever he be!
>
> O, what if the fowler my blackbird has taken?
>     Then sadness and sorrow shall be all my tune,
> But if he is safe, then I'll no be forsaken,
>     And hope yet to see him in May or in June.
>
> For him through the fire, through mud and through mire,
>     I'll go, for I love him to such a degree
> That was constant and kind, and noble of mind,
>     Success to my blackbird, wherever he be.
>
> The birds of the forest are all met together,
>     The turtle has chosen to dwell with the dove,
> And I am resolved, in foul or fair weather,
>     Once more in the springtime to follow my love.'

The song has not been dated exactly (though recent research by Peter Davidson pushes it back as far as the 1640s). It seems to have been popular around 1715, when there was a spate of 'Blackbird' satires: this was the year when '*The Tale of the Raven and the Blackbird* by the Author of the *Blackbird's Song*' (not this one) appeared in London. The fact that the native bird is 'known as a stranger' in England suggests a perceived change of heart among the English, who have denationalized themselves like Mackay of Scourie in *The Grameid*, by failing to recognize a native king.[85]

The accession of Anne defused Jacobite xenophobia, and this was one of the reasons her twelve-year reign produced an interlude of consent to the new regime on the part of many natural Jacobites. Anne was portrayed in terms calculated to emphasize her native status: at the beginning of her reign she told Parliament that she knew her 'heart to be entirely English', a phrase which was seized upon:

> Begin, Great Queen, the *Stuart's* steps to tread . . .
> And let thy *Living* Worth Exceed the *Dead*;
> Happiest of Princes in this Climate Born,
> Entirely *English*, above thy Enemies Scorn . . .

proclaimed 'the Golden Age', a poem of November 1702 which portrayed Anne as a 'Second Restoration of the Stuarts', a *renovatio* of Astraea, and thus a legitimate exemplar of the iconography of her father's dynasty. Anne was certainly strongly aligned with the imagery of her predecessors, even to the extent of Swift's compliments on her hunting. Some Jacobites read into her assumption of such status (restoring the Royal Touch, for example, albeit in a simplified ritual) a willingness to restore her half-brother which was perhaps never there. Despite the poetic and medallic portrayal of Anne as an 'Entirely English Heart' or 'The Golden Age Restor'd', some were not convinced:

> 'Tis She, that wou'd, for ev'ry slight Offence,
> Depose a True Hereditary Prince;
> That would *Usurpers* for their Treason Crown,
> Till Time and Vengeance drag them headlong down,
> And *Exil'd Monarchs* Reassert their rightful Throne.
>
> William Shippen, 'Faction Display'd'

Writers like Shippen saw Anne for what she had been, one of the instruments by which William had gained and held power.[86]

But one of the virtues Anne undeniably had was that she was an easier subject for Stuart typology than her predecessor. Matthew Prior found no difficulty in establishing her as Augustus, with himself in the role of Horace, in 'An Ode, Humbly Inscrib'd to the Queen – On the Late Glorious Success of Her Majesty's Arms, 1706', even though the young

---

85 Ellis, *Poems on Affairs of State* 6: p. 263; *A Collection of Loyal Songs* (London, 1694); *The Tale of the Raven and the Blackbird* by the Author of the *Blackbird's Song*, 2nd edn (London, 1715); Crofton-Croker, *Historical Songs*, pp. 117ff.; this set of 'The Blackbird' is sung by 'The Corries' in *Stovies* (1980); another is published by Hogg in *The Jacobite Relics*, 2 vols. (London, 1819–21), II: p. 68.

86 Ellis, *Poems on Affairs of State*, 6: pp. 449, 453, 465, 487, 648, 651; E. P. Thompson, *Whigs and Hunters* (Harmondsworth: Penguin, 1975), p. 29.

James was a military leader on the other side in the War of the Spanish Succession.

James's image-makers had not been idle either. The 1697 Roettiers medal which emphasized the patriotic and Roman aspects of the young prince amid 'images of adversity and triumph', was followed by portrayals of James as the sun which 'will soon rise and revitalize the earth', and the 1708 'Cuius Est' medal, which showed the young king on one side and on the other a map of Britain surrounded by waves on which were ships: either those of the navy his father had done so much to found, or those of the French who were to try and land him in Scotland that year. In any event they were 'walls of oak': metaphors for the Stuart oak, the oak of rescue and England's royal tree. The exiled king was still commonly seen in terms of a renewed fertility which had been mocked by the famines of William's reign ('thirteen years I wanting bread', as one Scots song describes it), and which Anne's reign had failed to deliver due to persistent war. On the other hand, a restored James would bring peace:

> The Lads with curling Ivy bound
> The Maids with flowry Garlands crown'd,
> To their great Pan shall yearly Honours pay,
> And consecrate with Mirth, the *Restoration* Day.[87]

And it was peace, or more precisely withdrawal from war, which James VIII and III sought when he made the attempt of 1708, and with French help (despite Roettiers including 'King of France' among his titles in a French-struck medal) attempted to secure the Scottish throne.

## Scotland and the Union

> Shall Monarchy be quite forgot,
>     and of it no more heard?
> Antiquity be razed out,
>     and slav'ry put in stead?
> Is *Scots* Mens blood now grown so cold
>     the valour of their Mind
> That they can never once reflect
>     on old long sine, &c?
>
>                 *The true Scots Mens Lament for the Loss of*
>                 *the Rights of their Ancient Kingdom*)

---

[87] Frank H. Ellis (ed.), *Poems on Affairs of State* 7 (New Haven and London: Yale University Press, 1975), p. 174 ; Woolf, *Medallic Record*, pp. 46ff., 55; *Second Book of Scottish Pasquils*, p. 96; cited Monod, *Jacobitism and the English People*, pp. 66, 74, 75.

Here lyes the unnatural nephew, sone [sic],
Ambitious as wes Absolon . . .
Scotland rejoyce, now quyte of a most cruel foe,
O! starved in Caledon, and martyred in Glenco.

Epitaph on King William III

God Bless preserve and home in Safety Bring
James 3d Great Britain France and Irelands King
Head of the Church the Christian faith's defender.
Plagued by rebellious Whiggs and term'd Pretender
Of Scotland Prince and Stewart Royall Pearle
Duke Rothsay, Carrick Cunninghame Kyles Earle . . .

'To the Royall? or health of the day
being the 10th of June 1711'[88]


The Union of Scotland and England remains a matter of live debate: that such is the case indicates that it is an event still central to the mythology of Scotland and Britain, as much as to their history. Particularly in Scotland, it endlessly reproduces itself as a typological paradigm of vice or virtue, loyalty or corruption. The Revolution was the catalyst for an absorption of England's peripheries, both internal and external, into the new power core: the once Parliamentarian South East consolidated itself at the heart of a new regime which favoured the ruralism of Stuart iconography as little as it did the typological royalisms of Scotland and Ireland. This centre of authority created its own validity in its development of the constitutional sovereignty of a 'free' Parliament. Out of the invasion of a usurper, persecution and violence in Ireland and constitutional pressure on Scotland, grew doctrines of liberty and limited popular sovereignty, backed up by a tenfold increase in the number of capital crimes which helped underwrite the legitimacy of the state. This is not simply a modern gloss: the intimate relationship between the identification of criminality and the identification of political legitimacy was well understood. In John Gay's *Beggar's Opera* the unwritten constitution of the regime generates its own justification through the unstable words of its defenders: not the certainty of legitimacy promised by the Stuart text, but the shifting, money-oriented accretive petty treachery of Peachum, Walpole, or the pirates in *Polly*. These are alike masters of words without value. Unlike the typologies of the past, the new regime invents its authority as it goes along.[89]

---

[88] Woolf, *Medallic Record*, p. 39; National Library of Scotland, Rosebery Collection 117; *Second Book of Scottish Pasquils*, p. 97; National Library of Scotland MS 1696, p. 65; *Second Book of Scottish Pasquils*, pp. 73, 82, 97.

[89] Frank McLynn, *Crime and Punishment in Eighteenth-Century England* (Oxford: Oxford University Press, 1991 (1989)), p. ix (there were three times as many capital crimes in 1760 as in the late

This is the state and the myth we inherit, much changed, but discernible still in the sacral quality of parliamentary sovereignty in a centralized state, which in the publicity for the tercentenary of the Glorious Revolution mentioned Scotland only in its complicity, and Ireland not at all. The centripetal tendencies of British constitutionalism are largely rooted in 1688, when a revolution at the core of government came over the next seventy years to absorb all the disparate claims of its peripheries.

In 1689, William of Orange's coup d'etat had been accepted in Scotland, and it was on the basis of this acceptance in the Claim of Right that Westminster came gradually to exert political pressure on Scotland which encouraged it to conform further. The rejection of the Act of Settlement by the Scottish Parliament, followed by a strong nationalist reaction, was a rebuff to attempts at gradual absorption which led in their turn to a political crisis and the agreeing of the Treaty of Union.

One of the methods by which pro-English and pro-Union feeling attempted to gain ground in Scotland was by a propaganda war which ran throughout the 1690s and early 1700s. Many pamphleteers and popular song-writers argued that Scotland had always been subject to England; patriotic writers took the opposite line. Post-Revolution pro-Union pamphleteering had started in Scotland as early as the Claim of Right convention in 1689, when *A Letter to a Member of the Convention of States in Scotland*, after beating out an insistent anti-Jacobite mantra of '*popery* and *Slavery* . . . *Popery* and *Tyranny*', went on to argue that James's return would 'cut of all Hopes of an Union' with England. The author was probably right, as James's supporters in Scotland argued on compatible lines. By the mid-1690s, a full-scale battle was raging between those who saw Scotland as a subject state of England in historical terms, and those who saw Scotland as a historically free nation. Both sides emphasized history: and the fundamental shape of the conflict (in which the pro-English side prevailed, with marked consequences for future historiography) was often one which could be traced to a battle between foundation-myths. British-based Stuart Arthurianism appears to begin to wither in Scotland in the 1690s, for the Stuart cause was in process of hardening into the patriotic cause. With this came a slow shift in Scottish Stuart typology, which distorted the pan-British imagery and interests of the dynasty in eventual favour of a more democratic and localized view. The icon of the Highlander as patriot, for example, suggested the deliberately partialized view that all Lowlanders favoured the Union, while the image of Stuart king as Highland cateran suggested that he was a folkloric type of social bandit rather than the rightful head of the British state. The

seventeenth century, but there were three to four times more crimes which *could* attract the death penalty); John Gay, *Dramatic Works*, ed. John Fuller, 2 vols. (Oxford: Clarendon Press, 1983).

complexity of British Jacobite politics was decentred in favour of the centring of the periphery of Scotland, and within that periphery another periphery, that of the Gaeltacht: ironically expressed not in Gaelic, but in English and Scots, the languages of the supposedly treacherous Lowlands.[90]

Because of the conflation of Jacobite and patriotic feeling, high and low culture were brought together in a more pronounced fashion than in England. An example of this is 'Belhaven's Vision', where a speech of Lord Belhaven's in the Estates against the Union was versified and passed into popular currency. Its main themes were the Roman and Celtic qualities of the Stuarts and Scotland, and the vision of history as a struggle for liberty, an image long part of Scottish national typology:

> The Sun two thousand times did fly
> Round the twelve Chambers of the Sky,
> Since *Fergus* form'd our MONARCHY;
>   And to this Hour,
> Our Laws have been controuled by
>   No foreign Pow'r ...

> Our *Stewarts*, unto peaceful JAMES,
> *Gordons, Kers, Campbels, Murrays, Grahams,*
> Hero's from *Tyber* known to *Thames*,
>   For Freedom stood;
> And dy'd the Fields, in purple streams
>   Of hostile Blood.

Scottish history is presented as heroic; but it was now in the grip of a destruction of its own ultimate value by the power of money: 'Antiquity ... razed out' as '*The true Scots Mens Lament*' put it, in favour of commercial advantage: 'What shall become now of our Crown ... Shall we it for Tobacco sell / and never once repine?' This theme was widely taken up, and Belhaven's versified paraphrase, 'Shall it be told, / We, for a little shining Clay, / A Kingdom sold', echoed in many contemporary productions, continues powerfully to inform a Scottish vision of Union as betrayal and loss.[91]

If anti-Union writers centred themselves at the periphery of Scotland, those who favoured Scotland's absorption into the British state could

---

90 *A Letter to a Member of the Convention of States in Scotland*, By a Lover of His Religion and Country (n.p., 1689), pp. 6–7; Sir Charles Petrie, *The Jacobite Movement: The First Phase 1688–1716* (London: Eyre and Spottiswoode, 1948), p. 226; Murray G. H. Pittock, 'Hits and Myths of the Union', Election Essay, *Scotland on Sunday*, 5 April 1992, p. 15.

91 LORD BELHAVEN'S SPEECH IN PARLIAMENT, The Second Day of November 1706 ... To which is subjoined, BELHAVEN'S VISION. A Poem. Edinburgh: A. Robertson, 1766; William Donaldson, *The Jacobite Song: Political Myth and National Identity* (Aberdeen: Aberdeen University Press, 1988), p. 9; NLS Rosebery Collection, 117.

equally play on Scottish fears of being peripheral. Propagandists like Defoe tried to engender support for the Union by arguing that only thus could sympathizers with the centre join it, and not themselves remain compulsorily marginalized. In other words, it was to Unionist as much as nationalist advantage to conflate Scottish nationalism with Jacobitism. As Defoe put it:

> scot, ... a Name that Foreigners can't find
> While mixt with English het'rogeneous kind,
> But now by Trade, inform the distant Poles,
> That Britain is the World of Gallant Souls.

Thus those who sympathized with the centre's priorities could have no part in them without the Union. On the other hand, those who opposed Union were by that token diehard peripheralists, that is closet Jacobites. Defoe underlines this: '... the design was to defeat the endeavours of Union only, in order to bring in French bondage, and King James VIII'.[92] In 1708, this argument revealed its core of truth when anti-Union feeling came close to restoring James in his northern kingdom.

If there was a political dimension to the way in which circumstances in Scotland reinforced the image of the Stuarts as patriot-kings linked to a native foundation-myth, there was also a religious one. The disestablishment of the Episcopal Church in 1689 had helped to ensure that virtually all its ministers nonjured, and just as unlikely political alliances were formed across class boundaries, religious alliances seem to have crossed denominational ones. Anne's royal proclamation of 1704 against Popery in Scotland was least effective in Buchan, Deeside and Strathbogie: precisely those areas where Episcopalianism was strong, and potentially able to shelter its Roman Catholic fellow-sufferers. After 1689 these two churches more than ever shared an ideology of royal authority: in 1693 James may have been allowed by the Papacy to continue to nominate bishops in the nonjuring 'British Catholic' churches as well as Roman Catholic ones. Nonjurors in England and Scotland alike remained true to caesaropapism.[93] Since James was now an exiled monarch whose authority was no longer (save in theory) political, there was perhaps little difference apparent in practice between the Henrician and Gallican interpretations of his authority in ecclesiastical matters. This was reinforced by a drift in Episcopal mysticism towards 'foreign influences ... most of the authors whose works became popular belonged either to

92  Daniel Defoe, 'A Scots Poem, or a New Year's Gift, From a Native of the Universe, to his Fellow-Animals in Albania', Ellis, *Poems on Affairs of State* 7: pp. 239, 266n.
93  Peter F. Anson, *Underground Catholicism in Scotland 1622–1878* (Montrose: Standard Press, 1970), 102; cf. J. H. Overton, *The Non-Jurors: Their Lives, Principles and Writings* (London: Smith, Elder & Co., 1902), pp. 87–9.

pre-Reformation or to Roman Catholic Christianity', while Thomas (later Bishop) Deacon of the English nonjurors remarked that 'when I came to consult history, the less defensible I found the Church of England'. Archbishop Fenelon of Cambrai was more of a spiritual leader than the juring Archbishop of Canterbury in the heartland of Scottish Episcopacy, while James's dual claim to nominate Roman and British Catholic bishops was not undermined by the caesarist responsibilities of real power: the contradiction between political and ecclesiastical claims which had disabled toleration in 1687/8 was no longer present. Both faiths (or variants on a faith) were persecuted by the new regime; and both (though Episcopalianism more fully) associated themselves with the cause of the exiled king.[94]

Such were the political and religious parameters of Scottish Jacobitism at the time of the Union, after a decade or more of steady conflation between the nationalist and Stuart causes. As this ideological alliance gained ground, an intensifying and a glorifying of Scotland's marginal status took place which was to give a distinctive and enduring cast to Scottish Jacobitism. The strong linkage of national to dynastic questions brought steadily together the interests of Episcopal bishop, Catholic seminarian, Scottish aristocrat, patriotic farmer and those further down the social scale who had suffered both through the famines of 'King William's lean years' which killed 100,000, and also under the stress of economic change in the era of Union. An analysis of the kind of men recruited to the Jacobite army in 1745 bears this out clearly: getting on for half the army was the result of crossclass Lowland recruitment, at odds with the myth that it was a Highland force (though this itself apparently grew from the Jacobite image of Highlander as patriot).[95]

The role Jacobite sympathizers in Scotland assumed was very close to that defined by E. J. Hobsbawm as 'social banditry', the crossing of social divisions in its performance only serving to raise its profile further. Hobsbawm suggests nine points as central to the social bandit's image, among them the following:

> He is a victim of injustice.
> He rights wrongs.
> He takes from the rich to give to the poor.
> He never abandons his community and is supported by it.
> He dies only through treason.

---

[94] Broxap, *The Later Non-Jurors*, 66; G. D. Henderson (ed.), *Mystics of the North East* (Aberdeen: Third Spalding Club, 1934), pp. 14, 15, 18.
[95] Bruce Lenman, *The Jacobite Risings in Britain 1689–1746* (London, 1980), 75; cf. Jean G. McCann, 'The Organisation of the Jacobite Army, 1745–46', unpublished Ph.D. thesis (Edinburgh, 1963).

These roles exist within a political programme in which banditry acts as a radical force while posing as a reactionary one:

The bandits of the kingdom of Naples ... who rose against the Jacobins and the foreigners in the name of Pope, King and the Holy Faith were revolutionaries ... They rose not for the *reality* of the Bourbon kingdom ... but for the ideal of the 'good old' society ... Bandits in politics tend to be such revolutionary traditionalists.[96]

It is easy to apply this model to the Jacobite cause, not only with regard to criminality (Jacobite smuggling being a particularly good example), but also to the Jacobite army. 'Court, country and city / Against a banditti' was indeed how the centre viewed the peripheral threat, irrespective of whether the 'banditti' were figures like Col. John Roy Stewart or the meanest ageing labourer in the fighting tail of Glengarry. Nor did supporters of the 'banditti' entirely reject this characterization, for *Rauberromantik*, bandit romanticism, surrounds the poems of Macpherson and the earlier verse of the Jacobite age, such as 'MacPherson's Rant/Lament', a popular song melded with a high cultural account of a Highland hero betrayed in the heart of his own (Jacobite) country in 1700:

> The reprieve was comin o'er the brig o Banff
>   To set MacPherson free;
> But they put the clock a quarter afore
>   And they hanged him on the tree.

MacPherson's breaking of his fiddle at the foot of the gallows ('He took the fiddle into baith of his hands / And he broke it ower a stane') presages the defiant motif of the Irish song 'The Minstrel Boy' ('The harp he loved ne'er spoke again / For he tore its chords asunder'). In both cases, personal integrity defies its end, whether '"There's nae ither hand shall play on thee"' ('Lament') or 'no chain shall sully thee' ('Minstrel Boy'). The central folk instruments of Scottish and Irish culture (fiddle and harp) become synecdochal expressions of national resistance.

Popular or folksongs about MacPherson, long circulating widely in the North East, confirmed his social bandit status:

> I've lived a life of strut and strife,
> I die by treachery;
> It burns my heart that I must depart
> And not avenged be.[97]

---

[96] E. J. Hobsbawm, *Bandits* (London: Weidenfeld and Nicolson, 1969), pp. 21, 35, 112.
[97] David Buchan, *Scottish Tradition: A Collection of Scottish Folk Literature* (London: Routledge & Kegan Paul, 1984); 1745 set of 'Lillibullero' in Hogg's *Relics*, second volume.

Long before the era of ballad-collecting, Jacobite culture was turning towards vernacular and popular cultural art forms to express itself. The gentry and officer-class were themselves classed as 'social bandits' by their enemies, being in frequent danger and sometimes attainted. The core regime was just as ready as the nationalist periphery to conjoin Lowland and Highland, rich and poor: the one in order to demean the social alliance of Jacobite 'banditti', just as the other sought to emphasize its simple patriotism. The 'Highland Laddie' icon (discussed fully in Chapter 4) could be perverted by the crude anti-Scottish humour of such prints as *Sawney on the Boghouse*, but its original purveyors used it as a vision which united sexual virility, hardy but honourable poverty and spiritual renewal. The Highlander was classless, since each was a 'gentleman', and could thus well stand in symbolic relation to that cross-class group in both Highlands and Lowlands who rejected the 'parcel of rogues' who had 'bought and sold' their country. Threadbare as he often was, the Highlander was a gentleman due to his birth and honour alike. Here lay a nexus of 'social bandit' oppositionalism, one of the roots of that 'Jacobitism of the Left' understood by the Scottish Renaissance and now re-emerging as a historical concept:

> Far on the *Cairnamount* I spy'd,
>     in careless Dress a Highland Laddie,
> Who briskly said wer't thou my Bride,
>     I'd row thee in my Highland Pladie.
> *O my bony, bony Highland Laddie*
> *O my bony, bony Highland Laddie*
> *When I am sick and like to dye,*
>     *Thou'lt row me in thy Highland Pladie.*
>
> No *Butter-Box* [Dutchman] he seem'd to be,
>     no *English-Fop*, nor Lowland Laddie,
> But by his mein he was well known,
>     to be some Gentie Highland Laddie.
>
> Chorus [98]

On the Cairnamount, the border between Highland and Lowland, the virile patriot, who is 'Gentie' despite being neither rich Dutchman nor English fop, presents himself as the spirit of noble outlawry to the erotic intoxication of his female Lowland visitor (Scotland herself, like the image of Hibernia in the *aisling* poems of Ireland):

---

[98] Cf. Donaldson, *The Jacobite Song*, 56; Dr Frank McLynn is the originator of this phrase (cf. 'The unWhigging of the Jacobites' (profile), *Times Higher Education Supplement* 23 September 1988, p. 18).

His Quiver hang down by his Thigh,
    his Mein did show his Bow was ready ...

Political threat and sexual promise are united in a vision which blends
traditional themes of unsuitable Lowland/Highland marriages (such as
'Bonnie Lassie, Come to the North Hielands') with a message of liberation
on a communal as well as personal basis. High culture unites with the folk
voice on the level of both drama and message. Later, Charles Edward
Stuart was to present himself as the 'Highland Laddie': at the same time
(inaccessible) sexual icon, social bandit and rightful king. The longstanding folk link between the Stuarts and their people (James V was supposed
to have written 'The Gaberlunzie Man' while himself disguised as a
beggar) was adopted as the patriotic voice of the Jacobite cause in a
country dispossessed by post-Revolution economic crises and by Union,
where twenty per cent of the population may have been beggars, and
where many of these beggars (especially in the North East) could act as a
conduit for Jacobite messages, a practice recalled by the character of
Wandering Willie in Scott's *Redgauntlet*.[99]

Scotland's case was distinct from England's, but not altogether different. If nationalism in the one country encouraged a convergence of
interest between classes and registers, Stuart ruralism, that great seventeenth-century topos, achieved something of the same end in the other;
while within the cities themselves radical discontent often found itself a
Jacobite focus. Exclusion from government did to the Tories something of
what loss of government inflicted on the Scots. During the reign of Anne,
English Jacobite ideology was in suspended animation compared with the
rapidly shifting spectrum of sympathy in Scotland: thereafter it displayed
itself in comparable forms. The next two chapters deal with the poetic
expression of Jacobite ideology in England, where the traditional typologies of the seventeenth century were not so liable to be subsumed under the
democratic vision of nationhood emblemized in the Highland social
bandit's metonymic status as the patriotism of a whole nation.[100]

---

[99] Anson, *Underground Catholicism*, pp. 97, 99; NLS Rosebery Collection, 89; Donaldson, *The Jacobite Song*, pp. 49ff.

[100] For the distinctively nationalist character of Scottish Jacobitism, see my own *The Invention of Scotland: The Stuart Myth and the Scottish Identity 1638 to the Present* (London and New York: Routledge, 1991).

# 2

## The wee, wee German lairdie

### In pursuit of a patriot king

We are not of the King-killing train:
The seed of old *Oliver* we defy,
For High-Church for ever shall be my Cry
So drink to my Love o'er the Main.
                    'The Three Olives'

Great Britians [sic] scourge let all good men admire,
God's goodness now is cast into the fire.
Lett all true Brittains to Cancell his fame
Piss on his dust and shyt upon his name.
                    'An Epitaph [?] on a Geordie'

Put on his bobwig pin burnt with the weather
And his grog run coat in which he came thither
With his Horns in his head he will look very smart
And so drive him back in an auld turnip Cart.
                    Ballad of 1722

Would you see the Man of Sorrows,
Then behold great JAMES the just
                    Towneley MSS[1]

The xenophobic decade of the 1690s, when there were an estimated 25,000 soldiers from James's army out of service, Jacobite criminality was on the increase, and Jacobite songs circulating with remarkable freedom, gave way under Anne to an uneasy peace and Indian summer which marked

---

[1] Paul Kleber Monod, *Jacobitism and the English People* (Cambridge: Cambridge University Press, 1989), 51–2; Alexander B. Grosart (ed.), *The Towneley MSS: English Jacobite Ballads, Songs & Satires* (Printed for Private Circulation, 1877), p. 23; National Library of Scotland, ADV MS 19.3.44/141; Nicholas Rogers, 'Popular Protest in Early Hanoverian London', *Past and Present* 79 (1978), pp. 70–100 (96).

the years 1710–14 in particular.[2] During this time, as Harley and Bolingbroke were negotiating a Stuart restoration, there was a considerable
amount of tension but less overt Jacobite propaganda activity (in England
at least). Yet Jacobite-related issues could touch a raw popular nerve, as
when the High Church apologist Sacheverell's *The Perils of False Brethren*
(1709) sold 100,000 copies, 50,000 of these in its first three weeks (the
record of his subsequent trial sold only 1,500). The popular riots in
support of Sacheverell were one of the factors which led to the passing of
the Riot Act in 1715.[3] In Parliament, the gains made by Scots Jacobites in
the 1710 election led to toleration for the Episcopalians, but such events
were high profile in comparison with the quiet negotiations of Harley and
Bolingbroke with James, which broke down in March 1714, just a few
months before Anne's death.[4]

The elusive commitment of such plotting was lost in a hail of popular
protest in 1714–15, once it became clear George was going to succeed. A
tide of mediated song text, orally circulated but printed for such circulation, swept the Jacobite areas, and continued to do so for a decade. High
and folk culture communicated through a language of protest borrowed
by one from the other and returned to it in a fresh medium. It was an
example of

a two-way interchange: the chapbooks and the broadsides derived material
from tradition and they also sent material into traditional circulation. The
interactions of folk with high and popular literatures offer fertile ground for future
research . . .[5]

Francis Clifton's pastorals, of which thirty were printed in 1718 and ten
or twelve a year till 1724, allied high cultural form with the erotic
love-ballad. Clifton had a large network of ballad-singers, who distributed
his Jacobite material widely. His activities, and the activities of those like
him, caused considerable concern to the authorities. As Paul Chapman's
research indicates, a printer might employ two or three dozen ballad-
hawkers, each selling twenty-four copies of a song, implying over 700 sales
in all. But as many ended up in inns, their circulation was in effect far
greater, and they were undoubtedly sung in the streets, learnt and
repeated, as the concern of government reports bears witness: among the

---

[2] Paul Monod, 'For the King to Enjoy His Own Again', unpublished Ph.D. thesis (Yale, 1985),
p. 112; G. Ross Roy, 'Jacobite Literature of the Eighteenth Century', *Scotia* 1 (1977), pp. 42–55
(43).

[3] G. Holmes, 'The Sacheverell Riots', *Past and Present* 72 (1976), pp. 55–85 (85).

[4] Daniel Szechi, *Jacobitism and Tory Politics 1710–14* (Edinburgh: John Donald, 1984), pp. 67, 76;
H. N. Fieldhouse, 'Oxford, Bolingbroke, and the Pretender's place of Residence 1711–14',
*English Historical Review* 52 (1937), pp. 289–96 (289); 'Bolingbroke's share in the Jacobite
Intrigue of 1710–14', *English Historical Review* 52 (1937), pp. 443–59.

[5] Buchan, *Scottish Tradition*, p. 12.

more agitated of these is a claim that 30,000 Jacobite 'half pay poapers' [sic] have been distributed to alehouses in a week, '& so they go for good true news'. Thus ballads and broadsides created from the emotions of folk literature were returned to the realm of oral transmission via the printed text: and those without access to printing distributed manuscript material in this way. Visual as well as verbal Jacobite communication was employed: a 1720 woodcut of Clifton's showed 'a lady and a gentleman, roses, flaming hearts, a ship on the water, an empty throne, a crowned king hiding in an oak tree and a butler' [Ormonde]. If these were images attuned to demotic use, Mist's portrayal of James as sun-god was their high cultural equivalent (Monod, 'For the King to Enjoy his own Again', pp. 71, 78).[6]

James, 'the just Astraea', appears to have had quite a degree of influence in managing his own propaganda campaign, though perhaps never to the extent his son did in 1745–52 (Monod, 'For the King to Enjoy his own Again', p. 80). Jacobite drinking-glasses and swords accompanied the broadsides, but such accessories were subordinate to the power of the pen:

The same Government, that in 1715 boasted It self everywhere settled for ever, trembled before the End of 1716. What wrought this change but the Pen? & wou'd not the same Pen, had it been, as it might have been ... employed abroad, have blown up the fire it Kindled to the overthrow of the Usurper?

Mary Flint, quoted by Paul Chapman

Certainly, if weight of words had been sufficient for victory, the Jacobites would have had it.[7]

Opposition to the new king was very traditionally based: most of the areas which had been Royalist in the 1640s were Jacobite in 1714–15 (Monod, 'For the King to Enjoy his own Again', p. 168). The cries for Ormonde and Sacheverell from crowds in places as diverse as Tewkesbury, London and Birmingham (Monod, 'For the King to Enjoy his own Again', pp. 174, 181; *Jacobitism and the English People*, p. 222) indicated either their manipulation by aristocratic Jacobite elements or their own identification with the catch-phrases of Stuart ecclesiastical and political claims (indeed, Ormonde as the leading Anglican Jacobite might serve as a kind of surrogate for the Catholic monarch in High Church mobs). The private satire of disenchanted gentry which presented George as horned (symbolizing his cuckolding by Count Konigsmark who was thus supposed to have fathered George II – a Jacobite response to the warming-pan myth) found itself relocated on a folk-popular level in Jacobite

---

[6] Paul Chapman, 'Jacobite Political Argument in England 1714–66', unpublished Ph.D. thesis (Cambridge, 1983), pp. 10ff., 46, 148.

[7] Mary Flint, letter of 2 August 1745, quoted by Chapman, 'Jacobite Political Argument', pp. 21ff.

counter-theatre. Here George was presented as a cuckolded Lord of
Misrule: and in Lancashire and the West Midlands especially, this coali-
tion of thematic interest between cultures was strong. The revival of
Restoration Day and the flooding of London with white roses were both
the kind of events which, in either spontaneous or designed manner,
reinforced traditional images of the Stuarts. (Monod, *Jacobitism and the
English People*, pp. 210, 220, 222; Pittock, 'New Jacobite Songs of the
'Forty-five', p. 72n). The return of Oak Apple Day in particular (which
had gone into abeyance before 1714) turned popular attention towards
the native status of the Stuart kings and to the whole cycle of deliverance
and restoration thus symbolized. Xenophobia had returned to the agenda,
engendering a new Jacobite code, that of the 'Patriot King', a term used
by Bolingbroke in the spirit of double-entendre.[8] George was identified as
mediocre, ridiculous and above all alien, the 'turnip king', a man who
could not even speak English:

> Woes me, quoth the Shepherd, the Theme of my song,
> Great Jemmy the Lord of the Plain, he is gone,
> Hogan Mogan has seized upon all as his own . . .
> 'The Landlord'

This pastoral vision of James was in keeping with Stuart rural ideology,
and it was a vision which (as some later kinds of English ruralism were to
be) was reactive against foreigners:

> Come! – listen awhile, ev'ry Staunch, Honest Tory!
> And I'll tell you a strange, tragi-comical story;
> (it shall be, Sirs, however, no stranger than true)
> Of the Rump, – and the Dutchman, – the German, – the Jew.
>     Derry a down, Down, Hey Derry down.
> 'Great Britain's Remembrancer'

Such revived xenophobia was backed up by a strong appeal to the
patriotic qualities of the Stuart king. Britannia was one of the symbols
used to emphasize this (hence perhaps the anti-Britannia role of Dulness
in *The Dunciad*). Part of the pan-British iconography introduced by James
VI and I, a version of her (based on Frances, Lady Stuart) appeared on
the 1667 Peace of Breda medal, and thereafter (from 1672) on Charles II's
coinage. In 1713 she appeared as an explicit symbol of the new United
Kingdom, holding both a rose and a thistle, while her appearance with
'bright temples bound with *British* oak' emphasized her native qualities

---

[8] E.g. in Viscount Bolingbroke, *Letters on the Spirit of Patriotism* (London, 1749), p. 74. For
contemporary debate about this topic see the views of Christine Gerrard (since, I believe,
somewhat modified) on Simon Varey's arguments for Bolingbroke's ambivalence (Gerrard,
'The Patriot Opposition to Sir Robert Walpole: A Study of Politics and Poetry, 1725–1742',
unpublished D.Phil. thesis (Oxford, 1986).

and possible link to the Stuart cause.[9] Dr Archibald Pitcairne linked her with Aenean typology in the lines modelled on those from *Aeneid* ix lines 446–9 which appeared on Roettier's 1712/13 medal, 'James III and VIII Presented to Scotland':

> O pair divine, for if my verse can give
> Immortal life, your fame shall ever live
> While Banquo's line on Edin's rocky tower
> Shall dwell, or Stuart sway Britannia's power.

Britannia was an ideal vehicle by which to emphasize once more the native quality of Stuart kingship, an emphasis further reinforced by reference to other periods of Roman history:

> Nero possess'd Britannicus's Crown,
> George hath usurp'd unhappy James's Throne.

George was a Nero not only by virtue of ecclesiastical persecution, but also in terms of political usurpation, as is discussed more fully below – killer of Britannicus and the first Pope alike.[10]

The native patriotism of the Stuart dynasty was seen not only in alignment with Britannia, but in the growth about this time of another song, since made famous by the dynasty it opposed:

> God save the King, I pray,
> God bless the King, I pray,
>   God save the King.
> Send him victorious,
> Happy and glorious,
> Soon to reign over us,
>   God save the King.

This most famous of Jacobite songs ('Send him/her victorious' is the only line which now reveals its source) may (according to an 1814 controversy in *The Gentleman's Magazine*), have originated in either the reign of Charles II or James VII and II. It was possibly sung in St James's Chapel for the king when William landed in 1688, or again on James's return to London at the end of that year. In either event, it derives from a French song to Louis XIV:

> Grand Dieu, sauver le Roy!
> Grand Dieu, sauver le Roy!
>   Vive le Roy!

---

[9] Grosart, *The Towneley MSS.*, pp. 91, 110; Herbert M. Atherton, *Political Prints in the Age of Hogarth* (Oxford: Clarendon Press, 1974), pp. 90–3.

[10] Woolf, *The Medallic Record of the Jacobite Movement*, p. 66; Bodleian MS. Eng. Poet. e87 (Western MSS. 46482), p. 9.

> Qu'a jamais glorieux
> Louis victorieux
> Voie ses enemis
>     Toujour soumis.[11]

'God Save the King' became, in various sets, a popular song of support for the exiled native monarch in 1714 and the years that followed:

> God bless the happy hour may the almighty power
> Make all things well
> That the whole progeny who are in Italy
> May soon and suddenly
> Come to Whitehall.

Its power was considerable, and was at length recognized by the sincerest form of flattery, when it became, as had its subject, usurped by the Hanoverian regime.[12]

As opposed to this patriot monarch blessed by God, George was emphatically 'Nero', a usurping and anti-Christian tyrant. In Richard Savage's 'Britannia's Miseries' for example, he is 'her Nero' rather than 'her King' who is 'a Royal Exile made', while elsewhere Savage likens George to 'Pharaoh and his Host', with James playing the part of exiled Israel rather than Aeneas. Savage also foreshadows Johnson's prophecy that a plebiscite would lead to restoration, when he argues 'If Kings are by the Nation's Choice / Pray put it to the vote'. This populist strain was often characteristic of high cultural poetry like Savage's, which reiterated the potentially xenophobic view that James was 'our Native Prince, / And born a British King', while George was 'like Esop's Jay, drest up in borrow'd Plumes'. Bird and beast fable were characteristic of many differing registers in Jacobite satire.[13]

The 'borrow'd' quality of George's plumes (together with his being cuckold) suggested an artifice, a pretence and a sterility which was well matched in popular Jacobite organicism, with its vision of James as a 'vegetation god' figure (Monod, 'For the King to Enjoy his own Again', p. 1):

> Again our Country Swains shall plough and sing,
>     And reap the Product of the fruitfull Spring,
> The stars shall Shine, indulgent on our Isle,
>     And rural Pleasures round about us Smile,
>         The Lads with curling Ivy bound

[11] Grant R. Francis, *Romance of the White Rose* (London: John Murray, 1933), p. 85; *The Gentleman's Magazine* 1814 (2), pp. 42, 99–100, 323–324, 339, 430, 552; Woolf, *Medallic Record*, p. 45; Monod, 'Pierre's White Hat', p. 188.

[12] A set of this is printed in Woolf, *Medallic Record*, p. 45, and another in Hogg.

[13] *The Poetical Works of Richard Savage*, ed. Clarence Tracy (Cambridge: Cambridge University Press, 1962), pp. 16, 18, 19, 21.

> The Maids with flowry Garlands crown'd,
> To their great Pan shall yearly Honours pay
> And consecrate with Mirth, the *Restoration* Day.

This emphasis on restoration and fertility as opposed to usurpation and barrenness was itself linked to the royal oak ('the King of the Wood') and also to an image Paul Monod has called 'the smiling king in the flowering tree' who is also envisioned as 'the suffering King on the barren crucifix' (Monod, 'For the King to Enjoy his own Again', pp. 122, 135). This vision of a king exiled from possession to suffering could be readily aligned with the more political typology of Aeneas/Augustus. The two pillars of Stuart authority, political and ecclesiastical, reinforced each other's typologies in a fashion traditional since the Fourth Eclogue:

Augustus' returning light will work 'a double magic on Rome's people, preserving both the exterior and interior quality of their lives, landscape and ethos at once.[14]

This was all the more firmly emphasized by the largely pro-Stuart inheritance of the 1650s Horatian Ode, and the frequency with which Horace (especially *Odes* IV:5) was imitated in the eighteenth century by Jacobite writers:

> O Prince from English Princes Sprung,
> Why does thou stay from us so long;
> Thy Absence, James, thy Subjects mourn,
> And longing sigh for thy return . . .
>
> Till thou are here & like the Spring,
> Givest a new life to every thing.

James is both Horatian Augustus and fertility god, to exclude whom the usurper 'Our Senates bribed & places Sold', and on whose return 'The vocal Hills and Vales exulting, / Shall proclaim a STUART's reign'. Similarities in these lines to both Pope's *Epistle to Burlington* and *Windsor Forest* show how readily marginal literature might echo its canonical equivalents: 'And peace & plenty soon proclaim / Again a STUART's reign' as 'A Birth Day Ode' puts it. Pope's politics were clearly thought sympathetic by the Jacobites, as a broadside in celebration of James VIII and III's landing in Scotland makes clear, recommending Pope as a poet for the new king of equal worth to Dryden.[15]

The return of the true Augustus was linked to a series of prophecies circulated by the Jacobites to confirm their eventual success in advance. These were often conjoined with the foundation-myth and the native

---

[14] Michael C. J. Putnam, *Artifice of Eternity: Horace's Fourth Book of Odes* (Ithaca: Cornell University Press, 1986), p. 105.
[15] Grosart, *The Towneley MSS.*, pp. 3, 23, 40; *ADVICE to the MUSE, on the KING's Landing* (Perth: Robert Freebairn, 1716).

quality of the king, as in 'Merlyn's Prophecy dated in ye year 482, about the time of King Vortigern's Restoration to ye British Throne', which comfortingly promises that 'This Isle, her ancient glory gains / For lo! her own Augustus reigns'. Similarly 'An old prophecy made in ye year 1207 by Robt. de Cresley a British [n.b. not English – the claims of the Anglo-British foundation-myth may be being emphasized] Astronomer but found in Manuscript at Oxford 1641' suggests that 'Quarrels ... cannot end till Caesar hath his due', after mentioning 'Forreigners' and 'A Belgick Boar' as the main instigators of such dissension.[16]

The prophesied return is also the return of Astraea and Aeneas: indeed, James is passionately identified with this process:

> The wise & good like Him Thou dost engage,
> When with Astraea Thou adornst thy page,
> In pomp the Goddess does her charms display,
> And shines conspicuous, as the prince of day;
> A generous warmth to every breast imparts,
> And leaves her bright impression on our hearts.
> Loudly she calls on Exil'd Stuarts' name
> On Anna's Murder, & on Ormonde's fame:
> And seems to dwell upon the glorious Theme ...
>
> Immortal Maro after mighty wars
> With foreign foes & sad domestick jars
> Conducts his Heroe to ye Latian Throne,
> And does reward his Vertue with a Crown.
> Thine not inferior, & as Poets sing,
> Sprung from the ancient Race of Trojan king ...
>
>                               'To the Author of the Birth Day'

The concerns of Aeneas and Astraea were one: the return of Augustus. George represented only a perverted shadow of such an event, as in 'Upon the Thanksgiving Day', a poem which is ironically headed 'Iam redit et Virgo, redeunt Saturnia Regna':

> The Golden Age is now at last restor'd,
> Anne is no more, but George is Britain's Lord,
> Now Justice, Plenty, Joy, & Fortune smile
> With George's Genius on this happy Isle ...
>
> Here he hath brought the dear Illustrious House,
> That is, Himself, a close stool, & a Louse;
> Two Turks, three whores, & half a doz'n Nurses,
> Five Hundred Germans all with empty purses.[17]

---

[16] Bodleian MS. Eng. Poet. e87 (Western MSS. 46482), pp. 96, 169.
[17] Ibid., pp. 76, 125–7.

But when all this spleen was spent, George was still king. The second restoration was hoped for, even expected, but it was an ideal nevertheless. Perhaps the reality led to a subgenre of the Jacobite voice concerning itself more intensely with the Aenean experience of exile, rather than home-coming and success. Such poems dealt with reversals of Jacobite fortune, of which there were many. One famous example was 'Derwentwater's Farewell', traditionally supposed to have been written by that Earl on the eve of his execution:

> Farewell to pleasant Dilston Hall,
>   My father's ancient seat,
> A stranger now must call thee his
>   Which gars my heart to greet ...
>
> My tenants now must leave their lands
>   Or hold their lives in fear.

Derwentwater's only hope is that 'Some honest heart may then amend / For Ratcliffe's fallen line': the disinheritance of the nobleman parallels the disinheritance of the king, and can only be put right by an 'honest' patriot. 'Honest' was one of the code-words which indicated (Jacobite) patriotism.[18]

Whether or not 'Derwentwater's Farewell' was written by the Earl himself, it is a good example of cultural convergence in the Jacobite voice. The idea that it is the Earl's poem is itself a traditional one, and tradition also makes (as in the ballads recorded from the singer Agnes Lyle in the nineteenth century) Derwentwater a Scottish hero betrayed by a corrupt English court. Scotticisms (e.g. *gar*) appear in variants of Robert Surtees' set, such as quoted above. In the explicitly Scotticized ballad 'Lord Derwentwater' the same themes appear as in the poem, though the cultural context is altered. The young English nobleman of a hundred years before becomes a folk hero of the same order as Douglas or Wallace: the representative of high culture has entered folkways as a social bandit, betrayed and sacrificed, but not by his community:

> 'O all you lords and knichts in fair London town,
>   Come out and see me die;
> O all you lords and knichts in fair London town,
>   Be kind to my ladie.
>
> 'There's fifty pounds in my richt pocket,
>   Divide it to the poor;
> There's other fifty pounds in my left pocket,
>   Divide it from door to door.'[19]

---

18 Hogg, *Relics*, II: pp. 30, 268.
19 William Bernard McCarthy, *The Ballad Matrix* (Bloomington and Indianapolis: Indiana University Press, 1990), p. 17; Francis James Child, *The English and Scottish Popular Ballads*, 5 vols. (Boston and New York: Houghton, Mifflin & Co., 1890, 92), IV: p. 116.

Thus the fate of one of the leaders of the 'Fifteen, commemorated in a poem allegedly written by its victim, is within a century or less widely distributed within folk culture and altered to fit the parameters of that culture's politics (Agnes Lyle's radicalism and suspicion of English government, in this instance). In Scotland, the ballad-tradition made of the Earl a patriotic Scot: but versions of the ballad are found in the north of England, and even in Shropshire dialect. In most cases, Derwentwater is the victim of treachery. For such a ballad to have become widely distributed in oral tradition suggests that this Jacobite hero's fate was far from being a matter of indifference to ordinary people. Moreover, folk traditions about Derwentwater extended far beyond orally transmitted poetry. Classical portents which might have been supposed the prerogative of high cultural propaganda passed into the popular mind: the mysterious lights said to have been seen in the sky at the deaths of Kenmure and Derwentwater were known in the north as 'Derwentwater's Lights', and are mentioned by Collins in his 'Ode on Popular Superstitions'.[20]

Thus the Aenean poetry of exile was reflected in aspects of popular Jacobite festival just like the Horatian–Vergilian constructs of Augustan return. But unlike its counterpart, this verse of exile is found in more experimental forms. An example of this is 'King James's Sufferings Describ'd by himself', a dramatic monologue written up to fifty years before Warton's 'Dying Indian' (Pittock, 'New Jacobite Songs', p. 45n; Monod, 'For the King to Enjoy his own Again', p. 94):

> Eternal mind by whose most just Commands
> I feel the unjust strokes of wicked hands
> Inspire my fancy and Conduct my tongue
> Whilst I describe the hardest fate
> The greatest wrong ...
>
> And thou who did once sit on Israel's throne
> Learn me those Dollful strains –
> Thou sang on Jordan's plains
> Whilst thou did thy hard fate bemoan
> Pursued by the unnatural Absolom ...
>
> Pittock, 'New Jacobite Songs', p. 45

The references to David and Israel were common in this kind of poem: just as the returning Augustus was an excellent type for a restored king, so the troubles of David or the bondage of Israel in Egypt shadowed the experience of exile (as they had in the 1650s). They also provided a kind of scriptural gloss to the pious example of Aeneas, and in so doing empha-

---

[20] Cf. *The Poetical Works of Richard Savage*, p. 23; cf. *The Poems of Gray, Collins and Goldsmith*, edited by Roger Lonsdale, Longman Annotated English Poets (London: Longman, 1969), p. 492.

sized the link between pagan and Christian typological readings of the Fourth Eclogue.[21]

It was in these poems of restoration and exile that the two kinds of Jacobite lyric I defined in the Introduction as the erotic and sacred found their meeting-place. The lost lover, the lost Pan, the lost Aeneas were also the lost Christ and the lost David. Here too were points of interchange between the language and conceptions of embattled nonjurors and popular carnival.

This is an area I turn to now knowing that there is still significant controversy as to how far popular urban Jacobitism was the result of manipulation by a minority elite. George Tresidder has recently suggested that 'between 1714 and 1821 the urban lower orders had become increasingly politicized' and that at the former period demonstrations were not as 'decidedly popular in nature'.[22] This is not an untypical view.

But it is one worth disagreeing with. 'Party strife and fissures in the urban elite' undoubtedly contributed to popular Jacobitism, but they do not explain it. Seditious words prosecutions, for example, show a large number of working and lower middle-class Jacobites. The kind of things said, like the kinds of songs sung, show a consistency across social groups. As suggested above, Jacobite images often appear similar in differing cultural media.

Moreover, without entering folk culture but definitely moving outside the sphere of aristocrats and great merchants, journals such as *Mist's* peddled Jacobite propaganda to tens of thousands, who were presented with accounts of events in encoded Stuart typology:

Such Confusion, Despair, and Amazement, attend the Downfal of *South Sea*, that they look on one another as the *Trojans* did, when the Power of *Greece* first sat down before their City.

South Sea equals corruption, amazing to the Trojans (Britons) who hitherto had avoided it, but are now besieged by it. Britain is Troy – that is the 'patriot' and 'honest man' are Trojans: the rest, those who created and profited from South Sea are aliens, Greeks.[23]

This kind of code seems to have been accessible to a very wide audience. Playgoers had long been addressed as 'British Trojans', and the manner in which the Patriot opposition of the 1730s took up the Trojan example shows its continuing breadth of appeal. Hildebrand Jacob's *Brutus the*

---

[21] This poem, cited by Monod from *Loyal Poems* (Beinecke Osborn Shelves b.111, 10), seems to have been widespread in its circulation, also appearing in a Banffshire commonplace-book.

[22] George Tresidder, 'Coronation Day celebrations in English towns, 1685–1821: elite hegemony and local relations on ceremonial occasions', *British Journal for Eighteenth-Century Studies* 15:1 (1992), pp. 1–16.

[23] *A Collection of Miscellany Letters Selected out of Mist's Weekly Journal*, 2 vols (London, 1722), II, p. 34.

*Trojan* (1735), an interesting piece of this type, nevertheless detaches the 'British Trojan' from Stuart typology by having Brute fight the Picts and have his Trojans assailed by a Druid crowned 'with *Oaken* boughs' (the Druids hold council in a place 'shadow'd round with high impending *Oak*'). The Celtic margins where Stuart support was strongest were thus exiled from Patriot use of Stuart typology. Patriot use of traditional Whig Saxonicity also helped compromise such typology while adopting it.[24]

The manner in which such images were usurped suggests that they were widely understood. As Jacobite images, the level of their distribution implied at least limited knowledge of their typological language. In 1716, not only did the price of white roses quintuple in London, but there was 'an epidemic of Jacobite ballad-hawking', which was matched by itinerant singing men throughout the provinces. Poems like 'The Turnip Song: A Georgick' were calculated to appeal to popular tastes (Monod, *Jacobitism and the English People*, pp. 47–8, 58), while in Scotland 'Geordie Whelps' Testament' sold thousands. In 1715

> The street ballad-singers were irrepressible.
> They were the more audacious as they often sang
> words which were innocent in their expression,
> but mischievous by right application.

This was a standard tactic: using familiar airs with Jacobite sets or singing 'lost lover' ballads in code, with the intention of giving 'no handle to the law officers of the Crown'. But confidence seemed to run so high in 1714–16 that some singers were not as subtle as this. At Pye corner, there was a man bawling out pastorals 'on behalf of *dear Jemmy, lovely Jemmy*' who claimed to be 'Ballad-Singer in Ordinary in Great Britain' to King James, while 'The King shall enjoy his own again' was so continuously popular its effect was compared with '*Lillibullero*' (indeed it is strange that any who may acknowledge the popularity of this song in the 1680s should be able to view the Jacobite song as the isolated product of disenchanted aristocrats). Female balladeers were arrested for singing 'licentious' material about King George, and 'It was very observable that among the noisiest and most violent of the Jacobite mob or army were the "Charity School Boys"' (Mary Astell's association with charity schools is of interest here in a Jacobite context).[25]

---

[24] Roberta Florence Brinkley, *Arthurian Legend in the Seventeenth Century*, Johns Hopkins Monographs in Literary History III (Baltimore: The Johns Hopkins Press, 1932), p. 118 (in reference to John Banks' *Destruction of Troy* (1679)); Hildebrand Jacob, *Brutus the Trojan* (London: William Lewis, 1735), pp. A3r, A4v, 1, 100, 110.

[25] Dr. John Doran, *London in the Jacobite Times*, 2 vols (London: Richard Bentley and Son, 1877), I, 70–2, 236; cf. Ruth Perry, *The Celebrated Mary Astell* (Chicago and London: University of Chicago Press, 1986), p. 238.

Such practices were general in opposition counter-theatre in the Walpole era:

Ballads were still ... a political instrument of minor but distinct importance ... Hawkers urged them ... upon passers-by; and now and again a ballad-singer might be seen, entertaining a 'large crowd' with the newest ditty.[26]

The political language and code of such ballads have also been seen as echoed in the poetry of high cultural writers like Pope, while those like Pope's hero the Man of Ross who have not distanced themselves from folk culture, often protected and succoured it in a distinctively Jacobite way, an example of this being Sir Watkin Williams Wynn's support of traditional Welsh harpers like John Parry. Indeed, such support for folkways could be a sign of Jacobitism, especially when Whigs such as Fielding 'advocated an all-out effort to destroy popular culture and the folkways of the "lower orders"'.[27]The emphasis on protection of property in Whig law and the fear of rural disorder in the Black Acts were signs of establishment concern over lower as well as higher-caste Jacobitism. Episodes such as the distribution of Jacobite medals, prints and portraits by the Kentish smugglers seem to suggest that such concern was justified.[28] The steady rise in capital crimes from fifty at the Revolution to one hundred and sixty by 1765 was a sign of a regime on the defensive, itself politicizing crime as a kind of oppositionalism, and stigmatizing oppositionalism itself as crime. The link between the financial revolution's protection of property and the Jacobite critique's attack on that revolution and its consequences created a potential nexus of interest between Jacobite and criminal classes which was reinforced by the illegal status of both. The idea that crime was the result of destitution (caused by Hanoverian corruption) was found in the Jacobite press, while the illegality of the regime itself in Jacobite eyes made possible support for criminality as a function of the belief 'that all Hanoverian property was theft':

Since the post-1688 regime was illegitimate, it followed that in a sense all its property relations were bogus, and that the highwayman was merely claiming back what had been stolen.          McLynn, *Crime and Punishment*, pp. ix, 57

Some highwaymen at least shared this point of view, Thomas Neale comparing himself on the gallows to Lord Balmerino, who had likewise suffered under 'an illegitimate government', while Tim Buckley, who

---

[26] Milton Percival (ed.), *Political Ballads Illustrating the Administration of Sir Robert Walpole*, Oxford Historical and Literary Studies Volume 8 (Oxford: Clarendon Press, 1916), pp. xi, xxix.

[27] Peter Burke, *Popular Culture in Early Modern Europe* (Aldershot: Wildwood House, 1988 (1978)), p. 25; Frank McLynn, *Crime and Punishment in Eighteenth-Century England* (Oxford: Oxford University Press, 1991 (1989)), p. 96.

[28] Paul Monod, 'Dangerous Merchandise: Smuggling, Jacobitism and Commercial Culture in Southeast England, 1690–1760', *Journal of British Studies* 30: 2 (1991), pp. 150–82 (161).

specialized in holding up 'pawnbrokers and stockjobbers', and Butler, who fought in the 'Fifteen and was a spy for Ormonde, belonged to the same group, for which

There is abundant evidence that highwaymen were of a higher social and educational level than other criminals.

This 'higher' status (some highway robbers were ex-officers of King James) led to an association of the highwayman with gentlemanly acts, such as the release of debtors from prison, and gave them a legitimacy to challenge the regime in Jacobite eyes. As Chevalier Ramsay argued, if you deny hereditary right in kingship, you cannot have it in property: highway robbery was a quid pro quo for usurpation (McLynn, *Crime and Punishment*, pp. 57–60, 73).

This was almost certainly understood by John Gay, who in *The Beggar's Opera* created a text that not only united the oppositionalist modes of high culture with the songs of popular culture, but also created in 'Captain' Macheath an image of the (Scottish) social bandit while holding up a mirror to establishment corruption. Peachum's dictum that 'there is not a spot or a stain, but what it [money] can take out' combined with Jemmy Twitcher's remark that 'What we win, gentlemen, is our own by the law of arms and the right of conquest' indicate simultaneously the legitimacy and values of the new regime: if the state rests on 'right of conquest', why not the gains of the highwaymen? And if the core of conquered value was cash, was that not a legitimate aim for criminal and conqueror alike? Moreover, the dispossessed are criminalized by the system which manipulates them having overthrown them. To underline this point, Macheath is given the designation of an army officer (as indeed, such a highwayman might well have been), and we are told that 'gentlemen of the road' may be 'fine gentlemen'. This was true, and Macheath is quite possibly of a higher social class than Peachum. But the world of the play is an inverted hierarchy created through an illegitimate regime. When Macheath sings the air of *Lillibullero* it is accompanied by a set which deprecates the money-based society that the supporters of the song have generated. Other airs such as 'Gin thou wert mine awn thing' and 'Bonny Dundee' reflect a Scottish bias, later reinforced in *Polly* where 'O Jenny come trye me' is an adaptation of 'Jamie': a quasi-Jacobite erotic song later adapted by Burns. In *The Beggar's Opera*, the famous song 'Over the Hills and far away' also echoes the power and popularity of the erotic Jacobite song: a number of pro-Stuart sets to this exist considerably before Gay wrote, such as the following:[29]

---

[29] John Gay, *Dramatic Works*, ed. John Fuller, 2 vols. (Oxford: Clarendon Press, 1983), pp. 21, 22, 48, 85; *The Beggar's Opera*, ed. Edgar V. Roberts (London, 1969), pp. 22, 31, 63, 77, 82.

> Bring in ye Bowl, I'le toast an health,
> To one that has neither Land nor Wealth,
> The bonny'st Lad that ever you see
>     Is over the Hills & far away.
> Over ye Hills, & over the Dales,
> No lasting peace, till He prevails,
> Strike up, my Lads, with a loud Huzza'
>     A Health to Him that is far away.[30]

In this English version of 1714/15 (a Scottish version, 'He is over the seas and far awa', exists in a dated MS of 13 June 1710), exile, dispossession and poverty accompany the defiant drinking-song: a most suitable model for Gay. In mentioning 'excellent ballad-singers', his text makes particular reference to the cultural crossover it is celebrating. The presence of references to the Atterbury plot and airs like the '*South-Sea* Ballad' (popular after 1720) reinforce this point:

> The lucky rogues, like Spanish dogs,
>     Leapt into South-sea water,
> And there they fish for golden frogs,
>     Not caring what comes after.
> 'Tis said that alchemists of old
>     Could turn a brazen kettle,
> Or leaden cistern into gold,
>     That noble tempting metal.[31]

By using the air to this song, Gay invites his audience to project a shared language between such topical popular songs and the world of his drama, just as the play itself displays such a sharing of values between cultures onstage. Indeed, *The Beggar's Opera* made its way into the furthest reaches of Jacobite high culture: the Duke of Wharton for example 'thought of himself as Macheath' and his friends as his 'gang'. The Jacobite social bandit could be a model for the greatest peers.[32]

What Gay took advantage of was the language, in many cases the cryptic language, of dispossession and conspiracy as well as the emptiness of political promises of freedom and liberty (unless issued by a patriot king figure, like Cawwanhue in *Polly*). The codified and cryptic quality of Stuart language had come very much into the popular domain at the time of the Atterbury Plot, that 'caused great public interest in the hidden significance of an apparently innocuous vocabulary', which Swift mocked

---

[30] National Library of Scotland MS. 2092 f. 35.
[31] James Hogg, *The Jacobite Relics*, I, p. 139.
[32] Gay, *Beggar's Opera*, p. 46; Mark Blackett-Ord, *Hell-Fire Duke: The Life of the Duke of Wharton* (Shooter's Lodge: The Kensal Press, 1982), p. 221.

in *Gulliver's Travels* under the guise of the language of Lagado.[33] The ambivalence of such language could be an ambivalence of identical terms, where expressions meant their opposite: a paradigm of the usurping character of the Whig state played on by Gay. The feature of loyal inversion was one of the most frequent uses of this ambivalence:

> I toast, – come – here's the KING;
> I need no further ope the Scene
> All who know me-know whom I mean . . .

The speaker invites those who can to read him, read his identity: if they can do that, then they can read his text: to know the man is to know his king. Likewise, knowing who 'Britannia' loves is the knowledge of the kind of Britain you want. In the identity of the speaker resides the code, whether expressed verbally or visually, as in Clifton's 1720 woodcut, or in a mixture of the two, where pictogram and word mingle.[34]

The presence of such ambivalent material in differing media (the visual codes perhaps inheriting some of the fertility symbolism of seventeenth-century Stuart stumpwork) provoked a continuing Whig response. Chapbooks, which 'circulated in their thousands through the kingdom', were accompanied by Jacobite distribution to target groups, such as the Kent smugglers or Westminster weavers: and these were answered by Whig mockery of fertility or foundation-myth claims, as in 'The Stroler, To the tune of, *Aeneas Wand'ring Prince of Troy*' or 'Young *Perkin* a poor wand'ring Knight'. The former title confirms Jacobite success in adopting Aeneas as a solely Stuart archetype, and when such success proved too irritating to mock, Whig writers fell back on incremental history's victory over typology's claims to truth, since the Jacobites had 'nothing but a Tune / To support the 10th of *June* / And the Hopes of a Restoration'.[35]

In return, Jacobite writers attacked such Whig typology as existed, reserving some of their heaviest fire for Whig use of Roman themes, such as Addison's *Cato*, answered by 'Cato's Ghost. 1715':

> Oh! Addison, couldst thou not be content . . .
> Hadst thou no other way to rise to fame
> And Fortune, but by wounding Cato's Name:
> Mean & Injurious had but Cato lived
> In Brittain's happy Isle, how had he greived [sic],
> Greived for a King struggling in storms of fate,
> And gently falling with a falling state . . .

[33] Paul Langford, *Walpole and the Robinocracy*, The English Satirical Print 1600–1832 Series (Cambridge: Chadwyck-Healey, 1986), pp. 16, 17.

[34] Percival, *Political Ballads*, p. 131; Monod, *Jacobitism and the English People*, p. 71; Cf. 'The Highlander's Riddle', National Library of Scotland FB 1.162.

[35] Victor E. Neuberg, *Chapbooks* (London: The Woburn Press, 1972 (1964)), p. 1; Monod, *Jacobitism and the English People*, p. 47; *A Collection of State Songs* (London, 1716), pp. 4, 107.

That Secret plan of power delivered down,
From Age to Age, from father to the Son,
Is each man's rule of Action, & had he
Been subject to a King's Authority,
Even Cato's self had bled for Monarchy.

This anonymous reaction (one of many) to Addison's play makes the same equation between hereditary property in the private and national spheres as did Chevalier Ramsay. The point is not Cato's Republicanism: it is that he has been true to what he inherited, while Britain has inherited hereditary monarchy and not been true to it.[36]

Attacks on Addison were particularly important in order to maintain Jacobite control of classical typology, since viewed as a representative of Vergil, who had identified William with Augustus, Addison provided a strong challenge to such control: though his 'Augustan' qualities in the Hanoverian period are not altogether convincing, as Malcolm Kelsall has argued. But to Jacobite writers he was a threat to be resisted not only by contesting his use of typology, but also by democratizing an appeal to the hereditary principle which put Cato in his historical place and left him there: if monarchy is 'Each man's rule of Action' in Britain, Cato's political expectations are decontextualized. Paradoxically, the appeal to indefeasible monarchy is a democratic one.[37]

This democratic tendency is widely at work in Jacobite poetry, and is one of the elements enabling a link to be forged between the high culture of typological complaint and the world of popular protest. As suggested in Chapter 1, the stage was one of the places where dramatic code could meet with popular approval, where the audience could 'see the Senators / Cheat the deluded people with a shew / Of Liberty, which yet they ne'r must taste of' and hear appeals on behalf of 'this glorious Cause ... To do it right!' (Otway, *Venice Preserved* ACT I: lines 153–55, 216–17). Most of all, the theatre could present the moral of its play to the audience as a means of establishing popular consent to high cultural premisses. Paul Monod asserts this:

Without sympathy from above, popular political theatre could not have established such strong links with the formal stage.

(Monod, *Jacobitism and the English People*, p. 181)

This is perhaps why *Venice Preserved* may have been such a powerful expression of Stuart politics on stage, since its Epilogue had originally been written with them in mind:

---

[36] Grosart, *The Towneley MSS*, 101–2; Ramsay, cited in McLynn, *Crime and Punishment*, p. 58.
[37] Malcolm Kelsall, 'Addison and Classical Rome', unpublished B.Litt. thesis (Oxford, 1964), pp. 69, 173–6.

*The Text is done, and now for Application ,*
*And when that's ended pass your Approbation . . .*

*They'd use his Person as they've us'd his Fame;*
*A face, in which such lineaments they reade*
*Of that great Martyr's, whose rich blood they shed,*
*That their rebellious hate they still retain,*
*And in his Son would murther Him again:*
*With indignation then, let each brave heart*
*Rouse and unite to take his injur'd part;*
*Till Royal Love and Goodness call him home,*
*And Songs of Triumph meet him as he come;*
*Till Heaven his Honour and our Peace restore,*
*And Villains never wrong his Vertue more.*

This was the language of the Exclusion Crisis: but it served perfectly well for the time when the king had been permanently excluded.[38]

It was to the advantage of the Jacobites that plays or poetry written under Charles II or even Anne could be used to express opinion with little fear of censure, since the new regime accounted them respectable, even if they spoke an ideological language relevant to Jacobite claims. In some respects such language changed little: *The Kit-Cats. A Poem* of 1709 foreshadows precisely the language of *The Dunciad*:

> On the dark Margin of the stagnant Flood
> The Temple of the God of Dulness stood.

Likewise, the ambivalence of identical terms enabled single words or concepts to endure in Jacobite language as long as they endured in the language of the monarchy generally, though some terms, such as 'REDEAT', dramatically used in William King's 1747 oration and Charles's 1752 medal, were less ambivalent than others, being linked with the language of Aenean exile rather than Augustan government. New forms which developed after 1688, such as the 'lost lover' poems or the animal fable, did not detract from the old, but amplified their appeal, democratizing the indefeasibility of Jacobitism in an attempt to turn people's hearts against the '... Strangers in the *Place* / Your *Native Birds* were wont to grace'.[39] Poems like 'The happy Pair' emphasized that the exiled king was 'the Master of my Heart', echoing the terms of contemporary sentimental comedy (Monod, *Jacobitism and the English People*, 64–5), while also expressing them as biblical imagery:

---

[38] J. C. Ghosh (ed.), *The Works of Thomas Otway*, 2 vols. (Oxford: Clarendon Press, 1968 (1932)), pp. 207, 210, 288, 289.

[39] *The Kit-Cats: A Poem* (London, 1709), p. 8; Woolf, *Medallic Record*, p. 121; *The Blackbird's Tale* (London, 1710), p. 3.

> When will my lovely shepherd dear,
> To his lost sheep again return?

This is the provision of erotic access to the talismanic language of sacred kingship: the democratization of Augustus.[40]

The argument that Jacobite typology 'did not spring from an oral tradition' but was 'manufactured by educated men' ignores the mediated quality of many of these educated manufactures. Not only were balladeers used to provide an organized distribution pattern by Jacobite printers, but oral culture itself was already in a phase where it was naturally influenced by written culture: and that written culture itself (as in the case of the Scots vernacular revival) was defending its identity by attempting to enter and use both folk and popular forms.

Alehouses, where Jacobite poems were pasted up to be sung, formed a nexus for these cultures. The centrality of inns to Jacobite (as indeed to criminal, particularly highwaymen's) activity in the eighteenth century is an interesting and under-explored example of Peter Burke's contention that the inn was at the core of popular culture:

Ale-houses were a setting for popular art ... Broadside ballads were sometimes posted on the walls of inns so that people could join in the singing.

This is a general observation: but it is absolutely consonant with what is known about the distribution patterns of Jacobite propaganda in the eighteenth century, as, of course, is the idea of 'ruler as popular hero ... not infrequently contrasted with the actual king' which Burke discusses in detail. Jacobite ideologues found patterns in the cultural language of ordinary people well fitted to receive their message. It is already accepted that 'the community selects' from the material available to it, and that some of the selection is carried out by middle-class suppliers of oral culture (Mrs Brown of Falkland, for example).[41] At other times, chapbook makers may themselves be the products of oral tradition, as is the case with Dougal Graham, author of *The History of the Rebellion*. In the Jacobite period, selection and mediation worked in both social directions, and Jacobite heroes like Lord Derwentwater entered both oral and elite traditions. Even non-Jacobite historical ballads were affected: 'Chevy Chase' is an example of 'the Scottish traditional ballad' sung to the air of 'Derwentwater's Farewell' perhaps 'because it was already associated with the Stuart cause'.[42] In any case, those folkways which may themselves

---

[40] Monod, *Jacobitism and the English People*, p. 65.
[41] Burke, *Popular Culture*, pp. 74, 109, 115, 150, 152, 153; cf. David Buchan, *The Ballad and the Folk* (London: Routledge & Kegan Paul, 1972), pp. 6off.; Buchan, *Scottish Tradition*, pp. 9off.
[42] Alisoun Gardner-Medwin, 'A Ballad on the Battle of Otterburn: Scottish Folksong', in Alisoun Gardner-Medwin and Janet Hadley Williams (eds.), *A Day Estivall: Essays in Honour of Helena Mennie Shire* (Aberdeen: Aberdeen University Press, 1990), pp. 81–95 (94).

have been outdated versions of high culture already contained material
found in Jacobite literature: the use of a mock-title like 'Earl of Fingall' in
English popular culture may have been an example of this, while even a
poet on the fringe of the Jacobite cause like Prior shows an awareness of
folk culture in a poem such as 'Merry Andrew'.[43]

There was certainly a support for such culture among Jacobites. The
common status of potential criminality drove the classes together. If the
additional binding agent of nationalism was not as available in England as
in Scotland or Ireland, English upper-class Jacobites were still outsiders,
in religion not least. This status was strongly expressed in a continuation of
the retreat poetry tradition inherited from the Civil War:

> Give me, O indulgent fate:
> Give me yet before I die
> A sweet, yet absolute retreat . . .
> My unshaken liberty . . .

The Countess of Winchilsea holds additional interest as an author of
retreat poetry, as her outsider status as Jacobite was compounded by her
gender. Marginalized as a woman ('Debarred from all improvements of
the mind, / And to be dull, expected and designed'), she feels sympathy
not only towards the Stuart 'lonely stubborn oak . . . Sapless leaves all bent
and shrunk', but also with Mary of Modena, whom she had served as a
maid of honour: 'The sovereign mistress of my vanquished mind' as she is
in 'On the Death of the Queen' (1718). Woman, Catholic, and Stuart
queen, Mary is triply 'debarred' from acceptance on equal terms. Though
never explicitly linking these different ways of being an outsider, the
Countess writes of them in interchangeable terms: the women 'fallen by
mistaken rules, / And Education's, more than Nature's fools', could
equally well be Catholics, alike exiled from education and political rights.
Elsewhere she links her marginalization to the financial revolution, criti-
cizing in a poem like 'A Song on the South Sea', the male mercantile world
of stockbroking which has altered the age: 'And brokers all the hours
divide / Which lovers used to share'. Her plea for retreat, addressed to
another woman, is alike a refuge from political and personal feelings of
oppression. As in the case of Mary Astell, the feeling of being an outsider
by virtue of gender led to identification with the Stuart cause.[44]

The transition from Anne to George, and with it the end of any hopes
for a peaceful restoration of James, laid open the identity of Augustus as an
irritating wound for fifty years, to be plastered over by Hanoverians and
scratched by Jacobites, but not to heal. A pervading doubleness of intent

---

[43] Burke, *Popular Culture*, p. 40; *The Poetical Works of Matthew Prior*, p. 138.
[44] Anne Finch, Countess of Winchilsea, *Selected Poems*, ed. Denys Thompson, Fyfield Books
(Manchester: Carcanet, 1987), pp. 7, 14, 53, 57, 80.

kept the sore going. When Prior wrote in 1706 of 'boasted Brute' from whom 'Tudors hence, and Stuarts offspring flow', he reinforces in Anne a typology none of her successors could claim. She could perhaps be 'Envied Britannia, sturdy as the oak', but such identification with Stuart tree and Stuart icon could only suggest the necessity of a following restoration, if she were not to be the last of a line. Anne's 'English heart' and her role as 'Envied Britannia' seem implicit xenophobic rebukes to her officially chosen successor.[45]

Of course many made the transition, despite the difficulty of attributing traditional monarchical language to George (at least William could receive compliment through conquest – indeed, Prior saw no difficulty in this). Of course many did not 'disown / A foreign Lineage, and a plunder'd Throne' for all kinds of reasons. But the question remained, buoyed up by doubtful prophecy such as 'Merlin's' 'For lo! her great Augustus reigns' attached to verse such as 'The Landing':

> Appear O James approach thy native Shoar . . .
> And to their ancient state thy realms restore.

But the restorer of history, Augustus the returned Aeneas, was by now at Rome, the Roman king returned to exile from the land his ancestors possessed, the Blackbird (a term also used – by John Wesley's brother – of Atterbury), the Moorhen, the absent hero. The Augustan could fear the abyss, or he could be a follower of the lost Augustus who had already fallen down it: but either way, the absence of the king left an ambivalent fear in a political and ecclesiastical culture forced into hypocrisy in order to sustain the idea of a continuing regime.[46]

# The 'Forty-five

> Through every Scene thy rigid Fate I moan . . .
> *Increasing Taxes* and *declining Trade, Debts,*
> *Pensions, Bribes* no more disturb my Mind.
>                     'To Miss Polly Peachum'

> Great Charles will Britains scepter sway,
> And Hanoverians rue the Day,
> Over the Hills and far away.

---

[45] *The Poetical Works of Matthew Prior*, pp. 124, 166, 175, 176.
[46] *An Epistle from a Student at Oxford to the Chevalier* (London, 1717), p. 5; National Library of Scotland MS. 2092 f. 86; Doran, *London in the Jacobite Times*, I, p. 371.

Charley's red & Charley's white
and Charley is bonny O,
He is the Son of a Royal King
and I love him the best of any O.

When he came to Darby Town
Oh, but he was bonny O
The Bells did ring, & the bagpipes play
And all for the love of Charley, O.

                          Song recorded at Shrewsbury, 9 June 1750

O dinna greet sae sair, poor wife,
    For hunger ye mauna dee:
There's wealth o' beef on Culloden Moor
    To serve baith you an' me.
An' ye maun gird your barrels weel,
    An' fill them to the brim.
For there's a feast in fair Scotland
    Of the life blood and the limb.
And there is naught for thee, auld wife,
    An' your cursed rebel brood,
But to chew the banes your body bare,
    An' drink your ain heart's blood.[47]

In the first eight years of George I's reign, three Stuart restoration attempts failed. This proved deeply dispiriting for the Jacobite movement in the 1720s and 30s. A revival of hope came chiefly in the person of the young Prince Charles. Several years before the attempt of 1745 Jacobite attention was clearly shifting from James to his son, who was to be called 'Charles III' by the late 1740s, twenty years before his father's death (Pittock, 'New Jacobite Songs of the 'Forty-five', p. 38).

A shift in propaganda accompanied this shift in affection. The Stuart text did not alter its subject, but it changed its emphasis as it had fifty years before in the xenophobic period under William, and thirty earlier in its bias towards the culture of 'Popular counter theatre', which had been such a potent weapon in the era of the 'Fifteen: 'Between 1715 and 1722, popular Jacobitism disturbed the peace of almost every important English town.' In the aftermath of the 'Fifteen, the proportion of ordinary people arrested in 'seditious words' prosecutions may have climbed considerably. In 1689–1714, 56 per cent of such prosecutions in Lancashire, Staf-

---

[47] *A Collection of Poems on Several Occasions*, published in the *Craftsman*, by Caleb D'Anvers (London: Nicholas Amherst, 1731), p. 14; Grosart, *The Towneley MSS.*, pp. 1–2; Monod, *Jacobitism and the English People*, p. 216; *The Royalist* vi:4 (1895), p. 91 (the genuineness of this song (also in Hogg) is open to doubt: it may well be black propaganda).

fordshire and Gloucestershire were of people from a lower-middle class background or below; from 1715–52, the proportion rose to 76 per cent (Monod, *Jacobitism and the English People*, pp. 222, 225, 249), though Nicholas Rogers' less complete figure may compromise this picture, suggesting that as early as 1714–16 73 per cent of Jacobite prosecutions in Middlesex were of the lower orders.[48]

Charles's propaganda did not ignore this aspect of his support: he was portrayed in a more successfully radicalized form than either his father or grandfather had been. In the 'lost lover' poems in particular, Charles's sexual attractiveness lent greater force to metaphors of fertility and renewal, especially in combination with a military energy which clearly outgunned that of his father. More important than either of these things was his presence during the whole of a long campaign in which he led from the front, shared his army's privations, and was sheltered by its soldiers (notably Major Patrick Grant): whereas James had joined the 'Fifteen late, and had left Montrose in relative safety with a collection of magnates and senior officers in the spring of 1716. Charles presented a popular image, but there was a popular reality to match.

This emphasis on a democratic, accessible prince on sexually equal terms with his admirers was echoed in the upper register of Jacobite iconography also. Charles's use of Roman images was often one with a Republican tinge: even when acting as the official representative of divine right, the Prince was portrayed with a hint of radical chic (perhaps the partial move to English rather than Latin legends on his medals was an aspect of this (Woolf, *The Medallic Record of the Jacobite Movement*, p. 113)). To an extent, this was his own responsibility, since Charles controlled his propaganda portrayals in the 1745–52 period, the centre of this Republican phase: in 1749, for example, a Jacobite cartoon shows him with a 'liberty cap' (Monod, *Jacobitism and the English People*, pp. 80, 84).

Shortly after Charles was 'blooded' at the siege of Gaeta in 1734, he begins to be displayed as an adult Jacobite leader distinct from his father, appearing depicted under a star in the manner of Christ and Alexander the Great (Monod, *Jacobitism and the English People*, pp. 79–80). Such duality of pagan and Christian iconography was conventional enough in Stuart terms, but it was shortly succeeded by portrayals of Charles as a virtuous Roman: a *philosophe*, a figure at least potentially one of Enlightenment. This more republican mode was accompanied by his portrayal in tartan, emphasizing Scottish qualities in solidarity with the marginalized Highlander patriot icon. English Jacobites took up this 'barbarian' Charles as their own: Sir John Hynde Cotton ordered a full tartan set in 1743/4, and tartan waistcoats were worn by those who wished to taunt the

48 Nicholas Rogers, 'Popular Protest', p. 86.

Government. Thus both 'Roman' and 'barbarian' images of Charles passed into circulation, simultaneously emphasizing his qualities as states-manlike restorer of a fallen state and beggarly social bandit. As a result

> By the early 1750s, Charles Edward had established a unique iconographical place for himself. His images were more human, more active and less authori-tarian than those of his father. They mingled Republican classicism with tinges of romanticism to create the concept of a bold and virtuous 'patriot' Prince.
>
> Monod, 'For the King to Enjoy his own Again', pp. 155–6, 167, *170*

The classical image of Charles was in keeping both with the old patriot king idea and the traditional typologies of the Stuart dynasty, as well as providing a hint of Whig radicalism: 'Cato's self' would have been much more likely to bleed 'for monarchy', if the monarch himself were a Republican (as were in effect some senior Jacobites, such as the Earl Marischal).[49] The romantic, 'barbaric' image had a wider appeal, but it also possessed a kind of risque delight for English Jacobite gentry who not only slummed it in tartans, but provided other more refined Scottish codes to show their agreement with the tartan Prince's agenda, such as the planting of Scots firs, 'Charlie trees'. The classical imagery of retreat poetry was blended with the image of English gentlemen as wild High-lander. This is exactly the territory in which Scott's Waverley operates: though literary critics have as a result seen fit to accuse him of anachro-nism.[50]

Republican and 'barbarian' images reinforced one another to a certain extent, since both suggested metaphors of rebellious freedom from the current regime. Indeed, they were associated with rebel movements in Europe such as the Corsican nationalists: and this was true from at least the 1730s onward. Boswell even toyed with the idea of making Charles Edward king of Corsica. Later Pasquale Paoli was seen as a Jacobite figure, while it seems that the Whiteboys in Ireland were at least conscious of this kind of Jacobite ideology in the responses they made to authority.[51]

Although 'barbarian' images of Charles suggested that he stood for attacking authority, and Republican ones suggested that he would re-establish an authority of differing nature, the traditional attributes of the sacred king were not neglected: as suggested at the beginning of this chapter, emphasis was always more likely to change than the basic

---

[49] For Cotton's tartans, see the 1990 National Museums of Scotland Exhibition; for Marischal's Republicanism, see Frank McLynn, *The Jacobites* (London: Routledge and Kegan Paul, 1985).

[50] Mrs. Kit Sabin, Raemoir House, Raemoir, Kincardineshire in conversation, 1991; D. D. Devlin, 'Scott and History', in A. Norman Jeffares (ed.), *Scott's Mind and Art* (Edinburgh: Oliver and Boyd, 1969), pp. 72–92 (91).

[51] Monod, 'For the King to Enjoy His Own Again', p. 167; David Greenwood, *William King: Tory and Jacobite* (Oxford: Clarendon Press, 1969), pp. 170–1.

elements of Stuart self-portrayal. Charles's (successful) Royal Touch in Edinburgh in 1745 displayed the continuing power of belief in the sacramental authority of the royal house, even among the largely Presbyterian inhabitants of a relatively sophisticated urban centre: the popular opinion was 'that within a few days more than five hundred out of a thousand would be perfectly cured' (Crawfurd, *The King's Evil*, pp. 141, 157).

The poems which celebrated the Prince's landing showed a full-scale re-emphasis of the Stuart foundation-myth. 'Hail Glorious Youth! the wonder of the Age', which may have been composed in Edinburgh following the victory at Prestonpans, was headed with the eternal Stuart quotation: 'Iam redit et Virgo, redeunt Saturnia regna.' After a further identification with the Vergilian archetype ('Another Maro shall arise, whose pen / Shall place the Hero with immortal men'), the poem goes on to blend patriot Highlander imagery dating back to the *Grameid* with the story of the 'Godlike Man', Charles/Aeneas: 'O'er the black mountains see! the Sons of Fame / Fearless advance and catch the Glorious flame'. But this image of triumphant 'barbarians' rapidly gives way to a conventional description of the authority they are authenticating:

> See how Hereditary right prevails!
> And see Astraea lift the wayward scales!

This straightforward return to the reinforcing types of traditional imagery is accompanied in other poems by direct reference to the major Stuart texts of the last fifty years: 'And peace & plenty soon proclaim / Again a STUART's reign' says one 'Birth Day Ode' (definitely not by Cibber!) from Somerset, in clear imitation of Pope's *Windsor Forest*, while another poem asks whether Charles will 'Bid peaceful plenty wave upon thy plains/ The untouched harvest of the Golden Grain?', recalling the traditional Stuart fertility imagery used by Pope in his *Epistle to Burlington* (Grosart (ed.), *The Townley MSS*, pp. 33, 40, 62, 65, 67).

In an attempt to recapture the Stuart image of Britannia from the clutches of the Hanoverian James Thomson's 'Rule Britannia' (from *The Masque of Alfred* (1740)), parodies were written with the aim of reclaiming the song, just as the Whigs were at this time reclaiming 'God Save the King' from the Jacobites:

> When royal Charles by Heaven's command
> Arrived in Scotland's noble Plain; (2)
> Thus spoke the Warrior, the warrior of the Land,
> And Guardian Angels sung this strain;
> Go on Brave Youth, go combat & succeed,
> For Thou shall't conquer, 'tis decreed.
>
> Grosart (ed.), *The Townley MSS*, p. 61

Here, interestingly, the emphasis is more on the Scottish patriot icon, 'the warrior of the Land', giving the set a distinctively Scottish national slant to set against the native Britishness of the air.

Jacobite messianic propaganda was best realized in Scotland, where the returning king was truly a symbol of renewal and fertility to the whole nation (and some societies such as the Templars still seem to play on this mystic nexus of Stuart patriotism), while in England the political (not so much the religious) desires his return was seen to fulfil were more disparate ones. But such imagery remained central to Charles's activity in both kingdoms, whether in the democratic or erotic images of radical Jacobitism or in more traditional statements. His youth was a great asset to the revivifying of such typology. Captain David Morgan (executed for his part in the Rising) summed this up well in *The Country Bard* (1741):

> Happy that Breast where native Candour reigns,
> Informs the Thoughts and animates the Veins.
> Rev'rend to Age *whose unpolluted Youth*,
> In *Wisdom* walks and treads the Paths of *Truth*.

This is the only way to overcome the inverted world of tired Whig tyranny which Morgan invokes and Pope was shortly masterfully to unmask in *The Dunciad*. The 'Youth', who has the native, natural qualities of truth and wisdom can give a fresh start, and clean out the Augean stables of constitutional and literary mediocrity.[52]

From the beginning Charles inspired passionate loyalty: 'Oh were my pen a Sword, Thy foes I'd meet / And lay the Conquered world at Charles's feet' as one poem puts it. Hyperbole perhaps, but a hyperbole of intimacy which reached newly intense levels. It was in English as well as Scottish songs that Charles was 'The royal and charming Bright Laddy'. Even Whig satire on the Prince often acquiesced in these familiar metaphors:

> Over the water and over the lea,
> And over the water to Charley.
> Charley loves good ale and wine,
> And Charley loves good brandy.
> And Charley loves a pretty girl
> As sweet as sugar-candy.

The dividing line here between Charles's hearty sweetness and the gross indulgence intended to be lampooned is a thin one (Grosart (ed.), *The Townley MSS*, pp. 79, 86–7; Woolf, *The Medallic Record of the Jacobite Movement*, p. 130).

---

[52] 'The Golden Age and Sin in Augustan Ideology', *Past and Present* 95 (1982), pp. 19–36; cf. Peter Partner, *The Murdered Magicians: the Templars and their Myth* (Crucible, 1987 (1981)),

This intimacy personalized the Prince's love of his lost land: an adored youth who represented the coming of spring and was worthy of love by those who were not blinded by the chief vice of age, avarice:

> What's the Spring, breathing Jessamine and Rose,
> What's the Summer, with all its Gay train;
> What's the Plenty of Autumn to those
> Who have bartered their freedom for Gain.
>
> 'A Song' in Grosart (ed.), *The Townley MSS*, p. 85

The Independent Electors of Westminster (a largely Jacobite grouping) sang 'Highland Laddie' (Monod, 'For the King to Enjoy his own Again', p. 308), showing the widespread circulation of such erotic and demotic Jacobite verse in the era of the 'Forty-five. Such poetry circulated widely in both oral and quasi-oral transmission, as the song recorded from Shrewsbury at the head of this section suggests. The frequent use of folk culture's 'pervasive tendency to marshal its material ... in threes' in Jacobite poetry may be a partial sign of such transmission. In any event, Charles Edward was the only Stuart to enter such subgenres as nursery rhyme as a personal and intimate participant, not only in rhymes such as 'Elsie Marley', but in the role of secret lover in the familiarly structured 'The Secret':

> O hame came our good man at e'en, and hame came he,
> And there he saw fine riding boots where no boots should be.
>   'Wife', quo' he, 'How can this be?
>   How came these boots here wi'out the leave o' me?'
>     'Boots?' quo' she.
>     'Aye, boots', quo' he.
> 'Ye auld blin' donnert carl, and blin'er mought yoube,
> That's but a pair of milking stoups my minnie brought to me.'
> 'Far hae I travelled and muckle hae I seen,
> But spurs on milking stoups, saw I never nane.'
>
> O hame came our good man at e'en, and hame came he,
> And there he saw a man asleep where no man should be.
>   'Wife,' quo' he, 'How can this be?
>   You're hiding *Chairlie* i' the house, wi'out the leave o' me!'

Little could be more intimate than this: yet the husband is not angry at the suggestion of adultery (as in other rhymes on this model), perhaps because Charles's personal eroticism is too closely linked with the greater issue of community loyalty, as in 'Charlie is My Darling', likely to have been circulating at the time of the 'Forty-five, though the earliest recorded version we have is from 1775:

*Beauceant*, the modern Scottish Templar journal; David Morgan, *The Country Bard: Or, the Modern Courtney. A Poem.* (London, 1741), p. 19.

And Charley is my darling,
my darling, my darling,
And Charlie he's my darling,
the young Chevalier.[53]

The love – loyalty of a previous generation of Jacobite lost-lover poems is
intensified and democratized: the abandoned Britannia or Hibernia (in
the *aisling* poems) of this tradition can become a yet more intimate picture
of an ordinary woman. More spontaneous passion augments the elite
constraints of an earlier tradition: Charles becomes (especially in Scotland) a leitmotif of affection and political hope. Habitually, his personal
comeliness and lovableness is combined with his public role:

The man that should our king hae been,
He wore the royal red and green,
A bonnier lad you never seen
Than our young royal Charlie.

He is 'our', both king and lover, 'young' and 'royal', whose personal
appearance is the clue to his status: and he is dressed in Royal Stuart
tartan, emphasizing his intimate appeal.[54] Although songs like this had
been written about James, Charles is more at ease as its subject: both set
and air are more likely to be original than adapted from existing popular
tradition. Indeed, popular tradition sometimes appears to take over
Jacobite songs centred on Charles Edward to express its own concerns, as
in 'The Bonet O' Blue':

It was down in Green willow, a town in Yorkshire,
I lived in great splendour, and free from all care;
I lived in great splendour, had sweethearts not a few,
Till wounded by a bonny boy and his bonnet o' blue ...

I was instantly dressed, and quickly I came;
I stood with great patience to hear my love's name,
Charlie Stuart is his name, and I love him most true,
Once a prince of that name wore a bonnet o' blue.

The song claims not to be about the Prince: though originally this could
have been an oblique cover to avoid identifying the now-defeated Charles
(who tends to be more anonymous in later poems, as William Donaldson
has pointed out). It is close in structure to the 'Charlie is My Darling'
scenario: the woman speaker is even more intensely 'most true' when she

[53] Buchan, *Scottish Tradition*, p. 7; Eleanor Graham (ed.), *A Puffin Book of Verse* (Harmondsworth:
Penguin), pp. 109–10; T. F. Henderson, '"Charlie He's My Darling", and other Burns'
Originals', *Scottish Historical Review* 3 (1906), pp. 171–8 (175/6).
[54] 'Welcome Royal Charlie', set recorded by 'The Corries' in *Stovies* (1980).

hears the name, as if even an oblique reference has its own force.[55] Such were some of the feelings the young Prince aroused; and later he would be depicted in a passion of a different kind: the man of sorrows, robbed of the world for a heavenly reward. Charles's later depictions had much in common with High Church paintings (Monod, 'For the King to Enjoy his own Again', pp. 133–4).

But it was in the 1740s that Charles's charm and the strength of his propaganda made the greatest inroads, as his opponents knew. Their response to it was in many ways similar to that of the Williamite propagandists of half a century before. On the one hand, satire was employed to undercut Stuart claims even while appearing to acknowledge them; on the other, traditional typology was applied to the representatives of the new regime. In the last stages and aftermath of the Rising, it was Cumberland who served as the icon of Whig counter-culture. He was an even less convincing candidate than William had been in the 1690s: but it was just as necessary that such a candidate should be found. The satirization of Stuart claims could draw attention to their existence, even while rubbishing them. Partly this showed such claims themselves as ridiculous: but Hanoverian satire tended to hover uneasily between the typology and its (unworthy) representative when picking its target. In such circumstances, it was better to make at least a token gesture of claiming to be the legitimate inheritors of what was worth while in the typological tradition, and it was to this end that Cumberland is portrayed in a poem like *The Morning Star* (1746), which makes a neat allusion to the Astraea story (Morning Star = Venus = mother of Aeneas who = Augustus), while avoiding fully acknowledging it.

In *The Compliment*, another poem of the Rising's aftermath, Cumberland is lionized in the role of huntsman monarch (a typically Stuart image). It is telling and chilling that the animals which are the objects of his hunt are likened to people:

> Here drive the stag – Here kill the Hare –
> Hunt 'em, as *Rebels* in your Chace
> Thro' Woods and Hills, like *Highland Race*,
> With nimble Fear, they run, they fly,
> Till by superior Force they dye –

This was all too true. The Whig use of Stuart imagery gives itself away through the criterion of authority it uses: 'by superior Force'. It is remarkable how often Whig poetry uses as its justification for success precisely those premises which criminalized it in Stuart eyes. Yet perhaps there is a purpose for the use of 'Force' in this poem, for the glorification of victory

---

[55] John Ord (ed.), *The Bothy Songs & Ballads of Aberdeen, Banff & Moray Angus and the Mearns* (Edinburgh: John Donald, n.d. (1930)), p. 295.

and success in Whig verse challenges the ability of the elegant typologies it satirizes to alter the situation. Thus in the 1740s we see the Stuart cause, in Whig eyes, brought to the brink of Romanticism: 'old unhappy far-off things, and battles long ago'. Battles fought not at Actium or Philippi, nor between Turnus and Aeneas but Cumberland and Charles, marginalize by sheer force the intricate history of indefeasible right. The celebration of the triumph of Hanoverian force in the 'Forty-five paved the way for romanticization of the heroic and marginal quality of Stuart ideology and its defenders:

> Lord grant that Marshall Wade
> May by thy mighty aid
> Victory bring.
> May he sedition hush
> And like a torrent rush
> Rebellious Scots to crush
> God save the King.

The insertion of this brutish verse in an originally Jacobite anthem simultaneously encapsulated the disavowal and usurpation of Stuart typology practised by the post-1688 regime since its inception. 'God save the King' was now a loyal Hanoverian song, and its new set included a verse in praise of the crushing use of force against the grandson of that king whom conquering William had driven out sixty years before.

The irony was that Wade did virtually nothing of military significance in the Rising. It was Cumberland who became the new owner of Stuart images, the hunter and the celebrant of retreat:

> CAESARS of old, that *Actions* fought
> To *Villa's* for Refreshment sought –
> For *Heroes* scorn to make *Retreats*
> Except to Charming Country seats –

Cumberland appears here to be a natural successor to Stuart typology. But the tribute is more oblique than it appears: it is not the verdant retreat of nature which is celebrated, but the 'country seat', the virtue of which does not derive from its ruralism, but from the star quality of its occupant. It is the hero which determines the status of the retreat, not the retreat which affirms the qualities of the hero. Cumberland's 'scorn', like his 'force' is a commanding quality which lords it over the archetypicality of the images *The Compliment* places him among. Under guise of affirmation, Stuart typology is being deconstructed as effectively as were the Episcopal chapels of the North East.[56]

Some Stuart iconography, like the oak, is freely adopted into Hanover-

---

[56] *The Morning Star. A Poem.* (London, 1746); *The Compliment* (London, 1746), pp. 3, 5.

ian patriotism as a type of British (sea)power, becoming in Victorian times a constituent part of the vision of Britain as Athens (Themistocles' wooden walls equating with the Royal Navy). Burke's great defence of 1688 in *Reflections on the Revolution in France* uses the oak as an established image of British patriotism, and this adoption of the 'Royal Oak' and its 'gen'rous Fruit' by the Whigs was an unqualified success, owing not a little to its development in the Patriot opposition of the 1730s.[57]

Other Stuart images were only adopted in altered form, or attacked. The Whig opposition had already begun such a process: it is tempting to think that in James Thomson's *Castle of Indolence* the words of Indolence the Enchanter's lament for the passing of Astraea are meant to illustrate the folly of clinging to Stuart values:

> 'Outcast of Nature, Man! the wretched Thrall ...
> That all proceed from savage Thirst of Gain:
> For when hard-hearted *Interest* first began
> To poison Earth, *Astraea* left the Plain;
> Guile, Violence, and Murder seiz'd on Man ...

This appears to endorse a pro-Stuart account of 1688. But what does Indolence offer instead except a self-satirizing statement of the nonjuring position: 'the Best of Men have ever lov'd Repose: / They hate to mingle in the filthy Fray ...'. Thomson allows Astraea to be portrayed as primarily nostalgic, even paralysingly nostalgic. Those who support her ways uncompromisingly are what one might term contemplatives of the Stuart order, looking back on a lost world rather than building a new one. Their castles in the air of restoration are in effect castles of indolence.[58]

That it was necessary to level such accusations against a faltering cause is clear from the enduring strength of Astraean imagery, summed up in the strength and breadth of the reaction to an Oxford don's Latin oration in the late 1740s. The five REDEAT prayers in William King's 1747 Radcliffe speech, delivered in support of 'Astraea nostra', Charles Edward Stuart, made high cultural waves right into the 1760s. John Wilkes summed up Oxford Jacobitism in terms of this single speech, given a generation before:

Methinks I still hear the seditious shouts of applause given to the pestilent harangue of the late Dr King, when he vilified our great deliverer, the Duke of Cumberland, and repeated with such energy the treasonable *redeat*.

King's great restatement of the Astraea theme called forth not only a number of poems, both in his favour and against him, but also apparently sparked off a renewed wave of Jacobite propaganda using the very words

---

[57] *A Religious Ode Occasioned by the Present Rebellion*, By A Clergyman (London, 1745), p. 7.
[58] James Thomson, *Liberty, The Castle of Indolence and Other Poems*, ed. James Sambrook (Oxford: Oxford University Press, 1986), pp. 31, 161ff., 178–9.

of his speech. The medal struck for Charles's 1752 visit to England carried King's words, 'REDEAT MAGNUS ILLE GENIUS BRITANNIAE'; and a new spate of 'REDEAT' drinking-glasses followed. The feminization of some of Charles's portrayals in the aftermath of the 'Forty-five reinforced his image as the rightful Astraea. As Thomas Warton wrote of King's speech:

> He blends the speaker's with the patriot's fire . . .
> What Britons dare to think, he dares to tell.

> Bids happier days to Albion be restored
> Bids ancient Justice rear her radiant sword;
> From me, as from my country, claims applause,
> And makes an Oxford's, a Britannia's cause.

The power of the Astraea motif to stir up sympathy for the Stuarts remained considerable, even in the aftermath of Culloden.[59]

Conscious of this, opponents of the Stuarts were also conscious of the power of the connected images of Aeneas/Augustus, which, William III excepted, the post-Revolution regime had failed to adopt with any success. Of course Whig authors were influenced by the classics, and were themselves aware of the doubleness of Augustus: 'if that ambiguous name / Confounds my reader' as Edward Young writes. But they were less able to use Aeneas/Augustus in a political context than their rivals. Indeed, there was a tendency among some writers to tamper with the parameters of the foundation-myth in rendering British patriotism Greek not Trojan: emphasizing that at Troy the Greeks won, and thus once again underlining the role force and success have in replacing the inherited typology of legitimism. An example of this is found in a poem of 1749, 'Rebellion', later revised by Robert Southey, which displays some of the chief features of Whig propaganda, such as a reversal of Jacobite fertility symbolism, portraying instead the centres of Stuart support as barren and desolate:

> perpetual
> On Mountains where *continual* Winter reigns . . .
> over fruitless woody Wilds they go,
> And Mountains cover'd with eternal Snow.[60]

'Rebellion' presents Jacobitism as poverty and discord rather than fertility and renewal. But it is also marked in its tendency (admittedly not consistent) to identify the Jacobite forces at Prestonpans as Trojans fighting British Greeks. Balmerino is 'like Ajax . . . an Host', while of the brave Colonel Gardiner the author comments:

> So great Achilles heap'd the Trojan Plain,
> With Lycian and with Dardan Heroes slain.
>                                  'Rebellion', pp. 12, 29

[59] Greenwood, *William King*, pp. 198, 200, 203, 226, 238.
[60] Edward Young, 'Satire IV' in *Bell's Poets of Great Britain*, vols. 84–7 (London: John Bell, 1877), 86: pp. 108; National Library of Scotland, MS. 300, pp. 7–8, 112n.

Although Gardiner is elsewhere described as 'Hector' ('Rebellion', p. 44), the poem sounds a note which can be heard in anti-Jacobite poetry from Prior's 1690s poem on the Siege of Namur onwards, and which may have anticipated the nineteenth-century vision of Britain as Athens, so different from the Trojans of the seventeenth. In such circumstances, continued insistence on a Trojan reading may mean a Jacobite or at least opposition Whig position is being indicated.[61]

Gray's 'The Bard' is a poem which toys with such readings. The prophetic Bard echoes Dryden's *Aeneid*, and in referring to the 'long-lost Arthur', resuscitates another Tudor and Stuart foundation-myth, which is then linked to 'Britannia's issue': the 'Youth of Form Divine' seems to suggest to the reader the person of Charles Edward Stuart, especially since 'Dryden uses the phrase "form divine" twice in the description of Aeneas' vision of the future leaders of Rome', while the suggestion has been made that the 'Elegy' itself refers to the trial of the Scots peers in 1746. Certainly the villagers ('village Hampden', 'mute inglorious Milton' and 'Cromwell') all seem to belong to the other side, while the fact they have 'Forbade to wade through slaughter to a throne' reminds us of the civil discord caused by the recent Rising. Gray is no Jacobite, but he writes in consciousness of Jacobite language and allusion: what else lies behind the Celtic nationalism of 'The Bard'? In the 1750s it becomes safer to use Jacobite language in order to refer to the romantic qualities inherent in its marginalization, now that political threat is becoming depoliticized by defeat. In this Gray, who was 'excited by Macpherson' anticipates the elegiac Jacobite codes of *Ossian*.[62]

Awareness of Jacobite language remained strong among its opponents because it continued to express Jacobite allegiance or identity in traditional terms. *Ascanius, or the Young Adventurer* (1746) portrays Charles as Aeneas' son, heir to the foundation story (copies of the book have 'C.P.' and the feathers of the Prince of Wales blocked in gold). *Aeneas and his Two Sons* (1745/6) criticizes 'the ridiculous false Aspersions cast upon the unfortunate old *Aeneas* and his Family', archly underlining all the while the contemporaneity of Vergilian typology:

there are many Gentlemen now in *Great Britain* and *Ireland*, who have been in *Italy*, many who have had opprtunities of being personally acquainted with *Aeneas* and his Family ...

'Aeneas' is, repeatedly, 'that unfortunate Exile', while George is 'GERMANICUS', his foreign-ness emphasized. *Aeneas and his Two Sons* is not a

---

61 *The Poetical Works of Matthew Prior*, with a Memoir and Critical Dissertation by the Revd George Gilfillan (Edinburgh: James Nichol, 1858), pp. 49ff.; cf. Richard Jenkyns, *The Victorians and Ancient Greece* (Oxford: Basil Blackwell, 1980).
62 *The Poems of Gray, Collins and Goldsmith*, ed. Roger Lonsdale, Longman Annotated English Poets (London: Longman, 1969), pp. 7, 107–8, 128, 129, 196–7.

particularly inventive text, but it takes for granted the inherited language of Jacobitism in order to trigger response and recognition of 'Aeneas' in the person of the exile oversea, who has not yet come home.[63]

*Ascanius, or the Young Adventurer* and *Aeneas and his Two Sons* were by no means the only books printed at the time which take for granted Stuart rights to the foundation-myth inheritance. Charles is elsewhere portrayed as 'Alexis', an Ascanius/Aeneas hero with a teasing anonymity half-conferred on him, while James's own 1743 proclamation emphasizes the specifically Scottish foundation-myth. So entrenched were these kinds of images, that they could even be used humorously in Jacobite correspondence, as in William King's 1737 letter to Swift, which enthuses for a government 'headed by a king fashioned of oak ... I would have such a King as *Jupiter* gave to the Frogs', commenting that 'Happy had it been for the world, if the long Catalogue of *Roman* Emperors ... had been of the Wooden Species!' Jacobite iconography was not without its humour.[64]

English Jacobitism thus sustained two major languages. The Stuart text told its story in both high and popular forms. The former, often elegantly expressed, depended on learned conceptions of history, authority and the state born out of longstanding justifications of Anglo-Scottish kingship; the latter drew deeply on common feeling and popular superstition concerning the nature of kings and kingship. The former offered a definitively typological account of history, disallowing the usurpation of this account by the apologists of 1688; the latter was almost archetypal, as if drawn from the pages of *The Golden Bough*. Both sacralized their object in paradoxical terms – Christian and pagan, messianic and erotic – promoting a vision of Stuart kingship at once aloof and (especially in Charles Edward's case) intimate. Combining the magisterial and personal in this way generated a pathos and sublimity in Stuart language that influenced and was readily absorbed by Romanticism, which had ample room for both. The dual language of the Stuart text, archetypical and historical at once, premissed enduring nostalgia after the abatement of its force.

But its force was great, based as it was on a deliberate complementarity between diverse registers. For to divide Jacobite culture into elite and popular forms is to ignore the political link between 'the book of the people' and a politically marginalized gentry and aristocracy, so well articulated in our own century by Yeats, whose Red Hanrahan is a composite creation of two eighteenth-century Jacobite poets.[65] From

[63] *Ascanius, or the Young Adventurer* (London: T. Johnston, 1746); *AEneas and His Two Sons* (London: J. Oldcastle, 1745/6), pp. ix, xxxii, 35, 40.
[64] Col. James Allardyce (ed.), *Historical Papers Relating to the Jacobite Period 1699–1750*, 2 vols. (Aberdeen: Spalding Club, 1895), I: 177; Cited in Greenwood, *William King*, p. 77.
[65] W. B. Yeats, *The Collected Poems* (London: Macmillan, 1950), p. 276; Mary Helen Thuente, *W. B. Yeats and Irish Folklore* (Totowa, New Jersey: Barnes and Noble, 1981 (1980)), pp. 198ff.

James V as Gaberlunzie man to Charles as poor Highlander, there were Stuart leaders available who objectively fulfilled the role of sacred leader and accessible lover that their dual textuality required. Likewise the reactionary quality of the 'social bandit' ethos and the cross-class criminalization carried out by the Whig government reinforced bonds of common circumstance to join elite and popular texts and oral culture. Both spoke of a context they shared: demanding restoration of justice and order alike denied by the perceived disruptiveness of political and financial revolution. It was not till the Stuart text was decontextualized by failure that it was ripe for romanticization: but such romanticization took implicit account of the duality of what it romanticized. The Noble Savage epitomizes the convergence of initially differentiated expressions of Stuart support: Jacobite nobles were outlaws, and 'savages' gentlemen. For every Highlander was claimed to be a gentlemen, and many a gentleman died like a Highlander if he fought for the king. So while there was a political reality to sustain the expression of such reciprocity, the two languages of the Jacobite cause found common voice in pursuing a single aim.

# 3

# The codes of the canon

## John Dryden

I must now come closer to my present business: and not think of making more invasive Wars abroad, when like *Hannibal*, I am call'd back to the defence of my own Country. *Virgil* is attack'd by many Enemies ... their principal Objection being against his Moral ... we are to consider him as writing his Poem in a time when the Old Form of Government was subverted, and a new one just established by *Octavius Caesar*: In effect by force of Arms, but seemingly by the Consent of the *Roman* People.
Dryden's Preface to the Aeneid

> Not Great *Aeneas* stood in plainer Day,
> When, the dark mantling Mist dissolv'd away,
> He to the *Tyrians* shew'd his sudden face,
> Shining with all his Goddess Mother's Grace ...
> Britannia Rediviva[1]

Dryden's is the only major poetic career to span both Civil War and Revolution. Yet despite the fact that he has often been portrayed as a poet whose reaction to these turmoils was that of the Vicar of Bray, recent criticism has uncovered a consistency in his underlying approach to political change, a 'longing for an irrecoverable past' 'already detectable in the Hastings elegy [of 1649]', and directed towards the 'golden dayes' of 'the court of Charles I, where ceremony and the arts had been prized as they would never be again'. This view sees Dryden as basically always a Stuart royalist in waiting, whose ambivalence towards Cromwell in 'Heroic Stanzas' is a kind of counterpart to Marvell's 'Horatian Ode'.[2] As in Marvell's poem, Dryden's view of Cromwell shows particular reservation over the dictator's warlike qualities:

---

[1] *The Works of John Dryden*, volume 5, ed. William Frost, textual editor Vinton A. Dearing (Berkeley, CA and London: University of California Press, 1987), pp. 277–8, 343.
[2] Winn, *Dryden and His World*, p. 55; Zwicker, *Politics and Language*, p. 81.

94

His grandeur he derived from heaven alone,
For he was great, ere fortune made him so;
And wars, like mists that rise against the sun,
Made him but greater seem, not greater grow.

The comparison of Cromwell with the sun is a traditional royal image: but the 'mists' of his self-created wars distort that brightness, appearing to amplify it, but in reality obscuring it: a seeming not a growing. This reading connects with the 'sullen interval of war' which *Astraea Redux* characterizes as the Cromwellian period, while others among Dryden's seeming compliments to the dictator are reversed, 'Our cross stars denied us Charles's bed' because 'faction seized the throne', reflecting directly on:

He fought, secure of fortune as of fame,
Till by new maps the island might be shown,
Of conquests, which he strewed where'er he came,
Thick as the galaxy with stars is sown.

War, the chief justifier of Cromwell's success, not only distorts his apparently royal grandeur, but also creates its own fortune, sowing the stars of destiny. But these stars are 'cross', keeping the faction-ruled land away from the intimate satisfaction of 'Charles's bed', with its accompanying promise of a 'general peace'. Charles's return is guarantor of the circularity of peace implicit in the *renovatio* of Astraea, which is the counterpart to Cromwell's possession of 'a fame so truly circular'. Cromwell's fame is 'circular' because it arose through war and perpetuates itself through the 'new maps . . . Of conquests'. But this self-creation, 'Like that bold Greek who did the East subdue' is limited in its duration and effectiveness: while the monarchical paradigm of Astraean justice is eternal. 'The stars' who 'sullenly obey' the 'foreign conquests' of Cromwell, do so only while his strength can ensure their obedience:

His latest victories still thickest came,
As near the centre motion does increase;
Till he, pressed down by his own weighty name,
Did, like the vestal, under spoils decrease.

Eventually Cromwell perishes under the weight of his own warlike success; and in doing so he is likened to the treacherous virgin Tarpeia, who betrayed Rome to the Sabines. There is something ultimately self-destructive about the 'truly circular' nature of Cromwell's fame. War breeds death, the 'lawless savage liberty' as *Astraea Redux* puts it, 'Frosts that constrain the ground and birth deny', but the renewing monarchy of Astraea brings both spring and life. Charles is the opposite of Cromwell, the bringer of peace rather than war, the agent of destiny rather than its grim master:

> How shall I speak of that triumphant day,
> When you renewed the expiring pomp of May!
> (A month that owes an interest in your name:
> You and the flowers are its peculiar claim.)

This renewing monarchy is hinted at in the earlier 'Heroic Stanzas':

> And wars have that respect for his repose
> As winds for halcyons when they breed at sea.

The apparent compliment glosses the fact of its purport: that Cromwell's death is linked to the end of war, an abating of winds which give way to the 'kindly heat of lengthened day' which characterizes Astraea's return in *Astraea Redux*.[3]

Thus it is possible to see the Dryden of 1658 as, albeit politically carefully, consonant with the Dryden of 1660, indeed with the Dryden of 1690. Just as Cromwell is the 'bold Greek', Alexander, who takes the realm by right of conquest, so in Dryden's later poem 'Alexander's Feast', the Alexander-like triumph of William (a comparison which emphasizes the theme of conquest – one William disliked) is contrasted to the fate of Darius, in words which liken the Persian monarch to James II and VII:

> By too severe a Fate,
> Fallen, fallen, fallen, fallen,
>     Fallen from his high Estate,
>       And weltring in his Blood:
>     Deserted at his utmost Need,
> By those his former Bounty fed . . .[4]

William and Cromwell alike are both 'Alexanders' (Greeks as opposed to British Trojans, it is worth noticing), who succeed by right of conquest. Thus in Dryden's (as indeed in other) poetry of the 1650s, the right of conquest theme later applied to William is foreshadowed in the treatment of Cromwell. There was of course a Royalist tradition that Cromwell's success in war did not create destiny, but was a result of the surrender of that destiny to the power of the Devil. The dictator's crucial victories at Dunbar and Worcester both occurred on 3 September, and on the same day he died, seven years after the latter victory: a convenient period for Faustian rumour. Thus his victories can be seen as reflecting a surrender to demonic seduction: and this may be hinted at in Marvell's *Ode*, where the upright sword of the last line (a sign of Cromwell's perpetual war-likeness over which the poet has reservations) is an inverted cross.[5]

---

[3] *The Oxford Authors: John Dryden*, ed. Keith Walker (Oxford, New York: Oxford University Press, 1987), pp. 1ff. References to 'Dryden' in the text are to this edition.

[4] Winn, *Dryden and His World*, p. 493; *The Oxford Authors: John Dryden*, p. 547.

[5] Andrew Marvell, *The Poems and Letters*, ed. H. M. Margoliouth, 2 vols. (Oxford: Clarendon Press, 1971), I: pp. 91–4.

It would of course be wrong to see either Marvell or Dryden as totally engaged in a cryptic destruction of Cromwell's reputation. But it might also be wrong to see Dryden engaged in a Royalist *volte-face* in 1660 and afterwards. In much earlier poetry such as 'Upon the Death of the Lord Hastings', Dryden had used imagery which foreshadowed the politics of the Restoration, comparing Hastings' death to that of Charles I:

> But hasty Winter, with one blast, hath brought
> The hopes of Autumn, Summer, Spring to naught.
> Thus fades the Oak i' th' spring, i' th' blade the Corn;
> Thus, without Young, this *Phoenix* dies, new born.

The death of the royal oak and the encroachment of the Cromwellian winter are as present here as in the poetry of 1658–60, with this difference: that in *Astraea Redux* the Phoenix is reborn (Winn, *Dryden and his World*, p. 51).

The return of Charles II saw Dryden adopt the explicitly Vergilian pose which was to be reflected in post-1688 visions of the Jacobite Aeneas. *Astraea Redux* makes clear Dryden's centring of himself within this tradition (Winn, *Dryden and his World*, p. 106). Compared to 'banished David', Charles is also the Aeneas 'Forced into exile from his rightful throne', who has returned in a Christlike fashion as 'The prince of peace . . . A gift unhoped'. Dryden does refer to the hope that Charles will 'foreign foes assail', but the restoration of peace is the keynote to the poem, a restoration which, as a Pax Britannica, is likened to Augustus' closing of the Janus gate, and the Pax Romana: 'The British Amphitrite . . . With the submitted fasces of the main' welcoming the returning 'great monarch' in a reversal of Aenean exile: 'As you meet it, the land approacheth you'. Dryden concludes in lines which make the Vergilian quality of the poem explicit:

> Oh happy age! Oh times like those alone
> By fate reserved for great Augustus' throne!
> When the joint growth of arms and arts foreshow
> The world a monarch, and that monarch you.[6]

'Arms and arts' is a phrase which echoes the first line of the *Aeneid*. Thus in the last lines of welcome to Charles II there is a foreshadowing of the translation which Dryden would later write in reference to James' departure:

My Translation of Virgil is already in the Press . . . I have hinder'd it thus long in hopes of his return, for whom, and for my conscience I have suffered, that I might have layd my Authour at his feet . . .

---

[6] *Oxford Dryden*, p. 17.

Writing in 1697, almost forty years after *Astraea Redux*, Dryden hints that he would have liked to see the triumph of Book XII accomplished by Aeneas/Augustus (in the person of James) before releasing the volume. As it is, it stands as a prophecy, yet unfulfilled (Winn, *Dryden and his World*, p. 485).

Prophecy and the mystic power of the Stuart monarchy are linked by Dryden in 'To his Sacred Majesty, a Panegyric on his Coronation', where Charles is greeted in Frazerian terms:

> And opened scenes of flowers and blossoms bring
> To grace this happy day, while you appear
> Not king of us alone but of the year.

Charles's presentation as flower-king and year-king is associated with his tree, the oak, and its religious aspects (Aeneas had of course taken the Golden Bough from the Nemean oak to enter the underworld):

> Thus from your Royal Oak, like Jove's of old,
> Are answers sought and destinies foretold:
> Propitious oracles are begged with vows,
> And crowns that grow upon the sacred boughs.

The Royal Oak was depicted on one of the four triumphal arches of Charles's coronation, which took place on the mythically appropriate St George's Day, thus rendering Charles both patriotic emblem and patriotic saint, secular and sacred sovereign of England (he had of course been crowned in Scotland a decade earlier).[7]

The link between Charles and the oak could also be made on the level of popular patriotism, which associated English royalty with the oak (Elizabeth had been sitting under one at Hatfield House when she learnt of her succession to the throne), and the Druidic sacred oak of native Britons. This was already foreshadowed in Charles's taking refuge in Stonehenge after the battle of Worcester, mentioned as an additional justification of his claims to hereditary right in Dryden's poem 'To my Honoured Friend Dr Charleton' (1663).[8]

But the central thrust of Dryden's royalism remained its Vergilian theme, as he admitted in the prefatory letter to *Annus Mirabilis* (1666), when he owns Vergil 'my master ... I have followed him everywhere ... my images are many of them copied from him' (Dryden, p. 28). Indeed, Dryden shows a marked consistency in his imagery. In *MacFlecknoe*, one of the earliest poems to feature an anti-Aeneas, Dryden exposes Shadwell in terms he had earlier used to compliment Cromwell, thus revealing their ambivalence: 'His rising fogs prevail upon the day', just as Cromwell's mists of war distort the light of the sun.[9]

---

[7] Ibid., pp. 18, 20, 865n.     [8] Ibid., p. 21.     [9] Ibid., p. 143.

James is heir to the language Dryden uses of Charles. 'Prologue to the Duchess on her Return from Scotland' was printed as a prologue to *Venice Preserved* in May 1682. Implicitly comparing the Exclusion Crisis with the Interregnum, it associates James's exile with barrenness, and his return with fertility: 'Our fruitful plains to wilds and deserts turned, / Like Eden's face, when banished man it mourned' on James's departure; but now 'The famine past, the plenty still to come', the Duchess's return with her Duke ensures that 'for her, the ground is clad in cheerful green'. Restored from 'cruel exile' 'The queen of beauty, and the court of love' bring fertility back to the land. It is noteworthy that here, as in the explicitly Jacobite 'Lady's Song', Dryden's language is to be later borrowed by the Jacobite poetry of Major General Alexander Robertson of Struan, for example in his poem on the exile of Pan and Syrinx.[10]

In the 1680s, Dryden's use of political language amplifies itself to include both Puritan typology in *Absalom and Achitophel* (Winn, *Dryden and his World*, p. 350) and the beast-fable in *The Hind and the Panther*.[11] The former poem allows Dryden to resuscitate the Davidic king imagery of the 1650s: and the biblical episode chosen is especially appropriate since the rebellious Absalom dies in the branches of an oak, the royal tree overcoming rebellion (Winn, *Dryden and his World*, p. 352). The latter makes use of the beast-fable as both popular literature and political allegory:

The beast fable was popular during the Restoration – new editions of Aesop were published regularly throughout the period – and enjoyed a privileged generic status. On the one hand, such fables were held sufficiently simple and obvious to form the characters of children, on the other, they were considered an ancient vehicle of wisdom, especially such wisdom as penetrated and opposed political deceit and hypocrisy.

The last word here is the one which offers a keynote to the politics of Aesopian fable: it was frequently anti-Whig, for it was the Puritans and their perceived descendants who were held to exemplify 'political deceit and hypocrisy' (Bywaters, *Dryden in Revolutionary England*, pp. 22–3).

Thus in constructing *The Hind and the Panther*, Dryden backgrounded his high Vergilian pose in showing a sensitivity to more popular contemporary modes of political understanding and comment. The dual role of the Aesopian story, its 'popular generic status' as both elementary moral and exposing political fable, was to be crucial to the popularity of the beast-fable in post-Revolution propaganda. The dual voice of the Stuart cause could perhaps find a means of suitable expression in Aesopian beast-fable,

[10] Ibid., pp. 217, 321; Alexander Robertson of Struan, 'The Consolation. An Eclogue', in *Poems* (Edinburgh, 1749), pp. 88–92.

[11] David Bywaters, *Dryden in Revolutionary England* (Berkeley, CA and Oxford: University of California Press, 1991), pp. 22ff.

a genre which, as the great Scots poet Robert Henryson had earlier found, was well able to conceal under its generalities piercing criticism of political abuse. 'The Wisdom of the Ancients has been still wrapt up in *Veils* and *Figures*' as Dryden's political ally, Roger L'Estrange, wrote in the preface to his 1692 translation of Aesop (Cited, Bywaters, *Dryden in Revolutionary England*, p. 23).

In this context, Dryden's achievement in *The Hind and the Panther* lay not only in lifting religious controversy and beast-fable out of the margins of poetic high culture, but also in blending them with a deeply political reading conveyed in a canonical text. Dryden here as elsewhere formed an ordering syntax for the subsequent vocabulary of Jacobite critique.

Even in this poem, however, Dryden does not abandon the Vergilian model he was at the same time strongly exercising in poems like 'Threnodia Augustalis', which reaffirmed the Caroline age of 'Nature's golden Scene' and repeated the *Astraea Redux* image of 'The *Fasces* of the Main' to exemplify the transfer of power from Charles to James. As Stephen Zwicker has observed, the use of the *Aeneid* in part three of *The Hind and the Panther* 'to raise issues of invasion and conquest, of property and prosperity, of political deceit and political legitimacy' foreshadows Dryden's fears of and later concern for, questions of 'invasion and conquest' brought to a head in 1688.[12]

These fears are seen in *Britannia Rediviva*, the title-page of which bears a Vergilian legend from the *Georgics*, emphasizing the birth of the young Prince and the washing away of the ancient crimes of the Trojans (Dryden's politically unstable fellow-countrymen, the 'Jews' of *Absalom and Achitophel*, 'a headstrong, moody, murmuring race' (Dryden, p. 180)). The new James is both a new Augustus and 'a second *Constantine*' (Dryden, p. 213), thus emphasizing once more the sacred typology of Tudor religious claims – perhaps a strange thing to do, since Dryden was now a Roman Catholic. The young Prince is also the 'Great *Aeneas*', typological successor to the ancient Trojan (Dryden, p. 214). Although the Vergilian epigraph does no more than associate the birth of the new Prince with a washing away of the treacheries of the past, Dryden intensifies the connexion in language which renders the young James a Christlike as well as an Aeneas-like figure:

> Let his Baptismal Drops for us attone;
> Lustrations for Offences not his own.
> Let Conscience which is Int'rest ill disguis'd,
> In the same Font be cleans'd, and all the Land Baptiz'd.
>
> Dryden, p. 216

---

[12] *The Works of John Dryden*, vol. 3, ed. Earl Miner, textual ed. Vinton A. Dearing (Berkeley and Los Angeles, CA: University of California Press, 1969), pp. 92, 107; Zwicker, *Politics and Language*, p. 153.

There is an unspoken link here between the atoning waters of baptism (itself an extension of the doctrine of baptismal regeneration, unwelcome to many of the sectarian beasts of the political forest) and the blood of Vergil's epigram, suggestive of a connexion between baptism and the Atonement, conjoined in the blood and water which flowed from the dead Christ's side. Dryden's images make of James Francis Edward a sacrificial Christlike prince, but they also suggest an underlying violence, a catastrophe to come.

That catastrophe came within six months. In a few months more, Dryden had ceased to be Poet Laureate. His replacement by Nahum Tate was a fitting epitaph on Stuart support of art and letters, as perhaps Dryden obliquely hints in a *Discourse of Satire*:

For setting prejudice and Partiality apart, though he is our Enemy, the Stamp of a *Louis*, the Patron of all Arts, is not much inferior to the Medal of an *Augustus Caesar*. Let this be said without entering into the interests of Factions and Parties.[13]

As in Atterbury's Preface, the reader seems intended to bring to these lines the consciousness that the age of Augustus Caesar has passed.

Despite Whig speculation that Dryden might turn coat and back the new regime (Bywaters, *Dryden in Revolutionary England*, p. 34), he remained loyal to the royal language and persons of the Stuart line. As he puts it in the Preface to *Don Sebastian*:

Certainly, if a Man can ever have reason to set a value on himself, 'tis when his ungenerous Enemies are taking the advantage of the Times upon him, to ruin him in his reputation. And therefore for once, I will make bold to take counsel of my old Master, *Virgil*, *Tu, ne cede malus; sed, contra, audentior ito*.

Both *Don Sebastian* and *Cleomenes* were viewed as Jacobite plays, and contributed to the Jacobitism of the stage in the 1690s. It was once again to Vergil that Dryden turned to deliver his verdict on the new regime. In all of Dryden's Vergil, in the *Pastorals*, *Georgics* and *Aeneid*, 'versions of usurpation' are present in the vocabulary; and in the last-named poem, as I suggested in Chapter 1, Dryden found a metaphor as appropriate for Revolution as *Astraea Redux* had been for the Restoration (Bywaters, *Dryden in Revolutionary England*, pp. 1, 7, 75, 126).

It is well to tread carefully here. Dryden's *Aeneid* can be read, though not thoroughly read, as alluding to William. For example, Augustus' accession is described as a 'Usurpation' upon the 'Freedom' of the Roman people, which, coupled with Dryden's lengthy comparison of Aeneas and Augustus and the presence of William's hooked nose in the illustrations of Aeneas, suggest an identification of William with a usurping Augustus/ Aeneas figure. Douglas Brooks-Davies has suggested the presence of a

13 Bywaters, *Dryden in Revolutionary England*, p. 137.

Jacobite Turnus, and Stephen Zwicker opines that 'Dryden condemns Aeneas for William's crimes'. But Dryden is contrasting as well as condemning:

*Aeneas*, tho he married the Heiress of the Crown, yet claim'd no Title to it during the life of his Father-in-Law.

Here Dryden does not condemn Aeneas, but by praising him, contrasts him with William: 'Dryden condemns William by enforcing the difference between the pious Trojan and English parricide.' So William is an unrighteous Augustus, an anti-Aeneas: rather than merely reflecting the failures of Aeneas, William also exemplifies his own, and is thus attached to typology by antithesis. Dryden uses Aeneas to expose William's actions through both analogy and disparity.[14]

But Dryden's pyrotechnics do not stop here. Typological disparity is confirmed by historical disparity: Augustus did not claim the throne during his uncle Caesar's lifetime (James was William's uncle as well as his father-in-law). So *unlike* Aeneas, William has usurped his father-in-law's crown, and *unlike* Augustus, he has usurped his uncle's authority. Moreover, Dryden's comparison of William with Brutus and Cassius in *Don Sebastian* (Bywaters, *Dryden in Revolutionary England*, p. 37) brings to mind the fact that these traitors were the slayers of Caesar and defeated by Augustus. Thus William can neither satisfactorily be the exiled Aeneas or the restored Augustus, although he is compared to both. Dryden makes such comparisons only to destabilize them, as in the Dedication where he suggests that when Vergil wrote

the old Form of Government was subverted . . . and a new one just Established . . . In effect by force of Arms, but seemingly by the Consent of the *Roman* People.
                                            Dryden, *Works*, 5: p. 278

William is likened to Augustus by such a comparison, but the analogy subverts his legitimacy. Yet on the next page the regime that Augustus replaced is identified as the usurping one: Marius and Sulla are described as 'Usurpers', while '*Pompey*, *Crassus* and *Caesar* had found the Sweets of Arbitrary Power'. Thus Caesar's chief opponent (Pompey) and Caesar himself are linked as 'arbitrary' rulers: the concept of legitimacy is smudged as a result. The Pompeians whom Augustus fought and the Caesareans whose interests he emblematized are alike 'arbitrary', and, as Dryden tells us, '*Virgil*' 'was not an Arbitrary Man' (Dryden, *Works*, 5: p. 283). Why then did he support Augustus? Because although he could be seen as restoring the unjust kingship of Tarquin ( = William as in Arthur Mainwaring's 'Tarquin and Tullia'), Augustus also restored (in the eyes of

---

[14] Ibid., pp. 189n, 190n; Zwicker, *Politics and Language*, p. 67; Frost (ed.), *The Works of John Dryden* 5: p. 284.

his apologists, such as Vergil) the true constitution of the Republic. Is this then a compliment to William, that he restored English freedom and liberty? Not at all, as we learn from Dryden's use of that great Jacobite exemplar, the 'Honest Man':

an Honest Man ought to be contented with that Form of Government, and with those Fundamental Constitutions of it, which he receiv'd from his Ancestors, and under which he himself was Born ...                    Dryden, *Works*, 5: p. 281

These lines anticipate the arguments from inherited value later used by apologists for a Jacobite Cato (see Chapter 2). Octavian Augustus could be seen as inheriting both Republicanism and Caesarism from his ancestors, and his restoration of both forms of government followed due form, in a way William's did not (Augustus, for example, did not claim the office of Pontifex Maximus (significantly now held by the Pope) till the death of his opponent the triumvir Lepidus in 12 BC). This 'Office of the High Priesthood, with which Augustus was invested' (Dryden, *Works* 5: p. 285) parallels both Aeneas' piety (though Vergil died seven years before Augustus assumed Lepidus' title) and the sacred authority of Henrician claims to be head of the British Patriarchate, claims inherited by James and mentioned in *Britannia Rediviva*, but effectively sidelined by William. Even though '*AEneas* could not claim to be *Priam's* Heir in Lineal Succession', this 'Lineal Succession' has been disrupted by war in a way Britain's has not; Aeneas does not claim the Trojan throne (unlike his Dutch successor), and his power comes by divine plan. It is, I think, Aeneas' prime virtue, pious duty, which excuses the arbitrariness of James (to which the subtle Dryden is no doubt pointing) and exposes that of William. Indeed, Dryden specifically defends Vergil's choice of piety as the prime Aenean virtue: 'a thorough Virtue both begins and ends in Piety'. Aenean piety is the prototype of Augustan high priesthood and Papal title. So when at the beginning of his translation Dryden writes 'his banish'd Gods restor'd to Rites Divine', he draws attention to Aeneas' establishment of worship at Rome, an establishment succeeded by that Roman Catholicism banished by an impious William. This association of pagan and Christian Roman religion could not only be made through the sequence of Augustan and Papal title, but also through Vergil's own mediaeval role as quasiChristian prophet, and the providential status of Rome, in both sacred and secular terms, in political theory such as that of Dante.[15] Dryden's typological commitment here can be seen as a confirmation of the claims of Catholicism set out in *The Hind and the Panther*. The 'group of engravings with altars, sacrifices, and divining scenes dedicated to Roman Catholics' in the *Aeneid* emphasizes the point; while Aeneas'

[15] Dryden, *Works*, 5: pp. 283, 343.

descendant's role as founder of Britain lends an independent value to the notion of a British Patriarchate to rival the Roman one: a theological theme of high Anglicanism inherited by the Nonjurors.[16]

The main text of the translation shows 'unfailing' attention to making Vergil's language contemporary in its application. The opening lines, with their talk of 'settl'd sure Succession in his Line' and the 'Expell'd and exil'd' nature of Aeneas (Dryden, *Works* 5: p. 343) expand the language of the original considerably in order to draw attention to the events of 1688/9, while a mention of marriage-rites in Vergil becomes 'Succession, Empire, and his Daughter's Fate' (an apparent reference to Mary's treachery). In Book VII, 'magnum bellum' becomes 'waste' and 'change the state'. Dryden turns parts of Vergil's text into a litany of treason and mutability: when Neptune '... saw the *Trojan* Fleet dispers'd, distress'd / By stormy Winds and wintry Heav'n oppress'd', it seems not only a comment on French naval difficulties in the 1690s, but a prophecy of the 'protestant winds' that thwarted the return of the Jacobite Aeneas in the next half-century. Whatever the temporal trials of exile, though, the eternal fate of traitors is a worse one:

> Then they, who Brothers better Claim disown,
> Expel their Parents, and usurp the Throne;
> Defraud their Clients, and to Lucre sold,
> Sit brooding on unprofitable Gold ...

In Vergil, the brothers are hated, the parents beaten: in Dryden, they are respectively 'defrauded' and 'expelled', as Zwicker points out (Maitland also seems to be drawing political attention to this passage in his 1691 Preface).[17]

Manipulation of Vergil's text rams home the parallels and constructs a metaphor to challenge the legitimacy of the post-Revolution state. In Book x for example, Dryden expands two words in the Latin, meaning 'to carry off plunder' into these lines:

> Hard and unjust indeed, for men to draw
> Their Native Air, nor take a foreign Law
> Realms, not your own, among your Clans divide ...

This kind of appeal to contemporary xenophobia, though it can be applied against Aeneas, mainly works in his favour (he is, after all, a British Trojan). Venus, who is 'queen of love', like Mary of Modena in Dryden's 'Prologue to the Duchess' ('queen of beauty, and the court of love' (Dryden, p. 217)), complains to Jove in terms which clearly empha-

---

[16] Zwicker, *Politics and Language*, pp. 66–7, 192.
[17] Ibid., pp. 120, 196, 202, 253; *The Works of John Dryden* 5: pp. 348ff.; National Library of Scotland Deposit 221/62, 2rff.

size the royal, godly and native authority of the rightful Aeneas (Dryden, *Works* 5: p. 353):

> But we, descended from your sacred Line,
> Entitled to your Heav'n, and Rites Divine,
> Are banish'd Earth, and, for the Wrath of One,
> Remov'd from *Latium*, and the promis'd Throne.

But this right, emphasized through Aeneas' piety, is in the jeopardy of exile throughout most of the narrative. As Aeneas himself says (Dryden, *Works* 5: p. 369):

> What thanks can wretched Fugitives return
> Who scattered thro' the World in exile mourn?

Such fugitives run many risks. Ilioneus' fear for Aeneas: 'But if, O best of Men! thy Fates ordain / That thou art swallow'd in the *Lybian* Main ...' (Dryden, *Works* 5: p. 367) gives in Dryden's rendition a close echo of his own translation of Archibald Pitcairne's lines on Viscount Dundee:

> O last and best of *Scots*! who didst maintain
> Thy Country's Freedom from a Foreign Reign ...
> Dryden, *Works* 3: p. 222

Dryden expresses Ilioneus' concern for Aeneas in the language of an already final Jacobite fate: that of Dundee at Killiecrankie. This is consistent with a treatment of Vergil's epic which throughout lays emphasis on Aenean exile and loss rather than Augustan success and gain. As Zwicker puts it:

The neutral future, the promised day, the destined land – these and a number of Virgil's other topoi are consistently darkened and undercut. We are made to fear the active malignance of gods who in Virgil are detached or indifferent. Such language as 'dark futurity', 'fate's irrevocable doom', and 'fatal place of rest' shapes our perception of the fates in Dryden's translation.

This dark mediation of Vergil's text colours Jacobite literature's sense of robbery and betrayal, and finally, in work such as Macpherson's, its nostalgia. For Dryden too is beginning to be nostalgic, and Earl Miner's idea of the *Aeneid* as functioning 'to strengthen the Catholic claims of antiquity and cultural superiority' is amply fulfilled by a translation which celebrates these things in terms of loss and retirement from public life. But the elegiac quality of Dryden's translation is provisional in the context of the 1690s. There was still hope, if not for the ageing former Poet Laureate, then for those for whom he wrote.[18]

This hope expressed itself in the cunning doubleness of Dryden's post-

---

[18] Zwicker, *Politics and Language*, pp. 203, 229n; Winn, *John Dryden in His World*, p. 485.

Revolution rhetoric. While William is the 'present deity' of 'Alexander's
Feast' (itself a title suggesting the possibility of change), the poem also
marks an atrocity of Alexander's army, the firing of Persepolis, and does it
in terms quite consonant with a Jacobite reading:

> And the king seized a flambeau with zeal to destroy;
>> Thais led the way,
>> To light him to his prey,
> And, like another Helen, fired another Troy.
>
> Dryden, pp. 546, 549

The firing of Persepolis destroyed numerous treasures of Persian art; the
firing of Troy is the central episode of anguish in *Aeneid* II: what were the
British Trojans to make of such a comparison?

In 'The Lady's Song' (Dryden, p. 321) the unidentified Phyllis seems, in
symbolizing the deserted land, to anticipate the Britannia lost-lover
ballads of the eighteenth century, while the 'May-lady to govern the year'
being chosen in the first stanza is a representation of Stuart ruralism and
fertility symbolism, but also surely of the Blessed Virgin, Queen of the
May, whom Dryden had before (in *Britannia Rediviva*) associated with
Mary of Modena. The Aenean James of that poem, 'a pre-Christian type
of Christ' is paralleled by the Messianic appearance of Aeneas in *Aeneid*
I: line 834. Yet perhaps in protective ambivalence, a subsequent verse of
'the Lady's Song' has recently come to light which casts doubt on the
explicit Jacobitism of the earlier verses.[19]

John Dryden ends his poetic life in the age of Revolution as he began in
that of Interregnum: by using the rich ambiguity of the symbolism of
sovereignty to confirm and evade political commitment. He remains very
much the public poet of times of uncertainty. The language Dryden
chooses for this public expression owes much to Vergil's diagnosis of
kingship, as recognized in modern classical criticism.[20] The Vergil who
italianized Aeneas and alienized Turnus (Cairns, *Virgil's Augustan Epic*,
p. 122) is followed by Dryden in his gentle playing on the growing
Jacobite xenophobia of the 1690s. Political poetry without jingoism is hard
to write; and it is a measure of Dryden's triumph that he managed to write
thus for more than half a century. That encoding and its splendid
classicism were legacies to subsequent Jacobite literature; and there was
always enough sympathetic (and hostile) deciphering available to make
Dryden's Jacobitism clear. That is how this book sees him, not compromised in equally strong allegiance to James and William, as William J.

[19] Paul Korshin, *Typologies in England 1650–1720* (Princeton: Princeton University Press, 1982),
    p. 5. I am indebted to Howard Erskine-Hill for information concerning the differing version of
    'The Lady's Song'.
[20] Francis Cairns, *Virgil's Augustan Epic* (Cambridge: Cambridge University Press, 1989), pp. 1ff.

Cameron argues, but rather knowing how to speak and what to say in an age that demanded either silence or propaganda of its political writing.[21]

*The Secular Masque* perhaps provides a fitting epitaph to this career of speech, where royalist form comments obliquely on royalist sentiment: 'peace, the lazy good' has fled comments Mars, while the presence of Janus reminds us not only of the 'old age' and the 'new', but the Janus gate of peace and war itself, closed by Augustus. But 'The warrior god is come'. 'Love will have his hour at last', Venus (mother of Aeneas) insists; but for now 'the queen of pleasure' is fled, her 'lovers were all untrue', like those who 'Deserted at his utmost need' the James/Darius of *Alexander's Feast*. Yet what will war achieve: those of Cromwell and William having 'brought nothing about'. The futility of the history Dryden has lived through is perfectly balanced: James and Charles, Mayking lovers of the land were betrayed in their peaceful aims; but Cromwell and William have caused war for no positive end. Will 'Love . . . have his hour at last'? For an old man, the answer is compromised and affirmed by the cyclical quality of the changes he has seen. The Janus gate of the seventeenth century has been a revolving door. Dryden offers such uncertainty an elegy:

> All, all of a piece throughout;
> Thy chase had a beast in view;
> Thy wars brought nothing about;
> Thy lovers were all untrue.
> 'Tis well an old age is out,
> And time to begin a new.

Dryden did no more than begin it, dying in the month of his earthly king and the Queen of Heaven, 1 May 1700 (Dryden, pp. 547, 855–7).

# Alexander Pope

The *Aeneid* was evidently a party piece, as much as *Absalom and Achitophel*. Virgil was as slavish a writer as any of the gazeteers.                    Spence, quoting Pope

> But Britain, changeful as a Child at play,
> Now calls in Princes, and now turns away.
> Now Whig, now Tory, what we lov'd we hate . . .
> *Imitation of Horace*, Epistle II

---

[21] William J. Cameron, 'John Dryden's Jacobitism', in Harold Love (ed.), *Restoration Literature: Critical Approaches* (London: Methuen, 1972), pp. 277–308 (277).

Loud thunder to its bottom shook the bog,
And the hoarse nation croak'd, 'God save King Log!'

*The Dunciad*

not a King of Whigs, or a King of Tories, but a King of England. Which God of his
mercy grant his Present Majesty may be ...                    Pope to Atterbury, 1717[22]

Alexander Pope was a Roman Catholic. He remained so in the face of
major and adverse alterations in the legislation affecting Roman Catholics
throughout his life. There were considerable social and potential financial
rewards for apostasy: he did not take them. Yet by no means every book on
Pope considers the question as crucially important, or takes pains to
examine his devotional life. That there were many reasons for his conduct
apart from political ones need not be in doubt: but it is significant to this
writer at any rate that the diminishing of Pope's Catholicism and the
neglect of his Jacobite leanings seem connected critical phenomena.[23]

Pope continued to correspond with Atterbury 'after it became a felony
to do so'. The last of the above quotations thus emphasizes the ambivalence of patriot king imagery in Bolingbroke's circle before Bolingbroke
himself named the concept. Who is the 'Present Majesty' in a letter
between 'a Roman Catholic nonjuror' and an Anglican bishop later
suspected of trying to overthrow the Whig state? 'Here's to the King, sir
... Ye ken who I mean, sir'. Certainly, the 'certain laws, by Suff'rers
thought unjust' enacted by the 'Present Majesty' of the post-Revolution
state had done nothing to modify any hostility Roman Catholics might feel
towards it. The acts of I William and Mary 9 and II William III 4 deprived
Pope of rights of residence, worship and Catholic education before he was
ten years old; Anne continued the trend; I George I 2, 13 deprived him of
professional employment rights; I George I 2, 50, 55 appropriated the
majority of Roman Catholic estates; and IX George I 18 imposed financial
penalties on Roman Catholic worship. Pope had fewer civil rights than a
South African black at the height of apartheid: in such circumstances, it is
difficult indeed to avoid the conclusion that he cannot have been sympathetic to the regime. Nor was it a question of Walpole alone; it was the
Revolution and the Act of Settlement that made Roman Catholic life 'a
long disease' of potential civil oppression, even where sanctions were not
enforced. That such elementary points can be omitted from discussion of

---

22 Zwicker, *Politics and Language*, p. 233 n116; *The Poems of Alexander Pope*, ed. John Butt, one-
   volume Twickenham Pope (London: Methuen, 1963), pp. 641, 735 (future reference in the
   text is to this edition); Pope to Atterbury, November 1717 (*Correspondence* I, p. 454).
23 Maynard Mack's *Alexander Pope: A Life* (New Haven: Yale University Press, 1985) offers a
   more satisfactory account of Pope's religious position.

Pope is evidence of the grip Protestant Whig historiography has on literary criticism.[24]

In such circumstances, satire is born. Toleration, liberty and freedom of property were already Whig concepts self-satirized for Roman Catholics by the hypocrisy of their application. Pope was thus well-placed to inherit Dryden's double mantle of language and its political applications. In 'Messiah: A Sacred Eclogue, in Imitation of Virgil's Pollio' (1712), Pope follows Dryden in seeking Astraean return:

> All Crimes shall cease, and ancient Fraud shall fail;
> Returning Justice lift aloft her Scale . . .[25]

This Astraean return will take a predictable form:

> Then Palaces shall rise; the joyful Son
> Shall finish what his short-lived Sire begun . . .
> (Pope, p. 192)

The 'short-lived Sire' may be James's reign of 1685–8; 'the joyful Son' would be James III and VIII, poised to succeed the ailing Anne. Such a restoration would bring with it the usual restored fertility:

> Waste sandy Vallies, once perplex'd with Thorn,
> The spiny Firr and shapely Box adorn . . .
> (Pope, p. 192)

The fir tree's Jacobite symbolism has been already referred to; it is also worth noting that the Blessed Virgin is the rose without a thorn, and that Christ was crowned with thorns: an event alluded to in a Jacobite context in Pope's grotto, as Maynard Mack has pointed out. The thorn as a symbol of infertility is everything that is unChristian and, by implication, offends against the sacred majesty of the Stuart king.[26]

In addition, although the restored fertility of the land is intentionally based on the Fourth Eclogue, Pope makes a significant innovation in that he suggests that part of the renewed fertility will come about as the result of deliberate cultivation: in this sense the 'shapely Box' is a forerunner of 'the Slope' which 'laughing Ceres' will 're-assume' in *Epistle to Burlington*. Jacobitical garden codes both modified and exemplified Vergilian and biblical fertility prophecy. Vergil's ground 'unprompted by the hoe' becomes a process of more planned renewal.[27]

The prophecy of restored fertility itself encodes a restored crown: 'Thy

24 Maynard Mack, *Alexander Pope: A Life*, pp. 265, 579; *The Poems of Alexander Pope: Imitations of Horace*, ed. John Butt, Twickenham Pope Volume IV (London, 1939), p. 169.

25 *The Poems of Alexander Pope*, p. 190.

26 Brean S. Hammond, *Pope* (Brighton: Harvester, 1986); also discussed in Maynard Mack, *The Garden and the City*.

27 Vergil, *Pastoral Poems* (Harmondsworth: Penguin); *The Poems of Alexander Pope*, pp. 192, 594.

*Realm* for ever lasts! thy own *Messiah* reigns!' concludes 'Messiah' triumphantly. The 'Incence of the breathing Spring' will return for ever: and in the use of the word 'incense', Pope doubly emphasizes the political consequences he has in mind. Frankincense is the symbol of God's presence, thus of the returning Messiah; but it is physically used as such a symbol only in High Church and Roman Catholic ritual in the West. Thus the word indicates not only Messianic return but the rehabilitation of Catholic worship. The returning vigin Astraea ('A *Virgin* shall conceive, a *Virgin* bear a Son!') will restore both fertility and true religion, while the 'LIGHT HIMSELF' of 'Messiah' is the hopeful counterpart to the 'Universal Darkness' which Pope later feared (Pope, pp. 189, 194).

Of course the Astraean image was used to support the Hanoverian regime, though perhaps in little depth until the 1730s. But Pope's satirical consciousness of this only underlines his Jacobitical intentions. His note on Astraea in 'Epistle to Augustus' reflects the devaluation of the concept in Hanoverian usage: '*Astraea* A Name taken by Mrs Afra Behn, Authoress of severall obscene Plays, &c' (Pope, p. 645). As Manuel Schonhorn points out:

For Pope the cycle is complete. His Augustan Age has brought the return of a demoralized and salacious goddess, signifying through his allusive authority the full decay of classical values for his time.[28]

That Pope should find in Astraea (particularly in the ultimate anti-Astraea of Dulness) a focal point for such comment on decay is significant in any evaluation of his political sympathies.

*Windsor-Forest*, published in 1713, has already attracted considerable attention as a Jacobite or quasi-Jacobite poem (not only for its dedication to a Jacobite peer), with emphasis falling on the doubleness of the William the Conqueror figure as both William I and III (that the latter did not like to be called a conqueror only makes this a more effective insult on Pope's part).[29] But it is possible to see the poem as a textured Stuart argument on rather more than this single level. Placing itself in the tradition of *Cooper's Hill* (a poem with which it advertises its intertextuality), *Windsor Forest* belongs to a subgenre already heavily embroidered with Stuart ruralist royalism. This in its turn emphasizes the safety of rural retreat in comparison to the noisome dangers of a disorderly city (from which of course Roman Catholics could be excluded at whim). *Windsor Forest* opens:

[28] Manuel Schonhorn, 'Pope's *Epistle to Augustus*. Notes Towards a Mythology', in Maynard Mack and James A. Winn (eds.), *Pope: Recent Essays* (by several hands) (Brighton: Harvester, 1980), pp. 546–65 (565).
[29] Woolf, *Medallic Record of the Jacobite Movement*, p. 25; cf. Howard Erskine-Hill, 'Alexander Pope: The Political Poet in His Time', *Eighteenth-Century Studies* 15: 2 (1981/2), pp. 123–48.

Thy Forests, *Windsor*! and thy green Retreats,
At once the Monarch's and the Muses' Seats ...

An Edenic quality is presented from the beginning in the 'green Retreats', emphasizing their resistance to a world '*Chaos*-like together crush'd and bruised', such a world perhaps as is represented in *The Rape of the Lock*, where the centrality of zeugmatic effect in rhetoricizing the poem displays the disharmony between the Edenic and its materialist violation: 'Puffs, Powders, Patches, Bibles, Billet-doux'', 'Forget her Pray'rs, or miss a Masquerade' (Pope, pp. 222, 225).

If this seems over-speculative, there is plenty of harder evidence in *Windsor Forest*. Pope's repeated use of the oak as a symbol may suggest a generalized British patriotism: but the oak was still strongly associated with the deposed Stuarts, as the 1690s medallic record makes clear (see Chapter 1). The presence of broken or uprooted oaks in the Williamite iconography of victory adds another layer to Pope's satire on 'Our haughty *Norman*'. Oaks are thus symbolic both of the Stuart dynasty and its conquest from abroad: indeed, just after Pope first praises the oak in line 31 comes the famous couplet:

Rich Industry sits smiling on the Plains,
And Peace and Plenty tell, a STUART reigns.

The compliment of course is primarily intended for Anne; but it would be extraordinary to deny the possibility of ambivalence.

The oak reappears as the guarantor of British naval power in line 219:

Thou too, great Father of the *British* Floods!
With joyful Pride survey'st our lofty Woods,
Where tow'ring Oaks their growing Honours rear,
And future Navies on thy Shores appear.

James II and VII was the founder of the Navy in its modern form, and remained such an enthusiast for it that he is rumoured to have cheered the English fleet at La Hogue in 1692, to the considerable discomfiture of his French allies. His successors also retained a soft spot for the service. In these lines, Pope seems to quiver on the verge of hinting at a restoration by armed force: the 'thy shores' is ambiguous (Thames or England, Oak or Stuart), and the 'growing Honours' of 'tow'ring Oaks' suggest, in the context of Williamite iconography, a restoration of Stuart fortunes. The oaks are no longer 'bent and broken', and the navies which appear on 'thy shores' (as in the 1708 medal of James III and VIII) may not be British ships built of oak, but French ones led by the Royal Oak. It may be objected that the compliment to Stuart fortunes is intended for Anne; but Pope insists on the futurity of his compliments, and the Stuart line had no future without restoration.

*Windsor Forest* contains many other hints of Jacobite sympathy, such as
the 'naked Temples' of line 68 (abandoned in the aftermath of William's
invasion, and thus linked to Catholicism and Dryden's 'banished Gods'),
or 'At once the Chaser and at once the Prey' (line 82), a reference to
William being thrown by his horse and killed (both William I and III died
in this way). Perhaps the reference to William II *Rufus*'s murder in line 83
can be taken to apply to the 1696 Assassination plot; perhaps to William's
rumoured homosexuality (a preference which was also Rufus's); perhaps
to neither. Whichever is the case, the consistent praise of retreat, the
linking of Stuart power with fertility, and the strong presence of Stuart
iconography all indicate a strongly Jacobite theme in *Windsor Forest*.

*The Rape of the Lock* has been identified by Douglas Brooks-Davies as a
Jacobite-inclined poem (in *The Mercurian Monarch* (1983)). Brooks-Davies
draws particular attention to the symbolism of the sun as a device for
representing the changing fortunes of Stuart absolutism: arguing for
example that the declining sun of Canto III heralds the approach of a
corrupt parliamentary sovereignty.[30] But once again, this is a poem
textured with Stuart symbolism on many different levels: after all 'This
verse to CARYLL, Muse, is due' perhaps in a political as well as personal
sense. The mock-heroic epic's central action, the severing of the lock, is
clearly linked to the fall of Troy, with the scissors acting the part of Trojan
horse. The term Pope uses to describe them, 'fatal Engine', is a direct
borrowing from the description of the horse in Dryden's *Aeneid* II:345,
while the image of the Trojan horse might suggest the conquest of the
British Trojans by William, emphasized perhaps in the line 'By Force to
ravish, or by Fraud betray' (Pope, p. 224). The use of the *Aeneid* throughout as the major epic source suggests the importance of both 'Force' and
'Fraud' in the taking of Troy (the Lock): great strategy and petty strata-
gem are linked by zeugma to criticize the social order to the top:

> Here Thou, Great *Anna*! Whom three Realms obey,
> Dost sometimes Counsel take – and sometimes *Tea*.
> Canto III, lines 7–8

Which is which doesn't seem to matter to Anne, but it does to the victims
of the state mentioned a few lines later:

> The hungry Judges soon the Sentence sign,
> And Wretches hang that Jury-men may Dine ...

Again, refreshment is linked to government, but with clearer import:
justice, like counsel, occupies the spaces between personal indulgence. It
can be no more than implied that Anne's governmental decisions are as

---

[30] *The Poems of Alexander Pope*, pp. 197, 202; Douglas Brooks-Davies, *The Mercurian Monarch: Magical Politics from Spenser to Pope* (Manchester: Manchester University Press, 1983), pp. 181ff.

arbitrary as the legal ones of the courts, but that implication alone is damaging enough, whatever Pope's lightness of tone and touch conceal.

The death of Queen Anne and George's accession could only serve to deepen such disenchantment. Among Pope's circle such feelings expressed themselves in familar terms:

Arbuthnot, writing to Swift in November 1714 ... borrowed Panthus's lament for Troy ... to express his sense of the passing away of the age of Queen Anne:

> fuimus Troes, fuit Ilium et ingens
> gloria Teucrorum: ferus omnia Iuppiter Argos
> transtulit; incensa Danai dominantur in urbe.[31]

The departure of the last Stuart is once again envisioned in the prototype of the Fall of Troy, as sure as the Baron of Bradwardine's 'Fuimus Troes' is his elegy on the 'Forty-five in *Waverley*. Arbuthnot was not just 'borrowing' classical typology: he was writing in established code (as he knew, one of his brothers having fought at Killiecrankie before serving as an agent for King James (Mack, *Alexander Pope*, p. 191)).

Pope was to write in it in greater detail. His vision of Caryll in autumn 1715 as an Aeneas returning to his inheritance was unusually timely given the season's political events, and it was only one of many allusions that Pope would make which, like the poetry of retreat itself, conflated personal virtue with the language of public politics. As Howard Erskine-Hill notes, Pope concludes the *Epistle to Burlington* with 'an unmistakable allusion to Dryden's version of the *Aeneid*, Book VI, in which Anchises foretells to Aeneas the destiny of Rome'. Rome's 'Imperial Arts, and worthy thee' (Dryden) becomes Pope's 'These are Imperial Works, and worthy Kings', and this is only the culmination of a general echo of the whole conclusion of the prophecy in the preceding lines.[32] Dryden's 'thee' is Aeneas; Pope's 'Imperial Works' are, as has often been pointed out, those which George II did not do. Of course he did not: he was an anti-Aeneas. The true 'Kings' of Pope's last line are those who *do* such works, true Aeneases, the Stuarts of the prophecy of lines 173–6:

> Another age shall see the golden Ear
> Imbrown the Slope, and nod on the Parterre,
> Deep Harvests bury all his pride has plann'd,
> And laughing Ceres re-assume the land.

Fertility, rather than Timon's waste, is a central image of Stuart restoration: the golden age which a returning Astraea will bring, accompanied by the fertility of Ceres (here as in 'Messiah' linked with sensible garden-

---

[31] *The Poems of Alexander Pope*, pp. 218, 227; F. P. Lock, *Swift's Tory Politics* (London: Duckworth, 1983), pp. 68–9.

[32] Howard Erskine-Hill, *The Social Milieu of Alexander Pope* (New Haven and London: Yale University Press, 1975), pp. 72, 324.

ing: the 'Slope'). Pope is practising intertextuality not only with Dryden, Vergil (and Horace, as Howard Erskine-Hill points out), but with himself in 'Windsor Forest' where 'O'er sandy Wilds were yellow Harvests spread'.[33]

Moreover the poem's allusions to Lord Burlington's own tastes and interests are suggestive. Originally written in commemoration of Burlington's publication of 'Palladio's Designs of the Baths, Arches, Theatres, &c of Ancient Rome', the *Epistle* commemorates the *renovatio* of Augustan and Stuart art in Burlington's interests. Palladio had learnt extensively from Vitruvius, as had that most typical of Stuart architects, Inigo Jones, whose designs Burlington had also published: and Vitruvius had dedicated his book on architecture to Augustus. In this context, Pope's allusion to the 'Works' 'worthy kings' slyly reflects on George's inappropriateness as an Aeneas/Augustus of either politics or architecture, as displayed by a Burlington who shows that 'Rome was glorious, not profuse'. Since Burlington himself was an ambivalent political figure, the nature of Pope's addresses to him become highly suggestive:[34]

> Jones and Palladio to themselves restore,
> And be whate'er Vitruvius was before:
> Till Kings call forth the 'Ideas' of your mind ...
>
> Bid Temples, worthier of the God, ascend ...

The call to 'restore' imports a significant verb into an apparently innocuous context: to restore Jones and Vitruvius is to restore the Stuart and Augustan age, and perhaps not in architecture alone. The 'Temples' such architecture might build will be 'worthier of the God'; and such lines attract little attention despite the fact they are addressed by a Roman Catholic to an Anglican whose Nonjuror-linked chaplain kept a Mass book in his desk.[35] Moreover, they echo the lines about 'ruin'd Temples' in *Windsor Forest* which allude to the period of Williamite conquest. The restored temples, 'worthier of the God' in a new Augustan age which has brought back Jones and Vitruvius, speak across more than thirty years of poetic cipher to the 'banish'd Gods restored to Rites Divine' of Dryden's Aeneas/Augustus. To add yet another Augustan flourish, Pope mentions the obscure Sabinus ('Thro' his young Woods howpleas'd Sabinus stray'd') who 'dedicated a lost book on gardening to Maecenas' while informing us that without sense in gardening 'Nero's Terraces desert their

33 *The Poems of Alexander Pope*, p. 195ff.; Erskine-Hill, *Social Milieu*, p. 325.
34 *The Poems of Alexander Pope*, p. 588ff.; cf. the recent work of scholars such as Jane Clark and Richard Hewlings in this area.
35 *The Poems of Alexander Pope*, p. 595; Mr Lawrence Smith has recently uncovered these facts about Lord Burlington's chaplain in a paper given at the Society of Antiquaries on 26 February 1993.

walls', in Nero citing a well-worn cipher for George (that this couplet may be political is suggested by the use of Versailles as an exemplar in the previous line). Even in describing architecture and gardening in the abstract, the metaphor of 'by force betray' is never far off, unless it be truly resisted by an organic gentry ideology:

*Architecture* and *Gardening*, where all must be adapted to the *Genius* and Use of the Place, and the Beauties not forced into it, but resulting from it.

This could very well stand as an expression of Royalist retreat ideology of the 1650s, such as that of the Irish poet Sir John Denham, who may have been responsible for the building of Burlington House in the reign of Charles II. Dryden had indeed drawn attention to Denham's *Cooper's Hill* in his Preface to the 1697 *Aeneid*, and Pope had consciously used it as a model for *Windsor Forest*.[36]

Similar notes of dissent and suspicion towards the current regime's forcibly imported values are voiced elsewhere in the Epistles, for example in *Bathurst*, with its attack on the financial revolution ('Blest paper-credit! last and best supply! / That lends Corruption lighter wings to fly', and praise of the Man of Ross, representative of a rural culture of retreat in touch with the common man (Pope, pp. 574, 582). By contrast, William receives (especially in minor poetry such as 'Receipt to Make Soap' or 'Verses to be placed under the Picture of England's Arch-Poet' (Sir Richard Blackmore, the Williamite propagandist), short shrift indeed (Pope, pp. 475, 494).

The patriot verse of the later Pope is itself double-edged, as particularly in the case of 'One Thousand Seven Hundred and Forty', where the last lines, such as 'on one alone our all relies' can be taken as referring either to Frederick or James. The use of visual symbols rather than words (Pope uses a sun to illustrate the Patriot King's integrity) is a particular feature of Jacobite propaganda in the 1720s and 30s, as discussed above. Moreover, the rhetoric of 'honesty' is a Jacobite one, rendering the last lines wholly ambivalent:

> Whatever his religion or his blood,
> His public virtue makes his title good.
> Europe's just balance and our own may stand,
> And one man's honesty redeem the land.

The land must be redeemed from 'An Atheist court, a thief's administration', and it is a 'just balance' of nicety indeed to conclude whether Pope expects this to be done by Frederick or James. The ambivalence of such open language would itself seem unnecessary unless intended (and this is a

---

36 *The Poems of Alexander Pope*, p. 591; *The Poems of Alexander Pope: Epistles to Several Persons (Moral Essays)*, ed. F. W. Bateston, Twickenham Pope Volume III-ii (London, 1951), p. 133.

good reason for suspecting its politics when it appears), though it is fair to note that Pope seems opposed to restoration by war:

> To purge and let thee blood, with fire and sword,
> Is all the help stern S[hippen] wou'd afford.

This is not enough, and will not restore peace to the corrupted land (Pope, pp. 827–31).

*The Dunciad*, of course, is Pope's ultimate poem on the subject of Aeneas. It not only makes extensive use of parallels with the *Aeneid* (notably in the 1743 version Book vi, suggesting increasing gloominess on Pope's part), but also is itself almost an anti-*Aeneid*, portraying an underworld from which there is no emergence:

The Action of the *Dunciad* ... is the removal of the Imperial seat of Dulness from the City to the polite world: as that of the Aeneid is the Removal of the empire of *Troy* to *Latium*.

Dulness's 'good old Cause' (a phrase deliberately reminiscent of the self-identification of the Cromwellian/Puritan side in the Civil War) is that of the 'Saturnian age of Lead', the reverse of Astraea's golden promises, 'redeant Saturnia regna', emblemized in the potential return of what Jacobite writers were calling not 'pius Aeneas', but that 'Godlike Man' of 'Another Maro's . . . pen', Charles Edward Stuart.[37] *The Dunciad* can be seen as containing an annotation of what fugitive Jacobite writers were saying: a defence of their dispossession against the official scribblers of the Whig state. The concept of Dullness itself dates back to the first decade of the eighteenth century and, like William King and Jacobite writers before him, Pope uses the language of broadly accessible Jacobite culture:

> Loud thunder to the bottom shook the bog,
> And the hoarse nation croak'd, 'God save King Log!'
>                                                          (*Dunciad* ii, lines 329–30)

*The Dunciad* is a patchwork at times of a popular literature it is simultaneously describing with hauteur.

It is also a poem structured around the highly charged high cultural text of Vergil. The structure of the *Aeneid* and *The Dunciad* are, as Douglas Brooks-Davies notes, parallel, *Dunciad* i following *Aeneid* i and ii, ii following v, and iii, vi. *Aeneid* vii–xii feature less: Brooks-Davies suggests that this is so we do not see the '"foreign Prince" take possession of Latium' (Brooks-Davies, *Pope's Dunciad and the Queen of Night*, p. 51), but it may rather be emphasizing that there is no re-emergence from the underworld.

---

[37] *The Poems of Alexander Pope*, pp. 345, 725; Alexander B. Grosart (ed.), *The Towneley MSS: English Jacobite Ballads, Songs & Satires* (Printed for Private Circulation, 1877), p. 62.

In the 1743 *Dunciad*, Cibber is compared to Mezentius, Vergil's exemplar of bad kingship, while the 1728 poem opens with the clearly Vergilian 'Books and the Man I sing'. The Dunces' games satirize the sacred rituals of *Aeneid* v, thus becoming 'a mock commemoration of George I' (Brooks-Davies, *Pope's Dunciad and the Queen of Night*, p. 55), while Cibber is 'the young Aeneas' of iv: 290. The deliberate echoes of Vergil's poem set the context for these allusions. In the 1743 *Dunciad*, sixteen out of thirty-seven direct references are to *Aeneid* vi, twelve out of the last seventeen in the poem: thus emphasizing a downward drift into the underworld. The epic is not completed with the last six books: and this discontinuity of tradition separates Pope from Vergil: where is the golden age, where are the 'household gods' of an older religion and tradition, where is Aeneas, where is kingliness, where is the king? The zeugmatic bifurcations between ideal and reality of Pope's earlier mock-epic become intensified into an absorption of one by the other: playful tension is replaced by total usurpation and decay. The 'Saturnian age of Lead' is the direct antithesis of Astraea's: and it has come because 'Dunce the second reigns like Dunce the first' (I, lines 6, 26). The 'tall May-pole' which 'once o'erlooked the Strand' (II, lines 24, 372) is banished, and with it fertility. The dinginess, darkness and vileness of the city reflects its role at the leading edge of social change accompanying the Whig regime:

the London of Grub Street, the bankers and merchants, and a corrupt court, a labyrinthine complex of mud, dirt, decay, mist and darkness.
(Brooks-Davies, *Pope's Dunciad and the Queen of Night*, p. 15)

Although Pope in the 1743 *Dunciad* includes some lines which appear to show reservations concerning the Stuarts ('For sure, if Dulness sees a grateful Day, / 'Tis in the Shade of Arbitrary Sway' (IV, lines 181–2), the James whom the goddess praises (James VI and I), is praised for his qualities of genuine as opposed to false learning, while the context of deepening darkness only suggests how much worse things are getting now. The question is not whether Pope unreservedly recommends the exiled dynasty; but whether his reservations about it were less intense than his extreme dislike of the alternative. In 1743, he was also writing the 'Fragment of Brutus, an Epic' of the origin-myth: its fragmentary state is a metaphor of the 'grat Anarch's' victory: 'The Patient Chief, who lab'ring long, arriv'd / On Britain's Shore ... with fav'ring Gods' was never to come, the winds staying Protestant. Just as in his self-comparisons to Dryden in the notes to *The Dunciad*, Pope's intertextuality here is suggestive.[38]

Recent criticism often accords with Valerie Rumbold's contention that

[38] *The Poems of Alexander Pope*, pp. 350, 351, 372, 775, 782, 836.

Pope 'could not offer a shared sense of dynastic and political loss' with 'Virgil and Atterbury', 'refusing the role of Jacobite court poet' while remaining sympathetic. There are those on each side, like Douglas Brooks-Davies and J.A. Downie, who emphasize or are sceptical of Pope's Jacobitism, though none goes as far as contemporaries such as Oldmixon, who remarked that 'This Papist Dog . . . has translated HOMER for the use of the PRETENDER'.[39] As I remarked in Chapter 1, it is difficult to sympathize with those whose criteria for Jacobitism are public statement, armed insurrection, or laying oneself open to capital charges. In England in particular, only hotheads, the unwise or the unlucky fell into these categories. Pope was not among them, though some of his friends were, and on occasion, as Maynard Mack argues, even he can be construed as making directly sympathetic statements, whether in his grotto or correspondence. The Jacobites thought of him as a potential laureate, and as late as 1745, so Howard Erskine-Hill informs us, 'an anonymous Jacobite seems to have quoted from Pope's Epilogue to the Satires in an appeal to the English to join the army of Prince Charles Edward Stuart'.[40] Pope numbered many Jacobites among his friends; he appeared in Atterbury's defence; he had a relative arrested on suspicion of Jacobitism; the regime kept him under surveillance and occasionally thought of taking him into custody. He knew he had to be careful and he was. The Horatian satires of the 1730s were one of the ways in which he sustained criticism through typology; and as I hope to have shown, there were others.[41] But Pope must have known better than to risk having anything more than a question-mark set against his allegiance. That question-mark still stands, and I think it better to interpret it as the necessary avoidance of an answer than a coincidental and recurrent uncertainty. The mockery of 'On a Lady who P–st at the Tragedy of Cato' ('Let others screw their Hypocritick Face / She shews her Grief in a sincerer Place') undermines the play's propagandist claims, while 'Epitaph. On John Lord Caryll' speaks clearly of a lost (Jacobite) ideal:

> A manly Form; a bold, yet modest mind;
> Sincere, tho' prudent; constant, yet resign'd;
> Honour unchang'd; a Principle profest;
> Fix'd to one side, but mod'rate to the rest;
> An honest Courtier, and a Patriot too;
> Just to his Prince, and to his Country true:
> All these were join'd in one, yet fail'd to save

[39] Valerie Rumbold, *Women's Place in Pope's World*, Cambridge Studies in Eighteenth-Century Literature and Thought (Cambridge: Cambridge University Press, 1989), pp. 184, 241.

[40] Brean Hammond, *Pope*, pp. 9, 25; Mack, *Alexander Pope*, p. 261; Erskine-Hill, 'Alexander Pope: the Political Poet in His Time', p. 140.

[41] Mack, *Alexander Pope*, pp. 189, 402, 403, 405, 579, 775.

> The Wise, the Learn'd, the Virtuous, and the Brave;
> Lost, like the common Plunder of the Grave!
>
> Pope, pp. 278–9, 283

Pope was this kind of 'Patriot'. Lord Caryll became Secretary of State to King James in Saint-Germain, a Prince not 'Born for First Ministers, as Slaves for Kings', like his German successors, but one fit to bring 'Imperial works' to 'happy Britain' (Pope, pp. 595, 797). That Pope's 'Britain' was less and less 'happy' seems his judgement on the reality of this wish.[42]

# Jonathan Swift

> And every stinking weed so lofty grows,
> As if 'twould overshade the royal rose,
> The royal rose the glory of our morn,
> But, ah, too much without a thorn.
>
> 'Ode to Dr William Sancroft'

> Under the rose, since here are none but friends
> (To own the truth) we have some private ends.
>
> 'An Epilogue to a Play for the
> Benefit of the Weavers in Ireland'

> And oh! how short are human schemes!
> Here ended all our golden dreams.
> What St John's skill in state affairs,
> What Ormonde's valour, Oxford's cares
> To save their sinking country lent,
> Was all destroyed by one event.
>
> Verses on the Death of Dr Swift, DSPD

I look upon the coming of the Pretender as a greater Evil than any we are like to suffer under the worst Whig ministry that can be found. Swift, writing in 1716[43]

Swift's sympathy towards Jacobitism is harder to locate than Pope's. Though his position as 'the conspicuous adherent of disgraced ministers and a discredited cause' places him in the same company as Bolingbroke or Ormonde in 1715, the assumption has been that this 'Hanoverian tory'

---

[42] For a discussion of this cf. Christine Gerrard, 'Pope and the Patriots', in David Fairer (ed.), *Pope: New Contexts* (New York and London: Harvester Wheatsheaf, 1990), pp. 25–43 (35).

[43] Jonathan Swift, *The Complete Poems*, ed. Pat Rogers (Harmondsworth: Penguin, 1983), pp. 63, 228, 495: future references in the text are to this edition. Lock, *Swift's Tory Politics*, p. 133 (*Correspondence* 2: 239).

was ... theoretically unable to come to terms with the Revolution, but in practice equally unable to support the restoration of the Pretender.[44]

What is made of this depends on the respective emphasis placed on the definitions of 'theory' and 'practice', particularly in the case of Swift's peak period of political activity, the last four years of Queen Anne. In 1710–14 he was very close to an administration which expended a considerable amount of theoretical gesturing, and a more limited ration of practical activity, in the direction of a Stuart restoration. Swift subsequently claimed to have known nothing of Harley's and Bolingbroke's negotiations with James; and indeed he seems to have been not a little naive about various other areas of this last Tory administration's activity. That he was entirely ignorant, is as likely as Pope's innocence in the matter of Atterbury; and the Whigs were of this opinion concerning Harley's creature. Swift's post was opened in 1715, so it is hardly surprising that his correspondence at the time contains judiciously pro-Hanoverian references. To judge him on this is to mistake the risks of expressing Jacobite sentiment.[45] Attacks on him such as *Dr S-'s Real Diary* (1715) and *An Hue and Cry after Dr S-t* (1714), doubted both his judiciousness and his Hanoverianism, asking

> If *Levi's* Sons still sing their ancient song,
> *That all are slaves, and Kings can do no Wrong?*

Swift must have been aware that his social and political environment smelt of sedition. Oldisworth, his successor as editor of *The Examiner*, joined the Rising of 1715,[46] while Arbuthnot's letter to Swift of November 1714, quoted above in discussion of Pope, is a clear encoding of political sympathy for the Stuarts under the cloak of Panthus' lament for Troy. Yet though the smell of cordite surrounded him, Swift's hand held no smoking gun. It may seem pointless to pursue his politics further at this remote date.[47]

There are nonetheless two routes of enquiry worth taking to intensify if not to press home suspicion of Swift's politics: back towards his early record, forward to his subsequent satire. Swift's position in 1689 seems to have been as equivocal as it was in 1714/15, as reflected in the remark attributed to him on the Revolution, 'that the receiver was as bad as the thief'. F.P. Lock judges that he 'probably would have been in favour of a

---

[44] R. B. MacDowell, 'Swift as a Political Thinker' in Roger McHugh and Philip Edwards (eds.) *Jonathan Swift 1667–1967: A Dublin Tercentenary Tribute* (Dublin: Dolmen Press, 1967), pp. 176–186 (179, 186); Lock, *Swift's Tory Politics*, p. 72.

[45] Lock, *Swift's Tory Politics*, p. 119.

[46] *A Farther HUE and CRY after Dr. S–t.* Timothy Brocade. 2nd edn (London, 1714), p. 13; Lock, *Swift's Tory Politics*, p. 71n.

[47] Lock, *Swift's Tory Politics*, pp. 68–9.

Regency' and that his poem to Sancroft exemplifies 'a favourite Swiftian belief, that defeat may be a greater kind of victory than earthly success', itself a rather jacobitical sentiment (Lock, *Swift's Tory Politics*, pp. 82, 84).In the 'Ode to Dr William Sancroft' after his nonjuring as Archbishop of Canterbury, Swift praises 'the divinity of retreat' which Sancroft has taken from 'the pollution of these days' where truth is obscured:

> How shall we find thee then in dark disputes?
> How shall we search thee in a battle gained,
> Or a weak argument by force maintained?

Whatever Swift's reservations about James's conduct, these lines suggest grave doubts concerning William's usurpation and the settling of religious and constitutional disagreements by armed force, doubts which Sancroft, criticized for his lack of action at the time, may well have shared.[48]

Despite the fact that he nonjured, Sancroft, an old man when he died in 1692, was never seen as an effective leader for the Nonjurors. There are signs in the poem that Swift, who had a lifelong concern for Anglicanism, was distressed by the events which led to the creation of a nonjuring church within a church. Had the Revolution divided the society it sought to unite?

> Necessity ... Say, why the church is still led blindfold by the state?
> Why should the first be ruined and laid waste,
> To mend the dilapidations in the last?
> And yet the world, whose eyes are on our mighty prince,
> Thinks heaven has cancelled all our sins ...
>
> And divine SANCROFT, weary with the weight
> Of a declining church, by faction her worst foe oppressed,
> Finding the mitre almost grown
> A load as heavy as the crown,
> Wisely retreated to his heavenly rest.                    Swift, pp. 64–5

In the first stanza the suggestion is surely that this is a Revolution too far, that it has damaged the Church it sought to protect, and that a confusion has arisen over what is truth in Church and State alike, through the (false) conflation of William's force and Heaven's bounty ('Thinks heaven has cancelled all our sins'). 'Faction her worst foe' has seized the Church, in leading part of it to nonjure. Swift's views on this are shortly made more explicit:

> The mitre, which his [Sancroft's] sacred head has worn,
> Was, like his master's crown, enwreathed with thorn.
>                                         Swift, p. 66

---

48 Patrick Fagan, *A Georgian Celebration: Irish Poets of the Eighteenth Century* (Dublin: Branar, 1989), p. 103.

The close links between high Anglicanism and the caesaropapism of the
Stuarts are re-emphasized here by Swift in a manner which reveals his
understanding of the Nonjurors' actions. The 'master's crown' remains
mildly ambivalent, possibly referring both to James and Christ: it is
Sancroft's duty to suffer both like his heavenly and earthly master. Not to
nonjure would be to betray his king, an apostasy from catholic truth as
revealed in the caesarean papacy of England. Swift here writes in the vein
of Henry Lolie, who preached before Charles II at Breda in 1649, likening
his father's death to the crucifixion.[49] Swift seems to have found it easier to
be critical of James's secular than of his sacred role: indeed, as with Pope's
Catholicism, it is in Swift's sincere high Anglicanism that we may find the
engine for his views:

> Pity a miserable church's tears,
> That begs the powerful blessing of thy prayers.
> Some angel say, what were the nation's crimes,
> That sent these wild reformers to our times;
>   Say what their senseless malice meant,
>   To tear Religion's lovely face:
> Strip her of every ornament and grace,
> In striving to wash off the imaginary paint . . .

The fear of Anglicanism's being a stalking-horse for Catholicism is rejected
here by Swift, but in terms which would have done nothing to ease the
minds of 'wild reformers': Sancroft, who has 'retreated to his heavenly
rest' is being asked to intercede with 'the powerful blessing of thy prayers'.
Swift's own High Church sympathies are revealed here: a dead and saintly
archbishop is being begged for prayers of intercession by his Church, no
doubt 'powerful' because (at least implicitly) of his own works of super-
erogation (Swift, p. 67).

Swift's dislike of the Revolution may have been more social and religious than political, but he nonetheless seems to avoid discussing it in such a
way as to compliment William. As F.P. Lock points out:

In the 'Ode to the King' attention is as much as possible deflected from the (to
Swift) problematical conflict between William and James to the much more
straightforward . . . contrast between William III and Louis XIV . . .

(Lock, *Swift's Tory Politics*, pp. 88–9)

National chauvinism came more naturally to Swift than zeal for disposing
of a patriot king. Although he had thought Viscount Dundee 'the best
man in Scotland' at the time of the 1689 Rising, Swift in general does not
seem to have cared for the Scots, as these verses on the Union suggest:

---

[49] Lock, *Swift's Tory Politics*, p. 83; for a discussion of the Breda period in 1649, see Ronald
Hutton, *Charles the Second King of England, Scotland and Ireland* (Oxford: Oxford University Press,
1991 (1989)), pp. 45–8.

> The Queen has lately lost a Part
> Of her entirely *English* heart,
> For want of which by way of Botch,
> She piec'd it up again with *Scotch*.[50]

Swift has no time for the 'crazy double-bottom'd Realm' which results, but this is very much a case of Jacobite-aligned politics arising from chauvinistic reasons. It is not perhaps till after the loss of 'our golden dreams' in 1714 that Swift becomes more clearly political in his reaction to a state from whose power structures he is now excluded:

> With horror, grief, despair the Dean
> Behold the dire destructive scene:
> His friends in exile, or the Tower,
> Himself within the frown of power . . .
>                            Swift, p. 495

The impeachment of Ormonde and the rumour of a £500 reward for Swift's arrest both added to the pressure and sense of final exclusion. The intensity with which Swift's interests subsequently turned to Irish politics has about it the quality of transference. It is thus interesting to note which shape it took: as John Redmond later said of the Dean, 'he did as much as any man in history to lift Ireland into the position of a nation'.[51] A more recent and neutral observer agrees:

That he [Swift] had a perfectly genuine belief in the moral right of Ireland to be legislatively independent of the English government of the day is beyond doubt.
                            Lock, *Swift's Tory Politics*, p. 162

Swift linked this passion for Irish rights to an English form of anti-government protest, implying that his concern for Ireland's role in the Whig state was a reflection of his concern for England's (about which he could now do nothing). *The Drapier's Letters* were themselves a reflection of the attitudes of the Whig state, as was *A Modest Proposal*, which ironically suggested that the ethos of the English financial revolution was insufficiently prevalent in Ireland, and that its greed could be more properly combined with traditional racist contempt to create a distinctive 'new' Irish policy.

In alluding to *The Drapier's Letters*, Swift aligns his political attitude with that of the Irish royalist Sir John Denham's most famous poem:

---

[50] Norval Clyne, *The Scottish Jacobites and Their Poetry* (Aberdeen, 1887), p. 16; Ellis, *Poems on Affairs of State* 7: pp. 283–5.
[51] Swift, *Complete Poems*, p. 855n; J. E. Redmond, *Historical and Political Addresses* (Dublin, 1898), p. 123: cited in McDowell, 'Swift as a Political Thinker', p. 186.

This hill may keep the name of Drapier:
In spite of envy flourish still,
And Drapier's vie with Cooper's Hill.
                                    Swift, p. 379

In what sense does Swift hope that this will be true? Surely not only in an adjectival, but also in a political sense. The honest tradesmen's names and roles may betoken a resistance to the Whig newfangleness of Wood's halfpence of the same mould as the traditionalism of the 1650s, while in a more nationalistic sense, Swift's attack on Wood's coinage was the fore-runner of Scott's Malachi Malagrowther letters a century later: in both cases a currency controversy serving as a surrogate for the suppression of national rights. The Letters even threaten the possibility of the Irish turning to Jacobitism should their natural rights be frustrated. Swift's connexion with the culture he wished to defend and represent is indicated in a neat piece of irony in Letter 6, where the Drapier suggests that he might have been better employed 'in writing "Proverbs" or "Ballads" instead of pamphlets'. Such 'ballads' might of course have been used as mediated texts to exactly the same political end as the letters themselves.[52]

In Swift's most famous satire, *Gulliver's Travels*, images of discontent with the Whig state abound, with Gulliver, its enlightened representative, perpetually in agreement with what he has previously found distasteful. In Lilliput, the Franco-Jacobite threat is mockingly explored in the war with Blefescu, while in Laputa, the intellectual trends of the present day are attacked. The Brobdignagian king bears more than a passing resemblance to the peace-loving patriot king ideal sought in similar language by patriot and Jacobite opposition alike in the 1730s. Such a figure is a giant among men, while the squabbling and treacherous antics of the current British state are fit only for Lilliputians. Swift takes apart the current polity's actions both in Gulliver's experiences and in his opinions, doubly destabil-izing his narrator as a result. Perhaps it is over-reading to point out that the Hanoverian dynastic badge was a horse: but the Houyhnhnms are every bit as genocidal towards the Yahoos as Protestant Britain is to the Irish.

There is some limited evidence to suggest that Swift was prepared to cross not only class (as in his imprecation to the Irish weavers to speak 'Under the rose, since here are none but friends') but cultural barriers in Ireland, particularly those between English and Irish language poetry. This is especially relevant to my discussion of the latter in Chapter 5, as Irish poetry was heavily Jacobite at this stage in the eighteenth century. In 1713, J.G. Simms observes:

[52] Nigel Wood, *Swift* (Brighton: Harvester, 1986), p. 115.

Catholics did little to conceal their Jacobite sympathies. Most protestants were Hanoverians and distrusted the diplomacy of Swift's Tory friends ... Catholic Ireland was excited by the prospect of a Stuart restoration [following the Treaty of Utrecht]. Recruits were flocking to join the Irish regiments in France, hoping to be back at home within a year.

Following the frustration of Catholic hopes in the 'Fifteen,

In Munster, the 'hidden Ireland' kept alive the traditions of Irish poetry. Egan O'Rahilly found shelter in the Kerry glens ... Elsewhere in the province Sean Clarach McDonnell and other aisling poets romanticised the cause of the Stuarts.[53]

Swift almost certainly knew Irish poets writing in Irish in this tradition. At Quilea, he 'met blind harpers', while there is a persistent tradition that he also met Turlough O Caroloa, whom he may have made use of in his poem 'The Description of an Irish Feast' translated from the original Irish. Although Swift with his customary paradoxicality observed that 'It would be a noble achievement to abolish the Irish language in this kingdom ...', it has also been noted that

his conception of the power and prestige of the satirist agrees closely with that held by the Gaelic poets ... his reputation for wit and wilful eccentricity, so similar to that of many Gaelic poets, has won him a permanent place beside them in Gaelic folklore and the Anglo-Irish continuum ...[54]

In other words, Swift as a cultural hero has been mediated between high Anglophone and folk Gaelic-speaking culture in Irish interpretation: and there is some evidence that he himself participated in this process.

In addition to his encounters with Irish bards, Swift kept up

a cordial correspondence with Sir Charles Wogan, the celebrated Jacobite soldier, who wrote to him at great length on the troubles of Irish Catholics ...

It is in this kind of area that generalizations such as Linda Colley's categorization of non-Roman Catholics as 'Protestants' break down, as this book should already have demonstrated. For, while non Church of Ireland Protestant denominations universally favoured Hanover, there were marked Jacobite leanings in that church itself, 'the strong anglicanism' of their party being 'associated with an anti-Hanoverian spirit not far removed from Jacobitism'. Ormonde was the icon of High Church Ireland, and Ormonde's impeachment and subsequent appointment as

[53] Swift, *Complete Poems*, p. 228; J. G. Simms, 'Ireland in the Age of Swift' in McHugh and Edwards, *Jonathan Swift 1667–1967*, pp. 157–75 (157, 159, 175).
[54] Simms, 'Ireland in the Age of Swift', p. 166; Swift, *Complete Poems*, p. 221; cf. Austin Clark, 'The Poetry of Swift', in McHugh and Edwards, *Jonathan Swift 1667–1967*, pp. 94–115 (109); Vivian Mercer, 'Swift and the Gaelic Tradition', *Review of English Literature* 3 (July 1962), pp. 69–79 (69).

Captain-General and Commander-in-Chief of James's forces underlined
these sympathies: Swift thought the Jacobite General 'a persecuted and
noble figure', and here perhaps we can hear echoes of his earlier sympathy
towards Sancroft.[55] The Dean exhibited in his poetry a certain relish for
any ill fate overtaking zealous Hanoverian Protestants in a way not
entirely dissimilar to more central Jacobite satirical verse such as 'The
Cameronian Cat':

> This Protestant zealot, this English divine
>     In church and in state was of principles sound;
> Was truer than Steele to the Hanover line,
>     And grieved that a Tory should live aboveground.
> Shall a subject so loyal be hanged by the nape,
> For no other crime but committing a rape?
>                           'An Excellent New Ballad: OR THE TRUE ENGLISH DEAN
>                                                   TO BE HANGED FOR A RAPE'

Swift is simultaneously identifying the corruption and hypocrisy of enthusiastic Protestantism in a manner clearly consonant with more direct
political satire. The poem's moral is, implicitly at least, a bitter one:

> Our church and our state dear England maintains,
>     For which all true Protestant hearts should be glad;
> She sends us our bishops and judges and deans,
>     And better would give us, if better she had ...
>                                            Swift, pp. 445–7

The doubts Swift may have had about that 'church and ... state' (as
Yeats put it, 'what if Church and State / Are the mob that howls round the
door?') he had long expressed by the time he came to write this poem. Are
the 'true Protestant hearts' those which belong to the administration
which has not only threatened the Church of England, but split it, as the
Stuart kings had never done? Is the link between Church and State
maintained in the wrong terms and at too high a price? And are enthusi-
asts for it, like the hanged Dean Sawbridge, of necessity hypocrites?
Swift's description of the Whig state in 'Verses on the Death of Dr Swift,
DSPD' very much suggests that he has these kind of reservations in mind:

> When up a dangerous faction starts,
> With wrath and vengeance in their hearts:
> *By solemn league and covenant bound,*
> To ruin, slaughter, and confound ...
>                                            Swift, p. 495

---

[55] Simms, 'Ireland in the Age of Swift', pp. 161, 166; Swift, *Complete Poems*, p. 925n; Greenwood,
*William King*, p. 15.

This use of the terms of the 1640s (alluding specifically to the 1643 Solemn League and Covenant, the fulfilment of whose terms implied the destruction of Anglicanism) shows Swift's alignment with those who saw the Church in danger in the early eighteenth century. In the chants of 'High Church and Ormonde' even jurant Anglicans could happily link Jacobite and Anglican sentiment: fear and dislike of Dissent could make the restoration of a Roman Catholic monarch (aided by his unimpeachably Anglican general) seem far better than the current state of affairs. To compare the Whig state with the politics of the 1640s was standard practice in Jacobite propaganda, and Swift's brief use of the convention here is of a piece with his other oblique commentaries on the post-Revolution polity.[56]

In 1737, Dr William King, whose satirical style was much influenced by Swift, sent the Dean his article calling for a new government for Corsica (= Britain) 'headed by a king fashioned of oak ... who, by the way; possessed his Empire by Divine Right', while the next year Swift gave King the manuscript of 'Verses on the Death of Dr Swift' in order that he might 'supervise personally' its publication. In the case of King as in that of Barber, the jacobitical Lord Mayor of London, Swift's friends and correspondents, like Pope's, showed on occasion a strong interest in a Stuart restoration: and in King's case, there was enough confidence in Swift's sympathies to communicate this to him in a plain, albeit playful, manner.[57]

But the verdict on Swift's Jacobitism must be a more open one. His oppositional praise in Aenean terms of 'Our eldest hope, divine Iulus' in 'On Poetry: A Rhapsody' (Swift, p. 534) remains poised between Charles Edward and Frederick, guarded, as so much else in his work, into irretrievable ambivalence. Swift's well-known penchant to delude renders him a suspect partisan to a yet greater degree. But it can be fairly said that he displayed consistent reservations over half a century about the kind of state the Revolution had brought about; and that in particular his churchmanship grieved over the lost unity, principle and power of Stuart Anglicanism. There is little in his work to suggest affection for the Stuarts, but his attitude to their replacements was a stronger one:

> But now go search all Europe round,
> Among the savage monsters crowned,
> With vice polluting every throne
> (I mean all kings except our own) ...
>
> Swift, p. 533

---

[56] Monod, *Jacobitism and the English People*, p. 204; W. B. Yeats, *The Collected Poems* (London: Macmillan, 1950), p. 327.
[57] Greenwood, *William King*, pp. 78–9.

This is Swift in Pope's Burlingtonian mode, complimenting the unique worthiness of the Hanoverian monarch in order to expose his inadequacy. As William King said, this poem shows 'the use and power of irony'. But that 'use and power', Swift's special genius, can in the environment of his politics only let us share his doubts: it does not readily show certainties.[58]

# Samuel Johnson

Augustus still survives in Maro's strain,
And Spenser's verse prolongs Eliza's reign,
Great George's acts let tuneful Cibber sing,
For Nature form'd the Poet for the King.
                                    'Epigram on Colley Cibber'

How just his Hopes let *Swedish Charles* decide,
A Frame of Adamant, a Soul of Fire,
No Dangers fright him, and no Labours tire ...
The vanquish'd Hero leaves his broken Bands,
And shews his Miseries in distant Lands,
Condemn'd a needy Supplicant to wait,
While Ladies interpose, and Slaves debate.
                                    'The Vanity of Human Wishes'[59]

Samuel Johnson stands a generation's distance from Pope. His distempered Toryism is much more outspoken than Swift's, and his politics seem easier to identify. Boswell, who had prayed for King James as a boy until an uncle had given him a shilling to pray for King George (which led him to philosophize that 'thus are all true Whigs made'), bears lavish witness to Johnson's repeated Jacobite sentiments. Johnson's description of George II as an 'unrelenting and barbarous' king on the occasion of the execution of Lt-Col. Dr Archibald Cameron in connexion with the Elibank Plot in 1753, Johnson's identifying the 'Forty-five as 'a noble attempt' and his 1777 statement in support of a referendum to restore the Stuarts: all point unequivocally to Jacobitism. Reading Johnson thus is to see him as a nonjuror of robust and provocatively pro-Stuart views.[60]

[58] Dr William King, *Political and Literary Anecdotes of His Own Times* (London: John Murray, 1818), p. 15.
[59] *Samuel Johnson: The Complete English Poems*, ed. J. D. Fleeman (London: Allen Lane, 1974 (1971)), pp. 53, 88. Reference in the text is made to this edition.
[60] Boswell, *Life of Johnson*, 1: 147, 3: 155, discussed in Howard Erskine-Hill, 'The Political Character of Samuel Johnson' in Isobel Grundy (ed.), *Samuel Johnson: New Critical Essays* (London and Totowa, NJ: Vision and Barnes & Noble, 1984), pp. 107–36 (112, 115, 117).

Admittedly, such an an assessment derives substantially from the pages of Boswell; and it has been argued that Boswell deliberately coloured Johnson's politics in order to echo his own views. Moreover, some of Johnson's comments are far more equivocal: for example his protestation that he would not have held up a finger to alter the fate of battle at Culloden. But it is true to say that Johnson was viewed askance by authorities other than Boswell. In the controversy surrounding the grant of a pension to Johnson in 1762 (a grant which itself had been opposed on the grounds of the recipient's political sympathies), Churchill accused him of loving 'the STUART he forsakes', while the status of Johnson's earlier 'Marmor Norfolicense' as a Jacobite tract was, as Howard Erskine-Hill has pointed out, well understood at the time. The line concerning 'the Lyon' whose 'Veins a Horse shall drain' is a straightforward image of the weakening of the British Lion by the Hanoverian horse-emblem, meta-phoricized as the cure proffered by a false doctor. The poem also belongs to a Jacobite subgenre: that of the ersatz prophecy, and in this context is an interesting example of Johnson's own use of more popular modes in an apparently high cultural poem, itself a Jacobite technique. The year before, 1738, Johnson's poem 'London' had praised retreat from the 'Vice and Gain' of the Hanoverian capital to 'some happier Place'

> Where Honesty and Sense are no Disgrace;
> Some pleasing bank where verdant Osiers play,
> Some peaceful Vale with Nature's Paintings gay;
> Where once the harrass'd Briton found Repose,
> And safe in Poverty defy'd his Foes . . .
>
> Johnson, p. 62

This harping on retreat, the praise of rural absence (linked with the 'Honest Man' tag) rather than civic presence underlines London's status as a centre of corruption, while the 'Poverty' of the rural Briton is a mark of his integrity in much the same way as the poverty of the Highlander patriot icon marked his exemption from the seductive power of the gold of England and the financial revolution. Eleven years later in 'The Vanity of Human Wishes', corruption has grown to include the whole world in 'the gen'ral Massacre of Gold'. This 'gen'ral Massacre' is in part the conflict of human corruption in pursuit of an elusive or false good, and throughout the poem there are hints that Johnson intends the Jacobite attempt of 1745 to be among the vain wishes uppermost in his readers' minds, rather as Voltaire uses Charles Edward's misfortunes as an example of how all is not for the best in this best of all possible worlds in *Candide*:

> Let Hist'ry tell where rival Kings command,
> And dubious Title shakes the madded Land,
> When Statues glean the Refuse of the Sword,

How much more safe the Vassal than the Lord,
Low sculks the hind beneath the Rage of Pow'r,
And leaves the wealthy Traytor in the *Tow'r* ...

                                        Johnson, p. 83

In the original MS of this poem, 'wealthy' is 'bony', a reference to the
Scots lords tried and selectively executed in 1746/7, an act of which we
know Johnson disapproved (Johnson, pp. 169, 209n). In the final version
this is less explicit, but there are no other prominent and contemporary
traitors who might be meant. The opening of the passage, with its mention
of 'rival Kings' and 'dubious Title' underscores the fact that these lines can
be read as a cumulative reference to the dynastic struggle whose tragic
outcome they end by commemorating. 'Dubious Title' is ambivalent: the
title may be in doubt pending the outcome of the conflict, or it may be that
the 'madded Land' is shaken by the rule of a usurper of 'dubious Title',
while 'the Rage of Pow'r' reflects the mercilessness of the government, and
matches well with Johnson's sentiments on Archibald Cameron's execution in 1753.

When we learn that the skulking 'hind' escapes 'Confiscation's Vultures'
we are reminded of the Acts of Attainder passed in the Rising's aftermath:
the 'wealthy', like the 'bony Traytor', where these are not the same, cannot
escape 'the Rage of Pow'r'. Although this 'Rage' is mocked as that of 'our
supple tribes' (line 95) anxious only to sell their votes, there is still danger
in it, not unlike that of the days when 'Rebellion's vengeful talons seized on
Laud' (line 168). Anger and rage is associated with both the contemporary
regime and the Cromwellians: an oblique reference similar to that made by
Swift in aligning Whigs and Covenanters.

The passage on 'Swedish Charles' unites both past and present in
Johnson's concerns. Ostensibly dealing with Charles XII of Sweden,
Johnson's verses can be as readily applied to a more recent and familiar
prince of that name. The 'vanquished Hero' who had to show 'his Miseries
in distant Lands' could also refer to Charles Edward's being driven from
France in 1748 under the terms of the Treaty of Aix-la-Chapelle, which
condemned him to be a wandering and 'needy supplicant'. Moreover, in
1745 Charles Edward had already been compared to the Swedish
monarch: and here the Stuart prince seems to hover on the edge of the text,
much as the 'Forty-five hovers on the margin of voicing itself through the
theme of the poem. Johnson's clear social conservatism, his emphasis on the
corrupt capital and clear indication of interest in the political events of the
last few years, all inch towards the hint of a sympathy which bears in mind
along with other futile vanities, the vain attempt of the year 1745.[61]

---

[61] Erskine-Hill, 'Political Character', pp. 121, 123; 'The Political Character of Samuel Johnson:
     *The Lives of the Poets* and a Further Report on *The Vanity of Human Wishes*', in Eveline

Johnson's *Dictionary*, designed to defend moral consistency in the knowledge that the quest for linguistic purity is vain, shows a characteristic
degree of suggestiveness in the language it uses on politically sensitive
subjects. The Church is primarily defined as 'catholick', and the quotation
on church government appears to offer equal value to presbyterian,
episcopalian and Papal/conciliar methods. Atterbury is quoted in support
of the definition of 'Church-Authority'; 'Presbyter' defined as 'priest' gets
an approving quote from Hooker: as an example of 'presbyterianism', a
disparaging one from Butler. 'Whig' is 'the name of a faction', 'Tory' is
famously 'one who adheres to the antient constitution of the state, and the
apostolical hierarchy of the church of England'. 'Nonjuror' is defined as
'One, who [thinks] James II unjustly deposed', while 'Nonjuring' is
illustrated by a quotation from Swift which qualifies it by the adjectives
'pious, learned, and worthy'. As Howard Erskine-Hill has pointed out, the
attitudes which are reflected in this persistent hinting can be found
elsewhere in Johnson's work. In *Lives of the Poets*, for example, the Civil
War of the 1640s leads to the victory of 'the usurping powers', and
Johnson's treatment of the writers who had to deal with the crisis of the
1688 Revolution is circumspect and awkward, suggesting a degree of
sympathy towards a 'regulated loyalty' for James, but not supporting his
excesses. Yet Johnson's phrasing clearly indicates a lack of desire to justify
the Revolution even when he shows reservations about James. His language is circumspect: 'a new government was to be settled' and 'King
James' was 'irremediably excluded'.[62] Throughout the language is given
to betray his morose assessment of the rewards of those in public service
under any monarch, as outlined in 'The Vanity of Human Wishes':

> What gave great Villiers to the assassin's knife,
> And fixed disease on Harley's closing life?
> What murdered Wentworth, and what exiled Hyde,
> By kings protected and to kings allied?

It seems from this that no Stuart king could ever be a sufficiently merit-
orious exponent of Stuart principles for Johnson: and perhaps this reveals
something of his political position, since the *Lives* evince more admiration
for those who loyally served James than they do for the king himself,
especially his public administration, which Johnson finds tainted, in
common with so much of government.

There continue to be suggestions concerning Johnson's conduct in 1745,

Cruickshanks and Jeremy Black (eds.), *The Jacobite Challenge* (Edinburgh: John Donald, 1988),
pp. 161–76 (161).
[62] Samuel Johnson, *A Dictionary of the English Language*, with a preface by R. W. Burchfield
(London: Times Books, 1979). Facsimile edition; Johnson, *Lives of the Poets*, 1: 9, 2: 35, 170–1,
287 in Erskine-Hill, 'Further Report', pp. 162, 165.

when he adopted a low profile, if not disappearing altogether. A similar gap occurs in the case of William King, but there is no evidence that he was directly involved with the Rising. Sir Charles Petrie points out that Johnson had a full set of arms, suitable for a Jacobite officer, which he kept with him all his life: and in later years, he showed considerable interest in retracing Charles Edward's footsteps in the Highlands. Boswell's reportage of Johnson's Jacobitism, combined with the hints in his own work, do little other than reinforce Petrie's speculations.[63]

Yet speculation it seems it must remain. It appears more likely to this writer that Johnson was a man of Jacobite ideals who distrusted their reality. In this view Jacobitism becomes part of the displaced baggage of human disappointment: the Stuart cause is wise, but every step taken to achieve its ends is vanity. It is an image of lost perfection, like the Fall. Johnson's reported comments on a referendum to restore the Stuarts support viewing him as an idealist: for there he makes (in Boswell's words) a clearer statement of Jacobite commitment than at any other time, but does so in terms which prioritize restoration being achieved by a simple mechanism of formal assent: a clean-cut statement of principle, remote from the slipshod compromises of high politics and intrigue which Johnson distrusted:

If England ... were fairly polled, the present king ... would be sent away to-night, and his adherents hanged tomorrow.[64]

But this clarity does not and cannot exist in the political world Johnson knew, and its very impossibilism should reveal to us the remoteness of his own Jacobite beliefs from any of the available routes for their realization. If Johnson was indeed right about the result of such a referendum, his views must have been widely shared: and in his regret for the Fall of 1688 while supporting no strategy for its realistic reversal, Johnson was perhaps no more than a typical English Jacobite. In time, it might even become a Fortunate Fall.

---

[63] *Samuel Johnson: The Complete English Poems*, ed. Fleeman, p. 86; Charles Petrie, *The Jacobite Movement: The Last Phase* (London, 1950), pp. 203–10; Greenwood, *William King*, p. 176.

[64] Cf. Howard Erskine-Hill, 'Political Character', p. 115; 'Samuel Johnson' in *The Royalist* v:2 (1894), pp. 25–30 (28); R. E. Francillon, 'Underground Jacobitism', *The Monthly Review* 21 (1905), pp. 17–30 (17).

# 4

## Jacobite political culture in Scotland

### Prosperity to Scotland and no Union

When Southward I do set my Face
And cast my Eyes on Edinburgh
I cannot look upon that Place
But straight it strikes my heart with Sorrow
To see a house stand empty now
Where men had wont to be right gaudy
And in their best apparel show
Before that seat should hold my Ladie
O my Bonie bonie Highland Ladie (2)
May Heaven direct what I affect
And send me home my Highland Ladie.
                    'The True Scotsmans Lamentation'

   The trumpet sounds at Burreldales,
      Says, 'man and horse mak' ready',
   The drums do beat on Staneman Hill,
      'Lads, leave your mam' and dady;'
   The pipes do play at Cromlet Banks –
      'Lads, leave the Lews o' Fyvie,'
   The trooper to the fair maid said –
      'O lassie, I maun lea' you'
                    'The Trooper and the Maid'

   It was a' for our rightfu' king,
      We left fair Scotland's strand:
   It was a' for our rightfu' king
      We e'er saw Irish land, my dear,
      We e'er saw Irish land . . .

   The sodger frae the wars returns,
      The sailor frae the main;
   But I hae parted frae my love,

Never to meet again, my dear,
Never to meet again.
                    'It was a' for our Rightfu' King' (Capt. Ogilvie)[1]


Scottish Jacobitism had always possessed an additional dimension, extended and consolidated by the events of 1707. The Stuart cause was bound up inextricably with the national question: Scottish Jacobitism aspired to a totalizing view of a free, familiar and traditional Scotland. It shared its main symbolic features and levels of register with English Jacobitism: but whereas in England the language of familiarity and intimacy with the departed dynasty was used to bridge gulfs between high and folk culture, creating a cross-class alliance of Stuart sympathy, in Scotland this intimacy was an extension of the national debate, especially among those not members of the established church. Experience of suffering, defeat and loss was shared on a national and ecclesiastical level by Roman Catholics and Episcopalians. In Scotland Episcopacy had not merely split in 1688–9, as had the Church of England: it had been largely destroyed. Only generations of a popular history which assumes Scots were Presbyterians en masse has succeeded in distancing us from this destruction, leading us to forget that fourteen bishops and a thousand priests dwindled to four and forty-two in the next hundred years.[2]

In political terms, the appeal of the Stuarts to gentle and simple alike was equally strong. Apart from a few strands of Cameronian nationalism, the Stuarts were the only available vehicle for anti-Union feeling (indeed, some Covenanting nationalists backed them for this reason), an ideological counter-core for those who wished to preserve Scottish cultural and political identity in the face of the pressures of metropolitan conformity, themselves welcomed by many Scots. Thus an enormous weight of unchallenged expectation was placed, with varying degrees of idealism or pragmatism, on the Stuarts by those who opposed the Union. Even Presbyterian nationalists wavered as a result of 1707 from three generations of criticism and demand:

Many Presbyterians ... preferred the old Pretender: 'for' said they, (according to their predestinating principles) 'God may convert him, or he may have Protestant children, but the Union can never be good'.[3]

---

[1] National Library of Scotland, ADV MS 19.1.13, 54; John Ord, *Bothy Songs & Ballads of Aberdeen, Banff and Moray Angus and the Mearns* (Edinburgh: John Donbald, n.d. (1930)); Hogg, *Relics* i: p. 186.

[2] The Revd W. Perry, DD, *The Oxford Movement in Scotland* (Cambridge: Cambridge University Press, 1933), p. 36.

[3] George Lockhart of Carnwath, cited in William Donaldson, 'The Jacobite Song in 18th & Early 19th Century Scotland', unpublished Ph.D. thesis (Aberdeen, 1974), p. 45.

It was in terms like these that the Jacobite cause merged with the national one. James was not the symbolic leader of the nation alone; he was the nation – and Jacobite poetry in Scotland can be marked by a passionate patriotism which does not distinguish the two:

> But there's a bud in fair Scotland,
>   A bud weel kend in glamourye;
> And in that bud there is a bloom,
>   That yet shall flower o'er kingdoms three;
> And in that bloom there is a brier,
>   Shall pierce the heart of tyrannye,
> Or there is neither faith, nor truth,
>   Nor honour left in our countrye.
>
> 'My Love he was a Highland Lad'

Here the 'bud' is the flower of Scotland: a symbol both of the nation and of the white rose king. As a rose, its bloom is beautiful, its thorns sharp: the former is the reborn fertility of the land and its returning king, the latter the forces (chauvinistically enough, Scottish ones) with which he will overthrow the Hanoverian monarchy. Moreover, the rose of Scotland and the king is also the mystic rose ('weel kend in glamourye') suggesting a mystic dimension inherent in the overarching identification of king and nation. In the last lines of the question, allusion is made to the myth of the Union, already in existence when the Treaty was passed: that (Lowland) Scotland had betrayed the virtues of its ancestors for English gold. The bud will bloom: but its blooming is conditional on a recrudescence of the national character, perhaps in the shape of the Highlander as hero: hence the erotic appeal to the king as 'Highland Lad', one similar to that of the quotation at the head of this chapter, where Edinburgh symbolizes the enslaved Lowland nation to be liberated. Empty, barren Holyrood Palace will once again receive the victorious Stuart, when Scottish hearts awake to their ancient virtues. The idea of the empty palace or house is a common one in Scottish Jacobite poetry, acting as an image of exclusion from the intimacies of possession and family. Such images find a tragic realization in the later Jacobite period and that of the Clearances:

> The glen that was my father's own,
> By his maun be forsaken;
> The house that was my father's home,
> Lies levelled with the bracken
> Ochone! Ochone! the glory's gone
> Stolen by a ruthless reiver
> Our hands are on the broad claymore
> But might has gone for ever.

> And thou, my prince, my injured prince
> Thy people have disowned thee,
> Have hunted thee and driven thee hence,
> With ruined chiefs about thee.
> Though hard beset, when I forget
> Thy fate, young helpless rover,
> This breaking heart will cease to be
> And all its griefs be over.

'The Highlander's Farewell'

Tragic as the loss is, it is, like Lord Derwentwater's, no worse than the king's ('If thou and I have lost our lives / Our king has lost his crown'). The 'rover' has been usurped by the 'reiver', the hunter has become the hunted, ownership is 'disowned'. The process of exile is complete.[4]

Earlier in the eighteenth century, the actuality of exile was not so fully realized, but its metaphors were powerful ones, more domestic than the Aenean symbolism of England. In 'This is no my ain House', politically bowdlerized by Allan Ramsay, the Hanoverian succession appears as a personal violation of the ordinary Scottish home:

> O this is no my ain house, I ken by the biggin o't;
> For bow-kail thrave at my door cheek,
> And thristles on the riggin o't.

Not only might one's house be altered or emptied, but it might be occupied by another:

> The adder lies in the corbie's nest,
>     Aneath the corbie's wame,
> And the blast that reaves the corbie's brood
>     Shall blow our good king hame.

Whig policies, here characterized in beast-fable terms, could only alienate fellow-Scots, resulting in increased Jacobite support (Hogg, *The Jacobite Relics*, I, pp. 53, 57).

The not uncommon personal or domestic intimacy of these songs intruded itself into the domain not only of home and its familiar appurtenances, but into the arena of human affections, in the famous erotic strain of Scottish Jacobite verse. 'The Trooper and the Maid', frequently sung in the north of Scotland until the present century, is a version of a muster song of the 'Fifteen, while 'The bonnie, bonnie banks of Loch Lomond' is a Jacobite adaptation of an eighteenth-century erotic song, with the lover dying for his king, and taking only the 'low road' of death back to Scotland:

---

[4] Hogg, *Relics*, I: p. 155; II: p. 185 (a version differing slightly from that quoted here).

> For me and my true love will never meet again
> By the bonnie bonnie banks o Loch Lomond.

This Jacobite soldier has died for a truer love, as another poem, set to a psalm-tune, makes clear:

> Great James, come kiss me now, now,
>   Great James, come kiss me now:
> Too long I've undone myself these years bygone,
>   By basely forsaking you.

The message could hardly be more direct (Hogg, *The Jacobite Relics*, i, p. 145).

Jacobite eroticism is often accompanied by a strong, even ferocious, nationalism which sits awkwardly with the Stuart aim of being restored in three kingdoms. (James VIII and III in fact issued a medal bearing the English coat of arms alone (though admittedly his touchpieces wore the opposite guise, bearing his Scottish title)). Such nationalism had its obvious roots in the Union:

> Scotland and England must be now
>   United in a nation,
> And we must all perjure and vow,
>   And take the abjuration.
> The Stuarts' ancient freeborn race,
>   Now we must all give over;
> And we must take into their place
>   The bastards of Hanover.
>                             'The Curses'

The Hanover line's illegitimacy is akin to that of Scotland being taken over by the English: the 'abjuration' is intimately connected to the process of Union itself (Hogg, *The Jacobite Relics*, i, p. 164).

More boisterous songs of anti-English resentment implied that Scotland alone would restore the Stuarts:

> Come let us drink a health boyes
> A health unto our King
> We'll drink no more in stealth boyes
> Come let our Glases ring
> For England must surrender
> To him they call'd pretender
> God save our Faith's Defender
> And our true lafull [sic] King.

The same air with a different set makes the message more explicit:

> Let our brave loyal clans, then,
>   Their ancient Stuart race
> Restore with sword in hand, then,

> And all their foes displace.
> All unions we'll o'erturn boys,
> Which caus'd our nation mourn, boys,
> Like Bruce at Bannockburn, boys,
> The English home we'll chase.[5]

Both songs identify the Stuart cause with a Scottish/English conflict, hence conflating Jacobitism with the view of Scottish history as a struggle for liberty. The latter song, written in 1714 in apparent expectation of a Rising, appeals to the image of Highlander as patriot, aligning his resurgent spirit with that of a new Scotland which will return to the ethos of 'Bruce at Bannockburn', setting aside the soiled surrender of 1707. But such optimism was not always without its self-irony, as in this translation of Horace which ends 'A new Ballad to the tune of Cheviots Chace Ao. 1717':

> our Gransyres they were papists all
> our fayrs Cromwellians
> ourselves we are confounded whigs
> begetting Hanoverians.[6]

If this sense of Scottish self-betrayal and self-disgust was accurate (and it has endured in Scottish thought to the present day), the adder was truly in the corbie's nest. The decline postulated here is not one of partial betrayal (the 'bought and sold' version of history) but universal inconsistency.

Such inconsistency made it difficult for Presbyterian nationalist writers to use the past with comfort: whereas the writer of the above lines may have been happy enough with the Catholicism of his 'Gransyres', such was not the case here. Even 'loyal Bruce and Wallace' were unsatisfactory icons of patriotism for the Presbyterian, since they lived in an age in which 'dismal darkness did remain / and overspread the nation', which was itself full of 'Palladins from Rome' and their 'prelatick scorpions' (a term which gives no confidence of subsequent sympathy towards Episcopacy). So the author of a Presbyterian nationalist tract like *Scotland's Glory and Her Shame* describes the Middle Ages; and the fact, secured by more recent historical scholarship, that the Catholic bishops had done much to fight Scotland's cause in the Wars of Independence can have done nothing to make such nationalism accord with the history from which its theology divided it.[7] Episcopalians and Catholics did not have such difficulties:

---

[5] Cf. John Ord (ed.), *The Bothy Songs and Ballads*, p. 20; Woolf, *Medallic Record*, p. 39; Hogg, *Relics*, I: pp. 100, 164; National Library of Scotland ADV MS 19.3.44/11.
[6] NLS MS 2092 f.49.
[7] *Scotland's Glory and her Shame*, By a Well-wisher to The Good Old Cause, 2nd edn (n.p., 1786 (1745)), pp. 8, 9.

Shall Monarchy be quite forgot,
  and of it no more heard?
Antiquity be razed out,
  and slav'ry put in stead?
Is *Scots* Mens Blood now grown so Cold
  the valour of their Mind
That they can never once reflect
  on old land sine, &c? . . .

  Why did you thy Union break
    thou had of late with *France* . . .

In this model for Burns' most famous song, history is no embarrassment; rather the loss of it is a standing reproach. The speaker is alienated from the British present, addressing it as 'you' in contradistinction to the 'thouing' of the Franco-Scottish past. 'Slav'ry' here is not the product of Catholicism, but of English rule: it is pre-Reformation Scotland which is praised for its valour. In mentioning (surprisingly) the Auld Alliance in terms of 'Union', the song refers to the dream of sixteenth-century Scottish Catholic monarchy: that Mary Stuart, Mary of Guise's daughter, should be queen (as she briefly was) both of France and Scots. 'Old Lang Sine' may have existed as a song with a non-political set of words before the eighteenth century; but in the early 1700s it became a widely distributed lament for antiquity, while its undertones of exile from history and from Scotland survive even in Burns' version:

  We twa hae paidlit in the burn
  Frae morning sun till dine;
  But seas between us braid hae roar'd
  Sin auld lang syne.[8]

As so often in Burns, the intimacy and domesticity of the Jacobite lyric's lament for a lost homeland and an invaded home is transferred, with an ease inherited from the codes of the subgenre, to a world of individuated grief, love and loss. The song which stages a grand finale to so many Burns suppers and Highland evenings is only a personalized version of Jacobite erotic loss: 'Is *Scots* Mens Blood now grown so Cold' the voice of doubt giving the lie to 'Will Ye No Come Back Again?'.[9]

National grief at the decline and passing of an idealized independent Scotland which once struggled for the liberty it now traded away (and the verb is significant, since the access to markets provided by Union could be paralleled in English Jacobite ideology with reactions to the financial

[8] NLS Rosebery 117; cf. Robert Burns, *Poems and Songs*, ed. James Kinsley (Oxford: Oxford University Press, 1992 (1969)), p. 353.
[9] NLS Rosebery 117; *Life and Songs of the Baroness Nairne with a Memoir and Poems of Carolina Oliphant the Younger*, ed. Revd Charles Rogers (Edinburgh: John Grant, 1896), p. 209.

revolution) often took the form of a nationalistic return to Scots vernacular. The high cultural side of the vernacular revival will be examined in
discussion of the age of Allan Ramsay in the next section: but it is
noteworthy that Jacobite song-culture in general can make the linguistic
equation Scots language = good, English language = bad. An example of
this is found in the fine song 'Lochmaben Gate', which although it cannot
be definitely dated, refers to a specific local event which occurred on 27
May 1714:

> I asked a man what meant the fray,
>     'Good sir', said he, 'you seem a stranger:
> 'This is the twenty-ninth of May;
>     'Far better had you shun the danger.
> 'These are rebels to the throne,
>     'Reason have we all to know it;
> 'Popish knaves and dogs each one.
>     'Pray pass on, or you shall rue it.'
>
> I look'd the traitor in the face,
>     Drew out my brand, and ettled at him:
> 'Deil send a' the whiggish race
>     'Downward to the dad that gat 'em!'
> Right sair he gloom'd, but naething said,
>     While my heart was like to scunner.
> Cowards are they, born and bred
>     Ilka whinging, praying sinner.

The non-partisan narrative voice ('fray', 'brand') is a literary English one,
as is the voice of the pompous Whig who presumes the narrator's complai-
sance. But as soon as the narrator begins to speak of his own politics, his
Scots intrudes, even in the verb of speech itself ('ettled'). Indeed, he seems
so angry ('my heart was like to scunner') that even when his direct speech
subsides back into reportage the Scots continues. Its presence is a measure
of emotion and patriotism, a rejection of cold blood in favour of Scots
passion. Although the vernacular is only lightly present, its voicing is
symbolic of an attack on the chilly metropolitan language of the
propaganda-sheet used by the disapproving Whig.[10]

Such favouring of the vernacular for patriotic expression was satirized
by the Whigs. In 'The pretended Prince of *Wale*'s New Exercise of the
SCOTCH Langboon', James VIII and III is transferred into a comic Scot:
'Take care on your Sell, sir noow'. For a marginalized Scottish nationalism to insist on the association of king and country in linguistic terms was
to risk the mocking intensification of that same marginality in the mouths
of its enemies. Charles Edward Stuart's subsequent populist use of the

---

[10]  NLS Rosebery 117; Hogg, *Relics*, 1: p. 133.

Highlander icon as an accompaniment to high cultural Roman republican and democratic images made the best of a position friends and enemies had alike placed him in.[11]

The image of Stuart prince as Highland/Scottish patriot was one bound to the erotic dimension of Jacobite lyric. When voicing Scottish nationalism in generic, totalizing terms, the Jacobite song drew on the imagery of home and exile, either laterally in current circumstances, or vertically through history. When writing in more personal terms of the Stuart prince as individual rather than comprehending symbol, the intimacy of domesticity becomes the freedom of lovers whose conjunction will restore the broken family, recentring in fulfilment of desire what had been decentred through loss. On a basic level this process draws attention to itself through citing the absent hero:

> Of no man we will stand in awe
> To drink his health that's far awa'
> He is over the seas and far awa . . .
> he is over the seas and far awa . . .
> Although his back be at the wa . . .
> Well [sic] drink his health that's far awa.

This song is far from being simply nostalgic: it is of a type later incorporated in one of the famous songs of *The Beggar's Opera*, as discussed in Chapter 2 (this set dates to 1710). As such it was the companion and forerunner of songs of a more definitively personal intimacy:

> Be gude to me as lang's I'm here,
>     I'll maybe win awa' yet;
> He's bonnie coming o'er the hills,
>     That will tak' me frae ye a' yet.
> For a' that and a' that,
>     And thrice as muckle's a' that;
> He's bonie coming o'er the hills,
>     That will tak' me frae ye a' yet.[12]

This kind of song (a variant of the famous 'Though Georthie reign in Jamie's stead', jacobinized by Burns as we shall see in Chapter 6) was in its turn adopted into an existing subgenre, the (poor) Highland lad meets (rich) Lowland lassie song. In the hands of Jacobite singers and writers this fabliau tale of rape, seduction or lovers' defiance was turned to a vision of sexual, personal and national liberation, which reached its expressive peak in the years after 1745. The Lowland woman, a paradigm of the Scotland which has been faithless, is returned to a relationship of true identity after yielding to the Highland patriot. As a result she is free

---

[11] NLS Ry. 124.       [12] NLS, S 2092 f. 35; Ord, *Bothy Ballads*, p. 196.

and happy, no longer 'following the G-man', but in escape from the prison
of Union:

> I crossed *Forth*, I crossed *Tay*
>     I left *Dundee*, and *Edinborrow*,
> I saw nothing there worth my Stay,
>     and so I bad them all Good-morrow.

> Chorus

> I will have no Commander, Man,
>     Captain, Col'nel, nor a Caddie,
> If all my Friends had sworn and said,
>     I'll have none but a Highland Laddie.

The woman in this song is active speaker as well as subject. She escapes the
Lowlands, rejecting its men, described in terms of the ranks in the British
Army. On the Cairnamount, at the border between Lowland and High-
land (from its peak five counties are visible), she meets, in the 'careless
Dress' of freedom, a Highland Laddie who is neither Dutch (*'Butter-Box'*),
English or Lowland. He too is a military man: but his armed readiness (to
conquer both her and Scotland) is emphasized in terms which serve as a
double-entendre for his fertility. His values are those of poverty and
freedom, not wealth ('Fop') and slavery: though he is 'Gentie', as are all
Highlanders. These points are emphasized in another song in the same
cycle:

> Now She's cast off her silken Gowns
>     that she wear'd in the Lowland
> And she's up to the Highland Hills
>     to wear Gowns of Tartain.
> And she's cast off her high-heel'd shoes
>     was made of the gilded Leather,
> And she's up to *Gilliecrankie*
>     to go among the Heather.

The woman's liberation from the trappings of wealth goes hand in hand
with freeing herself into fertility and fulfilment.[13]

Other love-songs like 'The Broom of Cowdenknowes', an early seventeenth-century seduction song, were adapted to Jacobite purposes; while
'Bonny Dundee' is found at this time as a song of erotic loss. A whole range
of political love-poetry is powerfully present before 1745:

---

[13] NLS ADV MS 19.3.44; 'The New way, OF THE BONNY HIGHLAND LADDIE-*To its own Proper
Tune, &c*', NLS Rosebery 89; cf. NLS MS 210 f. 21; NLS Rosebery III.a.10.75; William
Donaldson, *The Jacobite Song: Political Myth and National Identity* (Aberdeen: Aberdeen Univer-
sity Press, 1988), pp. 56–8.

O gin I live to see the day,
   That I ha'e begg'd, and begg'd frae Heaven,
I'll fling my rock and reel away,
   And dance and sing frae morn till even.
For there is ane I winna name,
   That comes the beingin bike to scatter;
And I'll put on my bridal gown,
   That day our king comes o'er the water.

This song, reputedly by the Countess Marischal, Lady Keith, sums up the replacement of loss by fulfilled desire which sits at the heart of the erotic Jacobite lyric.[14]

As suggested in the Introduction, there are two other great classes into which Scottish Jacobite song falls: the active and the sacred. The sacred song, which is often linked with erotic verse, is not often found in the vernacular, and has been seldom collected (perhaps because so many Jacobite verse selections follow Hogg's canon, which largely leaves them out). It seems centrally the unmediated voice of Jacobite high culture, not seeking folk cultural terms through which to defend its political identity, but celebrating instead its own underground continuance through biblical typology. In doing so, the sacred song referred back to the Royalist ideal of a Davidic king and forward to a second Stuart coming: it was a millenarian voice for royalty:

Long since our David Jordan mourning past
Down to the Ground his Tabernacles cast,
Oppressive Tyrants have usurp'd his throne,
And too, too long have made his kingdoms groans[sic]!
Our Nation's quite impov'rished, our trade
Is now quite sunk & subjects slaves are made.
Quite out their Lives hard-hearted Pharoh[sic] gnaws,
Exacts the bricks, & yet denys the straws.
Have Israel's nor Judah's men no thought
That David should be over Jordan brought?
Sure! Judah's men are his own flesh and bone,
Why then so slack to bring their king first home?
Is Zadok tongue-tied, Abiathar dumb ...
Why! why so slack in warning them become?
Let Cherethites & Pelethites combine
To right the long injured righteous Line!

This kind of mock-Dryden shows the Episcopalian voice at its most self-centred, an allusive gentry weeping into its commonplace books. But 'loving the man with the Gown' was an activity not confined to these, but

---

[14] Hogg, *Relics*, I, p. 46; for Jacobite version of 'Broom of Cowdenknowes', see Pittock, 'New Jacobite Songs of the 'Forty-five', *Studies in Voltaire and the Eighteenth Century* 267, pp. 1–75 (11); for an eighteenth-century version of 'Bonny Dundee', see NLS Rosebery III.a.10.31.

spread across classes, particularly in the Episcopal heartland of North-east Scotland.[15] Popular Episcopalianism could concentrate more on the Church as social rather than theological experience, as in this folk-song, 'The Last Speech and Dying Words of the Auld Kirk at Turriff', a dramatic monologue spoken by the ruined fabric of a church order destroyed in 1689, now both unhappy and obliquely repentant:

> 'Next came a race o' hectrin saints
> Wi' solemn leagues and covenants
> They learn'd my bairns like the ants
> Nae king to heed
> Ca'd them that own'd them malignants
> An' shed their bleed.
>
> Gin ye for parties preach and pray
> Or greedy seek owre muckle pey
> Turn careless o' your family
> Or proud and saucy
> Ye'll aiblins share the fate some day
> O' Piscopacy.

The very phrase of the title, 'Last Speech and Dying Words', seems to parallel the 'Last Words' of executed Jacobites, while the dramatic monologue format which confirms this parallel is a notable feature of sacred Jacobite verse. On occasion, as in 'The Remorse Anno 1715' it is used as a kind of public confessional for a King George figure to admit his faults:

> What horrors do this guilty soul affright;
> When darling sunshine yields to irksome night!
> Ah me the Ghosts of Butcher'd Britain,
> Whose dying words, methinks, do peirce [sic] the air?
> Their Blood to Heav'n for vengeance loud does call
> From the Brave Kenmure, to the Church-man Paul ...
>
> Why do I grasp a scepter not my own,
> While Subjects grumble, and the Heav'ns do frown? ...
>
> O Cousin James, take all, and make me free ...

This rather unlikely portrait of a sensitive and conscience ridden George I shows one of the reasons for the use of dramatic monologue (descended, as is clear here, from Elizabethan soliloquy) by the Jacobite song: the dramatic fashion in which it both expresses and summarizes hopes and ideals, while maintaining an intimacy more familiar from erotic Jacobitism.[16]

---

[15] Pittock, 'New Jacobite Songs', pp. 35, 37; Aberdeen University Library MS 2222.
[16] *The Greig-Duncan Folk Song Collection*, Volume 2, ed. Patrick Shuldham-Shaw and Emily B. Lyle (Aberdeen: Aberdeen University Press, 1983), pp. 588–9; NLS MS 1695/44.

This intimacy is found also in the active poetry of Jacobite resistance, linked in the example below to the already discussed image of the invaded home:

> And he's clappit down in our gudeman's chair,
>   The wee wee German lairdie,
> And he's brought fouth o' foreign trash,
>   And dibbled them in his yardie.
> He's pu'd the rose o' English loons,
> And broken the harp o' Irish clowns,
> But our Scots thristle will jag his thumbs,
>   The wee wee German Lairdie.

As in the case of the erotic song, the active Jacobite lyric was a fully mediated text: produced for or at least protected by nationalist high cultural elements, and distributed by ballads and singers in safe areas, either in broadside form or as pub wallpaper, a not uncommon way of providing drinking-songs. One of the chief examples of this sort of lyric was 'Geordie Whelps' Testament', distributed widely through Scotland at the accession of that king, both as an incitement to mock (one of the most effective forms of political satire) and to resist Hanoverian usurpation. George is presented as a small-time thief, who has corrupted and ruined the dwelling he has taken over. Domestic imagery once more intensifies the sense of violation inherent in the usurpation itself, and its consequences for Scotland:

> Wae worth the time that I came here,
> To lay my fangs on Jamie's gear!
> For I had better staid at hame,
> Than now to bide sae muckle blame.
> But my base, poltroon, sordid mind,
> To greed o' gear was still inclin'd,
> Which gart me fell Count Koningsmark,
> For his braw claise and holland sark.
>
> When that was done, by slight and might
> I hitch'd young Jamie frae his right,
> And, without any fear or dread,
> I took his house out-ower his head,
> Pack'd up his plenishing sae braw,
> And to a swine-sty turn'd his ha!
> I connach'd a' I couldna tak,
> And left him naething worth a plack.

The aims of a song such as this were perhaps threefold: to utilize the ancient sentiments of misrule festivals such as the Abbot of Unreason; to present the new 'domestic' monarch as a contemptible cuckoo-king of fear and hate; and lastly, to raise those who heard it to a defiance which its mockery might make them believe was not futile. To mock is to diminish: and this petty thieving Geordie began to seem quite a small target.[17]

Just as there are songs of action which raise such emotions, there are those which celebrate them once raised, such as 'Little Ken ye wha's Coming', an (original?) manuscript of which is dated 12 November 1715, with a note that it was first played by the Highland piper when the royal army entered Penrith:

> Little ken ye wha's coming
> Little ken ye wha's coming
> Jock and Tam an a's coming . . .

A list of magnates and clans who have joined the Stuart cause follows: but the implication of this first verse is that in effect the whole Scottish nation, 'Jock and Tam an a' ', has risen for the king.[18]

Given the failure of this and successive Risings however, there was a tendency for the song of action to retrench itself in the aftermath of defeat, and voice sentiments of defiance or fantasy. There are many examples of the former, including the famously ambivalent loyal toast:

> Here's a health to our King
> You know whom I mean
> And to every honest man
> That will do't again.

In the latter, dead heroes might emerge from the past precisely in order to 'do't again' for a less successful present, as perhaps in 'The Haughs o' Cromdale', where Montrose's 1645 victory at Auldearn seems conflated with the defeat of Major-Generals Buchan and Cannon by the government horse at Cromdale in 1690. As a result of this defeat, described in the first four stanzas of the poem, the spirit of an avenging Montrose returns to alter the outcome, like Arthur or Fionn returning in the hour of their nations' need:

> Thus the great Montrose did say,
> I say, direct the nearest way,
> For I will o'er the hills this day
> And see the haughs of Cromdale.
>
> They were at dinner, every man,
> When great Montrose upon them came;
> A second battle then began,

[17] Hogg, *Relics* I: pp. 84, 116–17.    [18] NLS MS 1695/152.

> Upon the haughs of Cromdale.
> The Grant, Mackenzie, and M'Ky
> Soon as Montrose they did espy,
> O then, they fought most valiantly!
> Upon the haughs of Cromdale.

There follows, in Gaelic-style traditional form, a list of all those who fought with the returning Montrose, a list which implies the unity of a large part of the nation: those mentioned could have raised a fighting force of more than ten thousand. There can only be one end:

> The loyal Stewarts, with Montrose,
> So boldly set upon their foes,
> And brought them down with Highland blows,
> Upon the haughs of Cromdale.

In such a fashion, wish-fulfilment is expressed for victory over 'Cromwell's men' or their successors. The patriot Highland army reverses the outcome of Cromdale in a revenant Auldearn, an original battle itself suitable for such a song because of its confused and divided military conduct.[19]

Along with such wish-fulfilment songs of self-irony occur, such as that on Sheriffmuir, 'There's some say that we wan, and some say that they wan, and some say that nane won at a' man', itself part of a subgenre of dialogue active Jacobite verse, which through an exchange between spectators neutralizes the political threat of what is being discussed. Some songs set such political threat in a broader context, such as 'ADVICE to the MUSE, on the KING's Landing', mentioned above, which places the restored 'GENIUS OF BRITTAIN!' in the context of a poetic revival, where 'New *Wallers* and new *Drydens* shall arise, / And sprightly *Pope* endeavour for the Prize' in a renewed Augustan age.[20]

The active song tradition, like the erotic, but only to a lesser extent the sacred, operated at these and other levels in three major modes of transmission. There was the Anglicized literary broadside or commonplace-book poem with (except perhaps on special occasions and at times of high tension) a limited circulation. There was the vernacular or partly vernacular broadside, distributed by balladeers, posted in alehouses, using folk tradition and entering the folk dimension; and there was that tradition itself, open to influence at this late stage from such mediated texts in written culture, but with its own, sometimes more oblique, manner of commenting on events, which could be manifest in the ballad-tradition. To an extent these divisions are artificial: but they enable us to see strands in the Jacobite song tradition later superbly married by Burns, whose roots in this tradition range from 'Tho Georthie Reigns in Jamie's stead' (which

---

[19] NLS ADV MS 19:3:44/68; Hogg, *Relics*, I, pp. 3, 5.
[20] Hogg, *Relics*, II: p. 1; NLS ADV MSS 19:1:13/63.

provides the air for 'A Man's a Man for a' That') to 'Such a parcel of Rogues in a Nation', the summary (again to an inherited air) of almost a century of lyric expression of the myth of Union.[21]

From the seventeenth century, patriotic Scottish high culture had been aware of the importance of popular and folk traditions in establishing a locale of speech and context for what it wished to say in defence of the nation. Fletcher of Saltoun was only one patriot who had a strong belief in the power of the popular ballad. Just as Jacobite high culture adapted to itself popular emblems (even Charles Edward Stuart sang Jacobite songs, repeatedly and with relish), so popular and folk culture found in the fate of Jacobite heroes a paradigm for the suffering of their more lowly supporters, and on occasion a fulfilment of folk prophecy:

> 'Inverugie, by the sea,
> Lordless shall thy lands be!
> And beneath thy ha'hearthstane
> The tod shall bring her bairns hame!'

The flight and proscription of the Earl Marischal and his brother in 1716 brought this about.[22]

It was the adoption of the vernacular as an engine of cultural defence which showed, however, the convergence across classes of nationalist ideals in the aftermath of Union. In order better to explain this crucial process in both differentiating the types and uniting the interests of the Jacobite song's central propaganda role, I now turn to Allan Ramsay and the vernacular revival. In fitting conclusion to discussion of the contemporary nationalist Jacobite song I quote one of the finest, first written before 1745, which combines sacred, erotic and active traditions in an appeal for restoration of the lost and paradisaical world of an independent Scotland and its dynasty:

> To daunton me, to daunton me,
> O ken ye what it is that dauntons me?
> Eighty-eight and Eighty-nine,
> Wi a the dreary years sinsyne,
> And cess, and press, and Presbytery,
> O these are the things wad daunton me.

> But to wanton me, but to wanton me,
> D'ye ken the thing that wad wanton me?
> To see gude corn upon the rigs,
> And banishment to a the Whigs,
> And richt restored whaur richt sud be,
> O siccan the things wad wanton me.

---

[21] NLS Rosebery 95.

[22] Norval Clyne, *The Scottish Jacobites and their Poetry* (Aberdeen, 1887), pp. 8, 11; Frank McLynn, *Charles Edward Stuart: A Tragedy in Many Acts* (London: Routledge, 1988), pp. 283–84.

But to wanton me, but to wanton me
D'ye ken the thing maist wad wanton me?
To see King James at Edinburgh Cross,
Wi' fifty thousand foot and horse
And the usurper forced to flee,
O sic is the thing maist wad wanton me.[23]

# Ramsay and the vernacular revival

Our antecessowris, that we sulde of reide
And held in mynde thar nobille worthi deid,
We lat ourslide, throw werray sleuthfulness . . .
*The Wallace*

'Renowned RAMSAY, canty Callan,
There's nowther Highlandman nor Lowlan,
    In Poetrie,
But may as soon ding down *Tantallon*
    As match wi' thee.

Ye gods who Justice Love look down
    and as you promised heretofore
would you all Scotland's wishes crown
    James with his Golden Reign restore.
Allan Ramsay

Since the early eighteenth century every revival of Scottish literature has been associated with a revival of traditional ('folk') literature and song, and this has gone hand in hand with antiquarianism.                 Tom Crawford[24]

The revival of antiquarian culture was a predominantly political act in post-Union Scotland. It took two major forms: the recrudescence, or perhaps more accurately the last stand of Scoto-Latin culture, and the revival of the vernacular. Those who were supporters of the former, like Ruddiman, were frequently associated with those who had an interest in the latter, like Ramsay. Ruddiman 'inspired a movement of Scottish patriotic publishing which at one time looked as though it would represent

---

[23] This set from G. S. MacQuoid (ed.), *Jacobite Songs and Ballads* (London, n.d.), p. 153.

[24] *The Bruce and Wallace*, new edn, ed. John Jamieson, 2 vols. (Glasgow, 1869), p. 3; *The Works of Allan Ramsay*, ed. Burns Martin and John Oliver, Scottish Text Society (New York and London, 1972), I: pp. 115, 196; Tom Crawford, review in *Scottish Literary Journal* Supplement 25 (1986), pp. 27–32 (29).

a major reaction to the Union', while Ramsay voiced a suitable speech for that patriotism to couch itself in.[25]

This relationship between Scoto-Latinity and a defence of the vernacular carried its influence forward to the age of Fergusson and Burns, finding echoes both in 'Scots poetry' and 'perhaps the vernacular classical architecture of some Edinburgh building of the 1760s' (Daiches, *The Scottish Enlightenment*, p. 19). As Paul Scott has pointed out, there was a strong cultural belief in an equation of Roman and Scottish virtues, and Scottish patriotism and Scottish classicism were to this extent ready fellow-travellers. Jacobite Latinity was no high cultural bolt-on accessory; it had a fundamental role to play in the vernacular revival of Scots. Freebairn may have lauded Scotland's classical heritage, but he also printed *The Bruce* and *Wallace* in 1714/15 as part of an appeal to the Scottish past and its language. Sir John Clerk of Penicuik had remarked that Middle Scots was '"genuine Saxon" in its purest form', and such comments could be held to justify a defence of Scots as more English than the English. Indeed, there is a hint of this in less nationalist circles throughout the century, as although there are famous lists of Scotticisms to be avoided, recent research has started to show that Scots survived in some form in Scottish grammar books until late in the eighteenth century at least.[26] Far from being, as Kidd argues, an 'archaism ... a vernacular dialect', Scots was still a developing language, whose pronunciation and syntax, if not its vocabulary or orthography, were still welcome in Unionist circles a hundred years after the Union.[27]

Aberdeen and the North East was both an area where Scoto-Latinity had one of its major strongholds, and where vernacular Scots was still widely spoken (this remained the case well into the present century). The universities and their hinterland had been an intellectual centre sympathetic to the Stuarts since the early seventeenth century, when the influence of the Aberdeen Doctors had helped to ensure that the burgh did not, alone of major towns in Scotland, sign the National Covenant, while two thousand men were raised for the king in the countryside. Charles II's Episcopal primate, Archbishop Sharp, was a Banff man educated at Aberdeen, while in the early eighteenth century Episcopal Jacobites continued to control both university colleges (appointments at Marischal being largely in the gift of the Jacobite Earl) until after the 'Fifteen. Three

---

[25] David Daiches, *The Scottish Enlightenment* (Edinburgh, 1986), p. 19.

[26] Paul Scott, in *Towards Independence* (Edinburgh: Polygon, 1992); Kidd, 'The Ideological Significance of Scottish Jacobite Latinity', in Jeremy Black and Jeremy Gregory (eds.), *Culture, Politics and Society in Britain 1660–1800* (Manchester and New York: Manchester University Press, 1991), pp. 123–48 (123); David Daiches, *Robert Fergusson*, Scottish Writers Series (Edinburgh: Scottish Academic Press, 1982), p. 15; I am indebted to the researches of Professor Charles Jones in the area of the survival of Scotticisms.

[27] Kidd, 'The Ideological Significance of Scottish Jacobite Latinity', p. 111.

professors at King's College, John Forbes of Corse, Henry Scougall and James Garden all contributed to the literature of the catholicizing Episco-palianism of the area. Thomas Ruddiman's 'own regent' at the university, 'heart of the North-East's traditional cult of Latin ... went with a deputation of professors to greet James Stuart at Fetteresso', while propor-tionately more recruits to the royal army came from the Aberdeen hinter-land than from anywhere else.[28] Ruddiman's own parents, from Tarland and Kildrummy, also came from this Episcopal heartland, and his back-ground and education, like that of Macpherson half a century later, must have done much to confirm and develop Jacobite prejudices (Daiches, *Robert Fergusson*, p. 28). The traditions of the North East intelligentsia and gentry inherited the aims of the class of royalist intellectuals, Latinists and Scots, which James had sought to develop in Edinburgh in the 1680s. Ruddiman, like Pitcairne, shared the 'Scoto-Roman ethos' of the leading figures of this school:

Grahame of Claverhouse, Sir George Lockhart and Sir George Mackenzie, to whose memory ... poems were written, symbolized for Pitcairne a culture over-whelmed in 1688.                                        (Duncan, *Ruddiman*, p. 18)

Claverhouse of course was celebrated as 'ultime Scotorum' by Pitcairne in his famous elegy translated by Dryden: the representation, in Latin, of the Scottish ethos: a perfect combination of the dual aims of the Scoto-Romans. Likewise, Ruddiman called that sturdy opponent of Union, Fletcher of Saltoun, 'Cato nostri seculi', as the Scoto-Roman critics of the new British state adopted Republican iconography to define their Jacobit-ism long before Charles Edward did. The typical plaint of such as Lockhart, Ruddiman or Pitcairne was that 'luxury and vanity' had replaced 'primitiveness and simplicity', the supersession of Scoto-Roman purity by Anglo-British imperial consumption (this thesis was widely reflected in more popular form in mediated texts). In this sense, their oppositionalism was similar to that of those who opposed the financial revolution in England. Pope's Man of Ross was the kind of character Scoto-Roman republicans would have admired.[29]

Ruddiman reinforced Episcopalian ideology in Edinburgh, where he came 'as a result of his meeting with Dr Archibald Pitcairne', sub-sequently co-operating with Freebairn to bring out an edition of Gavin

---

[28] Roger L. Emerson, *Professors, Patronage and Politics: The Aberdeen Universities in the Eighteenth Century*. Quincentennial Studies in the History of Aberdeen University (Aberdeen: Aberdeen University Press, 1992); Douglas Duncan, *Thomas Ruddiman* (Edinburgh and London, 1965), p. 11; G. D. Henderson (ed.), *Mystics of the North East* (Aberdeen: Third Spalding Club, 1934); David Stevenson, *The Scottish Revolution 1637–1644* (Newton Abbot: David and Charles, 1973); Julia Buckroyd, *The Life of James Sharp, Archbishop of St Andrews 1618–1679: A Political Biography* (Edinburgh: John Donald, 1987).

[29] Duncan, *Ruddiman*, p. 150; *The Poems of Alexander Pope*, p. 582.

Douglas's *Aeneid* (a patriotic Catholic bishop's translation into Scots of the major Stuart Latin text – an ideal choice), 'with a glossary of Douglas's Scots by Ruddiman' (Daiches, *Fergusson*, pp. 13–14). Douglas's epic was, in part at least, a patriotic statement to exhibit the potential of Scots, which was for the first time in the late fifteenth century being differentiated from the increasingly standardized English south of the Border. If Scots was to compete as an alternative standard rather than a provincial survival, it needed to scale the same heights of discourse as English aimed to do, courtesy of Mulcaster and others, in the sixteenth century. Douglas's *Aeneid* was a step towards that goal. Its popularity in the age of Ruddiman and Ramsay seems due to its identification as a meeting-point for vernacular and Latinist patriotism in the central story of Jacobite classicism. Ramsay's versions of Horace's *Odes* promoted the same end, but perhaps without the political edge Douglas provided: Ramsay even took 'Gavin Douglas' as his pseudonym when a member of the Jacobite Easy Club.[30]

This patriotic reaction had begun in anticipation of the Union in works like James Watson's *A Choice Collection of Comic and Serious Scots Poems Both Ancient and Modern* (1706), but within a short time afterwards had intensified in two directions. The loss of political power brought with it, as I suggested in Chapter 1, a move from incremental to typological historical consciousness: those writers who defined themselves as Scottish were robbed of cultural continuity upheld by political authority and its aesthetic apparatus of patrons, audiences and so forth, now that authority and its audiences were diluted into metropolitanism. As a result, they turned to the past, particularly selected prestigious past eras, as examples of a more perfect state of affairs which it was desired to recreate. At the same time, the publication of epics like Blind Hary's *Wallace* and Barbour's *Bruce* reminded residual patriotic audiences not only of the potential of the Scots language, but also the archetypicality of struggle with England as the defining syntax of patriotism. This essentially Jacobite reading defied the idea of Union as progress, and this kind of oppositional historiography (history as liberty) continued as a central expression of Scottish nationalism long after Jacobitism itself had become extinct as a political option.[31]

Such denial of incremental progress through the defiant recurrence of antiquarian value was accompanied by another classic response to loss of political power, as high cultural Scots wishing to continue the archetypal struggle and resist linguistic and cultural digestion by London, found a link with folk culture as the necessary defence mechanism. This folk link

---

[30] Alexander Manson Kinghorn and Alexander Law (eds.), *Poems by Allan Ramsay and Robert Fergusson* (Edinburgh and London: Scottish Academic Press, 1974), pp. ix–x.

[31] Daiches, *Fergusson*, pp. 11–12; Pittock, *Invention of Scotland*.

was joined in the vernacular revival's thought and praxis to the archetypicality of history as enshrined (for example) in the Wars of Independence. Thus Wallace, whose army had indeed largely consisted of 'the poor commons of Scotland' could be seen as the classic folk hero, defender of the people, while Bruce became an icon of royalist resistance. But their struggle was portrayed as the same struggle (doubtful in fact), and this community of interest was reflected in the place folk literature and associated mediated texts had in the patriotic voice of the vernacular revival.[32]

Just as Ramsay provided both versions of Horace and sets to folk airs, so Scoto-Latinity in general possessed a dual voice, that of classical authority and native patriotism, as can be discerned in this simile from Belhaven's famous speech against Union, itself more popular on the streets than in the Scots Estates:

our Ancient Mother Caledonia, like Caesar sitting in the midst of our Senate . . . breathing out her last with a *Et tu quoque, mi fili*.          Duncan, *Ruddiman*, p. 151

A slaughtered Caesar could only be avenged by a restored Augustus.[33]

Allan Ramsay, whom Ruddiman published, has been claimed to be 'almost singlehandedly' the author of the vernacular revival. Though this is an exaggeration, Ramsay did much to secure a connexion between the high ground of mediaeval Scots and current speech. In this, his place as 'a champion of Scottish folk-song and a wrecker of scores of such songs', Fergusson, Burns and Hogg were to be his inheritors.[34]

Ramsay's commitment to the vernacular was by no means absolute: he tamed it considerably in order to find an English market, introducing apostrophes for example, which suggested that Scots was a sloppy English rather than a differently spelt tongue. But nevertheless he maintained and extended a tradition which lay outside English cultural norms; nor should we altogether judge his Anglophonic moments unpatriotic, for Ramsay often couches nationalistic sentiment in English guise, as in 'Tartana, or the Plaid'. Here he attacks the 'base foreign Fashions' which have threatened the tartan (a reference to Union and the Highlander as patriot motif), while praising the colours of the plaid in terms suggestive of the renewing power of Stuart government:

> If lin'd with Green *Stuarta's* Plaid we view,
> Or thine *Ramseia* edg'd around with Blue;
> One shews the Spring when Nature is most kind . . .

[32] Geoffrey Barrow, *Robert Bruce and the Scottish Identity*, 3rd edn (Edinburgh, 1988), p. 88.
[33] LORD BELHAVEN'S SPEECH IN PARLIAMENT, *The Second Day of November 1706 . . . To which is subjoined*, BELHAVEN'S VISION. *A Poem* (Edinburgh: A. Robertson, 1766).
[34] Allan H. Maclaine, *Allan Ramsay*, Twayne English Authors Series (Boston: Twayne, 1985), p. 1; *The Works of Allan Ramsay*, I: pp. xviii, xx.

The conventional pastoralism of the imagery is nonetheless suggestive of the returning spring of Stuart propaganda.[35]

Discreet as he may be here, it is difficult to doubt Ramsay's politics. From the beginning (he arrived in Edinburgh as an apprentice wigmaker in 1701), his statements, actions and verse all point to a firm, often explicitly Jacobite, nationalism. Though this is sometimes expressed in prose which has been claimed to be a later forgery, there is no such doubt surrounding Ramsay's early membership of the patriot Easy Club in 1712.[36] The members of this forerunner of the famous Scottish clubs of the Enlightenment took pseudonyms, at first English, then subsequently Scottish ones. Ramsay was first Isaac Bickerstaff, then Gavin Douglas. On 5 November 1713, in recognition of the 'perfidy, pride, and hatred of England', the Club switched to Scottish names. Perhaps this decision was in honour of the death of Dr Archibald Pitcairne on 20 October. At any rate, less than a fortnight after it was taken (18 November), Ramsay's poem to Pitcairne's memory was read to the Club. It was headed by a quotation from Douglas's *Aeneid*, a compliment both to Pitcairne's leadership of the Scoto-Latinist group and his unswerving nationalism:

> Sum yonder bene for reddy Gold in Hand,
> Sold and betrasit there native Realme and Land.

This is immediately followed by a dedication to the rest of the Easy Club, thus implicitly separating them from the treacherous 'Sum yonder' of the Scotland outside their doors. The dedication is itself signed 'Gavin Douglas' (Ramsay's new pseudonym), and the poem which follows makes many little obeisances in the direction of the *Aeneid*. Pitcairne is carried to Dis's empire, where, like Aeneas in Book VI, he witnesses the punishment of traitors:

> ... observed a pool of boiling gold
> On which did float, those who their country sold.
> They howled and yelled, and often cursed the Gods,
> Who had not made them vipers, asps, or toads.
> Here he the faces of some traitors knew
> Who at the U(nion) did their hands embrew,
> In the heart blood of ancient Caledon,
> Which mortal wound makes her dear children groan.

The 'bought and sold for English gold' motif is obvious enough here. Pitcairne goes on to visit 'Those noble Scots, who for their country's good, / Had sacrificed their fortunes with their blood', and is approached by Bruce, who asks

[35] *The Works of Allan Ramsay*, I: pp. 27–30.
[36] For a doubtful early letter of this kind, see Andrew Gibson, *New Light on Allan Ramsay* (Edinburgh: William Brown; Belfast: William Mullen, 1927), p. 18.

> Tell me, how fares it with my *Albion* now,
> Can they with ease to the proud Saxons bow?

Pitcairne's answer blames the rage of party for overcoming native loyalty; he is then welcomed to Elysium by Wallace, Douglas, Graham and Belhaven.[37]

Ramsay's elegy clearly indicates the drift of the Easy Club's politics, which sailed closer to the wind in early 1715, when the Club sent an address to George I appealing for the repeal of the Union at a time when even Mar and his like were apparently in unconditional support of the new regime. In the *Address*, drawn up by 'George Buchanan' (the pseudonym is significant, given the historical Buchanan's rather limited support for the rights of kings), the Club describe themselves as 'true sons of Ferguson', alluding to the Scottish foundation-myth with its Jacobite implication of support for the native royal line. The appeal in general has something of the character of a threat: the suggestion that if the Union is not repealed 'the glory of the best of Royal families must fall' invites a jacobitical double reading. It functions either as a lament that if the Union continues, the Stuarts cannot be restored (as they might have been under the Act of Security), or as a veiled threat of reprisal: if you do not repeal the Union, you will be overthrown.

There is no evidence that the *Address* was ever sent, but it was symptomatic of the coded statements which followed in 'The Lamentation', a poem written on 9 November 1715, just before Sherriffmuir, in the form of a dialogue between 'George Buchanan' and 'Gavin Douglas'. 'Gavin' (Ramsay) speaks of the present as a time 'when grief and hope alternately go round'. The ambivalence of this statement immediately suggests a Jacobite reading: if the 'hope' is for a government victory, why not say so? Neither of the participants in the dialogue do say so however, 'Gavin' lamenting the 'destruction' and 'meagre famine' of the age, though saying the former must be seen in the context of what is 'ten times' worse; while 'George' suggests a cure:

> Yet often when disease,
> Does threaten death, to give the patient ease,
> From purple veins the lancet gives a pass
> To that base blood which would defile the mass.
> So may it hit.
> I know the horrid cause for which we smart
> The black idea's rivet in my heart.
> O may they only suffer by the rod
> Who with this cursed crime offended God.

[37] Alexander Law, 'Allan Ramsay and the Easy Club', *Scottish Literary Journal* 16:2 (1989), pp. 18–40 (19, 22, 26, 27).

The 'base blood' may be that of George, only fifty-eighth in line to the throne, whose son was in any case supposed by the Jacobites to be the bastard of Count Konigsmark. Of course the warming-pan story would allow the phrase to refer to James, but again we may ask why the reference should be so veiled if it is as virulently pro-Hanoverian as this would suggest. The references to 'horrid cause', 'black idea' and 'cursed crime' all suggest an existing grievance 'for which we smart'. 'Gavin' answers George's complaint with the words 'So may it end as I would wish'. There is ambivalence in the expressed hope which tells its own tale of 'hopes of New Succession / to free us frae oppress[ion] / & bring us Libertie'.[38]

Outside the convivial bounds of the Easy Club, Ramsay continued to mine a powerful vein of antiquarian vernacular nationalism, such as is found in 'The Vision', an early eighteenth-century example of mimic mediaevalism: Ramsay claimed it dated from 1300. As suits the period and Ramsay's purpose, the poem deals with the Wars of Independence; and Ramsay uses this struggle as an archetypical forerunner of Scotland's present political problems. 'The Vision' both proclaims the value of Scots and defines the essential Scottish political experience in a camouflaged form which enables Ramsay to 'throw a protective coloring over his bold criticism of the parliamentary Union of 1707' (Maclaine, *Allan Ramsay*, p. 104).

The poem itself is a pastiche dream-vision, where a wanderer falls asleep, and wakes to a vision of 'Scotland's Guardian Spirit'. This 'Spirit' gives a thinly veiled rendition of the Highlander as patriot image of Scotland's struggle:

> To hills and glens I me betuke,
>    To them that luves my richt;
>       Quhase mynds yet inclynds yet
>    To damm the rappid spate,
>       Devysing and prysing
>    Freidom at ony rate.

The 'prysing' of 'Freidom' which the Guardian Spirit attributes to those who live in 'hills and glens' is opposed to 'Our trechour peers': a standard Jacobite opposition of Highland poverty, simplicity and bravery to the arcane (and well-bribed) political manipulations of the Lowland establishment. Later it is made explicit that it is 'ilk clan / Thats to their nation trew': patriotism is the property of the Highlanders or those who sympathize with them. The Spirit foretells that hope can come to Scotland

> Quhen Scottish peirs slicht Saxon gold,
>    And turn trew heartit men;
>       Quhen knaivry and slaivrie,

[38] Law, 'Allan Ramsay', pp. 33, 38, 38–39; *The Works of Allan Ramsay*, III: pp. 152, 196.

> Ar equally sispysed,
> And loyaltie and royaltie,
> Universalie are prysed.

The struggle of the Wars of Independence, in other words, foreshadows
that over the Stuarts and Union. Reference to 'Saxon gold' evokes the
language of anti-Union mythology, while the contrasting opposition of
'loyaltie and royaltie' suggests pro-Jacobite feeling.[39]

At the close of the vision, the Spirit is recalled by a 'fair etherial dame'
to a Council where 'sum grit thing is desygned':

> 'Owre mountains be fountains,
> And round ilk fairy ring,
> I haif chast ye, O haist ye,
> They talk about your king'.

The returning king motif is taken up in the scenery which surrounds the
wanderer when awakes, that of returning spring:

> For Flora in her clene array,
> New washen with a showir of May,
>   Lukit full sweit and fair;
> Quhyle hir cleir husband frae aboif
> Sched down his rayis of genial luve,
>   Hir sweits perfumt the air;
> The winds were husht, the welkin cleird,
> The glumand clouds war fled . . .

Just as 'The Vision' seems to presage success in the Wars of Independence,
so it seems also to prophesy returning fertility to Scotland in a restoration
of political autonomy, surely linked to the may-king's restoration to the
sun of majesty. In such a context it is no surprise that the Spirit itself is
envisioned in the accoutrements of Jacobite patriotism: 'A Braid-sword
shegled at his Thie, / On his left Arm a Targe'.[40]

'The Vision' first appeared in Ramsay's two-volume collection of mediaeval Scots poems from the Bannatyne Manuscript: *The Ever Green*,
published in 1724. In the Preface, Ramsay writes in support of Scots:
'There is nothing can be heard more silly than one's expressing his
*Ignorance* of his *native Language*', and to this sentiment Ramsay was to a
degree faithful in both the high cultural poetry reconditioned here and the
Scots songs he chose elsewhere.[41]

In these, Ramsay frequently skirts well-known Jacobite material, using
songs of the time popular with Jacobite sets which he bowdlerizes (e.g.
'This is No my Ain house' and 'Auld Lang Sine'). But Ramsay's cultural

---

[39] *Poems by Allan Ramsay and Robert Fergusson*, pp. 35ff.     [40] Ibid.
[41] Ibid., p. x.

and political exchange with Jacobitism was a two-way process, for songs
like 'Lochaber No More' and 'For the Sake of Somebody' may have been
adopted by the Jacobites through Ramsay's versions of them (if indeed
they were not already in use), while 'O'er the Moor to MAGGY' may later
have transmuted itself into 'Over the Water to Charlie'.[42]

The Highlandization of Scottish identity, so typical of Jacobite propaganda, is prevalent to a marked degree in Ramsay, whose version of the
'Highland Laddie' (Ramsay II, p. 81) gels with the whole cycle of Jacobite
songs bearing this label. 'Tartana, or the Plaid', mentioned above, gives
'Precedence to Antiquity' in speaking of the Plaid as a universally Scottish
garment, a patriotic image fit for the use of any '*Caledonian* Beauties'.
Indeed

> We'll find our Godlike Fathers nobly scorn'd
> To be with any other Dress adorn'd ...

The subsequent decline from this unity of purpose is a sign of a diminishing store of true patriotic Scottishness. 'Tartana' is apparently a poem
written in defence of the national dress: but in choosing a dress worn not
by the nation as a whole but by its most disaffected part, Ramsay offers a
suggestive political message, hardly compromised by his nods in the
direction of anti-French feeling:

> With such brave Troops one might o'er *Europe* run,
> Make out what *Richlieu* fram'd, and Lewis had begun.

Since this passage follows the observation that 'foreign Chains with foreign
Modes take Place', it can be argued that Ramsay is offering the politicized
reader a delicate and witty choice between 'foreign' as referring to France
or England, before damping down the possibility of seditious reading with
a jingoistic couplet on the former. The poem itself ends with an ambivalent though decisive political message:

> I'll prove the Moral is prodigious strong:
> I hate to trifle, Men should act like Men,
> And for their Country only draw their Sword and Pen.

Those who wear the acclaimed tartan should be patriotic in their defence
of it. How they should best defend it is a matter for the reader to decide,
but a 'prodigious strong' hint is given by the 'Pen' which has written a
poem about those whose 'Sword' has so recently shaken the British state
('Tartana' was first published in 1721) (Ramsay, I, pp. 27–30).

If Ramsay makes use of the image of Highlander as patriot, he also
seems alert to the Jacobite topos of retreat, giving a codified account of the
significance of pastoral made manifest in his famous play *The Gentle*

[42] Maclaine, *Allan Ramsay*, p. 95; *The Works of Allan Ramsay*, I: p. 169.

*Shepherd,* which first appeared in 1725. Performed as a ballad-opera in 1729 (apparently at the request of the pupils of Haddington Grammar School who had seen and liked Gay's *Beggar's Opera*) *The Gentle Shepherd* praises pastoral withdrawal and speaks of the restoration of a true order, in the shape of Sir William, a knight who has been exiled after fighting for Charles I. The language used about Sir William is frequently applicable to a current Stuart exile of rather higher social station. In Act II scene i, where the subject of Sir William's return first appears, Symon the old shepherd says:

> Seeing's believing, Glaud, and I have seen
> Hab, that abroad has with our Master been;
> Our brave good Master, wha right wisely fled,
> And left a fair estate, to save his head:
> Because ye ken fou well he bravely chose
> To stand his liege's friend with great Montrose ...

All are full of praise for their 'Master': Symon goes on to say 'And good Sir William sall enjoy his ain', while claiming that his enemies 'dare nae mair do't again', a phrase which echoes the Jacobite drinking-song 'Here's to the King, Sir'.[43]

The return of Sir William and restoration of King Charles are hardly distinguished in the drama. In Act II scene iii, Mause, whom the ignorant think a witch, sings

> 'Peggy, now the King's come,
>    Peggy, now the King's come;
> Thou may dance, and I shall sing,
>    Peggy, since the King's come.'

Shortly afterwards Sir William appears in disguise, a common dramatic trick admittedly, but also a practice associated with both James V and Charles II. The knight is *'the loyal sufferer'*, who gives a long soliloquy in praise of retreat:

> Thrice happy life! that's from ambition free;
> Remov'd from crowns and courts, how chearfully
> A quiet contented mortal spends his time ...

Of course, this speech indicates that restoration of the crown and Sir William is nigh. The country gentleman is restored, abandoning his disguise, and the play moves to comic fulfilment:

> God save the King, and save Sir William long,
> To enjoy their ain, and raise the shepherd's song.
>                                         (v: iii: lines 170–1)

---

[43] *Poems by Allan Ramsay and Robert Fergusson,* pp. xxx, 54–5, 58, 66, 102.

The conflation of Sir William's restoration with the return of royal and national order (significantly the king is called 'The Lyon', a specifically Scottish title), liberates the pastoral for comic fulfilment, just as it liberates Scotland. The Jacobite notes in *The Gentle Shepherd* are sounded in a minor key: but the play makes it clear that only the return of Scotland's legitimate king can restore order, release possibility, and confirm the *status quo ante* so necessary to the timeless ideology of pastoral. Ramsay plays on the sentiments he knows a part of his audience may share.[44]

Ramsay the man was in most respects as politically careful as Ramsay the writer, his only major recorded indiscretion being a visit to the young Charles Edward Stuart in 1736 (McLynn, *Charles Edward Stuart*, p. 47). Ramsay had nothing to do with the military side of either the 'Fifteen or the 'Forty-five: but he drew his pen for his country, offering posterity a defence of Scots as a patriotic language. Albeit his defence was a conditional one, Ramsay nonetheless recovered, reanimated and renewed both demotic and upper-register Scots as nationalist expressions of resistance to metropolitan demand, a recentring of the margin to evade the core's control. Nor was Ramsay behindhand in his commitment to the Scoto-Latin ethos: though lacking education himself, his Scotticizing of Horace (as in 'Horace to Virgil, On his Taking a Voyage to Athens'), and the trouble he took to nourish the classical ethos in his son, suggest an interest parallel to that displayed by upper-class Jacobite Episcopalian culture.[45]

But chiefly Ramsay helped to initiate, not just on the level of political propaganda, but in the heart of the canon itself, a politico-cultural centripetalism, whose language and mores commenced the defence of a specifically Scottish literature at its hour of greatest danger. It is this Ramsay who is echoed in the Fergusson who both wants to write an epic of William Wallace and to defend Scots traditional music against classical influences. Writing in Scots, Fergusson aligns musical and military decline, again using the image of Highlander as patriot:

> At gloamin', now, the bagpipe's dumb,
> Whan weary owsen hameward come,
> Sae sweetly as it wont to bum,
> An' pibrochs skreed;
> We never hear its warlike hum;
> For Music's dead.

Fergusson's Latinizing of Edinburgh and Scotland as 'Edina' and 'Scotia' goes hand in hand with a rough, folk-oriented voice. Both are in tune with his 'North-east Episcopal outlook', and either gives the same political

---

[44] Ibid., p. 71.
[45] *Poems by Allan Ramsay and Robert Fergusson*, p. 28; Iain Gordon Brown, *Poet and Painter: Allan Ramsay, Father and Son* (Edinburgh: National Library of Scotland, 1984), p. 47.

message, whether in the guise of 'Black was the day, and cursed be the ground / Scotland was eikit to the Union's bond', or in Fergusson's lament for William Hamilton of Bangour, another high cultural Jacobite ideologue with Scoto-Roman leanings. But it is 'Elegy on the Death of Scots Music', quoted above, which reveals how deeply defence of the folk has already become embedded in a specifically Scottish literary canon:

> *Fidlers*, your pins in temper fix,
> And roset weel your fiddle-sticks,
> And banish vile Italian tricks
>   From out your quorum,
> Nor *fortes* wi' *pianos* mix,
>   Gie's *Tulloch Gorum*.

In the battle between traditional airs and the classical music becoming fashionable among the urban polite middle-class, Fergusson is on the side of the people. Being on their side is also being on the side of the past, an idealized nation and its idealized capital:

If in so many of the town poems Auld Reikie is equated with order and tranquility, purity and health, fair weather or indoor warmth, modern Edinburgh is its antithesis: counterpastoral ... Modern Whig Edinburgh, in the rhetoric of Mackenzie of Rosehaugh, Colvil, Pitcairne and William Meston, the new Babylon ...

In this mode, Fergusson's writing allies a defence of Scottish people and custom to 'the tradition of Episcopal religious satire'.[46]

Like Ruddiman before him and the family of Burns who followed him, Fergusson came from the North East, heart of Scoto-Latinity and the richest area for folksong in Scotland. Fergusson's own circle seem to have been responsible for the publication of a late and perforce anonymous Jacobite songbook, the *True Loyalist* of 1779.[47] There is no contradiction in eighteenth-century Jacobite patriotism between the defence of the Scoto-Roman ethos and the vernacular revival. After all, had they not been joined in the greatest period in Scotland's literature, when Bishop Douglas had translated the *Aeneid* into Scots as a patriotic gesture, and when the aureate verse of Dunbar had Scotticized the Latin tongue itself?

The Scoto-Roman ethos and the vernacular revival together laid the foundations for Scottish literature to continue, and marked it with a mythopoeic absorption in the past and a strong attachment to the validity

---

46 *The Works of Robert Fergusson* (Edinburgh, 1805), p. 136; Daiches, *Robert Fergusson*, pp. 4, 41; F. W. Freeman, 'Robert Fergusson: Pastoral and Politics at Mid-Century', in Andrew Hook (ed.), *The History of Scottish Literature*, volume 2 (4 vols., gen. ed. Cairns Craig) (Aberdeen: Aberdeen University Press, 1987), pp. 141–56 (142, 148, 149); *The Oxford Book of Scottish Verse*, ed. John MacQueen and Tom Scott (Oxford: Clarendon Press, 1966), p. 358.

47 *The True Loyalist* (n.p., 1779).

of folk culture. When, in Scott's *Antiquary*, Edie Ochiltree the gaberlunzie man mocks Oldbuck's amateurish classical scholarship, it is the friendly voice of a folk culture in dialogue with the education of a squirearchy from which in England it would have been as alienated as Caleb Williams himself.[48]

## The year of the Prince

He, that undismai'd durst land
    With Seven under his Command,
Resolv'd to rescue nations three
    That's the man shall govern me.
        Govern me &c.

Fierce as a Lion, unconfin'd
As an angel, soft & kind,
Merciful & just is he:
Glorious Charles shall govern me.
        Govern me, Govern me &c

'Song. Tune the Amazon'

He comes He comes
    The Hero comes
Sound Sound your Trumpets
    Beat Beat your Drums
From Port to Port, let Cannons Roar
His Welcome to the British Shore
    Welcome Welcome Welcome
His Welcome to the British Shore.

'An Anthem on the Prince's Landing in 1745'

Wha wadna fecht for Charlie
Wha wadna draw the sword
Wha wadna up and rally
At the royal prince's word.

Think on Scotia's ancient heroes
Think on foreign foes repelled
Think on glorious Bruce and Wallace
Wha the proud usurpers quelled.

Buchan song

---

[48] Sir Walter Scott, *The Antiquary*, ed. Andrew Lang. The Border Scott, 2 vols. (London: J. C. Nimmo, 1893).

'Watchman, what do you see?'
'I see An Udairn and Rubha Huinis,
Caolas Ronaidh with mist obscuring it.'
'Do you see the galley beside the Dun,
flying the white banner of Charles Stewart?
Mary Mother, may grace be doubled for him,
a price on his head and the enemy hounding him,
may the French host come over and help him!'

> Gaelic waulking-song

Fare-well Manchester, bonnie Charlie's calling me,
  I must haste away for my King to be . . .
I fall in war none be sore for my death
  I'll be true with my last breath to Manchester.

> Reputedly marching-song of the Manchester Regiment[49]

The Jacobite machinations of the early 1740s led to a fresh upsurge of popular literature. On the Prince's landing in Scotland in 1745, these outpourings grew to a flood. The royal forces, rapidly building on their initial success, soon controlled more territory than in any previous rising. As a result, Jacobite material not only circulated widely in their wake, but was also printed in the towns they controlled, and not only in broadside form, but in books such as *A Full Collection of All Poems upon Charles, Prince of Wales* (Edinburgh, 1745):

> Hail Glorious Youth! the Wonder of the Age,
>   The future Subject of th'Historian's Page;
> Oh best of PRINCES! best of PATRIOTS . . .

Such active Jacobite poems frequently took on the guise of personal praise and welcome of the young prince, who clearly inspired more directly passionate feeling than his father had done. The ideological intimacy of previous Jacobite propaganda transforms itself from design to impulse in celebrating the young and daring hero. Charles's own adoption of the guise of a patriot Highlander, his attempts to learn Gaelic and his decision to march with his men all intensified this feeling, as well as binding it closely to nationalism:

> Expect the PRINCE to his native Shore;
> When Lord and Laird falls in one,
> That Year the PRINCE shall gain his Throne.
> Then *Scotland* rejoice, from Bondage you're free,
> You're a Nation again, and ever shall be.

[49] NLS MS 2910 13v, 20r; Hogg, *Relics*, ii: p. 100; cited in William Gillies, 'The Prince and the Gaels', in Lesley Scott-Moncrieff (ed.), *The '45: To Gather an Image Whole* (Edinburgh, 1988),

Sometimes the fertility imagery attached to the Stuart cause is used to suggest a complete Messianic renewal linked to the restored independence of Scotland, almost as if it were an Israel restored to favour from the pages of Isaiah:

> All Beasts that go upon all Four
> Go leap and dance around;
> Because that the curst Union's broke,
> And fallen to the Ground.[50]

'The messianic nature of the Prince's appeal' was thus almost instantaneous, born out of his youth, the daring quality of his arrival, the propaganda and expectation already surrounding him and his assiduous cultivation of a patriot image, evident from his early insistence that 'I have come home'. Charles's cause and personality also stood to receive a boost from within the ranks of his army, where a significant number of Jacobite poets served. The most high-ranking of these was Alexander Robertson of Struan, Colonel in the Atholl Brigade and by courtesy Major-General; others included John Roy Stewart, Colonel of the Edinburgh Regiment, William Hamilton of Bangour, gentleman-volunteer and perhaps later Captain in Lord Elcho's troop of Lifeguards, Captain David Morgan of the Manchester Regiment and Captain Alexander MacDonald of Clanranald's Regiment, the Prince's Gaelic tutor. I shall be examining their poetry later in this section.[51]

Charles's wearing of Highland dress may have been responsible for the spate of 'Highland Laddie' poems which accompanied and outlasted his campaign. These lyrics, drawing as they do on the image of the patriotic male Highlander liberating and fertilizing a feminized Scotland, represent Charles as an integrated Gael, absorbed into the typology of his cause's own propaganda:

> Where ha'e ye been a' the day,
> Bonie laddie? Hieland laddie?
> Saw ye him that's far away,
> Bonnie laddie, Hieland laddie.
> On his head a bonnet blue,
> Bonnie laddie, Hieland laddie;
> Tartan plaid and Hieland trews,
> Bonnie laddie, Hieland laddie?

pp. 53–72 (70); William Harrison Ainsworth, *The Manchester Rebels* (Bury: Printwise, 1992 (1873)), p. 384.

50  *A Full Collection of All Poems upon Charles, Prince of Wales* (Edinburgh, 1745), p. 3; *Jacobite Songs* (n.d.), p. 8.

51  Hugh Douglas-Hamilton, 'The Titular Charles III and the Stewart Crown of Scotland', in Scott-Moncrieff, *The '45*, pp. 14–22 (19); Charles Edward Stuart exhibition, Museum of National Antiquities, Queen Street, Edinburgh, 1988.

This is a set presumably written after Charles's defeat; the anonymity of its subject acting as a useful camouflage to prevent the singer being technically guilty on a 'seditious words' or similar charge. On one level, though, Charles's very anonymity is a product of his absorption into the 'Bonnie Highland Laddie' cycle itself: henceforth he *is* the Highland Laddie. A subgenre originally dealing with sexual encounters between young people of divergent cultural backgrounds has become a political manifesto of royal and national identity. Such a takeover of a traditional format is yet another indicator of the 'mediated text' process, whereby high culture speaks in the folk voice in the cause of an outlaws' alliance. At the limits of this process, Charles almost becomes a supernatural figure detached from a political agenda:

> Up the airy mountain, down the rushy glen
> We daren't go a-hunting for Charlie and his men.[52]

This almost magical quality was on one level the desiderated correlative to the euphoria which greeted the prince's arrival. In Gaelic poetry in particular, the Jacobite leader embodies the heroic virtues of a super-naturalist past:

> The Prince will be crowned in triumph
> in the White House where the heroes dwell ...
> Barra waulking-song

This idealizing tendency, especially marked in Irish poetry, was also present in more conventional high cultural English language verse, though the heroic image of Charles could be vitiated by tonal lapses when it came to describing his enemies:

> An Angel Prince in person & in deed
> A Valiant Hero in highland weed
> His goodness will immortalize his name
> His glorious acts will sound his endless fame
> A Health to Charles our Princely Hero
> And to all his Royall Scots
> Who will kik[sic] off George our Nero
> With all his turks and German Sots ...

In less uncontrolled outbursts, Charles was identified as Ascanius, the son of Aeneas, or as 'Alexis', a coded reference which carried overtones of identity with both Aeneas and Alexander the Great.[53]

Despite inevitable differences of emphasis, one of the most powerful impressions given by Scots, Gaelic and English poetry of the time is the

---

[52] *Scottish Songs*, p. 258; F. W. Robertson, *The Scottish Way 1746–1946* (Rothesay, 1946), p. 25; Hogg, *Relics* I: p. 93.
[53] Gillies, 'The Prince and the Gaels', p. 61; Pittock, 'New Jacobite Songs', p. 28; AUL MS 2222.

similarity of Jacobite ideology across social and linguistic barriers. In the
era of the 'Forty-five,

Gaelic political mythology clung to the ancient notion that the just king's reign
was accompanied by plenitude and fine weather, while storms and poverty were
signs of something rotten in the state.

Such views (similar as they are to Lowland and Irish Jacobite ideology),
must have made a powerful appeal in the famine years of 1744–6. The
attribution of supernatural virtues to the Jacobite leader, and his use of
these virtues as a motor for liberation and plenty was the typological
fulfilment of such mythology, predicated of the Prince with great eagerness. This process is expressed in the Gaelic verse of Capt. Alexander
MacDonald (Alasdair MacMhaigstir Alasdair), who 'found a way to fuse
together his vision of the Stuarts, of Gaeldom, and of an ideal Scotland' as
well as in Lowland poetry in the vernacular:

> We daurna brew a peck o' maut
> But Geordie he maun ca't a faut,
> And to our kail we scarce get saut,
> For want o' royal Charlie.[54]

The combination of awe ('An Angel Prince') with intimacy ('royal
Charlie', 'Jamie the Rover'), characteristic of Jacobite verse in Scots is
found also in Gaelic poetry, where Charles after Culloden 'was no abstract
symbol of kingship ... but the more homely "Tearlach Ruadh"', a
companion in the sufferings of the Gael. Combined intimacy and aloofness
served to make the returning Astraea of godlike Charles a figure even more
intensely Christlike than his father (at least in propaganda terms). Charles
was both the glorious supernaturalist hero and the incarnate poor un-
clothed suffering Gael: a symbol of an ideal Scotland, and a paradigm of
the suffering reality. Both messiah and man of sorrows, the double dimension of Charles's campaign in reality as well as in propaganda no doubt
charged it with much of the appeal it still possesses. When Alexander,
Lord Forbes of Pitsligo, General of Horse in the royal army, wrote his
apologia for joining the Rising, he said that he could not rid his mind of
the phrase 'This is the heir. Let us kill him' used by Christ of Himself. In
such a guise, Charles renewed the strength of his father's cause. In the
words of Alexander MacDonald:

> The health of King James Stewart,
>   Full gladly pass it roun d!
> But if within you fault is hidden
>   Soil not the holy cup.

---

[54] Gillies, 'The Prince and the Gaels', p. 55; John Simpson, 'The Causes of the '45', in Scott-
Moncrieff (ed.), *The '45*, pp. 1–13 (12); Hogg, *Relics*, II, p. 144.

The health of Charles's father's cause is directly compared to the Eucharist, while Charles himself is the Jesus longed for by the Jacobite saint in the dark night of the Unclothing Act:

> O come, beloved, lest we faint,
>     Before our courage sinks through fear;
> As long as hearts are in our breasts
>     We're thine, beloved, far and near.

In 'A Song to the Prince', MacDonald sees Charles as an apocalyptic figure, returning to implement a day of judgement:

> Like the storms of March his aspect,
>     'Dog-toothed' through the beating rain;
> Sharp blade in his hand for slaughter,
>     Corpses hewn like autumn grain.
>
> In that day the man is fated,
>     Who an ugly red-coat wears;
> His black hat, broad-brimmed, cockaded,
>     Split like a cabbage round his ears.

Such will be the fate of unbelievers, but in 'Oran Mu Bhliadhna Thearlaich' ('A Song About the Year of Charles'), MacDonald emphasizes the reward of the faithful:

> With the King will come bright days,
> Frost and snow shall flee from us,
> Tempestuous skies he'll banish,
> With joy our pain shall vanish . . .

The origin-myths of the Scottish crown and their celebration by seannachies are recalled in MacDonald's praise of Charles as that 'Dear visage most royal, / From Banquo's proud lineage', while reference is made to James's birth on 'the tenth / Of June, that month of gold', in language which recalls the *renovatio* of Astraea. This, and the plea to 'Lead us from greedy Egypt here / To Canaan's promised country', display a common typology with Anglophonic Jacobite high culture, while warnings to the Campbells of the consequences to them of benefiting from the financial revolution show similar awareness of the universal language of Jacobite dissent:

> To abandon your King and your country for treasure,
> To sell for a bribe your own souls to the demons,
>     'Twas a sacrifice vile, though attractive the gain.
> May you meet the same fate as overcame Judas . . .[55]

---

[55] Gillies, 'The Prince and the Gaels', p. 69; John Lorne Campbell, *Highland Songs of the 'Forty-Five* (Edinburgh: Edinburgh University Press, 1933), pp. 59, 73, 115; *The Poems of Alexander MacDonald*, ed. Revd A. MacDonald and Revd Dr A. MacDonald (Inverness, 1924), pp. 69, 97, 118–19, 161, 321.

In 'Oran Araid', the Prince and the Gaels are shown in dialogue, with Charles promising that 'I myself your wounds will bind'. Alexander MacDonald knew the Prince well, and his idealizations are not simply those of remote valorization. As well as writing poetry which portrays Charles as a supernatural hero, MacDonald also produced erotic Jacobite songs such as 'A Waulking Song', where the Prince appears as a woman:

> O graceful Morag of the ringlets
> To sing thy praise is my intention.

In 'The Proud Plaid', erotic affection for the Prince is passionately expressed in terms which carry sacred overtones:

> Though you tear our hearts out,
>     And rend apart our bosoms,
> Never shall you take Prince Charles
> From us, till we're a-dying.
>     John Lorne Campbell, *Highland Songs of the 'Forty-five*,
>                                     pp. 89, 145, 159

Such intensity of sentiment is echoed by other Gaelic poets of the Rising, such as Rob Donn Mackay, who speaks of the star at Charles's birth as hitherto

> The sign that marked our Lord alone –
>     Ere Charles came to this country here –
> When went the men of wisdom great
>     To seek Him in Jerusalem.
>
> But now, O Prince Charles Stewart, if
>     King George's crown were on thy head
> We'd have a numerous company
>     Of courtiers wearing gowns and robes!

Charles's courtiers parallel the Magi; he is both the restored David and the messianic hope of Rob Donn's vision (Campbell, *Highland Songs*, p. 235).

Colonel John Roy Stewart's verse on 'Culloden Day' levels Christ's curse on the fig tree (Matthew 21: 19, Mark 11: 13) at an England which has caused so much rapine and grief to Scotland:

> Woe is me for the land where you've entered
>     You have now left it swept flat and bare,
> Without oats or crops standing,
>     Without choice seed in desert or ground;
> You've taken the hens from the henroosts,
>     Even our spoons you have stol'n –
> But the curse of the fig-tree be on you
>     Withered from bottom to top.

Here traditional Scottish Jacobite imagery of invaded domesticity is joined to the cosmic issues raised by the renewing power of the sacred king which his opponents have defied. Charles's reputation remained very high in Gaelic poetry written after the end of the Rising, and indeed even in poetry written by Gaels on the Hanoverian side during it, such as Duncan Ban MacIntyre who writes of those 'Who had come to win the kingdom / For their King and for the right cause', though he fought for the government at Falkirk! (Campbell, *Highland Songs*, pp. 175, 209). It is unlikely that MacIntyre was alone: the MacLeods raised Independent Companies with the white cockade to persuade recruits that they were to fight for the Prince when the opposite was the chiefs' intention.[56]

The degree of popularity Charles may have had among the common people on both sides of the Highland Line is further reflected in the early sets of songs such as 'Charlie is My Darling', which was conflated with the 'Highland Laddie' cycle:

> 'But when she came to Aberdeen
> this bony lowland lass,
> There she found her true love
> was going to Inverness.

Chorus

> 'And Charly is my darling,
> my darling, my darling,
> And Charlie he's my darling,
> the young Chevalier.
> earliest printed broadside version known (1775/6)

The popular song was also given to self-reflexively celebrate its own popularity, as in 'The Piper o' Dundee':

> He play'd 'The Welcome owre the Main',
> And, 'Ye'se be fou and I'se be fain',
> And 'Auld Stuarts back again',
> Wi' muckle mirth and glee . . .
>
> He play'd 'The Kirk', he play'd 'The Queer',
> 'The Mullin Dhu', and 'Chevalier' . . .

The piper's 'muckle mirth and glee' draws attention to the fact that these airs on their own could not be treasonable, but that he knew full well his audience could silently supply the sets to them which were. As to the 'folk' status of such songs, David Buchan has pointed out that the eighteenth century was a period when a writer might see work appear in three

---

[56] Jean G. McCann, 'The Organisation of the Jacobite Army 1745–46', unpublished Ph.D. thesis (Edinburgh, 1963), p. 14.

registers: book, broadside and in oral transmission. The success of the mediated text, dependent as it was to an extent on this cultural fluidity, seems to have been reaching a peak at the time of the 'Forty-five and its aftermath. As William Gillies says of Gaelic Jacobite poetry 'the vast majority of the poems ... have been preserved at some stage by oral transmission'. This was to be particularly pertinent in the case of Macpherson's use of the Ossian cycle for the purposes of a surreptitious Jacobite reading of the past, as will be discussed in the next section.[57]

Those poets who accompanied the Rising expressed in little the consistency of the Jacobite theme across social and linguistic boundaries. Robertson of Struan was an old man in 1745, having his poetic roots in the seventeenth century. But to some extent his imitation of the Cavalier mode may have been as much an ideological decision as an accident of his years. Poems like 'The Transport' seem to echo Carew:

> Immortal Gods alone can tell
> How we embrac'd, how oft, how well:
> How melting Tongues, Love's lesser Darts,
> Convey'd the Dictates of our Hearts!

Though speaking this familiar tongue Struan is little more than a versifier, when he turns his attention to the central political vision of his life what he says is of interest: the chief's outlook on Scotland's future expressed in the language of an English writer. The gulf between Struan's speech and concerns is vividly shown in the manner in which he can refer to Highlanders in his patriotic poetry, despite being one himself:

> No more we'll hear the noble Savage moan
> But see him scour the Fields were heretofore his own.

At other times, this remoteness of tone can collapse into much readier identification with his subject:

> Can poor Low-Country Water-Rats,
> Withstand our furious Mountain-Cats ...

Here Struan stands alongside those to whom he belonged and elsewhere patronized, in the common fight 'To shake off UNION's Slav'ry'.[58]

In this alteration of the gap between rhetoric and subject, Struan can make use of the traditional Highland flyting format in order to express the diction of English drinking-songs, as in 'ST—N, to his Brother DUNCAN

---

[57] T. F. Henderson, '"Charlie he's My Darling" and other Burns' Originals', *Scottish Historical Review* III: 10 (January 1906), pp. 171–8; Hogg, *Relics*, II: p. 43; David Buchan, *The Ballad and the Folk* (London: Routledge and Kegan Paul, 1972), p. 272 (cf. also *Scottish Tradition: A Collection of Scottish Folk Literature* (London: Routledge and Kegan Paul, 1984), p. 7; Gillies, 'The Prince and the Gaels', p. 60.

[58] Alexander Robertson of Struan, *Poems* (Edinburgh, 1749), pp. 29, 33, 48, 49.

VOIR, over a Bottle' (a poem which Germanically describes the High-lander as a 'GOTH'), or can introduce a note of broadside scurrility into pastoral:

> Thus parted CORYDON with her,
>   To whom he once was Cully;
> And to old JAMIE's does prefer
>   A Mode brought in by WILLY.

The fertility promised by the returning triumph of Jacobite pastoral has been temporarily abrogated by the homosexual interlude of William's usurpation. The pastoral form reflects ironically on its subject, and this point is driven home in another poem:

> JAMES was but ill depos'd, whose fruitful Cods,
> Scatter'd a generous Race of Demi-Gods,
> While t'other unperforming privy Prig,
> Could only with his Page retire and fr –.
>                     Struan, *Poems*, pp. 57, 83–4

In some of his verse, Struan is closer to Rochester than Carew; while he echoes Dryden not only in 'The Hind and the Leopard' but also in 'The Consolation. An Eclogue', which draws on the typology of 'The Lady's Song':

> When honest PAN withdrew from factious State
> (Curs'd was the Hour, and fatal was the Date)
> When virtuous SYRINX, vilest Rage to Shun,
> Fled to preserve herself and infant Son,
> Then our unguarded Flocks became the Prey
> Of rav'nous Wolves, and Men more Wolves than they ...

Elsewhere, Struan uses the voices of sacred and erotic Jacobite poetry to convey a message more direct than that of irony and typology, as in 'BRITANNIA, to her BELOVED in *Spain*':

> THOU, JAMES of my Heart!
>   Who art ne'er in the Wrong,
> Why dost thou not part?
>   I have mourn'd for thee long ...
>
> Come, our Church to restore,
>   And quell, with thy Rod,
> Those who nothing adore
>   But Gold for a God.

This kind of Jacobite song diction is modified by the more formal Struan voice in poems such as 'An Ode to the Duke of Berwick', 'Epitaph upon the Captain of Clanranald' or 'To the learned and ingenious Doctor

Pitcairn'. Struan also writes beast-fables and Jacobite psalms, imitations of
Horace and a translation of *Aeneid* v: a wide range of voices with a central
sentiment (Struan, *Poems*, pp. 26–7, 89, 120, 123, 128, 131, 188, 224, 228,
301–44).

'Struan's Farewell to the Hermitage' combines the imagery of retreat
poetry with a destabilizing voice which violates the peaceful ambience of
the retreat, turning it into a nightmare of violence, suggestive of the loss of
the Highlands (Struan lived in a very remote area) as a safe haven from
Hanoverian power:

> Lo! while the furious Horsemen prance,
>     Poor Peasants gasp beneath their Feet:
> Yet Cruelty sits smiling on their Cheeks,
> To hear the Orphan's Cries and Widow's Shrieks.

The aftermath of Culloden and the Clearances themselves seem presaged
in such lines:

> A barb'rous unrelenting Throng,
>     Cut down your Bow'rs with ev'ry Tree,
> Revenging your melodious Song,
>     Meerly because you sung for me.

'My spotless Cell' has become 'a Den of Thieves': 'Farewell my sweet, my
innocent Retreat' exclaims Struan in a poem which violates expectations
of the blissful security of retreat, as well as foreshadowing the nostalgic
poetry of exile which came after (Struan, *Poems*, pp. 242–6). Military
defeat has made the retreat itself unsafe, there is no metaphor to hide in:
Scotland is barren, as is cleverly pointed out in 'Advice to a Painter', with
its high cultural form encompassing popular Jacobite imagery, the artistic
expression of everyday deprivation:

> Limner, would you expose ALBANIA's Fate,
> Draw thou a Palace in a ruin'd State,
> Nettles and Briers instead of fragrant Flow'rs,
> Sleet, Hail and Snow instead of gentle Show'rs,
> Instead of Plenty all Things meagre look,
> And into swords turn Plough-Iron, Scythe and Hook.

Messianic prophecy is wittily reversed: having left Scotland barren, the
Anti-Christ of Hanover can only expect that farm implements will be
turned into weapons, as there is nothing else left to use them for. Yet this
image of putative resistance serves only to confirm barrenness, a barrenness paralleled exactly in the sufferings of the king:

> Then sacred JAMES, let not thy Lot,
>     Tho' seemingly severe,
> Make thee suspect thy Cause forgot,
>     Thy Crosses nobly bear . . .

Without this exiled messiah, the suffering land cannot be at peace. Struan combines Horatian retreat and Judaeo-Christian allegory: James is Pan is also David: 'confounded be their vile Intent / Who DAVID's Life pursue' (fittingly for Struan's art, this occurs in a drinking-song). Yet a strong element of pagan fertility-imagery naturalizes the messianic king, in the interests perhaps of uniting caesaropapist Episcopalianism with ancient associations of the fertile renewal of good kings, as in 'On the Approach of the 29th of MAY, A HYMN' or 'To Strephon':

> The graceful Oak, that long has stood
> The Glory of the humbler Wood,
> In Time we'll feel the fatal Knife,
> And fall with Shrubs of shorter Life . . .

Such a fate can only be avoided by the 'providential Spring' of Struan's 'Holy Ode' (Struan, *Poems*, pp. 127, 140, 231, 233, 234, 291).

The co-existence of the classical and Christian ideals in Struan's work is not unusual in Jacobite ideology, as we have seen: but Struan presents this thematic alliance of antiquity and sacramentalism in a distinct way. He plays with the forms his education inherits, in order to join both wit and seriousness in an attack on what for him was a lifelong wrong to be put right:

> Tenacious of his Faith, to aid the cause
> Of Heaven's Anointed, and his Country's Laws,
> Thrice he engaged, and thrice, with STUART's Race,
> He fail'd; but ne'er comply'd with foul Disgrace . . .
>
> There's nothing dignifies so much this Dust,
> As that, like God, he aim'd at being just.
> 'Epitaph on himself', Struan, *Poems*, pp. 299–300.

William Hamilton of Bangour was another Jacobite by conviction who served in the Prince's army. Like Struan and others, he combined the inheritance of a classical education with a sensitivity to his country's culture. Apparently an ideologically committed Jacobite from an early date, Hamilton's earliest verse is 'a translation in heroic couplets of the final third of Book x, the *Aeneid*, "the Episode of Lausus and Mezentius"'. This passage, with its study of Mezentius as a type of bad and tyrannical kingship to be replaced by Aeneas, was, it has been argued, favoured by Jacobite writers as a code of opposition to the post-1688 regime. While Hamilton continued in this classical vein (one of his works in exile was a translation of the first scene of Racine's *Mithridate* with Jacobite overtones), he was also alert to his own national tradition in folk and high cultural forms: indeed he mediates between the two in the interests of the Jacobite idea. Half of the poems Hamilton wrote between 1720 and 1730

presuppose a musical setting: poems like 'the Maid of Gallowshiels'
deliberately exploit 'ancient national culture' while making sly digs at
contemporary politics: 'the monarch's face' sits 'refulgent on the brass' of a
coin whose metal portrays George's fatness.[59]

Although Hamilton had a hand in the vernacular revival, he also
developed (as did those he knew, Ramsay and Ruddiman) the elite vision
of a Scottish identity inherited from the mediaeval court and developed by
James VII and II in the 1680s. Poems like 'The Episode of the Thistle'
praise the Order and its revival, singing nationalist compliments to
'godlike Wallace' and 'Great Bruce'. The Saxons or English are identified
as the common enemy, while St Andrew in the poem 'shrewdly anticipates
the unwelcome counsel bestowed [on Charles Edward Stuart] to settle for
the Scottish throne and desist from invasion of the southern kingdom'
(Bushnell, *William Hamilton of Bangour*, pp. 27–9, 45, 46, 49). The poem's
use of the Wars of Independence as an archetype for Scottish struggle was
widespread at the time, in works like William Hamilton of Gilbertfield's
*New Edition of the Life and Heroick Actions of the renown'd Sir William Wallace*
(1722) as well as Ramsay's 'A Vision', discussed in the previous section.
Subsequent changes to Hamilton of Bangour's poem made it even more
Jacobite.

Hamilton came from a family with strong Jacobite connexions (his sister
married the 6th Earl of Carnwath, a veteran of the 'Fifteen), and it was no
surprise when Hamilton himself visited Charles Edward in Rome in
1740/1, nor when he enlisted in Lord Elcho's Lifeguard troop on 17
September 1745. After Culloden, Hamilton may have been John Roy
Stewart's companion in flight. During the campaign and after, Hamilton
wrote some of his most outspoken Jacobite material, such as his superb
classicizing of Prestonpans ('Over GLADSMUIR's blood-stained field /
SCOTIA, imperial goddess, flew') and his 1747 imitation of Psalm 137,
ferociously nationalistic:

> If thee, *O Scotland*, I forget,
>     Even with my latest Breath;
> May foul Dishonour stain my Name,
>     And bring a Coward's Death ...
>
> Remember *England's* Children, Lord,
>     Who, on *Drumossie* Day,
> Deaf to the Voice of kindred Love
>     'Raze, raze it quite', did say.

Given the role of such infamous Scots as Major Lockhart after the battle,
Hamilton can only (surely?) be espousing a psychological definition of

[59] Nelson S. Bushnell, *William Hamilton of Bangour: Poet and Jacobite* (Aberdeen: Aberdeen
University Press, 1957), pp. xi, 10, 19, 20, 94.

nationality, like James Philp fifty years before. Despite his lament 'On Gallia's shore we sat and wept / When Scotland we thought on', Hamilton was able to return home in 1750, after three and a half years exile in Sweden.[60]

Others were not so lucky. Following the defeat of the Rising, Jacobite poetry of erotic loss becomes increasingly charged with the distress of exile, and its concomitant desires. Not only does the abandoned country long for its Prince; the exiled Scot longs for the country he has had to abandon, which itself becomes an imagined land of nostalgia:

> Hame, hame, hame, Oh, hame fain wad I be
> Hame, hame, hame, to my ain countrie!
> The green leaf o'loyaltie's beginning for to fa',
> The bonny white rose it is withering an' a',
> But I'll water't wi the blood o' usurping tyrannie,
> An' fresh it will blaw in my ain countrie.

Here landscape itself is jacobitized, exhibiting the priority of ideology over reality in the 'ain countrie', where remembered foliage and flowers are symbolic as much as recalled, and the metaphor of renewing fertility is explicitly metaphorical: as it should be in such an imagined realm.[61]

At the same time as exile produces a broadening of the erotic Jacobite subgenre, the active Jacobite song exhibits defiance or poignancy, as respectively in 'Hail Wallace' or 'Carlisle Yetts':

> My father's blood's in that flower tap,
>     My brother's in that harebell's blossom;
> This white rose was steeped in my luve's blood,
>     And I'll aye wear it in my bosom.

Though this poem deals with active reality rather than ideological desire, it displays the feminized speaker and imagery common in the latter: in such grief, we can discern the beginnings of sentimentality as the active song moves from masculinized liberating violence to feminized grief and nostalgia. The substitution of loss by desire was no longer so practical when the desire's fulfilment (the return of the Jacobite leader) had led to further loss. Only nostalgia could cauterize such a double wound, and in this direction the Jacobite song gently moved in the years following Culloden.[62]

The aftermath of the battle raised much contemporary indignation, even among Whig Scots like Smollett, whose 'The Tears of Scotland' ('Mourn, hapless Caledonia, Mourn!') was reprinted among Jacobite

[60] Ibid., pp. xi, 48–9, 63, 73, 83–4; Murray Pittock, 'New Jacobite Songs of the 'Forty-five', p. 58n; Bishop Robert Forbes, *The Lyon in Mourning*, ed. Henry Paton, Scottish Text Society, 3 vols. (Edinburgh: Edinburgh University Press, 1895), I: p. 228.

[61] *Songs of Scotland*, p. 150.        [62] AUL MS 2740/4/18/2; Hogg, *Relics*, II: p. 198.

songs in *Poems on Several Occasions* (1750). *The Book of the Lamentations of Charles the Son of James* (1746) illustrated the sense, which some seem to claim came considerably later, of a turning-point in Scotland's historical struggle for liberty:

> Thy freedom, Scotland! in one fatal hour
> Is sacrific'd, alas! to lawless pow'r.
> *The Lyon in Mourning*

In the face of such disappointment and defeat, there was an inevitable search for scapegoats, a favourite Jacobite hobby in any case (there were also counterbalancing martyrs, like Lord Balmerino). Lord George Murray, always distrusted by some among the Jacobite leaders was one, while a much more univocal candidate was Col. John Murray of Broughton, the Prince's Secretary, who turned King's Evidence to save his life:

> To all that virtues holy ties can boast
> To truth to Honour & to Mankind Lost
> How hast thou wandered from the sacred road
> The path of Honesty & the pole of God
> O fallen fallen from the High degree
> Of spotless fame & pure Integrity ...
> *For Mr S.M. [Secretary Murray] on his turning Evidence:*
> *Quantum mutatis ab illis*

This poem, widely circulated, was first published in 1747, the year of Lord Lovat's execution: he was the most distinguished Jacobite Murray had sent to execution. Murray's name appears many times subsequently as a leitmotif of betrayal, for example in the mock-lullaby 'Charlie Stuart', where the widowed Jacobite mother sings to her baby, reminding him of his duty in the struggle for liberty:

> 'On Darien think, on dowie Glenco,
>  'On Murray, traitor! coward!
> 'On Cumberland's blood-blushing hands,
>  'And think on Charlie Stuart.[63]

But despite the defiance of *Loyal Songs* (1750) and *The True Loyalist* (1779), 'Charlie Stuart' was increasingly being recalled in terms of a decaying eroticism:

> O Yellow-hair'd Laddie when wilt thou return
> To ease thy poor subjects who are sadly forlorn.
> 'The Yellow-hair'd Laddie'

---

[63] *Poems on Several Occasions* (n.p., 1750), p. 27; Forbes, *The Lyon in Mourning*, I: p. 226; *For Mr S.M. on his turning Evidence: 'Quantum mutatis ab illis'* (London: Cooper, 1747); Hogg, *Relics*, II: p. 94.

If Charlie was 'like a trueborn Scot', this was increasingly the case in terms of exile and defeat. The ideology which Jacobite song-culture had supported was in decline. Cumberland himself had satirized the image of prince as patriot in his own singing of 'Will you play me fair, Highland Laddie, Highland Laddie?' This was a mockery; but in it we see the first foreshadowing of George IV's appearance in Highland dress in 1789 and Victoria's Balmoralism. The iconography of Jacobitism was losing its oppositional force, a process socially accelerated by the ravaging of the Highlands, the effective proscription of the Episcopal Church and the abolition of heritable jurisdictions. Jacobite ideology could no longer be protected by the lairds, the nonjuring church, the singing men, smugglers and Jacobite agitators of remoter Scotland: the social system which supported such activity was broken. Nostalgia triumphs, not just over the lost dynasty, but over the nexus of its social and ecclesiastical support. Although Gaelic poetry such as Ross's 'An Suaithneas Ban' ('The White Cockade') can continue to express strong Jacobite feeling, the lyric in general becomes more delicately sentimental:

an empire of the affections at once grand and remote; an ardour so personal and intimate that it can only be expressed by a woman (and it is notable how many later Jacobite songs do imply a female singer); and a prince so perfect and so fragile that he cannot even be named.[64]

We are on the verge of Flora MacIvor by the fountain; a political sublimity to be usurped successively by sentiment and Romanticism.

Scottish nationalist Jacobite iconography was housetrained. Barely twenty years after Culloden the British state and army were drawing on the Highlander as patriot image in a conjunction which both sentimentalized the Scottish past and ignored the Scottish present. Yet although 'In the Garb of old Gaul' (set by Major Reid) was to be symbolic of 'a surprising reversal' from the Highlander as papistical slave to guardian of British liberty (Donaldson, 'Bonny Highland Laddie', p. 45), certain aspects of the Jacobite critique survived in Scotland: notably the language of exile and an antipathy to the economic (and sometimes imperial) priorities of the British state. This critique, born in the 1690s, reinforced by Culloden and its aftermath, was bitterly justified by the Clearances. In the popular imagination, the Clearances follow directly on from Culloden, and are not separated from it by fifty years: this idea is, as I argue elsewhere, due to a surviving 'Jacobitism of the Left', a nationalist resistance to dispossession which has always sat ill with the shortbread tones of Tory kitsch.[65]

[64] NLS MS 2910 16r, 30r; William Donaldson, 'Bonny Highland Laddie: the Making of a Myth', *Scottish Literary Journal* 3:2 (1976), pp. 30–50 (40, 47); Campbell, *Highland Songs*, p. 287.

[65] Pittock, *Invention of Scotland*, Frank McLynn (profile), 'The unWhigging of the Jacobites', *Times Higher Education Supplement*, 23 September 1988, p. 18.

But the dominant note, particularly after 1760, was the 'loss ... institutionalized by the imperial note of gain' (Pittock, *The Invention of Scotland*, p. 72) into a romanticization of defeat. As Tom Crawford writes:

By the third quarter of the century, Jacobite and anti-Jacobite sentiment tended to become subordinate to a new loyalty to Scotland conceived as part of the super-nation, Great Britain.

Yet even this tendency, the tendency of sentiment to gloss over a past which could no longer challenge or surprise, was not without its own ambivalences. James Macpherson did much to revivify the Celtic image of Scotland while proclaiming its doom, rather in the manner of the Celtic Twilight more than a century later. But the doom Macpherson proclaimed was one inflicted not by the lapse of centuries and the end of the Fianna, but by British troops fifteen years before. At Ruthven, in Badenoch, where Macpherson grew up, the Jacobite army rallied for the last time, before dispersing, on 17–20 April 1746.[66]

## Macpherson's protesting lament

Once the proud seat of royalty and state,
Of kings, of heroes, and of all that's great;
But these are flown, and Edin's only stores,
Are fops, and scriveners, and English'd whores.

O Scotland! Saxons dare deride ...
                                          'The Hunter'

We shall pass away like a dream ... Our name may be heard in the song, but the strength of our arms will cease.                                          *Ossian*

He wrote of ancient tragedies: 'A tale of the times of old!'; but the spirit which throbs through these lays is the dirge for the ancient civilisation which in his own day and in his own strath he saw dominated and depressed by the coarse, dull emissaries of the raw materialistic civilization of the south.

                    George Pratt Insh, *The Scottish Jacobite Movement*[67]

---

[66] Thomas Crawford, 'Political and Protest Songs in Eighteenth-Century Scotland 1: Jacobite and anti-Jacobite', *Scottish Studies* 14 (1970), pp. 1–33 (33); McLynn, *Charles Edward Stuart*, p. 262.

[67] Fiona Stafford, *The Sublime Savage* (Edinburgh: Edinburgh University Press, 1988), p. 57; James Macpherson, *Ossian*, ed. Otto L. Jiriczek (Heidelberg, 1940): facsimile of 1762/3 edition (future references in the text are to this edition; George Pratt Insh, *The Scottish Jacobite Movement* (Edinburgh & London, 1952), p. 174.

James Macpherson is a rare example of a British writer whose reputation has been made the object of cultural warfare. Since their appearance, *Fingal* (1761) and *Temora* (1763) have been repeatedly attacked as forgeries (usually by those who would not claim to know the language of any originals). This is still (despite the beginnings of a tentative revisionism) their place upon the doorstep of the English canon, locked out by reason of their perceived spuriousness. On the other hand, in the Gaeltacht (and indeed at first elsewhere in Scotland), there has been greater reluctance to convict Macpherson of faking his epic. Thus, from the beginning, it has been the perceived status of Macpherson's art which has been the issue, not the great influence of that art itself (a fact more acknowledged than discussed). Given the date of his epic's original appearance, the decade of Bute and Wilkes (a controversial time to be Scottish), it is clear that Macpherson's status is as much cultural as literary. Rejection of Macpherson is rejection of Gaelic epic, of the Scot on the make, of his Celticism as anything more than a post hoc construct (as in Lord Dacre's strictures on him in *The Invention of Tradition*); acceptance of him entails hostility to all these cultural and literary–linguistic judgements. But this conflict was not evenly balanced: those who accepted Macpherson could always be convicted of chauvinism by those who chauvinistically opposed him, since to be a chauvinistic Englishman has always been more acceptable than to be a chauvinistic Scot in the dimensions of British cultural judgement. Johnson's belief in a 'Scotch conspiracy in national falsehood' is only more politely stated in Leah Leneman's recent judgement that the Highlanders' refusal to call *Ossian* a forgery 'in their own way ... helped in the creation of the myth'.[68]

The view that Macpherson was a forger throve on his lack of manuscript evidence for the epics he produced (despite his rather peculiar promise to provide it). In that it did so, it overlooked the orality of the culture on which Macpherson drew almost entirely: and this only a few years before the great era of ballad-collecting and the defence of folkways under attack.

It can be argued that Macpherson's work both suffered and succeeded by reason of its author's ability to bridge cultures at a crucial time. Macpherson was a Highlander, born in Kingussie, brought up in Badenoch; his clan served as a regiment in the royal army of 1745. As a child of seven in Ruthven, Macpherson witnessed at least two of the events of the Rising: General Cope's advance in 1745, and Major-General Gordon's attack on the government forces in Ruthven Barracks in 1746. Fiona Stafford suggests that Macpherson may have 'joined his six-year-old

---

[68] Bailey Saunders, *The Life and Letters of James Macpherson* (London, 1894), p. 252; Leah Leneman, 'Ossian and the Enlightenment', *Scotia* XI (1987), pp. 13–29 (28). For Macpherson revisionism, see the work of Fiona Stafford and Howard Gaskill (ed.), *Ossian Revisited* (Edinburgh: Edinburgh University Press, 1991).

cousin, Allan Macpherson of Blairgowrie ... hurling stones at the troops
who were setting fire to the Chief's house' after the failure of the Rising.
Despite the destruction of the social order of his clan and the defeat of its
Cause, Macpherson's departure from Badenoch to be a student at King's
College, Aberdeen, in 1752 seems to have been the leaving of a childhood
paradise (though he later returned to be a schoolmaster at Ruthven). Yet
the environment at King's was far from wholly alien. As a student,
Macpherson was able to experience the last stages of Scoto-Latin culture.
Although the universities in Aberdeen had been largely purged of Jacobite
elements following the considerable support James had derived there in
the 'Fifteen, the city and its hinterland provided a regiment in 1745,
commanded by Lt-Col. James Moir. In Aberdeen Macpherson absorbed
the 'discipline of the classical scholarship of the Episcopal North-East',
and here it is possible that distance lent enchantment to his view of the
Highlands, and determined him to advertise 'that civilisation ... the
legends and the traditions of his own people' to the world.[69]

As the possibility of a successful Rising faded, a more depoliticized
Scottish patriotic voice was making itself heard in Home's *Douglas* (1756)
and James Stone's translation of a Gaelic ballad in *The Scots Magazine* in
the same year, with its classicizing tone:

Stone himself drew attention to the Homeric parallel by commenting on the
similarity between the Gaelic story of Fraoch and the Greek Bellerophon.

Such straws in the wind may have presented Macpherson with his opportunity to glorify his periphery and display Highland Scottish culture to the
world as a patriotic act, albeit one ostensibly depoliticized (Stafford, *The
Sublime Savage*, pp. 63–4).

It is certainly interesting that Macpherson's early poetic ventures reflect
both his Highland and North East experience. In 'The Hunter', Macpherson idealizes 'Donald', the archetypal Highlander. The portrait
seems understated, but is in fact highly political: of Donald's 'gun, a plaid,
a dog, his humble store', Fiona Stafford remarks that the first two are 'the
distinctive features of the Highlander most feared by the British Government', and in fact at that time banned (Stafford, *The Sublime Savage*, p. 53).
In the poem, 'the Highlands become a kind of Paradise, which must then
be lost', while Highland Donald is portrayed as coming to the aid of King
Fergus (a crucial name from the foundation-myth) to defeat the English,
freeing Scotland from 'Hateful slavery and the aspiring Rose'. Stafford
remarks that

By celebrating a Scottish victory over the English, led by a Highlander in full
tartan dress, Macpherson was attempting to reverse the double disgrace of the
1707 Union and the '45 Rebellion.     Stafford, *The Sublime Savage*, pp. 52, 55, 57

[69] Stafford, *The Sublime Savage*, pp. 18, 20; Insh, *Jacobite Movement*, p. 169.

'The Hunter', like Ramsay's 'Vision', is a poem which sets in the past its encoded references to the present: Donald, not 'basely sold / To sordid interest and the love of gold' represents antique patriotic virtue which this language pointedly bemoans the lack of. Yet the conclusion to the poem is more resigned than that of earlier eighteenth-century patriotism. The English leader prophesies of the Scots that 'Fair Liberty to them shall lose its charms', while the English themselves have 'schemes ... To change their steely points to ... gold'. The archetypical story of King Fergus may foreshadow the struggles of the present, but not their outcome. While appearing to call Scotland to action, 'The Hunter' stifles that call in the reference of its conclusion to Scotland's current position, expressed with the status of prophecy by the ancient enemy. An aura of inevitability surrounds the inevitable (Stafford, *Sublime Savage*, p. 58).[70]

If 'The Hunter' displays Macpherson's use of the motif of Highlander as patriot, 'On the Death of Marshal Keith', written at Ruthven, and published in *The Scots Magazine* for October 1758, pays its respects to one of Aberdeen and the North East's most famous heroes, whose statue stands today in the town square in Peterhead. A resigned conclusion is supplied here also: Keith's passing is the passing of a whole way of life:

> But, chief, as relics of a dying race,
> The Keiths command, in woe, the foremost place;
> A name for ages through the world revered,
> By Scotia loved, by all her en'mies feared;
> Now falling, dying, lost to all but fame,
> And only living in the hero's name.
>     See! the proud halls they once possessed, decayed,
> The spiral tow'rs depend the lofty head;
> Wild ivy creeps along the mould'ring walls,
> And with each gust of wind a fragment falls;
> While birds obscene at noon of night deplore,
> Where mighty heroes kept the watch before.

This is the end of nostalgia: longing cut off by mortality. Macpherson is beginning to shape images which will become a metaphor for the entire Celtic / Scottish experience in the Ossian poems. The hero who brought fear to Scotland's enemies is 'falling, dying': a phrase Fiona Stafford sees as echoing the 'fallen, fallen from that high estate' of the ode to Secretary Murray discussed in the last section (Stafford, *Sublime Savage*, p. 48). As 'relics of a dying race', the Keiths represent the last of the patriots, the last of the true Scots, now 'only living in the hero's name'. The lamenting note of Ossian is our contemporary, for Ossian

---

[70] Cf. Derrick Thomson, 'Macpherson's *Ossian*: Ballads to Epics', in Bo Alanquist, Seamus Ó Cathan and Padrag Ó Healain (eds.), *The Heroic Process: Form, Function and Fantasy in Folk Epic* (Dublin, 1987), pp. 243–64 (248).

represented the spiritual strength of the old Celtic civilisation of the Highlands of Scotland reinforced by the old scholarly civilisation of the Episcopal North-East.

Insh, The Jacobite Movement, p. 187

Both these traditions were of course joined in the first half of the eighteenth century by common political goals.

The stage was set for Macpherson to transmute the folk-cultural idiom of ballad into the high cultural one of epic: to crystallize the aesthetic possibilities of a tradition both politically threatened and exhausted. Without betraying Jacobite sentiment or the image of Highlander as Scottish patriot, Macpherson was preparing a rendition of his own politically and culturally marginalized background in terms which would seize metropolitan attention by adopting one of its genres, forcing the periphery above the horizon of post-Culloden dispossession, and, just as importantly, portraying Scotland as an anti-Enlightenment culture in the heart of the age of Enlightenment.[71]

This task involved altering the boundaries of genres and presenting the imagery of periphery in a guise suitable for wider attention. It was in the creation of an epic out of what were not in dimension epic sources that Macpherson's 'forgery' lay. He presumed a degree and more than a degree too far in this transmutation. For he was no Homer, nor was his Ossian even secondary epic, since Macpherson's own self-consciousness, his division between the needs of the nation and those of the market allied to continuing political vulnerability to charges of Jacobitism, all militated in favour of a poem contrived in tone as well as in genre.

Yet this is perhaps as far as Macpherson's 'forging' goes. It is a forgery not entirely unlike Stephen Daedalus's pledge to forge in the smithy of his soul the uncreated conscience of his race. Macpherson had a close relationship with the bards of the older Gaelic tradition, 'a prime example being the Badenoch poet Lachlan Macpherson of Strathmashie'. During his research trip to the Highlands in 1760–1, Macpherson talked to poets such as John MacCodrum, who knew many lays of the Fianna, as well as producing more contemporary material:

> Earnest prayer we'll offer, and help will be coming,
> Ten thousand French will come, at their feet will the ball be,
>   Charles will be their leader, ready for the slaughter,
> Armed in every way, to waulk the cloth from Cataibh;
> And when the sow's been singed and her brood of piglings salted,
> The broadsword and the plaid ne'er again will be forbidden.

Lorne Campbell, Highland Songs, p. 253

Macpherson's 'elaborate process of culling from the ballads, making an English epic, and translating it back into Gaelic, had already begun'. The

---

[71] Pittock, The Invention of Scotland, p. 73.

nationalistic quality of the whole enterprise was underlined by Macpherson's view 'that the Irish Ossianic ballads were ultimately borrowed from Scotland'.[72] There were, of course, many sites linked with Fionn (Fingal) and the Fianna in Scotland; and, moreover, a messianic tradition of the returning Fionn which rivalled that of Arthur:

People ... believed equally strongly [with the Scriptures] in the Gaelic Messianic tradition that puts Fionn, lying in Tom na h-Iubhraich, near Inverness, in the role of sleeping warrior who will one day reappear to restore the Gaels of Scotland to their former greatness.[73]

The link between the heroic legendary tradition of the Fianna and that of the Stuarts, evident from the seventeenth century, was built on by Macpherson. In *Fingal* and *Temora*, the Fianna act as surrogates for the cause of Scottish Jacobite nationalism. That these supposedly ancient fragments of Celtic epic were meant to stand in representational relationship to more recent conflicts was further demonstrated in Macpherson's classicizing, which 'frequently evoked passages from Virgil and Homer'. On one level these comparisons function as the provision of exalted company against which the patriotic epic can measure its 'moral superiority'; on another, Macpherson's choice of Vergilian parallels bears a close relationship to the exile and defeat metaphors of the *Aeneid*, already present in the Stuart myth and its ideology:

In *Fingal* ... the choice of Virgil's 'fortia facta patrum' (the brave deeds of the forefathers) has ominous undertones. The words come from the gold plate at Dido's banquet in *The Aeneid*, 1, [line] 641

These words are prophetic of Dido's death and Carthage's ruin, just as the appearance of Crugal in *Fingal* 22 can be paralleled with that of Hector's ghost presaging Troy's ruin. As Fiona Stafford points out, the use of Vergil's Troy rather than Homer's emphasizes the sense of doom in the poems (Stafford, *Sublime Savage*, pp. 70–1, 147).

Both Troy and Carthage are, of course, catalysts of exile for Aeneas, each disproving in turn that it is for him an 'abiding city'. Macpherson's own chief, Cluny (whose lands the poet helped restore in 1784), had died in exile in 1756, and the metaphor of exile had already become emplaced in Jacobite poetry. Just as the exile of 1688 and accompanying hopes of restoration had been linked to the *Aeneid*, so the eighteenth-century experience of diaspora underlined its force as a Jacobite text. The 'old Trojans' of Jacobitism aligned their fate with that of their leader. Macpherson's use of Vergil's Troy is not merely the adaptation of the Scoto-

---

72 Thomson, 'Macpherson's *Ossian*', in Alanquist et al. (eds.), *The Heroic Process*, pp. 244, 256, 261–2.
73 John MacInnes, 'Twentieth-Century Recordings of Scottish Gaelic Heroic Ballads', in Alanquist et al. (eds.), *The Heroic Process*, pp. 101–30 (105).

Roman ethos to the needs of Celtic patriotism, but is an analogue of the world of contemporary experience which underlies *Fingal*.[74]

The preface to *Fingal* makes two major assertions which place it in a patriotic context. First, Macpherson denies Tacitus' opinion ('that the ancient Caledonians were of German extract') in claiming that they were universally Celts. The identification of Scotland as entirely Celtic was almost always one which sought to minimize divisions between Highland and Lowland in the interests of patriotic unity: the Highlander as patriot. Scott's mixed vision of Scots as Germanic and Celtic was by contrast a paradigm of his evolutionary Unionism, as in *The Antiquary*, where Saxon Oldbuck scorns Celtic Hector's enthusiasm for *Ossian*.[75]

Secondly, Macpherson asserts the decline of Celtic civilization, arguing that 'the genius of the highlanders has suffered a great change within these few years', a change attributed to the penetration of the financial revolution and a weakening of traditional bonds. Although Jacobitism is understandably never mentioned, this is a classical Jacobite critique (Macpherson, *Fingal*, p. xv).

Having set the stage for an epic of Celtic decline appraised from a patriotic standpoint, Macpherson embarks on his text:

They [the heroes] stood on the heath, like oaks with all their branches round them; when they echo to the stream of frost, and their withered leaves rustle to the wind.

The association of oaks with Gaelic heroes is appropriate in terms of the oak's symbolic role in both Stuart and Celtic mythology. Set in a withered and decaying landscape, they reflect the epic's central theme, defeat:

I joined the bards, and sang of battles ... Battles! where I often fought; but now I fight no more! The fame of my former actions is ceased, and I sit forlorn at the tomb of my friends.

Passages like this hint at a contemporaneity of almost autobiographical proportions between the schoolmaster of a broken clan and the bard of the lost Fianna. The oak itself is now the victim of 'The unconstant blast', a cipher for the uncertain future of a threatened Gaeldom, whose 'years have passed away in battle', and whose 'age is darkened with sorrow'. 'And here my son will rest', Fingal says, 'they have fallen like the oak of the desert'; 'a thousand ages oaks are burning to the wind':

We shall pass away like a dream ... Our names may be heard in the song, but the strength of our arms will cease.

Macpherson, *Fingal*, pp. 24–5, 49, 51, 70, 74, 79, 84

---

[74] Saunders, *Macpherson*, p. 280; Sir Walter Scott, *Waverley*, ed. Claire Lamont (Oxford: Oxford University Press, 1981), p. xviii.

[75] Macpherson, *Ossian*, p. iii; Saunders, *Macpherson*, p. 24.

The prolonged elegiac quality of *Fingal*, reflected in its landscapes and metaphors ('an oak of the desert'), distorts epic imagery even while claiming it. The energy and scope Macpherson was seeking in this genre is dissipated in the process of its own expression. *Fingal* is an *Aeneid* of the first four books, when the last eight are already over. Lively observation and symbolic force are set aside in the interests of a stylized vision of landscape, absorbed in the performance of pathetic fallacy:

> Raise high the stones; collect the earth: preserve the name of Fear-comhraic.
> Blow, winds, from all your hills; sigh on the grave of Muirnin.
> The dark rock hangs, with all its wood, above the calm dwelling of the heroes.
> The sea, with the foam-headed billow, murmurs at their side.
> Why sigh the woods, why roar the waves: They have no cause to mourn.

Yet mourn they do; despite the rhetorical attempt at balance in the last line, Macpherson's Scottish landscape is withered and lost, a country choking on its lack of autonomy, where 'autumn leaves lie thick and still', as a more recent rendition of Macphersonian scenery puts it. Such imagery prepares us for the Scotland to come, the earliest and grandest of heritage theme parks, the sublimity of whose (unpopulated) landscapes lies at the heart of their popularity:

Autumn is dark on the mountains; grey mist rests on the hills. The whirlwind is heard on the heath. Dark rolls the river through the narrow plain. A tree stands alone on the hill, and marks the slumbering Connal. The leaves whirl round with the wind, and strew the grave of the dead. At times are seen here the ghosts of the departed.[76]

Macpherson's distorted epic is in the process of killing history. The heroic actions of the Gaels in time are elegized by the permanent sublimities of their barren landscapes throughout eternity. The Burkean sublime, with which Macpherson was acquainted, absorbs and entombs the heroic lay.[77] The grandeur of loss is eternal; the victories of the past, transient. Scotland is converted into spectacle, moved out of time, its history ended. Macpherson's Jacobite sympathies exhaust themselves in elegy, to become a tale whose only historical presence is in the time taken for its telling: ' "Pleasant are the words of the song", said Cuchullin, "and lovely are the tales of other times" ' (Macpherson, *Fingal*, p. 35). This is the process of forging heritage from history: the replacement of the exploration of other events and times as contextualizing and being contextualized by one's own, with a historicity which discretely reproduces detached packages of the past, fictively arranged to occupy the present only in the scope of time

---

[76] Kenneth Simpson, *The Protean Scot: The Crisis of Identity in Eighteenth-Century Scottish Literature* (Aberdeen: Aberdeen University Press, 1988), p. 66; 'The Corries', 'Flower of Scotland', *Live From Scotland Volume 1* (1974).

[77] Thomson, 'Macpherson's *Ossian*', p. 258.

taken for their presence as entertainment. The National Trust for Scotland video at Culloden is the true inheritor of Macpherson in its elegy for Gaeldom which aestheticizes Jacobitism out of Scottish history: 'This was the last battle of the Highlanders against the Strangers' lisps the video Ossian-wise. We are moving from Lochiel to 'Lochnagar'.[78]

Macpherson perhaps spoke truer than he knew in providing an ambience for the romanticization of Scottish culture. The 'exiled hero and the loss of paradise' had a strong contemporary application, but its implications for a future where there was no possibility of reclaiming that paradise were bleak ones. Macpherson's own successful career in the British state and Empire (despite the frequent repudiation of his work as 'a piece of Scotch impertinence') was itself paradigmatic of the implicit exit of his epic from historic Scotland. Although he continued to have the reputation of a 'notorious Jacobite', and used Gaelic 'to convey any confidential information', Macpherson's epic and his life were at least in part attempts to capitalize on the decline of the system he had spent so much effort in heroicizing. Confirming its importance to his audience, he immediately lamentingly reassured them that this importance was no more.[79]

Macpherson's poetry was central to a more general realignment of Celtic/Scottish images and ideas in British consciousness which confirmed their conversion from political opposition to aesthetic accessory for a North British identity. Early translation into the major European languages broadened *Ossian*'s scope so that it might represent a new universalizable image of the Celt, transmissible throughout Europe as a tribute to a remote past, the same remote past whose oral culture the first folklorists were already collecting. The Jacobite language of exile is conformed to more general themes of primitivism and cultural loss. 'But we are old, O Usnoth, let us not fall like aged oaks', Macpherson writes: the heroic image of Celt and Stuart conjoined in a lament which secured much to the historically uncomprehending eye of Romanticism, a comfortably vague Gaeldom of 'old, unhappy, far-off things, / And battles long ago'. Not so long ago.[80]

---

[78] Soundtrack, 1984 National Trust for Scotland video at Culloden Battlefield Centre.

[79] Stafford, *The Sublime Savage*, pp. 178, 182; Saunders, *Macpherson*, pp. 183, 225.

[80] Saunders, *Macpherson*, p. 236; *Temora* (in Macpherson, *Ossian*), p. 189; *The Oxford Authors: William Wordsworth*, ed. Stephen Gill (Oxford: Oxford University Press, 1990 (1984)), p. 319.

# 5

# Jacobite culture in Ireland and Wales

## Stuart cause and Irish myth

And O! may heaven's supreme decree
Restore the youth to love and thee!
    From realms afar I see him come,
    With might to right his injured home,
    To hush thy wail, to cheer the Gael,
    And sweep the foe o'er ocean's foam.

John Clarach MacDonnell,
'Reply to the Lady of Alba's Lament'

Like Aengus Oge he bears command,
Or Louis of the trenchant brand,
Or Daire's son, the great Conroy,
Brave Irish chiefs, my royal boy! . . .

Or Conall, who strong ramparts won,
Or Fergus, regal Rogia's son,
Or Conor, Ulad's glorious king,
Whom harp-strings praise and poets sing . . .

John O'Tuomy, 'The Lady of Alba's
Lament for King Charles'

A film of enchantment spread, of aspect bright
from the shining boulders of Galway to Cork of
    the harbours;
clusters of fruit appearing in every treetop,
acorns in woods, pure honey upon the stones.

. . . in the name of the faithful king who is soon to come
to rule and defend the triple realm for ever.

Aogan Ó Rathaille, 'The Vision'[1]

---

[1] Edward Walsh, *Reliques of Irish Jacobite Poetry with Metrical Translations*, 2nd edn (Dublin: John O'Daly, 1866), pp. 35, 37; Sean Ó Tuama (ed.), *An Duanaire 1600–1900 : Poems of the Dispossessed*, tr. Thomas Kinsella (Mountrath, Portlaoise: the Dolmen Press, 1980), p. 155.

Perhaps the central question about Irish Jacobitism after the siege of Limerick is why it was, to paraphrase 'Silver Blaze', the dog that did not bark in the night. Ireland should have been a heartland of militant Jacobite activity. Instead, whatever the sentiments of its Roman Catholic inhabitants, in military terms it remained almost quiescent during the period of the great eighteenth-century Risings.[2]

And it was not as if Ireland was militarily insignificant. The massive emigration of the nineteenth century and the effects of industrialization on England's population obscure the fact that Ireland was much closer to her neighbour in terms of population size between 1600 and 1800 than she has been since: something which makes the Hibernophobia of the Civil War period more understandable, at least in one dimension. Even on the accession of George III:

Ireland still ranked second among all the political units under his domain in population, in revenue and expenditure, and in volume of trade.

So why did such a big dog fail to bark? In this chapter I shall try to answer that question, first from the point of view of Jacobite ideological theory in Ireland, then from the effects of its practice.[3]

As in Scotland, the Jacobite agenda in Ireland was from the beginning deeply affected by nationalist demands. That this was the case was clear as early as James's arrival there in 1689:

When James II landed in Kinsale in March 1689 he had little choice but to put himself at the head of what had become a predominantly Catholic nationalist movement.

The demands on the king made by the Irish parliament were stringent, and placed James under almost as much pressure, of a different kind, as his father had endured in the 1640s.[4]

Irish poetry of the time (discussed in Chapter 1) can give priority to discussing setbacks in national rather than dynastic terms, and this trend was a continuing one. Enthusiasm for the Stuarts remained strong in Irish Jacobite poetry, but their role is iconic to an even greater degree than elsewhere. In Ireland as in the rest of the British Isles, James and Charles display the qualities of a fertility god, as in Aogan Ó Rathaille's 'The Vision', quoted above; but the position of the Irish nation in the major *aisling* tradition is central. True affection for the lost Stuart is less readily evident than a portrayal of James or Charles as heroic cipher, myth of the

---

[2] Cf. Frank McLynn, 'Ireland and the Jacobite Rising of 1745', *Irish Sword* 13 (1979); '"Good Behaviour": Irish Catholics and the Jacobite Rising of 1745', *Eire-Ireland* XVI :2 (1981).

[3] Francis Godwin James, *Ireland in the Empire 1688–1770* (Cambridge, Massachusetts: Harvard University Press, 1983), p. 1.

[4] Ibid., p. 15.

past returned, to overthrow British incremental history through Irish typological redemption:

> The *Aisling* proper is Jacobite poetry; and a typical example would run somewhat like this: The poet, weak with thinking on the woe that has overtaken the Gael, falls into a deep slumber. In his dreaming a figure of radiant beauty draws near. She is so bright, so stately, the poet imagines her one of the immortals. Is she Deirdre? or Cearnaut? or is she Helen? or Venus? He questions her, and learns that she is Erin; and her sorrow, he is told, is for her true master who is in exile beyond the seas ... the poem ends with a promise of speedy redemption on the return of the King's son.[5]

In certain respects, this model is very close to the lost lover ballad circulating in England at the time (though one of the most famous of these, 'The Blackbird', is apparently Irish). But the fate of the Gael and the national status of the woman are more central than the return of the king. The poet's interrogation of the woman focuses the poem not on her love for the lost ruler, but her own nationhood, which although implied by the lost lover ballads, is seldom dwelt on. As Daniel Corkery suggests, 'the place that the Stuarts themselves occupy in the Scottish poems is occupied in the Irish poems by Ireland herself' (Corkery, *Hidden Ireland*, p. 134): and though this is exaggerated, it emphasizes one of the distinct qualities of the *aisling*.

This accords with the development of the *aisling*-style vision into the characterization of Ireland as Cathleen Ni Houlihan in the nationalist literature of the late nineteenth and early twentieth century. Maud Gonne's vision of Cathleen in the opening of her autobiography, *A Servant of the Queen*, is close to that of the fair oppressed of the *aisling*, while in Yeats' *Cathleen Ni Houlihan* (1902), Cathleen appears on the landing of the French in 1798 to encourage Irish youth to sacrifice itself for her, the mystic Nation. Fourteen years later they did so, and Padraig Pearse fulfilled the metaphors of heroic nationalism Jacobite poetry had displayed two hundred years before:

> When he [Pearse] opened Scoil Eanna in September 1908, he put ... a large mural of the young Cu Chulain taking arms ... to recreate and perpetuate in Eire the high tradition of Cuchulain ... the noble tradition of the Fianna ... the Christlike tradition of Colm Cille ...[6]

Pearse's use of heroic identities was a way of maintaining the idea of typological return and victory over incrementality. In the same way, the identification of the Stuart king with Conall or Fergus in poetry such as

---

[5] Daniel Corkery, *The Hidden Ireland: A Study of Gaelic Munster in the Eighteenth Century*, 2nd edn (Dublin: M. H. Gill & Son, 1925), p. 129.

[6] Philip O'Leary, '"What Stalked Through the Post Office?": Pearse's Cu Chulainn', in John T. Koch and Jean Rittmueller (eds.), *Proceedings of the Harvard Celtic Colloquium* III (1983) (Cambridge, Massachusetts, 1983), pp. 21–38 (23).

John O'Tuomy's 'The Lady of Alba's Lament' mythologizes Charles Edward in order to increase his quota of heroic Irishness. Such heroic Irishness exists to overcome the British state in the interests of a feminized Ireland, sacrifice for which is the raison d'etre of nationalist heroics. The ersatz sacramentalism and romanticized violence of Pearse's doctrine of blood-sacrifice, which leave their fearful legacy today, are recognizably related to Stuart metaphors of suffering and renewal through armed support for the king, Ireland's dutiful son or lover in the eighteenth century as Pearse was in the twentieth. The strength of a feminized vision of the Irish identity endures from the era of the *aisling*:

> 'Alas!' she said, 'my nation's grief,
>     My prostrate host, my heroes dying.
> My wandering exiles, bard, and chief,
>     In distant regions sadly sighing –
> The slaves that plain in Saxon chain,
>     My SON exil'd o'er Ocean's water;
> While beauty's wail o'erloads the gale,
>     O heaven relieve thee, Erin's daughter!'
>                 Sean Clarach MacDonnell, 'Aisling Air Eire'

The cure 'heaven' might send would be 'one hero avenger', as in 'The Cruel-Base-Born Tyrant'. But this avenger, the *ri*

was an abstraction, the eighteenth-century equivalent of *an tairmgear-tach* (the prophesied one) or Aodh Eanghail of earlier times.[7]

  The 'prophesied saviour' figure, with its roots in Irish mythology, thus has a role to play both before and after the Stuarts in the imagery of Irish nationalism. The Jacobite *aisling* endured a surprisingly long time: as late as 1840 (according to Diarmuid Ó Mathuna) a poem calls 'To banish the foreign hosts of Calvin' in favour of the cause of 'James, the lawful monarch'; but already nineteenth-century figures like Daniel O'Connell were replacing the returning king in 'the political *aisling*'. The central format of Stuart poetic ideology in Ireland thus had an independent life of its own, adaptable to other nationalist circumstances . The *aisling* was a subgenre always potentially semi-detached from the Stuart cause to which it often referred. This semi-detached quality made the *aisling* metaphor an aesthetic object in itself, not merely the means to an expressed end:

though James Francis Edward Stuart and his son . . . were once real men in a real world, in *aisling* poetry they are no more substantial than the poet's heavenly visitant in female form.

7 Edward Walsh, *Reliques*, pp. 19ff., 21, 23; Brian Ó Cuin, 'Irish Language and Literature 1691–1845', ch. 13 in T. W. Moody and W. E. Vaughan (eds.), *A New History of Ireland 4: Eighteenth-Century Ireland 1691–1800* (Oxford: Clarendon Press, 1986), pp. 374–423 (407).

This insubstantial quality strengthens the fluidity of allegory: the trans-
formation of the 'allegorical lady' into the 'poor old woman' of nationalist
Ireland can be traced through the moveable feast of the *aisling*'s politics.[8]

In cultural terms, similar connexions between high and folk Jacobitism
can be seen in Ireland as elsewhere in mainland Britain. The *aisling* poets
sometimes wrote for such noble patrons as survived the massive Protestant
takeover of land (Froude estimates that 90 per cent of Irish land was 'held
by Protestants of English or Scotch extraction' by 1703 (Corkery, *Hidden
Ireland*, p. 30)). But by their very bardic status, such poets possessed the
kind of cultural networking found in societies with greater orality. They
were also part of an oppressed community, and some were themselves
among the very poor.

The role folk-singers had in propagandizing the Stuart cause in Ireland
was borne witness to as early as 1654, when the Cromwellian administration ordered

all harpers, pipers, and wandering musicians ... to obtain letters from the local
magistrate before they were allowed to travel.[9]

'Travelling harpers' were 'the ideal carriers of treasonable messages',
which in their turn became 'epic appeals to nationhood and love of
liberty'. Even when composed in a high cultural context, such appeals
were 'universally known and sung all over the country'.[10] As in Britain,
cultural frontiers were frayed by the shared outlawry of cross-class Jacobite sentiment: and this was possibly even stronger in Ireland than
elsewhere:

Colonel Maurice Hussey, himself a Jacobite, writes on the 26th of December,
1702, from Flesh Bridge: 'The Tories in the province are lately grown highwaymen ...'[11]

Lawless bands broadly sympathetic to the Jacobites remained common in
Ireland throughout the eighteenth century, the Whiteboys being the most
famous. A greater number of people had been dispossessed by circumstance in Ireland than elsewhere in the British Isles; and the same up-
heavals which sent half a million men abroad to join the Irish Brigades in
the course of the century had its effect in Ireland also.[12]

---

8  Diarmuid Ó Mathuna, 'A Late Aisling', *The O Mahony Journal*, 14 (Summer 1990), 15–21;
   Corkery, *Hidden Ireland*, p. 407; R. A. Breatnach, 'The Lady and the King', *Studies* 42 (1953),
   321–36 (321–2).
9  Bryan Boydell, 'Music before 1700', in Moody and Vaughan ch. 17, pp. 542–67 (559).
10 Patrick Gakin, *Irish Songs of Resistance* (London: The Workers' Music Association, 1955/6),
   p. 1.
11 *The Poems of Egan O'Rahilly*, ed. Revd Patrick S. Dinneen (London: Irish Texts Society, 1900),
   p. xxv.
12 Mark McLaughlin, *The Wild Geese*, Osprey Men at Arms Series (London: Osprey, 1980), p. 3;
   John Cornelius O'Callaghan, *History of the Irish Brigades in the Service of France* (Glasgow:
   Cameron and Ferguson, 1870), p. 163 gives 480,000 as the figure.

Insofar as crime was linked to a political agenda, songs were an effective means of communicating and confirming it, even after explicit Jacobitism was no more: in writing of Young Ireland, '*The Times* described the songs as far more dangerous than O'Connell's Parliament'. Jacobite songs survived in new sets, as Daniel Corkery remarks:

In the summer of 1915, in Kerry ... I heard an old illiterate woman break suddenly into one of them, changing, however, not without a twinkle in her eye, a word here, a name there, to make the poem fit with the fortunes of the Great War in its early phase.

No longer were the names in the songs those of 'Charles, son of Seamus', who would protect the Gael; but the structures continued nonetheless.[13]

British Jacobite airs were on occasion adapted into Irish song. 'The White Cockade' was probably the commonest example, used by the Irish Brigades as a tune to play men into battle: John O'Tuomy's 'The Lady of Alba's Lament' was to be sung to this air, and 'For the King to Enjoy His Own Again' was also used. But other popular airs also found their way into Irish tradition, such as 'The Soger Laddie' (air to John Clarach MacDonell's 'The Devil of Britain') and 'Over the Hills and Far Away' (the same author's 'King Charles'). 'Flowers of Edinburgh' and 'Charlie come over the water' were two other examples, while MacDonell also produced an Irish version of 'My Laddie can fight and my Laddie can sing'. Thus in performance clear evidence of interpenetrative connexion exists between the airs of Anglophone Jacobitism and the sets of Gaelic Ireland. This seems a prefiguration of

The cross-fertilization between Irish folk idioms and the international mainstream of European music [which] gave rise to the fashion of arranging folk-songs for sophisticated consumption ...

This process can be seen as reflected in Scottish folk-song: nearly half the songs collected by George Thomson were Irish. Ireland's awkward but important role in British politics may have been reflected in the part the ideology of her song-culture played on a wider stage.[14]

Irish Jacobite writers were conscious of a common Gaelic inheritance shared with Scotland: hence in 'Reply to the Lady of Alba's Lament', Charles's 'home' is the Gaeltacht without national distinction. These traditions were visible in a shared Jacobite ideology of sacred, sacrificial and renewing kingship, expressing itself in predominantly nationalist terms. Tiag MacDairc Mac Bruadighe's assertion 'that God' 'blesses the

---

[13] Gakin, *Irish Songs of Resistance*, p. 7; Corkery, *Hidden Ireland*, p. 136.
[14] Walsh, *Reliques*, pp. 107, 110; Corkery, *Hidden Ireland*, p. 258; Bryan Boydell, 'Music 1700–1850' in Moody and Vaughan ch. 18, pp. 568–628 (605).

reign of good princes, by a succession of peaceful and abundant seasons' was centrally a feature of the poetry of both nations.[15]

After 1690 there were also close links between the Irish bards and the Old Catholics, those earlier generations of predominantly English settlers. Aogan Ó Rathaille was close to Sir Nicholas Browne, who had been dispossessed in the aftermath of the Boyne. A whole nation had been affected by the defeats of 1689–92: 'the last phase of the Gaelic literary tradition begins in the shadow of the disasters of the Boyne, Aughrim and Limerick'. As in England and Scotland, common experience of outlawed status strengthened a unified Jacobite perspective on events: 'the only banner that promised another fight, if not the reversal of their hard doom, was that of the Stuarts'.[16]

These Stuarts were known by many names, illustrative of the variety of cultural roles they were fulfilling as icons of Irish nationhood. Charles was 'Saesar' (Caesar) frequently; also 'Charles Rex' or 'the Lion' (his Scottish title, interestingly enough), 'Angus Og ... Conall Cearnach, ... other heroes of the myths' (Corkery, *Hidden Ireland*, p. 132). Sometimes the absent Stuart had no name, reflecting the codified coyness of the Scottish erotic tradition:

> I'll not reveal my true love's name
> Betimes 'twill swell the voice of fame ...
> 'The Lady of Alba's Lament'

The erotic Jacobite tradition in Ireland does not focus solely on the abandoned quality of the female lover, however, but also on the fact that she is currently being violated, as in Ó Rathaille's 'Gile Nan Gile' ('Brightness most Bright'):

> When a man the most fine, thrice over, of Scottish blood
> Was wanting to take her [Ireland] for his tender bride.
>
> Pain, disaster, downfall, sorrow and loss!
> Our mild, bright, delicate, loving, fresh-lipped girl
> With one of that black, horned, foreign, hate-crested crew
> And no remedy near till our lions come over the sea.

The sense of darkness, rapine and thrall in Ireland's present position is particularly well-expressed in Ó Rathaille's *aisling* poems, and can only be dispersed by the hope of a returning and redeeming James, as in 'Mac An Cheannai' ('The Merchant's (Redeemer's) Son'), although here on

---

[15] John Daly (ed.), *Reliques of Irish Jacobite Poetry* (Dublin, 1844), p. 37n.
[16] R. A. Breatnach, 'The End of a Tradition: A Survey of Eighteenth Century Gaelic Literature', *Studia Hibernica* I (1961), 128–50 (128); Corkery, *Hidden Ireland*, p. 131.

hearing that 'the lover she cherished was dead', the woman (Ireland) dies.[17]

In other poems, Stuart sacramentalism and its effects are closely linked to Catholic nationalism, as in 'The Assembly of Munstermen':

> The Pope with the true clergy came to where the destruction was wrought;
>     In his right hand he held a seal (wax) and a candle;
> The boughs burst forth into blossom, and a cloudless heaven welcomes
>     The grace of the Son of God which is come unto us;
> Comes the wanderer without a blemish – though he has been evil spoken of –
>     To his rightful place in his full power and pure beauty;
> He will submerge the band who despised and struck at him,
>     And for that I will say nothing against him.

Ó Rathaille centres the importance of a Catholic as well as a Stuart restoration, conjoined in the Christ-king figure, in a way most English or Scottish Jacobites would have shied away from. James is a saviour-figure not despite his Catholicism, but because of it. Elsewhere he is looked on as the high king restored, the monarch whose marriage to the land will, in Frazerian terms, renew it.[18]

In later *aislings*, disillusion with the state of Irish and Stuart affairs can lead to the vision of a beautiful young girl being altered to one of a corrupted harlot. But a romantic *aisling* voice did survive after Ó Rathaille's death in 1729, though the 'rigid formula' of the subgenre was out of touch with reality after Culloden. Nevertheless, though the *aisling*'s nationalism and not its Jacobitism was perhaps to be its lasting legacy, poets like Eoghan Rua Ó Suilleabhain (1748–84) can still sound the right note. 'A Magic Mist' is a case in point:

> Gloomy my state, sad and mournful,
>     by horned tyrants daily devoured,
> and heavy oppressed by grim blackguards
>     while my prince is set sailing abroad.
> I look to the great Son of Glory
>     to send my lion back to his sway
> in his strong native towns, in good order,
>     to flay the swarth goats with his blades.

Ó Suilleabhain also associates Charles with the heroes of the Irish cycles, while even later writers such as Sean Ó Coileain (1754–1817) persist in this tradition, writing in 'An Bucheull Ban' 'one of the most perfect' *aislings*.[19]

---

[17] Walsh, *Reliques*, p. 35; Ó Tuama, *An Duanaire*, pp. 151, 153; *Poems of Egan O'Rahilly*, p. 17.

[18] *Poems of Egan O'Rahilly*, p. 107; Breatnach, 'The Lady and the King', pp. 325, 335.

[19] Breatnach, 'The Lady and the King', p. 323; Ó Tuama, *An Duanaire*, pp. xxiii, xxvii, 187, 189; Walsh, *Reliques*, pp. 63–5; Corkery, *Hidden Ireland*, p. 299.

Feminized Ireland, wooed by such heroes, was shortly to turn from the white to the black rose, 'Roisin Dubh', later Mangan's 'Dark Rosaleen', a focal-point of national renewal:

> O, the Erne shall run red
>     With redundance of blood,
> And gun peal and slogan cry
>     Wake many a glen serene
> Ere you can fade, ere you can die
>     My Dark Rosaleen!
>     My own Rosaleen!

Here the formula of renewing victory has shed its Jacobite character, but the passionate sacrifice for the feminized nation remains the poet's subject. Though there were other modes of Jacobite expression in Ireland – the use of biblical typology, Donough MacConmara's mock-*Aeneid* – it was the *aisling* which expressed the iconic quality of Irish Jacobitism in a stylized range of situation and symbol which was as much a commitment to renewing a nation as to restoring a dynasty.[20]

## Ireland's voice in Jacobite war

> An age is rip'ning in revolving fate,
> When Troy shall overturn the Grecian state,
> And sweet revenge her Conqu'ring sons shall call ...
> The banish'd Faith shall once again return,
> And vestal fires in hallow'd temples burn.
>
> Dryden, Aeneid, 1, lines 386–8, 398–9,<br>applied to the Irish Brigades

> To wage the fierce battle for Erin,
>     Comes the fiery Brigade of Lord Clare,
> 'Tis oft from their pikes, keen and daring,
>     The Saxon fled back to his lair ...
>
> May Charles have but courage to hasten,
>     With troops and with arms, to our shore ...
>
> We pray to the just Lord to shatter
>     Their hosts and their hopes to the ground,

---

[20] Ó Tuama, *An Duanaire*, pp. 103–4, 309; *The Oxford Book of Victorian Verse*, ed. Arthur Quiller-Couch (Oxford: Clarendon Press, 1912), p. 79; Douglas Hyde (An Craobhín Aobhun), *A Literary History of Ireland: From Earliest Times to the Present Day* (London: T. Fisher Unwin, 1899), pp. 102–3.

To rouse our green island, and scatter
The blessings of Freedom around!
Gaelic song on the 1744 invasion attempt

every right, that hereditary descent could give, the royal race of Stuart possessed
... all the enthusiastic sympathies of the Irish heart were raised for them ... and
all the powerful motives of personal interest bore in the same channel ... The
restoration of their rights ... would have been the certain consequence of the
success of the Stuart family, in their pretensions to the throne.

Daniel O'Connell

The Roman Catholic clergy have for three weeks past earnestly recommended
their people to behave themselves peaceably and quietly like good subjects, to
avoid like true Christians all riots, mobs, drunkenness or late hours, to give no
offence either in their words or actions to their neighbours, but to behave
themselves so in every respect, as to be worthy the favour and liberty they now
enjoy.        Open letter of Irish Catholic gentlemen in the 'Forty-five[21]

In the aftermath of the siege of Limerick, a significant Irish Jacobite
diaspora began to form abroad, of a size which soon overshadowed the
first flight of the Wild Geese in Cromwell's time. Throughout the greater
part of the ensuing century, the five hundred thousand who served in the
Irish Brigades of France and Spain provided a military threat which lent
reality to anti-Jacobite fears. The size of the Brigades was one of the first
signs that the British State was to fail in any attempt to incorporate
Ireland into its evolving imperial identity, a failure borne witness to in
Linda Colley's recent *Britons*, which deliberately excludes all discussion of
Ireland in order to maintain its protestant unionist thesis. As late as
1898–1900, Irish units fought for the Boers.[22]

Although the Brigades might have formed the spearhead of any pro-
Stuart French invasion force, their absence on the Continent was a
weakening factor in native Irish Jacobitism. Three Irish battalions fought
at Blenheim; at Ramillies, Lord Clare was Major-General in the French
forces; at Oudenarde James III and VIII himself had a brigadier's
command of the Maison du Roi, leading twelve cavalry charges against
the English lines; at Malplaquet the cry was that of Captain Cantillon,
'*Forward, brave Irishmen! Long live King James III, and the King of France*'.
Appointed to sail with James in 1708 were lieutenant-generals Hamilton,
Sheldon, Dorrington and Lord Galway; Major-General Fitz-Gerald and
Colonel Wauchop. Even given that the French army was grossly over-

[21] John Cornelius O'Callaghan, *History of the Irish Brigades*, pp. 193, 344, 603; Gerard O'Brien
(ed.), Tom Dunne (Associate Ed.), *Catholic Ireland in the Eighteenth Century: Collected Essays of
Maureen Wall* (Dublin: Geography Publications, 1989), p. 57.
[22] Mark McLaughlin, *The Wild Geese*, pp. 3, 33.

officered, the importance of the Irish within it is clear. Nor were these simply the rump of the Jacobite army which had left Limerick for France: new recruits kept coming in, the authorities on occasion stopping and arresting those en route abroad for service with the king's enemies (MacLaughlin, *Wild Geese*, pp. 9–10; O'Callaghan, *Irish Brigades*, pp. 226, 236–7, 269, 295).

Even after the 'Forty-five, where the Irish Picquets were commanded by Brigadier Stapleton, recruitment continued. Many Scottish Jacobite exiles gained commissions in the Brigades: a report on recruiting activity in Scotland in 1750 names Lt-Col. Ludovic Cameron, now Captain in the Brigades, Captain Donald McDonald, second son of Clanranald, Captain Donald McDonald of Lochgary, formerly Lieutenant in Loudon's, and the sons of Glengary and Coll McDonald of Barrisdale as recruiting agents. Their activity was judged 'a great encouragement to the revival and progress of Jacobitism & disaffection in Scotland'. The Brigades were seeking to recruit both Jacobites from the Gaeltacht and Lowlanders from the east coast, without distinction, for

The generality of shipmasters in the Ports of Aberdeen, Peterhead, Aberbrothick, Montrose, Stonhive & Leith are disaffected, and have been from time to time employed in bringing disaffected persons to the Countrey & carrying them off again with recruits for the French Service.[23]

This report is clearly consistent with the recruitment profile of the royal army in 1745, when three hundred and ninety volunteers came from Montrose: perhaps a quarter of its adult male population.[24]

Despite the report's typical exaggeration of the Jacobite threat, it bears witness to the fact that printed songs disseminated among the population were central to Jacobite recruitment: 'Songs put into their hands by the Priests . . . Rebellious & Scurrilous pieces printed in the years 1716 & 1746 . . . dispersed amongst them', were being used to attract the population to the Brigades (National Library of Scotland MS 98 f. 39). The use of Jacobite songs and symbols in Brigade recruitment and advertisement is a testament to their efficacy as ideological instruments; they were also central to the Brigades' own experience, as confirming the reason for and promising an end to their exile. At Fontenoy, 'The White Cockade' played them into battle, the emblem's colour reminding them of both the masters they served, Stuart and Bourbon, while the term 'wild geese' itself may derive from early eighteenth-century Irish verse. Irish poets had close links with the Brigades: Aogan Ó Rathaille wrote an elegy for Captain Diarmuid O'Leary, while the poet Laurence Whyte's half-brother (or

---

[23] National Library of Scotland MS 98 f. 39.
[24] Jean G. McCann, 'The Organization of the Jacobite Army 1745–46', unpublished Ph.D. thesis (Edinburgh, 1963), pp. 96–8.

uncle) was the Captain White who raised a company for King James, and died in the French service (1705). Swift was the correspondent, and Pope the friend of Sir Charles Wogan.[25] Consciousness of the Brigades was woven into Irish life: recruiting British troops in Ireland sometimes only led to desertions to the French service, and a hope for the return of the Brigades in triumph.

Those who stayed at home were not unnaturally proud of the achievements of Irish troops, and the patriotic centrality of such pride is evident as late as the Young Ireland movement, and Davis' moving apostrophe to Irish victory at Fontenoy. Not that Young Ireland was completely divorced from the era of the Brigades: Richard Nugent, their last surviving officer, died on 8 July 1859, while Daniel O'Connell's own uncle was Colonel of the late 6th Regiment: some of the Brigades having entered British service in 1794, after the fall of the Bourbons, in order to restore them.[26]

If supporters of the Brigades in Ireland looked to them as agents of 'a vague hope of . . . fortuitous return to a lost golden age', perhaps a similar tendency to liberating violence can be discerned in the Rapparees and Whiteboys of native social discontent. The latter had succeeded the former as a major threat by the 1760s, adopting white as their colour, perhaps in honour of the Bourbons and Stuarts, to whom they have been tenaciously, if tenuously, linked – rather like the Windsor Blacks: 'In the first major Whiteboy trial of 1767, a number of the accused testified that they had sworn oaths to the King of France and to Charles Edward Stuart.' Whiteboys were active in the core Jacobite areas, mostly in Munster and parts of Leinster, displaying many of the features common to the ideology of traditional Stuart ruralism:

contemporary agents . . . suggest that the organisation of the Whiteboys may have owed something to the traditional patterns of rural life, with its Mayboys, Wrenboys, Strawboys and their Captains.[27]

'The Hunting of the Wren' was a favoured radical Scottish song of the late eighteenth century; and popular Jacobite activity bore out such links in Munster, where '"The Blackbird", – with Allisdrum's March, the Flowers of Edinburgh, the White Cockade &c, was a favourite tune

[25] McLaughlin, *The Wild Geese*, p. 14; O'Callaghan, *History of the Irish Brigades*, p. 355; J. G. Simms, 'The Irish on the Continent, 1691–1800', ch. 19 in Moody and Vaughan, pp. 629–56 (636, 637n, 638–9); *Poems of Egan O'Rahilly*, p. 115; Patrick Fagan, *A Georgian Celebration: Irish Poets of the Eighteenth Century* (Dublin: Branar, 1989), p. 32.

[26] O'Callaghan, *History of the Irish Brigades*, pp. 633, 634, 638.

[27] Nicholas Canny, 'The Formation of the Irish Mind: Religion, Politics and Gaelic Irish Literature 1580–1750', *Past and Present* 95 (1982), 91–116 (111); Maureen Wall, 'The Whiteboys', in T. Desmond Williams (ed.), *Secret Societies in Ireland* (Dublin: Gill & Macmillan; New York: Barnes & Noble, 1973), pp. 13–25 (13, 16); Edith Mary Johnston, *Ireland in the Eighteenth Century*, Gill History of Ireland 8 (Dublin: Gill & Macmillan, 1974), p. 131.

among the old Jacobite natives'. It was not only the *aisling* which voiced
Jacobite sentiment, for 'till late in the last [eighteenth] century' defiant
nationalist-Jacobite songs continued to be sung in these country areas,
where Irish was a common anti-colonial code for communicating the
unsayable, though Jacobitism might also voice itself in English:

> I wish that day would come to pass,
> With all the Catholics going to mass!
>
> He *was* as fit to wear the Crown,
> As any *whelp* in London town;
> But of his right they cut him down,
> A noble Stuart born![28]

The oppositional strength of exile and outlawry was shared by
Whiteboy and Jacobite alike. Aodh Buidhe Mac Crutan's poem, written
while he was serving with Lord Clare in Flanders, expresses hope of return
to free Ireland, the hope 'the Munster poets still clung to' after 1745. They
were indeed 'justly discontented', in Edmund Burke's terms ('tracts on the
Popery laws'). In this, Irish Jacobitism both at home and abroad shared
the characteristics of peripheralization created by Whig laws in mainland
Britain.[29] Ireland shared the 'social bandit' ethos of Scotland and the
criminalization which created crossclass links in English Jacobitism. The
heroes Irish Jacobites clung to were largely in exile, but while in power
had themselves seemed to gesture in the direction of folk celebration,
which may have aided their subsequent popularity. Ormonde, even as
viceroy, wore 'the white rose himself on the anniversary of the birth of . . .
James III', and this is alluded to in the song

> Our noble Ormonde he is drest,
> A rose is glancing on his breast,
> His famous hands have doff'd his crest,
> White roses deck them over.
>
> O'Callaghan, *Irish Brigades*, p. 282

The air to this song seems to have been 'Away with Prince Hannover',
while 'songs of definitely English origin were sung to authentic Gaelic airs'
in cross-cultural interchange. The centrality of the ballad singer in
eighteenth and nineteenth-century Ireland was entirely compatible with
the wide distribution of both Whig songs like Wharton's 'Lillibullero' and
their Jacobite equivalents, as well as Scottish airs taken abroad. It was in

28  O'Callaghan, *History of the Irish Brigades*, pp. 269n, 605.
29  Brian Ó Cuin, ch. 13 in Moody and Vaughan, pp. 397, 406; Burke's Ascendancy attachment
to the Revolution blended with a sympathy for Catholic nationalism; he never lost his Irish
accent and is a marvellous example of a marginalized figure attempting to define the nature of
the political centrality he sought through a constitution whose effects he found hard to abide in
his own country.

the street ballads also that more conventional eroticism was to be found, as perhaps in the following:

> 'Twas on a summer's morning, as I walked along,
> Down by yon green valley, I heard a fine song;
> It was a fair damsel, and her voice rang most clear,
> Saying, 'How blest would I be if my darling was here.'

In such many different forms of 'the book of the people', nationalist sentiment on the margin defended itself against a centring metropolitan state, not only in the West but in Dublin itself, where the young Oliver Goldsmith lived from 1745:

and to this period belongs the oft-repeated legend of his ballad-making and subsequent strolls through the city to hear his songs performed.

Like Swift, Goldsmith may have had connexions with the nationalist culture which reflected itself elsewhere in the stylized protests of the *aislings* and the more fluid guise of a popular song proud of the achievements of the Irish Brigades abroad and of Ireland at home.[30] Although 'Ireland remained free from disturbance in 1745', a large 'number ... were leaving for France or Spain in the hope of obtaining commissions in the armed forces which would enable them to promote rebellions in Great Britain and Ireland': and this despite a frequently conciliatory stance towards the British state by the Catholic hierarchy, who had grown more cautious as the century progressed. Although 'the government ... was undoubtedly worried by the appeal that Jacobitism had ... for the "lower sort of people"', lack of Catholic enthusiasm, and publications like the 'Drapier's Letter' which argued that there was nothing to be gained for the working man in supporting the Jacobites helped to limit enthusiasm, in any case curtailed by the absence of key leaders abroad. Voltaire thought that the Irish 'had grown more attached to their rest and their possessions than to the House of Stuart', but the truth about the dog that did not bark is more complex than this. In 1745, the Stuarts did not come to Ireland, and those few troops of the Irish Brigades that joined them did so late in the day and far from their home. This was not, like 1689–92, a patriotic war: and although the majority of the Seven Men of Moidart were Irish, the evidence from the subsequent campaign is that they cared and understood little about Scotland or England; as little as Scotland or England cared for or understood them. The Stuarts were Fionn and Ossian: but while Macpherson froze them in the typologies they inherited,

---

[30] Colm Ó Lochlainn (ed.), *Irish Street Ballads* (Dublin and London: Constable & Co., 1939), pp. vii, ix, 26; W. B. Yeats, *The Collected Poems* (London: Macmillan, 1950), p. 276; Hugh Shields, *Oliver Goldsmith and Popular Song*, reprinted from *Long Room*, 1983 (Folk Music Society of Ireland, 1985), p. 5.

Irish poets disposed of the Stuarts themselves to rehabilitate typology for a fresh national challenge. The Stuarts were the vehicle of both Irish and Scottish nationalism: but while the former traded them in, the latter crashed them and never bought another. Irish Jacobitism was strong, but its strength was substantively that of its adjective.[31]

# Jacobite Wales

For the Days we've misspent,
Let us Truly repent,
And render to Caesar his due.
Here's a health to the Lad,
With his Bonnet and Plaid,
For the World cannot stain his True Blue.
For the World cannot stain his True Blue.

Cycle Club verse of 1745

May the brave Charles unsullied in grace,
be glorious and crowned with gold. O Stuart,
kindly and guileless our dear Prince curb
their fury.

Welsh Jacobite song of John Prys tr. A.G. Goyder

Owain is again ready for the day.
From his hideout in Snowdonia
He will come with his faithful band
To lead us at dawn to a free Wales . . .

Dafydd Iwan, 'Owain Glyndwr'

even in his exit, his [Owain's] name was on every one's lips; the prophets foretold his triumphant return and he became a subject of popular legend . . .[32]

There were three major reasons why Jacobitism in Wales differed from that in both Scotland and Ireland, lacking their social cohesion and popular force. First, the Stuarts were allied to Welsh sentiment neither

---

[31] Simms, ch. 19 in Moody and Vaughan, pp. 629–56 (635, 636); Frank McLynn, 'Good Behaviour: Irish Catholics and the Jacobite Rising of 1745', *Eire-Ireland* XVI :2 (Summer 1981), 43–58 (44, 51, 55).

[32] Peter D. G. Thomas, 'Jacobitism in Wales', *Welsh Historical Review* 1:3 (1962), 279–300 (289); John Prys, quoted by A. G. Goyder, 'Welsh Jacobite Societies', *The Stewarts* 11 (1) (1960), 16–21 (21); Robyn Gwyndorf, 'The cauldron of regeneration: continuity and function in the Welsh epic tradition', in Bo Alanqvist, Seamas Ó Cathain and Padraig Ó Healain (eds.), *The*

through nationality nor religion; second, Wales was already joined to England by the Tudor annexation, and there was no nationalist dimension to the events of 1688–1707, as in the other two countries; thirdly, Wales was less geographically remote than either Scotland or Ireland.

Despite their strong support for the Stuarts in the Civil War period, the gentry, even Jacobite gentry, in Wales was more Anglicized than in the other Celtic countries. Wales had been effectively settled for longer than Ireland; moreover, several generations of Irish settlers had gone native for religious and dynastic (including self-interested) reasons by the end of the seventeenth century. Scotland, as the wars of that century had shown, was still a country very much apart from England and English ways. Individual magnates could rule the entire country; archbishops could be murdered in daylight: and the native dynasty was perhaps best loved and worst reviled north of the Border. But in Wales these complications and extremes were much less marked, and not so linked to nationalism. The Stuarts were not co-religionists and were not Welsh either (though Humphrey Llwyd had claimed James VI to be 'a monarch of their own blood', emphasizing 'the Celtic origin' of the dynasty in 1584). The Welsh church had historic links with that of England, but did not suffer as did the Episcopalians in Scotland and the Catholics everywhere; and Welsh self-determination was not an issue in the political consciousness of the time. Moreover, in an era when it could take almost six weeks to get from Scotland to London, Wales' relative closeness to the centre of power was more marked than it is today. The power-structures of the Welsh gentry differed less from English ones than did their Scottish counterparts: though Sir Watkins Williams Wynn was a more powerful magnate than a baronet in England might have been, he and his Jacobite compatriots blend easily enough into an account of predominantly English Jacobite intrigue, such as Eveline Cruickshanks' *Political Untouchables* (1979). Wales, unlike any other country in the British Isles, did not raise one organized force for the Stuarts in five Risings, and was not at the heart of any plots. Welsh Jacobitism was politically, financially and militarily ineffective. The fact that some of the most central figures in Jacobite intrigue were Welsh noblemen is only another in the long catalogue of ironies of optimism which beset the cause of the exiled line.[33]

Jacobitism in Wales expressed itself in two main dimensions. On the one hand, there was the rural aristocratic Jacobitism of Wynn and his allies, such as the Duke of Beaufort, which was voiced chiefly through societies such as the Cycle Club and the Sea Serjeants. On the other there was the

*Heroic Process: Form, Function and Fantasy in Folk Epic* (Dublin, 1987), pp. 413–51 (443–4); J. E. Lloyd, *Owen Glendower* (Owen Glyn Dŵr) (Oxford: Clarendon Press, 1931), p. 143.

[33] Francis Jones, *The Princes and Principality of Wales* (Cardiff: University of Wales Press, 1969), p. 48.

Jacobitism of the poor, often the urban poor, similar to that found in Scotland and England, differentiated chiefly in terms of Welsh- and English-speaking elements.[34]

These two Jacobitisms are broadly similar in their make-up to those found elsewhere, but they appear to have left far less evidence behind them: perhaps because they were less prevalent, perhaps because cross-class links were less developed due to the lack of a truly native gentry with Welsh nationalist priorities. With the exception of isolated figures like Wynn, the Welsh aristocracy offered little patronage to Welsh letters. Whatever their perenially excellent reasons, Welsh magnates never convincingly put together an organized force, and seemed ineffective in recruiting radical Jacobite dissent among the poor. This was a significant group: as to an extent was the case in England, areas in Wales which had been Jacobite in the earlier eighteenth century, subsequently became Jacobin:

When jacobites looked for their areas of greatest support, they found them in those advanced regions where the jacobins of the 1790s would also hope for either votes or insurrections.          Jenkins, 'Tory Individualism and Town Politics', p. 122

This curious but apparently common phenomenon is discussed more fully in the next chapter. In Wales in particular, it was Freemasonry which helped to carry the old alliance between Jacobitism and radical discontent into the last quarter of the century.[35]

Although the aristocrats did not harness such feelings (for example as the fishermen of the Scottish ports or the Kentish smugglers were used elsewhere), there were occasional overlaps between their interests and the folkways of the rural poor, as evidenced in Wynn's retention of a Welsh harper, support for Welsh culture, and the use of Welsh itself in certain poems of the Cycle Club. Such evidence as exists from an earlier period may indicate that the 'joyous relief expressed by the bards in rhyme and song' at the Restoration was not an isolated event, and that the Stuarts were popular in the bardic tradition, popular sometimes beyond the point of truth: 'King James ... a Welshman by stock, a Welshman is he', as one remarked. It is interesting that the story of Edward I's massacre of the bards (so memorably commemorated in Gray's poem) dates from the early seventeenth century, and may thus be contemporary with bardic support for the Stuarts, while the bards experienced an eighteenth-century decline similar to that which took place in Ireland. There was in any event considerable cultural crossover with English material: 'recent research

---

[34] Philip Jenkins, 'Tory Industrialism and Town Politics: Swansea in the Eighteenth Century', *Historical Journal* (1985), 103–23.
[35] Philip Jenkins, 'Jacobites and Freemasons in Eighteenth-Century Wales', *Welsh Historical Review* 9 (4) (1979), 391–406 (392).

into folk-song origins tends to the view that many "Welsh airs" were adaptations of early English tunes'.[36]

The Cycle Club itself, founded on 10 June 1710, formed a focal point for north Welsh high cultural Jacobitism of a conventionally messianic (if rather rustic) kind: the Cycle Club medal depicts sheep on the hills with the legend 'Cognoscunt me meae' ('my own know me' [John 10]). Apart from Arthur, Wales already had a powerful typological returning hero in Owain Glyndwr, who had asked for the help of Robert III of Scots on the grounds of their common descent from Brutus, and who exemplified the hope of the 'Britons' and 'the Scottish race' to regain control over the 'whole island'. Although there is controversy as to how far Glyndwr was a folk hero before the Celticizing revival of the later eighteenth century, there is some evidence that this nationalist figure was linked, as he had been in his own lifetime, to a resistance voiced in Welsh culture, now favourable to the Stuarts:

No 'waster, rhymer, minstrel or vagabond' was to be allowed to maintain himself by 'making commorthas or gatherings upon the common people' – a plain indication that the cause of Glyn Dwr was dear to the bards and actively encouraged by them in their professional wanderings.

The returning and delivering hero (Arthur or Owain) could be used to link the poetry of the Cycle Club to the legendary expectations of Welsh culture. The 'resurgence of Welsh patriotism' in the latter half of the nineteenth century, expressed in the founding of *Cymru Fydd* ('Wales of the future') in 1886, drew heavily on this tradition:

As our forefathers longed for a Deliverer, so we in Wales today hope that there will always be men and women ready to lead their country and safeguard its inheritance.[37]

It was this longing which the Cycle Club poems framed, substituting (but only on occasion) an appropriate Welsh folk typology for that used by Jacobites elsewhere:

> This Owen [Glyndwr] is Henry the Ninth,
> Who dwells in a foreign land.

Yet although such poems are clearly attempting to connect with a folk tradition, it is unclear how far they succeeded in doing so. The secrecy and exclusivity of such as the Cycle Club and Sea Serjeants entitles one to doubt how far such views were mediated into or by folk culture, rather than simply being gesture politics. What is known of the regulations and

---

[36] Jones, *Princes and Principality*, p. 48, 51; Prys Morgan, *The Eighteenth-Century Renaissance: A New History of Wales* (Llandybie: Christopher Davies, 1981), p. 128.

[37] Woolf, *Medallic Record*, p. 65; Lloyd, *Glendower*, pp. 46, 55; Robyn Gwyndorf, in Alanqvist et al., *The Heroic Process*, pp. 413–51 (439, 443, 445).

proceedings of the Clubs suggests a limited membership and mainly convivial purpose expressed in terms similar to English Jacobite clubs (though the Sea Serjeants apparently admitted women). The Serjeants' examination for entry requested that the candidate should be 'of the Church of England as by law established': important perhaps because Wales had a distinctive claim to a share in Anglican theory, not only through the Welsh tradition of the 'Early British Church, founded by Joseph of Arimathea in the time of the Apostles', but in St David's function as a representative of historic ecclesiastical independence:

David was the most famous saint of the early British church, who could be taken as a permanent reminder that the Church in England and Wales could claim an ancestry independent of papal Rome. It may be for that reason that the Hanoverian court in London kept up the celebration of his festival.[38]

At the three-weekly meetings of the Cycle Club, songs such as the Anglo-Scottish lyric of Stuart patriotism, 'Robin John Clark', were sung:

> Ye true Bacchanals, come to John of the dale,
> And there we'll carous o'er a butt of good liquor;
> Bring with you no sharpers nor friends to usurpers,
> But such as will drink till their pulses beat quicker.
> Let the courtier who snarls at the friends of Prince Charles,
> And else who our houses and windows make dark,
> Ne'er taste of such pleasure, nor rifle our treasure,
> For this is the chorus of Robin John Clark.

Technically belonging to the class of songs of active Jacobite resistance, 'Robin John Clark' is in fact more of a drinking-song, and its popularity with the Cycle Club suggests the presence of rather passive as well as derivative attitudes. Wynn's second wife 'was a personal friend of Flora Macdonald' and burnt all her husband's papers on the night following his death, but whether or not these would have 'hanged half the county' as has been argued, is a moot point. Wynn was far more adept at intrigue than action.[39]

Fertile grounds for such intrigue appear occasionally in accounts of the clubs. Repeated rumours of French invasion coincide a little too neatly with the Serjeants' habit of meeting 'at Haverfordwest and other towns with tidal waters', while in Wynn's own North Wales, Jacobite belief survived a long time, particularly in Anglesey. However, the sentiments of John Prys in 1751 ('May the brave Charles, unrivalled in grace, be glorious and crowned with gold') were soon succeeded by attempts to link the Hanoverians to ancient Welsh descent, and seditious words prosecu-

---

[38] Goyder, 'Jacobite Secret Societies', pp. 17, 21; Morgan, *The Eighteenth-Century Renaissance*, pp. 17, 31, 57.
[39] Goyder, 'Jacobite Secret Societies', pp. 19, 20; Hogg, *Relics*, I: pp. 124–5.

tions appear to peter out by the 1760s. As suggested above, the Cycle
Club's own Welsh repertoire may show an attempt to reflect and encourage the views of a Welsh-speaking Jacobite area:

> The Hanoverian King with evil pride
> had formed the Duke
> (of Cumberland)
> From the loins of the Devil.

But here as so often elsewhere, the Jacobite topos in discussion is not one
with a convincing and contemporary Welsh dimension. Leaving aside the
messianic material, the sentiments expressed in the Club's songs seem
often secondhand. Perhaps even the duration of such clubs, the Sea
Serjeants lasting till 1862 and the Cycle Club till 1869, reflects their
essentially cosy and unthreatening qualities, more ends in themselves than
means to an end. Welsh Jacobitism displays the features of Jacobite
ideology known from elsewhere, but not its practical results. Methodism
has been blamed for killing off Jacobitism in Wales: if this was the case, it
did not face a sturdy opponent.[40]

---

[40] Goyder, 'Jacobite Secret Societies', pp. 16, 20, 21; Jenkins, 'Jacobites and Freemasons', p. 393;
Thomas, 'Jacobitism in Wales', pp. 292–93, 299; Jones, *Princes and Principality*, p. 52.

# 6

# The demon's light

## Revolution and continuity

My blessings aye attend the chiel
  Wha pitied Gallia's slaves, man,
And staw a branch, spite o the deil,
  Frae yont the western waves, man.
Fair Virtue water'd it wi care,
  And now she sees wi pride, man,
How weel it buds and blossoms there,
  Its branches spreading wide, man.

Burns, 'The Tree of Liberty'

To make the wrong appear the right,
  And keep our rulers in,
In Walpole's time, 'twas Jacobite,
  In Pitt's, 'tis Jacobin!

Edwarde Coxe (1805)

A young blacksmith wrote eight verses of doggerel in praise of the Radical cause
and the fight at Bonnymuir, all to be sung, as such amateur verse frequently was,
to the music of the Jacobite rant *Hey Johnnie Cope!*.       John Prebble

'The English people', Kersant had said, addressing the Convention in January,
1793, 'like all conquerors, have long oppressed Scotland and Ireland ... Since the
Union, Scotland has been represented in Parliament, but out of such proportion
to its wealth, its extent, and its population, that it does not conceal the fact that
it is nothing but a dependent colony of the English Government.'

Henry W. Meikle

When the Manchester Blanketeers of 1817 marched towards London, carrying
their petition for trade reform, they chose to follow Charles Edward's route
through Leek and Ashbourne to Derby ...       Paul Monod[1]

---

[1] *Burns: Poems and Songs*, ed. James Kinsley (Oxford: Oxford University Press, 1992 (1969)),
p. 721; W. G. Blaikie Murdoch, *The Spirit of Jacobite Loyalty: An Essay Towards a Better
Understanding of the Forty-five* (Edinburgh: William Brown, 1907), p. 153; Edwarde Coxe, quoted

Although Scottish exiles in the colonies tended to be loyalist in the American revolutionary period (perhaps on the principle that any king was better than none), the American War of Independence set in train the process of an awakening radicalism among Scots at home. Abroad, Scots fought in the war with French troops, and Charles Edward himself, offered a place as the figurehead of a provisional American government in 1775, followed the details of the ensuing war with avid interest, and with no sympathy towards the British crown (McLynn, *Charles Edward Stuart*, pp. 518–19). In Scotland, 'the cause of the Americans' was viewed with 'remarkably widespread sympathy', support which can be linked to 'Anglo-Scottish friction and Scottish disenchantment with the Union'. The old Jacobite typology of King Stork and King Log made an appearance in *The Scots Magazine*, and 'Scots emerged from the war in a mood to demand reform ... but not their own revolution'.[2] On the other hand, Scots in America seemed on the political verge of the rudderless nostalgia which endures among their communities today, as in the kind of romanticized conservatism of the magazine *Highlander*, which will not publish any articles on modern Scotland. As Andrew Hook puts it:

Scottish romance offered little or nothing in the way of a challenge or threat to the rationalism, moderation, or morality of enlightened modern society; it may present the reader with a vision of another, more dangerous, world of colour, excitement and high passion – but the location of that world is safely remote both in space and time.

Such was the beginning of the cult evident in 'the remarkable vogue enjoyed by Scottish literature in America from the 1790s until at least the death of Scott'.[3]

In Scotland itself, such comforting nostrums were to become equally familiar in the aftermath of the radical scare of the late eighteenth and early nineteenth centuries, as I discuss elsewhere (Pittock, *Invention of Scotland*, ch. 4). But in the meantime the American and French Revolutions were to provide an outlet for radical, and indeed nationalist, feeling in both Scotland and Ireland. The French Revolution transformed the symbols of a fading Jacobitism as the 'king of the wood', the Stuart oak, was transmuted into the new Tree of Liberty, a political symbol

---

in Frank McLynn, *Crime and Punishment in Eighteenth-Century England* (Oxford: Oxford University Press, 1991 (1989), p. 340; John Prebble, *The King's Jaunt* (London, 1988), p. 9; Henry W. Meikle, *Scotland and the French Revolution* (Glasgow: James Maclehose, 1912), pp. 163–4; Paul Kleber Monod, *Jacobitism and the English People* (Cambridge: Cambridge University Press, 1989), p. 341.

[2] D. B. Swinfer, 'The American Revolution in the Scottish Press', in Owen Dudley Edwards and George Shepperson (eds.), *Scotland, Europe and the American Revolution* (Edinburgh, 1976), pp. 66–74 (66, 73).

[3] Andrew D. Hook, 'Scotland and America Revisited', in Edwards and Shepperson, *Scotland, Europe and the American Revolution*, pp. 83–8 (88).

adopted from France. In 1792, a Tree of Liberty was erected at the Cross in Perch, and several others were put up later that year, including an attempt to plant a fir tree (a traditionally Jacobite symbol) as a Tree of Liberty in Dundee on 16 November. There were riots in Aberdeen, Perth and Edinburgh, where 'the first Society of the Friends of the People in Scotland met ... on July 26, 1792'. Their message was spread through 'ballads and songs', not only those of new-born revolutionary radicalism, but also of Jacobite protest, such as 'The Sow's Tail to Geordie'. The revival of such songs forged a link between Jacobite and Jacobin opposition to tyranny which finds its clearest expression in the poetry of Burns: a traditional voice in protest against the new-found British patriotism surrounding George III:

> For under him we sit and crack,
> In peace and unity compact,
> Whilst every nation's on the rack
> That does nae like our Geordie.[4]

Although Jacobin pamphleteers never suffered penalties as heavy as Jacobite ones had once done (Monod, *Jacobitism and the English People*, p. 338), the authorities' concern was evident: and the now more positive image of the Hanoverian monarchy came to their aid. There had been little need for intensive propaganda after the effective mid-century defeat of Jacobitism: indeed 'between 1745 and 1781 "God Save the King" received only ten formal performances in the London theatres'. But as defeat in America was succeeded by the French threat, 'over ninety such performances' took place between 1786 and 1800, while 'in the following two decades' this Hanoverian version of a Stuart song 'supplanted the more libertarian "Rule Britannia" to become the recognized national anthem'. Meanwhile Britannia herself became a more royal and state-oriented image after war with France began in 1793 (Colley, 'The Apotheosis of George III', pp. 102–3, 106).

Such strengthening of the British idea in the face of this new threat only further intensified the marginality of Scottish or Irish supporters of radical change. Britannia and 'God Save the King' had been images appropriated at the margins in order to demonstrate support for an exiled monarch, or at the least the nature of the political authority he represented. Though these images had been regained by the British state in the 1730s and 40s, they had never been such powerful evocations of Britishness as they now became. England's self-image consolidated a patriotic language which absorbed its margins in the face of a double threat: an ancient enemy

---

[4] Meikle, *Scotland and the French Revolution*, pp. 67, 86, 120,147; 1809 Dunbar poem cited in Linda Colley, 'The Apotheosis of George III: Loyalty, Royalty and the British Nation', *Past and Present* (1984), 94–129 (121).

exporting international revolution. To the Jacobites, France had been an (often unworthy) friend and ally exporting a reversal of 1688, which the new France (as Burke did not hesitate to point out) also intended to do. Louis XVI was not even closely linked with the Stuarts – he had rejected them, and perhaps 1789 was his punishment: in any case, it revitalized the French threat to the British state. To understand this process is to understand why Jacobitism and Jacobinism could draw on similar support and subscribe to a similar analysis among those discontented with the British state. True, many once-Jacobite aristocrats (to whom Burke appealed in his apostrophe to Marie Antoinette) fell into line with the new British patriotism: but among radicalized or nationalist elements in the Jacobite inheritance, the gulf between old and new political positions may have seemed far less marked (after all, there had been Jacobite republicans, like the Earl Marischal).[5] Occasionally it vanished altogether. At the time of the 1798 Rising in Ireland, the French considered restoring Henry IX to Wolfe Tone's disgust; while Henry himself was dramatically increasing his use of the Touch for the King's Evil at this time, perhaps in a last-gasp hope of being no longer merely king 'non desideriis hominum sed voluntate Dei', as his 1788 medal had proclaimed.[6]

In Scotland, enthusiasm for the Revolution in the once-Covenanting west went together with an appeal to Scots to support Wolfe Tone and the Irish revolt in terms of the Jacobite analysis of history as a perpetual struggle for liberty against England, shared now in the shared heritage of two Celtic nations: 'had Wallace died . . . had Ossian sung in vain?'. The consolidation of British patriotic language allowed the radicals to appeal to Scottish patriotic exemplars with full confidence in the contrast, since their own continuing importance as tools of confrontational protest was implicitly endorsed by the British state's own recourse to typological language. The radicals also took advantage of the fact such heroes were still an integral part of particularly Scottish culture: 'Blind Hary's *Wallace* . . . was . . . the favourite book of the "vulgar" in late eighteenth-century Scotland', as John Brims informs us.[7] As a popular hero betrayed by a false aristocracy (at least in the typological version of events), Wallace made suitable material for republican agitation. France's interests were aroused in the cause of a Scottish republic, and the United Irishmen made a 'decision to appeal to the Scottish republican tradition', presumably in an effort to link nationalist radicalism in the two countries. Yet this 'republicanism' could itself be of a rather uncertain kind: Paul Monod

---

[5] Frank McLynn, *The Jacobites* (London: Routledge & Kegan Paul, 1985).
[6] Woolf, *Medallic Record*, pp. 133–6; Monod, *Jacobitism and The English People*, pp. 107, 107n.
[7] Meikle, *Scotland and the French Revolution*, pp. 164, 171; John Brims, writing in Roger A. Mason (ed.), *Scotland and England 1286–1815* (Edinburgh: John Donald, 1987), pp. 247–261 (254).

argues that some of the United Irishmen favoured Henry IX's restoration.[8]

Thomas Muir appealed to the 'supposed principles of the ancient Scottish constitution', and it was held that the Union's 'aristocratic' political settlement was a betrayal in much the same way that the Jacobites had once argued that the Estates had sold out to greed, gold and power (indeed, the idea of the traitor who sells out is so entrenched in modern left-wing demonology that its prevalence in Jacobitism should alert us to those radical elements in its analysis that the Jacobins inherited). Although it has to be said that very many of the Scots radicals favoured revolution on a British basis (the same internationalist paradox that hamstrings Labour nationalists today), there were those among the United Scotsmen who had leanings towards

a French government which was becoming attracted to the idea of destroying the power of its most determined enemy by dismantling the British state and erecting in its place separate English, Scottish, and Irish republics.

In this context Jacobite-influenced nationalism could warm to the Jacobin critique, as in Burns' 'A Man's A Man for a' That' (called 'the Marseillaise of Equality') or 'Scots Wha Hae'.[9]

But Burns was only part of a broader perspective of protest against social and economic dispossession. As the age of the Clearances in Scotland began, the image of the Highland patriot was ripe to be radicalized in the cause of a new resistance to the incoming values of British change. In the early 1790s, both rural and urban Scots could choose to find in the past a vocabulary suited to a language of contemporary struggle for history as liberty. Agnes Lyle's renderings of the popular ballad-tradition in radicalized form show how a weaver's family of 1820 might use analysis appropriate to a Jacobite a century earlier, in order to evoke a consistency of resistance to tyranny:

The king in the repertoire is the king of England, hates Scots, and can't be trusted – not a bad summary of the way radical subjects north of the border viewed the Hanoverians[10]

Agnes Lyle's orality measures itself against the changing circumstances of British politics. In her ballad renditions, the English are portrayed as Tory and aristocratic, the Scots as radical and ordinary (an opposition also cunningly used by Burns to suggest the universal qualities of Scottish

---

8 Brims, in Mason, *Scotland and England*, p. 247; Paul Monod, 'For the King to Enjoy His Own Again', p. 20.
9 Brims, in Mason, *Scotland and England*, pp. 252, 255, 261; Meikle, *Scotland and the French Revolution*, p. 122.
10 William Bernard McCarthy, *The Ballad Matrix* (Bloomington and Indianapolis: Indiana University Press, 1990), p. 143.

patriotic radicalism). For Lyle, even Lord Derwentwater becomes, as mentioned in Chapter 2, a Scotsman, albeit a 'Scottish lord': yet his lordliness is that quality which he does not assert, but is robbed of by a treacherous English king. In fact, Derwentwater shows himself a true Scot in the nobility with which he accepts his loss of lordliness. 'A short, perfectly constructed ballad' as it is, 'Lord Dunwaters' may seem to be but part of the confused history of oral reportage: but it is also contemporary comment. The defendants in the radical trials were prosecuted by English counsel, as their Jacobite predecessors had been. Thus Derwentwater's departure from Scotland and his betrayal there can be read as symbolic as a rape of Scottish rights and identity by English demand (McCarthy, *The Ballad Matrix*, pp. 16–17, 30).

This process is at work throughout Agnes Lyle's repertoire, in which the abandonment of Scottishness is associated with a loss of radicalism resulting in a move towards Toryism and Anglicization. The Scottish patriot is the poor, simple and uncorrupted man, as he was in the Jacobite song. Agnes Lyle and women like her, whose orality was a function of female control over tradition (as also found in Jacobite families, where 'wives often outlived their husbands, and became the carriers of family political traditions') used the language they had inherited to describe a situation whose politics appeared to be entirely different.[11] Peter Womack has suggested that Gaelic was increasingly perceived as 'female space' after the 'Forty-five Rising; and this may also have been a process whose force was intensifying in oral culture outside the Gaeltacht. Agnes Lyle's ballads display a mixture of nationalism and cynicism: the one part of the inherited language of history as liberty, the other the exasperated accent in which it was expressed.[12]

It would be an exaggeration to suggest that the ballad-collecting of the late eighteenth century had been prompted to a major degree by the new and growing romanticization of the Jacobite threat. But clearly there was some connexion, not least because, as Dave Harker points out in *Fakesong*, so many more Scots than English were involved.[13] The close link between orality and high culture in Scottish literature, manifest not only in Burns, Scott and Hogg but long afterwards, was and is a relic of the mediated text and the vernacular revival as vehicles for Scottish patriotic reaction to the Union. Ramsay, Pitcairne, Ruddiman, Fergusson, Burns are all exemp-

[11] McCarthy, *The Ballad Matrix*, pp. 143, 156; Monod, *Jacobitism and the English People*, p. 307 (see also his chapter in Cruickshanks and Black (eds.), *The Jacobite Challenge* (1988)).

[12] Peter Womack, *Improvement and Romance: Constructing the Myth of the Highlands*, Language, Discourse, Society series, general editors Stephen Heath, Colin McCabe and Denise Riley (Basingstoke: Macmillan, 1989), pp. 134–40.

[13] Dave Harker, *Fakesong* (Milton Keynes: Open University Press, 1985), p. 40.

lars of the link between high and folk culture in the cause of resistance to metropolitan absorption; while later, nostalgic visions of Stuart and Celtic culture fed Romanticism, their emphasis on the heroicism of the primitive itself a propaganda inheritance from Jacobite ideology. 'No fatherland can exist without folk poetry' wrote a Finnish nationalist under Russian rule; and this echo of Fletcher of Saltoun's words about the importance of ballad and folk culture in defining Scottish identity after Union shows the dimension of Romanticism through which a radicalized as well as a romanticized Jacobite ideology entered the nineteenth century: 'if a man were permitted to make all the ballads he need not care who should make the laws of a nation!'.[14] Fletcher's comment was paraphrased by James Hogg in his introduction to the *Jacobite Relics* of 1819–21, when the Highlander as patriot had been formally adopted by the British state following his success in the Napoleonic wars. In Hogg's collection, the icon retains its two-edged quality of nostalgic preservation and continuing subversion. Both were present in Romanticism itself, and in the way the language of Jacobitism was adopted by radical and conservative (hence Burke's plangent lament for the Bourbons) alike in the era of the French Revolution. Haydn's 1790s arrangements of Scottish folk songs gave them an entrée to the salons of the Romantic era; but they were also plotting subversion below stairs.[15]

Besides Scottish and Irish Jacobins, there were those more centrally British who managed to favour revolutionary France and the last echoes of *de jure* Stuart right at the same time. Among the most notable of these was Joseph Ritson, who 'as late as 1778 ... published a pamphlet claiming Charles III was the legitimate King of England [sic]' (Monod, 'For the King to Enjoy his own Again', p. 472). Shortly afterwards, Ritson proved his politics 'strongly anti-aristocratic ... and fully in sympathy with the French *sansculottes*'. Since he 'hated George III', the common motivation for both sets of opinions was apparent. Discussing Robin Hood in 1795, Ritson wrote in favour of the social bandit ethos in a way which would have been instantly accessible to those who had adopted it in Jacobite terms, as well as to his Jacobin contemporaries. Ritson's verdict that 'all opposition to Tyranny is the cause of the people' confirmed for the language of Jacobite protest the same validity of critique as that allowed to the radicals. The Jacobite 'brier / Shall pierce the heart of tyrannye' in 'My Love he was a Highland Lad'; and now the Tree of Liberty promised to take part in the same common struggle. If 'all' opposition to tyranny was 'the cause of the people', then Jacobitism and Jacobinism were one, as

---

[14] Peter Burke, *Popular Culture in Early Modern Europe* (Aldershot: Wildwood House, 1988 (1978)), p. 12; Harker, *Fakesong*, p. 8.

[15] Burke, *Popular Culture*, p. 7.

Ritson perhaps intended his readers to understand, 'member of Godwin's circle' though he was.[16]

Ritson's *Scottish Songs*, which appeared in 1794 in two volumes, reflect his sympathies. A large number of songs, more than in any previous non-fugitive collection, were Jacobite: among them many of an active and revolutionary rather than sacred or erotic nature. Pieces such as 'On the Act of Succession', 'Tho' Geordie reigns in Jamie's stead', 'To Daunton me' and a Jacobite parody of 'Rule Britannia' all criticize the foundations of the British state, then being lauded as a bulwark against the Jacobins. Ritson's notes reinforce a partisan reading. James is 'the person whom his friends called James VIII'; 'King James VII was undoubtedly ... a popular character in Scotland: and *The 14th of October* (his birth-day) is still a favourite tune', while the Hanoverian hero Colonel Gardiner is dismissed as a man who only fought bravely out of 'a spirit of religious enthusiasm, and a bigoted reliance on the Presbyterian doctrine of pre-destination ...'. As far as the enduring claims of the Stuarts go, Ritson, in a passage echoed by Hogg, writes that 'the rival claims ... are not more to the present generation than those of *Bruce* and *Baliol*', but undercuts this by virtue of the reason he gives for it: 'the question of RIGHT has been submitted to the arbitration of the SWORD'. Hanoverian power is all that justifies Hanoverian legitimacy, the same power with which the regime is currently suppressing the Jacobins. Ritson emphasizes this point further when he describes Jacobitism as

a cause which they [the Jacobites], at least, thought right, and which others, perhaps, only think wrong, as it proved unsuccessful.

This was still a daring conclusion in 1794; and Ritson's comparison of Scottish and Irish music with its underlying pan-Celtic assumptions could hardly have been intended to calm British nerves either.[17]

But though individuals like Ritson combined Jacobite and Jacobin ideological features, what was politically important in the 1790s was not the last flickerings of Jacobite reality, but the continuing relevance of the Jacobite analysis to the grounds of radical discontent. Economic change had encouraged groups such as weavers to support Jacobitism heavily in the eighteenth century, just as they might encourage radicalism at the dawn of the nineteenth. Fear of social change had been an engine for Highland Jacobite support; now the Clearances were making that social change reality as those who controlled the Highland economy became further and further integrated into the British state. 'Scotland Free or a

---

[16] Harker, *Fakesong*, p. 18; Hogg, *Relics*, I: pp. 55–6; Arthur Johnston, *Enchanted Ground: The Study of Medieval Romance in the Eighteenth Century* (University of London: The Athlone Press, 1964), p. 120n.

[17] Joseph Ritson, *Scottish Songs*, 2 vols. (London: J. Johnson, 1794), I: pp. lix, lx, lxix; II: p. 79n.

Desert' proclaimed the radicals of the 1820 Insurrection: the fertility king was gone, but the barrenness caused by his absence endured.[18]

## Robert Burns

> Alas the day, and woe the day,
>     A false Usurper won the gree,
> That now commands the towers and lands,
>     The royal right of Albanie.
>
> We'll daily pray, we'll nightly pray,
>     On bended knees most ferventlie,
> That the time may come, with pipe and drum,
>     We'll welcome home fair Albanie.
>
> 'Scots Ballad'

> Satan sits in his black neuk,
>     My Bonie laddie, Highland Laddie,
> Breaking sticks to roast the Duke,
>     My bonie &c
> The bloody monster gae a yell,
>     My bonie &c
> And loud the laugh gaed round a' hell!
>     My bonie &c ...
>
> 'Bonie laddie, Highland laddie'

> But while we sing, GOD SAVE THE KING,
>     We'll ne'er forget THE PEOPLE!
>
> 'The Dumfries Volunteers'[19]

Burns, like Ritson, was a man of both Jacobite and Jacobin sympathies. His grandfather, a North Easterner, may have been 'out' in the 'Fifteen with the Earl Marischal: as Burns says, 'my Fathers ... shook hands with Ruin for what they esteemed the cause of their King and their Country'. Whether this was the case or not, their descendant prized that patriotic liberty as fiercely as he says they did. Burns' concept of 'Liberty' can be seen as linking the image of Scottish history as struggle with the new radical vitality of Revolutionary France. In poems like 'Scots Wha Hae'

---

[18] For a discussion of the Insurrection of 1820, see P. Berresford Ellis and S. Mac A'Ghobhainn, *The Scottish Insurrection of 1820* (London, 1970).

[19] Burns, *Poems and Songs*, pp. 299, 486, 605; David Daiches, 'Robert Burns and Jacobite Song' in Donald A. Low (ed.), *Critical Essays on Robert Burns* (London and Boston: Routledge and Kegan Paul, 1975), pp. 137–56 (146).

and 'Parcel of Rogues in a Nation', Burns updates the Jacobite critique
with more current ideas of political liberty. In Barbour, the Declaration of
Arbroath, the Community of the Realm of Scotland and the Jacobite
cause itself, Burns located concepts consonant with those of the 1789
Revolution. Barbour's 'fredome' becomes mixed with French 'liberte'. In
'A Man's a Man for a' That', Burns creates a universal paradigm out of
the historical struggle for Scottish identity. Scotland's history makes it
uniquely qualified to display radical value:

> Is there, for honest Poverty
>    That hings his head, and a that;
> The coward-slave, we pass him by,
>    We dare be poor for a that!
> For a that, and a that,
>    Our toils obscure, and a that
> The rank is but the guinea's stamp,
>    The Man's the gowd for a that.

It is perhaps no coincidence that this famous lyric of equality is linked by
both air and refrain to 'Tho Georthie reigns in Jamie's stead'. Burns is
drawing on features of Jacobite ideology such as the corrupting power of
gold, the idea of an aristocratic betrayal of the honest ordinary patriot and
the language of marginal resistance to the metropolis:

> A prince can mak a belted knight,
>    A marquis, duke, and a that;
> But an honest man's aboon his might,
>    Gude faith, he mauna fa that!

This invitation to the 'man of independant mind' to resist the beguiling
bribes of the monarchy of the British state (bribes once held by Jacobites to
have brought about the Union), is rendered in traditional language of
patriotic resistance: the 'honest man', a leitmotif of Jacobite expression,
and linked throughout to the 'honest Poverty' characteristic of the Highlander as patriot. The 'fools' who have 'silks' and 'knaves' who have 'wine'
are by implication English or Anglicized, just as the aristocratic oppressors
of Agnes Lyle's ballads are: 'The rank is but the guinea's stamp' suggests
the power of foreign gold to achieve this. The head stamped on the guinea
is that of George III, while the guinea itself is a coin which did not have an
equivalent in Scottish currency prior to 1707 (as, for example, the English
crown and the Scottish sixty-shilling piece had the same value). The very
Scottish terms of abuse levelled at the aristocratic parasites, 'yon birkie
ca'd, a lord ... He's but a coof' suggest their English qualities: what in
Scots is a 'birkie', is in English a 'lord': the nominalism of the British state
replaces the realism of the patriotic Scot, whose 'Man's a Man for a that'.
Such sturdily just appraisals of value, 'the pith o Sense', make Scotland a

suitable starting-point for universal radical change: 'That Sense and Worth, o'er a the earth / Shall bear the gree, and a that'. The 'He's comin yet for a that' of the Jacobite song becomes an 'Its', promising universal brotherhood rather than the restoration of kingly justice: but its genesis is the same. Jacobite language is made a contemporary vehicle for radical value.

Burns repeats this formula in 'the Tree of Liberty':

> Let Britain boast her hardy oak,
>     Her poplar and her pine, man,
> Auld Britain ance could crack her joke,
>     And o'er her neighbours shine, man.
> But seek the forest round and round,
>     And soon twill be agreed, man,
> That sic a tree can not be found,
>     'Twixt London and the Tweed, man.

Although 'Britain' is the entity ostensibly referred to here as radically backward, the Tree of Liberty cannot be found ' 'Twixt London and the Tweed', that is in England rather than Britain. The 'oak', with both its Stuart royalist and Druidical republican overtones is suggestive of a British past where the country 'ance could crack her joke, / And o'er her neighbours shine, man'. But British liberty lies in the past, not the present where it is replaced by English tyranny (as in 'Scots Wha Hae'). But 'Liberty', missing from England, can perhaps be found in the 'here' among the 'we' of this light Scots poem in established colloquial format:

> We labour soon, we labour late,
>     To feed the titled knave, man,
> And a the comfort we're to get
>     Is that ayont the grave, man.

The 'we' is that of the universal oppressed community, but not without its core Scottish character: the first two lines speak in English of the oppressor, the latter two in Scots make clear the fate of the oppressed. The 'man' refrain is characteristic in Scottish song, Jacobite song as much as any:

> O cam ye here the fight to shun,
>     Or herd the sheep wi me, man?
> Or were ye at the Sherramoor
>     Or did the battle see, man?

It is on such songs that Burns is drawing, with their implicit community of address, here offered to all the oppressed:

> Like brethren in a common cause,
>     We'd on each other smile, man;
> And equal rights and equal laws
>     Wad gladden every isle, man.

This stanza is echoed in the contemporary Common Cause movement for Scottish democracy, underlining Burns' placing of Scotland in the vanguard of international liberty, a place where 'Freedom' can sing 'a sang of liberty', two words joined both in 'The Tree of Liberty' and 'Scots Wha Hae'.[20]

'Scots Wha Hae' amalgamates the relatively innocuous 'Fredome' of Barbour's *Bruce* with the much more dangerous 'liberty' of contemporary (1793) language in a poem which, as Burns himself confessed, had Jacobite roots. The poem's air 'Hey tutti taiti', was rumoured to be that with which Bruce had marched into battle at Bannockburn, and a long Scots military tradition behind it.[21]

The poem begins with the community of address which characterizes both 'A Man's a Man' and 'The Tree of Liberty', uniting mention of both Wallace the popular and Bruce the royal hero in an appeal to the entire community of Scotland:

> Scots, wha hae wi' WALLACE bled,
> Scots, wham BRUCE has aften led,
> Welcome to your gory bed, –
>     Or to victorie.

The second stanza's 'chains and slaverie', reinforced in the fifth stanza's reference to 'chains', suggests contemporary reference not only to a Jacobin language of oppression, but perhaps also to the many Jacobites transported into slavery after the eighteenth-century Risings: such mentions are certainly more relevant to the eighteenth than the fourteenth century (despite Edward's habit of placing Bruce's family in cages). The fourth stanza makes the patriotic appeal to Barbour's 'Fredome is a noble thing' with quite obvious intertextuality:

> Wha for SCOTLAND's king and law,
> Freedom's sword will strongly draw,
> FREE-MAN stand, or FREE-MAN fa,
>     Let him follow me. –

'Scotland's king and law' is, as I have observed elsewhere, a Jacobite nationalist call for restoration of the true dynasty and nation, while the strongly emphasized 'FREE-MAN' finds his counterpart in the contemporary revolutionary 'Liberty' of the sixth (originally fifth and sixth) stanzas:

---

[20] Burns, *Letters*, I: 376, Daiches, 'Robert Burns and Jacobite Song', p. 141; Burns, *Poems and Songs*, pp. 425, 561, 602, 721.

[21] For a discussion of this see William Donaldson, *The Jacobite Song: Political Myth and National Identity* (Aberdeen: Aberdeen University Press, 1988), p. 87.

> Lay the proud Usurpers low!
> Tyrants fall in every foe!
> LIBERTY's in every blow!
> Let us DO – OR DIE!!!

The call appears to be that of Bruce, but the language of contemporary reference suggests the perpetual relevance of struggle against tyrants of all places and times. Burns has taken the idea of Scottish history as a struggle for liberty, linked both with the Wars of Independence and the Jacobites, and once again has used it as a source for a call to resistance and revolution in the age of the Terror. The 'proud Usurpers' are the Hanoverians as much as the Plantagenets; the 'Tyrants' are (as the poem implies if read carefully) generically English or Anglicized, the oppressing nation; while doing or dying for liberty has sharp political relevance in 1793, a relevance only mildly disguised by the historical setting. An early version of the fifth stanza reads:

> Do you hear your children cry:
> 'Were we born in chains to lie?'
> No! Come Death or Liberty!
> Yes, *they shall be free.*

This future tense is not primarily intended to remind listeners of a morning's victory in the summer of 1314, but is a call across history to revolutionary struggle. Shifts between past, present and future tense in the poem indicate that the perpetual struggle of Scottish history is the same whenever it takes place: history has modality, but liberty does not. The language speaks beyond situation to the essential struggle for freedom and national resistance which, in the light of developments in Scotland's ancient ally, is in the process of acquiring universal meaning throughout space as well as across time.[22]

Burns' use of Jacobite critique in a Jacobin context was one of the many routes he used in reconditioning folk cultural expression for high cultural needs which had grown beyond the parameters of the cross-class Jacobitism of the early eighteenth century. Burns reconditioned rather than simply documenting or collecting folk culture, as some of his contemporaries did: he sought to give new topoi to the traditional tongues, and his conflation of radical Jacobite and Jacobin sentiment was one of the more successful parts of this process.

But Burns did not limit himself to encoded renditions of inherited critiques: some of what he wrote remained, as in the case of his poem on Charlotte, Duchess of Albany at the head of this section, explicitly

---

22 Burns, *Poems and Songs*, p. 561; cf. *The Poems and Songs of Robert Burns*, ed. James Kinsley, 3 vols. (Oxford: Clarendon Press, 1968), II: p. 707 for editorial reference to the altered stanza in 'Scots Wha Hae'.

Jacobite – too Jacobite even for 1787 (it was published in 1843). Apart from such original poems, Burns also preserved or reconditioned large numbers of songs, such as 'Johnie Cope', 'Carl an the King come', 'Awa whigs awa', 'The White Cockade', 'The Battle of Sherra-moor', 'Killie-crankie', 'Bonie laddie, Highland laddie', and 'O Kenmure's on and awa Willie':

> Here's Him that's far awa, Willie,
>     Here's Him that's far awa,
> And here's the flower that I lo'e best,
>     The rose that's like the snaw.

Some of Burns' re-renderings are powerful, but, as above, he begins to reveal in his explicitly Jacobite poetry a growing emphasis on the senti-ments of departure and loss without commensurate hope and defiance. The Jacobite song is brought into the open by Burns, and he begins to make it respectable: but those songs which are respectable are sometimes so by virtue of their admission of defeat:

> Thou hast left me ever, Jamie
> Thou hast left me ever,
> Thou hast left me ever, Jamie,
> Thou hast left me ever.

Although poems such as 'A Birth-day Ode. December 31st 1787' show Burns' interest in Charles Edward as long as he is alive, the poet is fully conscious that the promised messianic return is awaited in vain by its ageing devotees:

> By yon castle wa at the close of the day,
>     I heard a man sing, tho his head it was gray,
> And as he was singing the tears down came,
>     There'll never be peace till Jamie comes hame –

Such sentiments are traditional in Jacobite rhetoric, but are not usually uttered by defeated greybeards. In the poem, all those who can fight are dead, and only those who cannot are left to weep: 'My seven braw sons for Jamie drew sword / And now I greet round their green beds in the yerd'.[23]

The same effect is visible in Burns' 'parcel of rogues in a nation', which so powerfully reworks the rhetoric of early eighteenth-century anti-Unionist and Jacobite propaganda:

> O would, or I had seen the day
>     That treason thus could sell us,
> My auld gray head had lien in clay,

---

[23] Burns, *Poems and Songs*, pp. 299, 413, 416, 420, 423, 425, 431, 453, 486, 498, 565; Daiches, 'Robert Burns and Jacobite Song', p. 146.

> Wi' BRUCE and loyal WALLACE!
> But pith and power, till my last hour
> I'll mak this declaration;
> We're bought and sold for English gold,
> Such a parcel of rogues in a nation!

Despite its defiance, this song ends in the impotent protest of an old man, whose 'auld gray head' can only complain 'till my last hour'. The age of the singer indicates the nostalgic idealism of his politics.

This sense of the singer/protagonist as ageing or doomed is strongly apparent in Burns' subtle farewell to the Jacobite cause, 'Ye Jacobites by name'. An apparently anti-Jacobite poem ('Your doctrines I maun blame') has such credentials undermined by the last stanza, where the speaker reveals himself as a fellow-sufferer in the cause he seemed to oppose, as William Donaldson first pointed out:

> Then let your schemes alone, in the State, in the State,
> Then let your schemes alone in the State,
> Then let your schemes alone,
> Adore the rising sun,
> And leave a Man undone
> To his fate. –

The 'Man undone' is himself a Jacobite, warning others that no hope can be expected from further Jacobite activity. The repetition of 'State' suggests the established nature of the power the Jacobites have to deal with; but the 'rising sun' image is ambivalent, since though it apparently refers to the Hanoverian dynasty, the 'rising sun' was also associated with Jacobite iconography. Although the Hanoverians are ascendant, they are so in terms of an ambivalent image: the 'Man undone' is thus singing of his own defeat in terms which might once have prophesied Jacobite victory. His reference to himself is intended to remind his audience (as I discuss more fully in *The Invention of Scotland*) that the Hanoverian victory has only been secured by creating many 'men undone', from the anonymous singer to the king himself.[24]

Despite such subtle reservations however, the 'undone' quality remains central, an apt counterpart to the impotent greybeards who voice Jacobite views elsewhere. The Jacobite cause and Scottish nationhood are definitively being presented in terms of loss, decline and defeat, a position summarized in Burns' lines on Stirling Castle:

> Here Stewarts once in triumph reign'd,
> And laws for Scotland's weal ordain'd;

24 Hogg, *Relics*, I: 57; Burns, *Poems and Songs*, pp. 507, 511; I am indebted to William Donaldson here, who first put forward these arguments in 'The Jacobite Song in 18th and Early 19th Century Scotland', his 1974 Aberdeen Ph.D. thesis; Pittock, *Invention of Scotland*, p. 82.

But now unroof'd their Palace stands,
Their sceptre's fall'n to other hands;
Fallen indeed, and to the earth,
Whence grovelling reptiles take their birth. –
A Race outlandish fill their throne;
An idiot race, to honour lost;
Who know them best despise them most.

The broken castle and the broken kingdom are one: the sense of invasion of native ownership and domestic rapine discussed in earlier Jacobite propaganda such as 'O This is No My Ain Hoose' is complete; or complete but for the Clearances.[25]

To some extent Burns' valetudinary qualities as a Jacobite bard may have been due to the fact that Jacobite culture was still 'hot': certainly his adaptation of 'The Sow's Tail to Geordie' into an innocuous love dialogue echoes Ramsay's cautious sets (which of course included 'O This is No My Ain Hoose'). But in his role as 'implicitly the voice of Scotland, explicitly the national poet', Burns' long farewell to the Jacobite cause was echoing events upon a larger stage. And yet his adaptation of Jacobite language to radical ends also foreshadowed a continuation of 'Jacobitism of the Left' into the nineteenth and twentieth centuries. Burns foreshadowed both the nostalgic Jacobitism of sentiment, and the capacity of its living analysis of Scotland's plight to inhere in the language of subsequent struggles. This was his triumph, and yet another aspect of his uncanny ability to be a ventriloquist for the culture he was transmitting to an altering audience.[26]

[25] Burns, *Poems and Songs*, p. 277.
[26] Daiches, 'Robert Burns and Jacobite Song', p. 144; cf. Mary Ellen Brown, *Burns and Tradition* (London and Basingstoke: Macmillan, 1984), p. 81.

# 7

# The tartan curtain

## James Hogg and a Jacobite canon

My country, farewell! for the murmurs of sorrow
   Alone the dark mountains of Scotia become;
Her sons condescend from new models to borrow,
   And voices of strangers prevail in the hum.
Before the smooth face of our Saxon invaders,
   Is quench'd the last ray in the eye of the free . . .
                    'The Harp of Ossian'

Donald was mumpit wi' mirds and mockery;
Donald was blindid wi' blads o' property;
Arles ran high, but makings war naething, man;
Lord, how Donald is flyting an' fretting, man.
Come like the devil, Donald Macgillavry,
Come like the devil, Donald Macgillavry;
Skelp them an' scaud them that prov'd sae unbritherly
Up wi' King James an' Donald Macgillavry!
                    'Donald Macgillavry'

Come o'er the stream, Charlie, dear Charlie, brave Charlie,
   Come o'er the stream, Charle, and dine with Maclean;
And though you be weary, we'll make your heart cheery,
   And welcome our Charlie and his loyal train.

And you shall drink freely the dews of Glen-Sheerly,
   That stream in the star-light when kings do not ken;
And deep be your meed of the wine that is red,
   To drink to your sire, and his friend the Maclean.
                'Maclean's Welcome'[1]

---

[1] James Hogg, *The Works of the Ettrick Shepherd: Poems & Ballads*, new edn with a memoir by the Revd Thomas Thomson (London, n.d.), pp. 417, 419; Hogg, *Relics*, II: pp. 90–2.

If Burns made Jacobite language the contemporary of the radical cause, James Hogg cultivated it as a revelation of the primitive, a disrespectable and forceful survivor of a past ardently present in the identity and sufferings of Scotland. Jacobitism was not anodyne heritage because its struggle was continuing, albeit in other guises. Hogg's insistence on making the past our contemporary, not a subject for valedictory regret, led him to be rebuked by many in his own age and misunderstood far beyond its confines.

By the 1790s, Jacobite lyricism was permissible as long as it was expressed in sentimental terms. Hogg was complicit in this, as can be seen from early songs such as 'Donald MacDonald', with a nostalgic emphasis on apolitical loyalty rather than ideology: 'What though we befriendit young Charlie? ... Had Geordie come friendless amang us / Wi' him we had a' gane away' (Hogg, *Poems*, p. 283). Yet some of the statements made by the Jacobite song remained too enduring in their critique of the British state to be saccharined into nostalgia. Where the sentimentalization of the Jacobite lyric accommodated itself to the changing boundaries of political loyalty following the 1789 Revolution in France, ringfencing as this did the dynastic quarrels of the past with a defence of the monarchical principle against the spectre of its overthrow, the more radical part of Jacobitism could, as we have seen, align itself with that very Revolution. Songs about clansmen, broadswords and loyalty to Charlie were getting more popular ('Wha wadna fecht for Charlie's right' was played in 1824 at the funeral of the last survivor of the 'Forty-five, RSM Peter Grant of the Monaltrie's and Balmoral regiment), but those which subjected the political and ecclesiastical establishment of the British state to Jacobite analysis seem not so welcome.[2]

When Col. Stewart of Garth wrote to Hogg in 1817 (the year of the last arrest for suspected Jacobitism), requesting a 'small collection' of songs on behalf of the Highland Society, the acceptability of the Jacobite lyric *in toto* was thus far from assured (despite Hogg's protest concerning the irrelevance of Jacobitism to his contemporaries in his subsequent Introduction). Stewart of Garth and the Society seemed to want a collection of a particular kind of song: one displaying 'wit and humour' in its language, and 'beauty' in its air. The letter to Hogg mentions music more often than words, and suggests also that the Society would like to see a balance between Whig and Jacobite songs.[3]

Over the next four years, Hogg produced his *Jacobite Relics* in satisfaction of this commission. In doing so, he pleased neither the Highland Society nor his reviewers. Despite omitting many offensive songs, and

[2] Pittock, *Invention of Scotland*, pp. 82–3, 103.
[3] William Donaldson, *Jacobite Song: Political Myth and National Identity* (Aberdeen: Aberdeen University Press, 1988), p. 95 (National Library of Scotland MS. 2245 f. 28).

bowdlerizing others (in 'You're Welcome Charlie Stuart', 'Britons' is substituted for 'Devils' and a stanza about 'The cruel bloody German Race' and its usurpation disappears), Hogg's work was attacked for a lack of 'taste and discrimination'. The Highland Society were dissatisfied by the large number of songs which failed to convey with proper romantic delicacy the plight of the dreamy loyal chiefs of sixty years since. The Jacobite songs which were wanted were those which would not bring a blush to Flora MacIvor's cheek. By 1820, Scott had already done much to emplace a fiction too potent for the historicity of Hogg's lyrics to disturb.[4]

The reception of the *Relics* has, as William Donaldson observes, adversely affected their reputation ever since. What Hogg had done offended because it exceeded his remit of selection: it became instead the creation of a Jacobite canon, notwithstanding omissions made by Hogg for what may either be political or personal reasons. Far from caressing the memories of wrongly placed loyalties at last redeemed by the solidarity of Highland troops in the Napoleonic Wars, Hogg's *Relics* gave room to far too many aggressive and disturbing voices. Some of these were, impertinently, his own, as found for example in 'The Highlander's Farewell' (discussed in Chapter 4), which spoke not only of Culloden, but of the contemporary Clearances raging in Sutherland, where between 1815 and 1821 794,000 acres of clan land were cleared for sheep, and 15,000 exiled. A generation of lairds (Stewart of Garth an honourable exception) who practised or condoned the Clearances were criticized by poems in the very book commissioned to celebrate Highland virtue. The belief that 'the departure of the redundant part of the population is an indispensable preliminary to every kind of improvement' was rejected by the Hogg who praised the 'Highland Elysium' of patriotic plenty in songs such as 'The Maclean's Welcome'. Hogg's ability to create Jacobite pastiche in a living tradition was masterly, 'Donald Macgillavry' deceiving, to Hogg's delight, even Jeffrey in the *Edinburgh Review*. Hogg's description of the piece as 'a capital old song, and very popular' in his notes, complete with some spurious discussion of likely Macgillavrys as its subject, served only to season further this apparently effortless literary deceit to which its author belatedly confessed in 1831. Under the guise of a primitive and unsophisticated patriotism, Hogg's poems and 'translations' from Gaelic 'originals' pointed out the nineteenth-century fulfilment of Jacobite prophecies of exile and exploitation: history revisited the present, loss was restated as contemporary; and these themes were borne out in many of the genuine Jacobite songs he published alongside his own renditions.[5]

The canonicity of the collection is, however, even more important than

[4] Donaldson, *Jacobite Song*, p. 101; MS. 2222, Aberdeen University Library.
[5] Pittock, *Invention of Scotland*, p. 107; Donaldson, *Jacobite Song*, p. 100.

its contemporary message. The *Relics* crystallized Jacobite song-tradition in print and bulk for the first and indeed only time. Subsequent anthologists either wrote their own (such as Harold Boulton's 'Skye Boat Song') or, more usually, borrowed wholesale from Hogg. There was no significant attempt to alter or expand Hogg's choice. What is known today of the Jacobite song (saving a few pieces by Lady Nairne and her successors – and some of hers were adapted rather than authored, such as 'Charlie is my Darling') is the version Hogg presents. His editorial choice modified a compendium of subgenres into a listed and limited corpus of printed texts. Subsequent editors leaned heavily on this, failing on the whole to reach further into MS or oral tradition. Nor was it that this was unavailable: it is not necessary to delve far into the collections of Scottish libraries or families to discover songs not in Hogg. The centrality of the *Relics* has helped to disguise such resources, and, as a nineteenth-century text, has helped to give rise to the myth that the Jacobite song is not contemporary.

Hogg's editorial policy, set out in his Introduction, is classically typical of the writer, in that it obscures sophistication through carefully calculated veering between the naive and the disingenuous. Hogg implicitly encourages confusion between the (few) Gaelic and the mass of Lowland songs in his edition: by terming Jacobite songs 'the unmasked effusions of a bold and primitive race', he seeks the complicity of his readership in viewing them as productions of the Ossianic Highlands and their heroic clansmen, rather than the dull and commercial Lowlands (Hogg, *Relics*, I, p. viii). Although what is explicitly stated in the Introduction indicates that Hogg knew precisely the geographical, political and linguistic boundaries he was dealing with, he nevertheless allows this image to remain: the songs are 'These strains that were chanted o'er many a wild heath' by 'noble Highlanders, sons of the North'. As Hogg well knew, few of these songs fell into that category (Hogg, *Relics*, I, p. vi).

This was the first disingenuity of the Introduction. Why did Hogg practise it? Three reasons suggest themselves. First, the expectation of his paymasters, the Highland Society. Secondly, the propaganda advantage of portraying Scots as Highlanders made evident through recent successes in the Napoleonic wars. The Jacobite image of the Highlander as patriot had already been partly usurped by the British Army and Empire, and was readily rehabilitated in support of those who had done penitence for their fathers' part in its reality by defeating Hanoverian Britain's chief enemy on the field of Waterloo. The Napoleonic Wars offered a splendid opportunity to renew the mystique of Jacobite loyalty in the service of the Hanoverian state, to which Celticism formed a picturesque accompaniment.[6]

---

[6] For an account of this see Prebble, *The King's Jaunt* (London, 1988).

Thirdly, and most interestingly, Hogg's motives may have been more specifically ones of Scottish patriotism. The Jacobite lyric's long portrayal of opposition to the Union as spiritually if not physically Highland was evident in poems like 'Donald Macgillavry', and Hogg's sly equation of Highlander as patriot with Highlander as author reinforces the authenticity of Jacobite propaganda. Indeed, Hogg elsewhere presents Wallace himself as a Highlander, one of the 'heroes of the plaided north', and this patriotic metaphor is as ubiquitous in his poetry as in that of any eighteenth-century Jacobite. For example, 'Lock the Door, Lariston', although a pastiche Border ballad, nevertheless Celticizes its Borderers in their struggle against the 'Saxon spears' of the English: reiving has become ethnic conflict. Hogg knew that the Highland patriot ethos was central to the subject-matter of the Lowland Jacobite song: his own poetry provides evidence enough of this. In his Introduction to the *Relics* he deliberately confuses subject-matter with origination.[7]

Thus Hogg's first disingenuity is one of authorship. His second is one of subject-matter. Having melded this with authorship in ethnic terms, he goes on to do so in socio-religious ones. Throughout the Introduction, Hogg implies that written song-collections are largely held by 'old Catholic families', associates Jacobite song-culture with Catholicism, and assures us that 'the horrors of the Catholic religion have ceased to oppress the minds of men', so that it is now all right to print these songs (Hogg, *Relics* I, pp. viii–xi).

As Hogg again knew, the principal religious group associated with Jacobitism was not the Catholics, but the Episcopalians (whose resulting disabilities did not fully disappear until 1867). Interestingly, Hogg virtually omits the sacred song (customary voice of Jacobite Episcopalianism) from the collection, just as he omits Episcopalianism from the Introduction, in an apparent desire to make the rather Gothic equation of Jacobite = Catholic.[8]

There were problems concerning the inclusion of the sacred song. It was more the voice of a disaffected few than the popular voice Hogg sought to project. Moreover, its airs were often adaptations of psalm or sacred tunes, and such still may have had power to shock, though the encoding of Jacobite messages in sacred music was a longstanding practice, as Ruth Smith has recently shown.[9] Nevertheless, Hogg's omission of the sacred Jacobite voice seems on balance a deliberate one, born out of more than its

[7] Hogg, *Poems*, pp. 377–80; James Hogg, *Selected Poems*, ed. Douglas S. Mack (Oxford: Oxford University Press, 1970), p. 142.

[8] Also discussed in Murray G. H. Pittock, 'The Making of the *Jacobite Relics*', *Studies in Hogg and his World* 3 (1992), 10–17.

[9] I am indebted to Ruth Smith's as yet unpublished MS of a book on political reading of eighteenth-century libretto; cf. also Monod, *Jacobitism and the English People*, p. 43.

lack of musical homogeneity with other songs (Hogg does after all include the odd sacred Jacobite skit to a psalm-tune, such as 'The Cameronian Cat', a fact he coyly acknowledges in the notes).

The editing out of the sacred tradition may thus be the second disingenuity Hogg practises: underlined by the fact that he claims in the Introduction that the songs he has omitted simply repeat the material he has decided to publish (Hogg, *Relics*, I, p. xii). The main text of Volume I of the *Relics* contains sixty-seven active/aggressive songs, sixteen erotic ones, four in the sacred tradition and three which are difficult to classify. A strong bias is thus evident in favour of those lyrics which reinforce the post-Waterloo image of the Highlander shown in the opening lines of Hogg's introductory verse epistle: 'To the sons of the men who ne'er flinched from their faith, / But stood for their sovereign to ruin and death, / These songs I consign'. Military glamour has earned the Highlander British society's respect: and the Jacobite canon sems to have been constructed by its editor to reflect this contemporary reality.[10]

Having distorted questions of author and subject, Hogg turns to context. Throughout the Introduction he protests that Jacobitism is a dead letter, as remote from contemporary politics as the Wars of the Roses (an example borrowed from Ritson, as pointed out in Chapter 6). Jacobitism is presented as an ideological position *held by the Hanoverians themselves*, who were in any case not really to blame for the severity of the suppression of the Risings. This is carried to the length of protesting too much, perhaps due to a desire to avoid any blame for some of the more forthright pieces in the collection (if so, it was a not altogether successful ruse). It is not echoed elsewhere in Hogg's work. There is nothing in the Introduction to the *Relics* of the 'disgrace of the British annals' which can never be blotted out, as Hogg elsewhere refers to the aftermath of the 'Forty-five. Nor is there anything of the consciousness of the fulfilment of Jacobite warnings in the Clearances evident in Hogg's poetry. The poems which Hogg himself composed for the *Relics* deceived reviewers precisely because their author had entered into Jacobite historical consciousness in a manner which would not have been available to him had he been an antiquarian only, celebrating a remote and curtailed past. Jacobitism for Hogg was not a heritage trail, and his attempts to render it so in his statements of editorial means and aims seem to earn their place mainly for the purpose of deflecting short-term criticism from their author, which they failed to do.[11]

Hogg's editorial statements of intent thus avoid three central questions about the Jacobite lyric: who wrote it, the nature of its analyses, and the

---

[10] Hogg, *Relics*, I, set of 'Cameronian Cat'.
[11] James Hogg, *The Three Perils of Woman*, 3 vols. (London, 1823), III, 345; Donaldson, *Jacobite Song*, pp. 103ff.

contemporaneity of their relevance. Hogg's Jacobite canon was too daring to earn him the favour he may have sought; but made crucial compromises even to be as far effective as it was towards such an end. Hogg had other reasons besides this for the disingenuousness of his Introduction: but the nature of his market was a major cause of it. His canon is the one we inherit; and, since no one has significantly altered or commented upon it till very recently, it is but too easy to forget the circumstances of its production. We are also prone to forget the slipperiness of Hogg as an artist. The *Jacobite Relics* are a work of art, of multiple narratives of contrived validity. Thus they are like other things Hogg wrote.

Hogg follows a process of coyness and slight evasion in his supporting notes also. If the text of the songs represents the canon of the Jacobite literary voice, the notes both reinforce the validity of that canonicity and provide a history to support it. Hogg's historiography, in fact, seems to lean slightly more to the Jacobite side than his Introduction warrants: but the quality of completion resident in all political history which is not contemporaneously politicized, makes his reading susceptible of a Romantic interpretation. The Stuarts are more gallant and anti-Hanoverian than they were in the Introduction: but those days are gone now, and in the past they must remain.

This feeling of completion is reinforced by Hogg's obvious reluctance to admit that the Jacobite canon is not frozen in the mists of time. For example, he avoids acknowledging Burns' authorship, even when patent, on more than one occasion; and of course, Hogg says nothing of his own ('Donald Macgillavry' is 'a capital old song' ). The narrator of Hogg's notes evades or lies concerning questions of contemporary authorship, making the outrageous statement that 'The Thistle of Scotland' is 'a modern song, and the only one that is in the volume, to my knowledge'. Who is this dogmatic, ignorant 'me'? An imp sent to tempt the reviewers, to seek their acceptance on their terms? The very title *Relics* belies the modernity of many of the songs Hogg chose: he is linking them to the vanishing past of the ballad-collectors.[12]

Yet, paradoxically, Hogg's own songs and many among the others chosen for the collection reflect a contemporary relevance at odds with the air of historical completion offered as their gloss. In this, they were more in keeping with Hogg the writer than Hogg the editor. Hogg's *The Three Perils of Woman* concludes with a vision of the post-Culloden world of surreal ghastliness, where the survivors of the new Scotland are a hypocritical Presbyterian employer, a perverted doctor, and Davie Duff the gravedigger, who lusts to cut off people's ears. In his masterpiece, *Confessions of a Justified Sinner*, Hogg presents his tale of double identity in the

[12] Hogg, *Relics*, I: pp. 280, 281.

context of Scotland's loss of her identity through the 1689 Revolution and
1707 Union, as I discuss at greater length elsewhere (Pittock, *Invention of
Scotland*, ch. 3). Despite or because of his sympathy with the Covenanters,
Hogg saw how establishment propaganda could alter the dimensions and
understanding of patriotic debate. Hence the unreliability of his nar-
rators, the distortions in their perception: his criticism of the Enlightenment for rejecting the supernatural in *Confessions*, his criticism of the
supernaturalist for rejecting empirical reality in *The Brownie of Bodsbeck*;
and his rejection, again in *Confessions*, of the incremental progression of
history in favour of the typological voice of the folk, the dispossessed of
Scotland:

> 'Oh! is there no day-spring for Scotland . . .
>
> The homes of my kinsmen are blazing to heaven,
>   The bright steep of morning has blush'd at the view;
> The moon has stood still on the verge of the even,
>   To wipe from her pale cheek the tint of the dew;
> For the dew it lies red on the vales of Lochaber,
>   It sprinkles the cot, and it flows in the pen;
> The pride of my country is fallen for ever . . .
>                     'Callum-a-Glen' (Hogg, *Poems*, p. 413)

In an age when suffering such as this was passed over in a society which
could nevertheless congratulate itself on its noble Scottish past, Hogg's
aim is to show 'manifestly how much an eye and ear-witness may be mistaken', despite good intentions. Authenticity is the preserve of those who
suffer and experience, rather than narrate and pontificate. When Hogg
writes of these things directly, his tone can change from elusiveness to
indignation:

No national calamity has ever given me so much pain as the total bereavement of
the brave clans who stood to the last for the cause of the house of Stuart. It is a
stain on the annals of our legislature which can never be blotted out.[13]

The 'stain' is of sin, the language of typological history: incremental
change can 'never' efface it, and even worse, it continues in the
Clearances:

> Oh-hon, an Righ! and the Stuarts of Appin!
> The gallant, devoted, old Stuarts of Appin!
>   Their glory is o'er,
>   For the clan is no more;
> And the Sassenach sings on the hills of green Appin.

---

[13] Hogg, *Three Perils*, iii, p. 65; *Poems*, p. 415.

The old songs were now more respectable to sing; but they still accused British respectability.[14]

## Sir Walter draws the tartan curtain

We are now all Jacobites, thorough-bred Jacobites, in acknowledging George IV. This seems to be one of the feelings that stimulate the people here, at the present time, to make such exertions.                    *The Edinburgh Observer*, 1822

We are THE CLAN, and our King is THE CHIEF
Sir Walter Scott

Sawney, now the King's come,
Sawney, now the King's come,
Down an' kiss his gracious hand,
Sawney, now the King's come ...

Tell him he can do nae wrang,
That he's mighty high an' strang,
That you an' yours to him belang.
Sawney, &c.

Swear he's great, an' chaste, an' wise,
Praise his portly shape an' size,
Raise his whiskers to the skies
Sawney, &c ...

satire on Scott's song of welcome
to George IV, 1822

Sir Walter had ridiculously made us appear a nation of Highlanders ...
James Stuart[15]

In 1820, central Scotland witnessed a Radical insurrection. Sixty thousand went on strike; many took up arms, leading to a skirmish with soldiers at Bonnymuir. The slogan of the Radicals was 'Scotland Free or a Desert', and although the outright nationalism of many who took part may be doubted or attributed to *agents provocateurs*, there was certainly a patriotic edge to the revolt. George IV, like George I and II before him, was portrayed as 'Nero', while

[14] Hogg, *Poems*, ibid.
[15] *The Edinburgh Observer*, quoted Prebble, *The King's Jaunt*, p. 123; Prebble, pp. 97, 100, 269; John Doran, *London in the Jacobite Times*, 2 vols. (London: Richard Bentley & Son, 1877), II: 378.

A young blacksmith wrote eight verses of doggerel in praise of the Radical cause and the fight at Bonnymuir, all to be sung, as such amateur verse frequently was, to the music of the Jacobite rant 'Hey Johnie Cope!'.

Jacobite symbolic language and sentiment appealed to a succeeding age of protest: in 1820, the patriotic rallying-cry of the Fiery Cross was used for the last time, at an election riot (Prebble, The King's Jaunt, pp. 8-9, 280).

The treason trials which followed the Insurrection were themselves reminiscent of the aftermath of the 'Forty-five, eliciting considerable popular support for the patriots sentenced to death. The voice of 1820 was Lowland, urban and radical: but it was a voice of Scottish protest, raised again in 1919 in the days of John Maclean. As such, it was an embarrassment to the establishment of a country whose rehabilitation from revolt had seemed complete after the loyal part Scottish troops had played in British wars since 1756.

The visit of George IV to Edinburgh in 1822 was the first occasion on which a de facto monarch had been north of the Border since the seventeenth century. Like his father, George had something of a sentimental liking for the Stuart cause: he had been the first Hanoverian to wear tartan, at a ball in 1789. The decision to come to Scotland, which produced a pathetic eagerness to please, was in fact something of an accident: an effort by the king's ministers to keep him out of the way. But whatever its cause, it was Scotland's opportunity to set the seal on its Britishness and loyalty to the new royal house. The man who was above all responsible for the narrative of pageantry which tried to secure this end was the already famous novelist Walter Scott.

In his fiction Scott had already begun to impose a historiography of his own upon the narratology of Union and the Jacobite cause. Whatever his secret Miltonic sympathies with the superseded, the central action of Scott's Scottish fictions is a triumphant recovery of unassailable incrementality from the charms of typological challenge. The recurrent horseshoe on the brows of Redgauntlet's family proves irrelevant beside the irreversible social change of eighteenth-century Scotland. Scott presents a pattern in which Scottish patriotism is characterized as childish, British patriotism as adult. Scott's Jacobites, Ravenswood, Redgauntlet or Vich Ian Vohr are mighty and seductive figures: but they have no part in the peaceable interchange of a civil society engineered by continual progress and development. Their touchiness, pride and headstrong lack of wisdom are the distinguishing qualities of adolescence: and Scott makes of the growth from Scottish to British, Jacobite to Hanoverian, a bildungsroman metaphor of the ultimate incrementality of growing up. Not only is this centrally the case in (for example) Waverley's emergence from adolescence: it is paralleled even in the case of that relatively worthy Jacobite, the Baron of Bradwardine. On arrival at Tully-Veolan, Waverley notices that a picture of the Baron at ten shows him just as he looks at present, emphasizing the immature qualities of his behaviour.[16]

Scott's reiterated conflict between constructs of 'old'/typological and 'new'/incremental in his novels underline their fictional appeal as the picaresque *bildungsroman* of nations. In *Waverley*, the 'old' consists of northern and Highland Scotland, the clans and the Scoto-Latinist intellectual tradition; the 'new' is Britain, settled prosperity and empirical common sense. As so often in his novels, Scott includes an apparent paradox in the construction of these premises: in *Waverley* it is the young who are chief among those attracted to the 'old': Waverley, Fergus and Charles Edward himself. This only underlines, however, the romance of the 'old', and its fitness for adolescent temperaments. The discarding of the 'old''s oldness is part of a process of renewal, of maturation, of adulthood in people as in nations. Those who refuse to grow out of the 'mode ... of melodrama', like Fergus, who even at his own execution remarks that it is 'well GOT up for a closing scene', must perish. The incrementality of British nationhood cannot tolerate the perpetual adolescence of egotism, quick temper and violence that Fergus and his politically pubescent ilk offer. As in *The Bride of Lammermoor*, the transition from 'old' to 'new' contains its reverse: newness can also be the process of getting older in a personal or constitutional sense. Scott's narrative confirms its own incrementality in plot, character, and historiography alike.[17]

At the beginning of *Waverley*, the 'oldness' of Jacobitism in England is strongly identified. Its military potential is lost, its supporters are ridiculous or naive antiquarians, and England grows more and more prosperous in the absence of the dynastic conflict it threatens. Waverley himself joins the British Army and heads north. On the borderland of Highland and Lowland, just north of Perth, he visits the Baron of Bradwardine, modelled on Col. Alexander, Lord Forbes of Pitsligo, and a classic example of an impractical Jacobite old-timer. Scott's constructs continue thus: the Baron is not a Celt, but a Saxon, descended from 'Godmund', a deeply unlikely name for a Scottish progenitor (as is 'Bradwardine' itself, as Claire Lamont notes (Lamont (ed.), *Waverley*, p. 475n)). Bradwardine's Saxonicity is a sign of one of Scott's persistent constructs: Lowlanders are Saxons, Highlanders Celts. This division is portrayed in his fiction as ethnic rather than linguistic: and one of its implications is that Lowlanders are more suited to British integration than Highlanders, being tempera-

[16] Donaldson, 'The Jacobite Song in 18th and Early 19th Century Scotland', unpublished Ph.D. thesis (Aberdeen, 1974), 434; Sir Walter Scott,*Waverley*, ed. Claire Lamont (Oxford: Clarendon Press, 1981), p. 58.

[17] Jane Millgate, *Walter Scott: The Making of the Novelist* (Edinburgh: Edinburgh University Press, 1984), p. 49 emphasizes this aspect of Fergus's character.

mentally more suited to unforced 'growing up'. True to type, it is Bradwardine who suffers least among the Scots for supporting the Rising.[18]

This view of Highlanders as immature and ethnically distinct from
other Scots (which seems to have played a significant role in justifying the
Clearances) had a long history, but it was by no means a commonplace of
the age: Hogg, as argued above, saw Scots as completely Celtic, as did
Scott when he wanted to make a different kind of political point. But in the
historiography of his fiction, distinguishing Highland and Lowland on
cultural and linguistic grounds would not have proved sufficient, as it
would have suggested that Scotland's divisions were circumstantial and
provisional, rather than deep-seated and permanent. Instead, Scott provided in *Waverley* a national faultline of 'old' Celts and 'new' Saxons, with
the Saxonicity of Bradwardine that which guarantees his eventual 'redemption' from romantic false consciousness.[19]

However, when Scott needed to use this consciousness for his own
purposes, the faultline disappears: the 'old' Scotland of Jacobite-
nationalist threat becomes an 'all' Scotland of romantic Celtification, as in
the political rather than historiographical reading of nationality prepared
for 1822. The methodology of Scott's fiction displaced the contemporaneity of Scotland's nationality; the methodology of his public relations
reaffirmed that contemporaneity, but only in displaced form. Scotland
was not a country of radical rising and continuing protest, of difficulty and
modernity; it was a sealed zone of Jacobite sentiment, served up to flatter
and comfort a Hanoverian king. Scott set the stage, and drew the tartan
curtain.

Not everyone applauded. Lady Nairne, who might be thought a fitting
accomplice to the Wizard of the North's rehistoricizing and decontextual-
izing, showed little interest in the King's visit: perhaps because of her still
genuine Jacobite feeling, while Patrick Walker's attempt to have King
George fly the Scottish quartering bespoke a persistent strain of (albeit in
this case token) nationalist resentment. But the massive boom in tartan
and the rise of a subsuming British patriotism which asserted 'that a
Jacobite king sat in London' was more typical. The *Edinburgh Observer*
emphasized the central quality of paradoxicality in this response, asserting
that 'upon the death of the last male heir to the Stuart cause ... the
Jacobite party had become completely triumphant' (Prebble, *The King's
Jaunt*, pp. 131, 178, 206, 242, 359). Jacobitism had become the apogee of
respectability. Scott himself

---

[18] Bradwardine was modelled on Lord Forbes of Pitsligo, whom Scott was well aware had
   suffered far less favourable treatment. See Pittock, *The Invention of Scotland*, p. 85; also Scott's
   Foreword to Alexander Lord Forbes of Pitsligo, *Thoughts Concerning Man's Condition and Duties in
   This Life*, ed. Lord Medwyn, 4th edn (Edinburgh and London, 1854).
[19] Cf. Pittock, *The Invention of Scotland*, pp. 86–8.

clearly wished to believe that the spiritual nature of a Stuart and therefore a Scottish monarchy, purified by exile and the blood of Culloden, had been made manifest in the fat form of the landlord of Brighton Pavilion.

Yet Scott appeared to want it both ways, protesting to George IV that 'Jacobitism still survived "to a wonderful degree in Scotland"' (Prebble, *The King's Jaunt*, pp. 18, 19). Even in George's confirmation as a Jacobite hero, a soupçon of danger lurked in the king's new status: enough to give the tang of pleasure to the romance of heritage.

As I have argued in *The Invention of Scotland*, the Celticizing glamour which accompanied the transference of Jacobite iconography to the new dynasty hid under its factitious show the lasting qualities of a radical Jacobite critique which it patronized. Scott and his recontextualizing allies were determined to make of the 'sixty years since' the Rising a chasm which jacobitical politics could not cross. Hence Scott's friend, Mac-Donnell of Glengarry, one of the most notorious clearers of the day, could be a peacock of tartanry: the politics and the image of Jacobitism had become utterly sundered. In the forty years after the King's visit, Jacobitism became 'a heritage trail into extinct history, the virtues of which could be patronized and the vices forgotten' (Pittock, *Invention of Scotland*, p. 90):

> Scottish romance offered little or nothing in the way of a challenge or threat to the rationalism, moderation, or morality of enlightened modern society; it may present the reader with a vision of another, more dangerous, world of colour, excitement and high passion – but the location of that world is safely remote both in space and time.

History's failures became futilities. And this is still the way Jacobitism is read today: backwards: the ultimate triumph of incrementality having been to display its opponent as the reverse of itself.[20]

As Dave Harker argues in *Fakesong*, Scott's constructs were part of a reaction against radicalization: in that they were such, they marginalized this element of Jacobitism in favour of its absolutist heritage. 'The old Trojans of 1745 nay 1715', to whom Scott had listened as a boy (Lamont (ed.), *Waverley*, p. xviii) had been absorbed into the contingent images of a new Britain whose Trojan qualities had nothing to do with the ideologues of its once exiled Aeneas. Scott's 'invention of tradition' laid the foundation for many others; and for the damaging assumption that all Scotland's myths of identity were fictitious and romanticizing marginalia to the central narrative of British development.[21]

[20] Andrew D. Hook, 'Scotland and America Revisited', in Owen Dudley Edwards and George Shepperson (eds.), *Scotland, Europe and the American Revolution* (Edinburgh, 1976), pp. 83–8 (88).
[21] Harker, *Fakesong*, p. 41; Eric Hobsbawm and Terence Ranger (eds.), *The Invention of Tradition* (Cambridge: Cambridge University Press, 1983): note particularly Hugh Trevor-Roper on Highlandism and tartanry, pp. 15–41.

# The end of an old song

Now the bricht sun, and the soft summer showers
Deck a' the woods and the gardens wi' flowers –
But bonny and sweet though the hale o' them be
There's ane aboon a' that is dearest to me;
An Oh, that's the white rose, the white rose o' June,
An' may *he* that should wear it come back again sune!

Lady Nairne, 'The White Rose o' June'

The bloom has faded frae her cheek
In youthfu' prime, in youthfu' prime;
And sorrow's with'ring hand has done
The deed o' time, the deed o' time.

Lady Nairne, 'The Lass of Livingstane'

John Sobieski and Charles Edward Stuart. The implication was unmistakable. They were the grandsons of the Young Chevalier; and they were legitimate. 'Will ye no come back again?' had ceased to be a rhetorical question.

William Donaldson, *The Jacobite Song*

Probably the last Nonjuror (if not the last Jacobite) in England died in the Charter House, London, in 1875 – the late Mr James Yeowell, for many years the worthy and well-known sub-editor of 'Notes and Queries'.[22]

True to Scott's presentation of events, the 1820s marked the beginning of Jacobitism's final acceptance by the British idea, as image if not as critique. The Jacobite portion of the gentry and aristocracy were now fully rehabilitated as Britons. Following the large-scale restoration of clan lands in 1784, George IV's Edinburgh visit (at which Lady Nairne's 'Wha'll Be King but Charlie' was played at the Hunt Ball) gave rise to a Memorial requesting the restoration of attainted peerages. In 1824, Parliament duly restored the peerage to Mar, Kenmure, Perth, Strathallan and Nairne (thus giving Lady Nairne her title!), and 'it was also proposed to reverse the attainder of Lord Strafford'.[23] In the same year, Marshal MacDonald and the Duke of Fitzjames were both present at the re-interring of James VII and II's remains; and this year also saw the death of the last survivor of the Rising, RSM Grant. In 1826, Airlie, Dalzell, Carnwath and Duffus were all restored, Lovat following in 1837, Niddesdale and Herries in 1841

---

[22] *Life and Songs of the Baroness Nairne with a Memoir and Poems of Caroline Oliphant the Younger*, edited by the Revd Charles Rogers, 2nd edn (Edinburgh: John Grant, 1896), p. 211. Donaldson, *The Jacobite Song*, p. 110; Doran, *London in the Jacobite Times*, II: p. 354.

[23] *Life and Songs of the Baroness Nairne*, pp. 50, 290n; Doran, *London in the Jacobite Times*, II: p. 379.

and Southesk in 1855. A claim made by Amelia Matilda on the Earldom of Derwentwater in 1868 was, however, rejected (Doran, *London in the Jacobite Times*, pp. 383–8, 400).

In England, the remaining members of the regular nonjuring church had been committed to the care of the Episcopal Church in Scotland by their last regular bishop in 1777; and in 1788, on Charles's death, the Episcopalians themselves conformed to the Hanoverian dynasty, though many individual members of the church did not. Lady Nairne's father, Laird of Gask and Captain of Gask's Troop in the Perthshire Horse in 1745, wrote thus to his chaplain on hearing the news:

Mr Oliphant presents his compliments to Mr Cruikshank, and as he has incapacitated himself from officiating at Gask, his gown is sent by the carrier, and the books he gave the reading of. As Mr Cruikshank has received his stipend to this Whitsuntide, there is no money transactions to settle between him and Mr Oliphant.

The Laird apparently found a replacement, but although old ladies continued to shuffle their feet at the back of churches when George's name was mentioned in prayers, the writing was on the wall. The last nonjuring bishop died in Ireland in 1805, and the disabilities lying on both Catholics and Episcopalians were gradually lifted, although the Episcopal Church did not become a member of the Anglican Communion until 1867, and 'the clergy ... were still debarred by statute from officiating for a single day in the Church of England till 1840'.[24]

Yet it is clear that a tradition endured. Almost as soon as what had been called (by its Primus, Jeremy Collier, in 1717) 'the Catholic Church in England' came to an end, it found a new form. Just as the Nonjurors had been sustained in their faith by the battle against Latitudinarianism, so Newman and the Tractarians raised the flag against Liberalism.[25] Keble's martyrological praise of Charles I in the *Christian Year* for 1827 was succeeded by attacks on the Glorious Revolution (though Lady Nairne, incidentally, was an opponent of Puseyism). Just as a nonjuring bishop had once confessed his fears of the indefensibility of the Church of England, so Newman's own defence of the Catholicity of the Thirty-Nine Articles became a step on his way to abandoning them (Gladstone at this time 'was prepared, if the Church of England were proved anti-Catholic, to go, not to Rome, but to the Episcopal Church in Scotland' – perhaps this was due to his Scottish background). In that Church, Archibald Penrose Forbes, a descendant of Lord Forbes of Pitsligo, who himself had been influenced by Archbishop Fenelon, defended and extended the ideas

---

[24] *Life and Songs of the Baroness Nairne*, p. 25; The Very Revd W. Perry DD, *The Oxford Movement in Scotland* (Cambridge: Cambridge University Press, 1933), p. 37.

[25] Henry Broxap, *The Later Non-Jurors* (Cambridge: Cambridge University Press, 1924), p. 39.

of the Oxford Movement, and 'patiently entertained . . . hope of reunion' with Rome. Caesaropapism reared its head again, but despite its new guise it had been badly (and perhaps irreversibly) damaged by the loss of its central raison d'etre: the sacramental monarchy. Before 1689, most of those monarchs most closely associated with the English Church hardly qualified as Reformers in the Continental sense of the term. Henry's hostile attitude to Luther seemed little changed by his own break with Rome; Elizabeth declined to eschew her crucifixes, and tried to keep Marian bishops (indeed, she wanted Archbishop Parker consecrated by such bishops in 1559, though this proved impossible). In 1561, she 'expressed her very great interest in a reunion of Christians and had seemed gratified at the approach of the nuncio', though mutual intransigence (as usual in such cases) ensured this came to nothing. The sacramentalism of late Tudor and Stuart imagery was intimately linked to the caesaropapist quality of those monarchies, a quality which could never properly be emulated thereafter. A sacred monarch excluded because of his steadfast adherence to religion may have been a compromise suited to a majority of Anglicans, but it damaged the original conceptualization of that Church's spiritual life; and a minority (a vast majority in Scotland) dissented from it for more than a century. In doing so, they strengthened both the language and principles of the Stuart cause, and preserved the Laudian inheritance (most clearly seen in the Nonjuring succession in America, with churches apparently dedicated to 'St William Laud').[26]

Jacobitism briefly raised its head again in secular politics in England in the late nineteenth century, where a whole Neo-Jacobite movement and press was brought into being: a Symbolist snook at the bourgeoisie, and a protest of 'neo-Platonic politics' against the growth of utilitarian scientism. The movement was divided between the sympathetic antiquarians in the Order of the White Rose, and the active restorationists of the Legitimist League. Jacobite candidates were selected to stand for Parliament, societies were formed and votes taken, and the sectarian Protestant press published cheap and popular thrillers such as Allen Upward's *Treason* and its sequel *Mary the Fourth*, which prophesied an invasion of England backed by 'Papal troops'. Many artists of the period, such as Ruskin, Whistler, Dowson, Lionel Johnson, Hubert Crackanthorpe and perhaps Yeats himself, were well-disposed towards or even active in, the Neo-Jacobite movement, which was a sufficient irritant to draw comment from abroad.[27]

[26] Broxap, *The Later Non-Jurors*, p. 66; Perry, *Oxford Movement*, pp. 61, 64, 76; John Jewel, Bishop of Salisbury, *An Apology of the Church of England*, ed. J. E. Booty, published for the Folger Shakespeare Library (New York: Cornell University Press, 1963), pp. xiff.

[27] Ian Fletcher, *W. B. Yeats and His Contemporaries* (Brighton: Harvester, 1987), 'The White Rose Rebudded: Neo-Jacobitism in the 1890s', pp. 83–123; Allan Upward, *Treason*, 3rd edn (London, 1904); *The Fourth Conquest of England* (London, 1905), pp. 44, 52.

Stuff and nonsense though this political Symbolism was on the verge of the twentieth century, it had important effects in the nationalist politics of Scotland and Ireland. In Scotland, Theodore Napier, an outspoken Stuart restorationist, was nonetheless a political activist who attracted the sporadic support of thousands of Scots, and whose paper, *The Fiery Cross*, was the first out-and-out nationalist publication in Scotland for a century and a half. Napier's anti-imperialism, his defence of the rights of small nations, and his awareness of the importance of a Scottish lobby in political publicity, were serious dimensions to his otherwise impossibilist Jacobitism. Ruaridh Erskine of Mar, John MacLean, Hugh MacDiarmid and Wendy Wood all inherited and developed the kind of radical Jacobite analysis to which Napier not inconsiderably contributed. Although the Scottish Patriots' enthusiastic 'discovery' of a 'legitimate' Jacobite heir at the end of the 1970s belongs to the realm of sugarplum fairy, the radical strain in the Jacobite analysis endures more convincingly in the development of political and cultural nationalism in twentieth-century Scotland. The Stuart cause is still an obsession with sections of the chattering classes, as the newspapers' frequent articles on the dynasty confirm, while the folksong revival (and its ersatz extension in 'Flower of Scotland' or 'Roses o' Prince Charlie') owes much to the syntax of the central nationalist voice of eighteenth-century Scotland.[28]

In Ireland, as argued in Chapter 5, Jacobite language readily transmuted into the mystic and sacrificial nationalism of the Plough and the Stars. The woman who once represented the beloved and longing country in the *aisling* poems can be aligned with Cathleen Ni Houlihan, and is fertilized by the bloodseed of recidivistic and brutal Republican martyrology. The analogy between Catholic and Jacobite martyrdom extends crookedly across history into the typological twisting of Pearse's bloodsacrifice or the H-block deaths of 1981. And the tongue of Loyalism, rooted in the events of 1689–91, confirms in its exemplars the mutuality of typological inheritance for both peripheries. Cuchulain as defender of Ulster has begun to appear on Loyalist murals; Pearse's own image is usurped in a reflection of the inherited language of his cause. The lambeg drums of Unionist opinion beat out the message of the siege of Derry: The Cry Was No Surrender. 'King James and all his Rebel Band' are with us yet; or, if preferred, 'King Billy . . . plundered and he burned and he killed King James's men':

> Roaming in the gloaming with a shamrock in your hand,
> Roaming in the gloaming with St Patrick's Fenian band
> And when the music stops – F—k King Billy and John Knox,
> It's good to be a Roman Catholic.

[28] Cf. Pittock, *The Invention of Scotland*, ch. 5.

Not only are the politics this book has concerned itself with directly and
destructively present with us in Ireland, but the means of transmission of
such sentiments are often the same as those discussed here: the popular
song. After the internments of the early 1970s, the following song spread
rapidly throughout Republican, Irish and eventually general oppositional
circles in the British Isles:[29]

> Through the crowded streets of Belfast
> In the dark of early morn,
> British soldiers came marauding ...
>
> Through the world the shout will echo:
> 'Cromwell's men are here again!'
> England's name once more be sullied
> In the ears of honest men.

That the world neither knows nor cares for 'Cromwell's men' any longer is
not relevant to the 'honest man' immersed in history's repetitions. As I
argued in Chapter 1, typological history is the voice of a national group
deprived of incrementality: and this is true for Ulsterman and Irishman
alike, as each frustrate the other's expectations.[30]

But it would be overly sentimental to discuss the legacy of the Jacobite
critique while ignoring the power of Jacobite sentimentality. Queen
Victoria's rehabilitation of the Jacobite song in 1842 was followed by the
adoption of Balmoral as a centre for the display of Hanoverian identity
reforged in the Stuart image: '"For Stuart blood is in my veins", said the
Queen, "and I am now, their representative and the people are as devoted
and loyal to me, as they were to that unhappy Race"':

In such terms, uttered by the Queen herself, did the Hanoverian dynasty finally
accept the loyalty they had spent so long suppressing. This was the consummation
Scott had sought from the 1822 visit ... Tartanry

Pittock, *Invention of Scotland*, pp. 103–4

If Victoria consigned Jacobitism to prime heritage in the songs and
portrayals she sanctioned or inspired, Albert, everywhere else a modern-
izer, appeared as a Fionn-like hunter, portrayed as spearing salmon
Redgauntlet-wise. Bad shot as he was, the Prince Consort's example
helped to create of Scotland a heroicized theme park where the hunter
might leave his jacobitized lodge to hunt in ossianized surroundings,
obligingly cleared of their inhabitants. The tangible result of this was that
by 1885 1.7 million acres of Scottish cultivable land was under deer (ten

---

[29] For a discussion of Irish Jacobitism's legacy to modern Irish nationalism, see above, ch. 5.
[30] The territorial questions raised by the religious division are symbolically alive in the demands
made by Orange marchers to march in Catholic areas.

per cent of the total).[31] Not only was Scotland viewed as an old-fashioned world of reassuring traditionalism; its landowners pandered to this image. Colonization by heritage altered the reality in favour of the moneyed fantasy:

This was the image of the Highlands as a wild place full of kilt wearing neo-brigands, and crooning lassies, where a man – well, a Very Important sort of Man – could rediscover the primitive blood-lust of the hunt.

The 'noble savages' were, if they stayed on the land at all, now the ghillies ('boys' – cf. colonial usage) of the noblemen pretending to be savages, who had in the shape of figures like the Sobieski Stuarts a frisson of Jacobite reality to tingle themselves with.[32]

These brothers, who came to prominence in the 1830s, pretended to be direct descendants of Charles Edward Stuart. Some believed, or affected to believe, them. Lord Lovat 'built them an amazing Celtic Xanadu' on Eilean Aigas, and they pandered to the sentimental Jacobitism of the Highland societies. Yet although their prime function was titillation, their own poetry, such as the unpromisingly named *Lays of the Deer Forest*, contains a strain of unabated anti-Union feeling at odds with some of those that eulogized them. The traditional emphasis on bribery and betrayal is distanced by the implicit heritage ('Lays'), but retains some force none-theless, as in these lines: 'Drop your cur-tails and snuff around the throne / Picking the bones and offal which may fall.' The Sobieski Stuarts were not immune from posing to bite the hand that fed them.[33]

Jacobite colour remains widespread in twentieth-century tourism and tartanry, but more meaningful legacies are disruptively submerged in minority nationalist and ecclesiastical traditions, with the notable excep-tion of Ireland, whose integration into Britain has always been so weak that the aboriginal divisions remain as keen as they were at the Boyne. For Jacobitism is, in its varied forms, the prime root and the first fruits of opposition to the British state; a language of dissent from the zeugma of Pope to songs of Burns, from the Quaker laird of Brux who took arms for the king to the Episcopal priest who gave the Last Sacrament in oatmeal and whisky to the dying on Culloden field.[34] Jacobitism is most centrally our contemporary as we are most centrally the inheritors of its enemies, of

---

31  Andrew Dewar Gibb, *Scotland Resurgent* (Stirling, 1950), p. 170.
32  Malcolm Maclean and Christopher Carrell, *As an Fhearann* (London, 1986), p. 39.
33  Donaldson, *Jacobite Song*, pp. 110, 113; John Sobieski and Charles Edward Stuart, *Lays of the Deer Forest*, 2 vols. (Edinburgh and London, 1848), 1: p. 368.
34  Bruce Lenman, 'The Scottish Episcopal Church and the Ideology of Jacobitism', in Eveline Cruickshanks (ed.), *Ideology and Conspiracy: Aspects of Jacobitism 1689–1759* (Edinburgh: John Donald, 1982), pp. 36–48 (45); George A. Burnet, *The Story of Quakerism in Scotland 1650–1850*, with an Epilogue on the period 1850–1950 by William H. Marwick (London: James Clarke, 1952), p. 162.

the Revolution settlement and its associated legislation, of the unwritten constitution ratified by Victorian apologists: just as history itself has been generated in the context of a British incrementality that can deny itself only in the patronage of hindsight. At the margin, in a Scotland torn between sentimental and meaningful belief in its own nationality, Jacobitism is a typology invoked in explanation of the national tendency always to retreat from Derby, while in more sinister media, the lambeg drums of Ulster beat out the message of the siege of Derry: the Cry was No Surrender. Even in English ruralism the note lingered:

Down to the age of Walpole and beyond, many Tories believed that if only the seditious dissenters, the monied upstarts and the factious politicians could be controlled, such an idyllic society would come into existence. Even today, one can still catch echoes of this old refrain ... This lingering distrust of the methods and principles upon which a system of representative government and an open commercial society must depend may have been the most important bequest of the royalist cause to future generations.

Such images, such problems are with us still. There is always a need for an Astraean *renovatio*; for justice is never found on the earth.[35]

[35] R. Malcolm Smuts, *Court Culture and the Origins of a Royalist Tradition in Early Stuart England* (Philadelphia, 1987), p. 291.

# Additional works

*An Account of the Proceedings of the Meeting of Estates in Scotland.* London, 1689.
*Act Extending Time for Restraining the Use of the Highland Dress.* Legitimist Jacobite League pamphlet.
Addison, Joseph. *Cato: A Tragedy.* London, 1713.
  *The Free-Holder.* London, 1761.
*Alexis, Or the Worthy Unfortunate. Being a True Narrative Of The Affecting Case of a Young Gentleman.* London, 1747
Allardyce, Mabel D. *Aberdeen University MacBean Collection: A Catalogue of Books, Pamphlets, Broadsides, Portraits. Etc., in the Stuart and Jacobite Collection Gathered Together by W. M. MacBean.* Aberdeen University Studies No. 126. Aberdeen: The University Press, 1959.
Allen, Robert J. *The Clubs of Augustan London.* Harvard Studies in English Volume VII. Cambridge, Mass. 1933.
Amherst, N. *Poems on Several Occasions.* London, 1720.
*Anatomy of the Scots Tory.* Edinburgh, 1719.
Anderson, James. *Scotland Independent.* Edinburgh, 1705.
Armens, Sven M. *John Gay–Social Critic.* New York, 1966
Mr Asgill. *De Jure Divino.* London, 1710.
Ashton, Robert. *The Battle of Aughrim.* Dublin, 1777.
Aveling, J. H. C. *The Handle and the Axe: The Catholic Recusants in England from Reformation to Emancipation.* London, 1976.
Axon, William E. A. *Stray Chapters on Literature, Folk-Lore and Archaeology.* Manchester and London, 1888.
Bacon, Peter. 'Dryden's Heroic Theatre'. Unpublished D.Phil. thesis. Oxford, 1986.
Barclay, P. *A Persuasive to the People of Scotland. In Order to remove their PREJUDICE to the Book of COMMON PRAYER.* 2nd edn. London, 1723.
*A Bibliography of the History of Wales.* 2 vols. Cardiff, 1962.
*Narrative of the Mutiny in the Black Watch in 1743.* Compiled By His Grace the Duke of Athole KT. Perth, 1893.
Blomfield, Reginald. *The Formal Garden in England.* 3rd edn. London, 1936.
Bold, Alan (ed.) *Sir Walter Scott: The Long-Forgotten Memory.* London and Totowa NJ, 1983.
Bolingbroke, Henry St. John, Viscount. *Letters of Lord Bolingbroke to Dr Jonathan Swift, DSPD.* Glasgow, 1752.

*Letters on the Spirit of* PATRIOTISM AND ON THE *Idea of a* PATRIOT KING. With an Introduction by A. Hassall. Oxford, 1926.

Bongie, Lawrence L. 'Voltaire's English, high treason and a manifesto for bonnie prince Charles'. *Studies in Voltaire and the Eighteenth Century* 171 (1977).

*Sir Robert Brass.* London, 1731.

*Britannia Excisa;* BRITAIN *Excis'd.* n.p., n.d.

Brock, William. *Scotus Americanus.* Edinburgh, 1982.

Brooke, Charlotte (ed.). *Reliques of Irish Poetry.* Dublin, 1789.

Brooks-Davies, Douglas. *Pope's Dunciad and the Queen of Night.* Manchester, 1985.

Brown, David. *Walter Scott and the Historical Imagination.* London, 1979.

Burness, John. *The Northern Laird, and his Tenant: A Tale.* Dublin, 1815.

Bush, George E. Jr. 'The Fable in the English Periodical 1660–1800'. Unpublished Ph.D. thesis. St. John's University, 1965.

*John Byrom and the Manchester Jacobites.* Exhibition Catalogue. City of Manchester Art Gallery, 1951.

Cannadine, David and Price, Simon (eds.). *Rituals of Royalty: Power and Ceremonial in Traditional Societies.* Cambridge, 1987.

Carruthers, R. *The Highland Note-Book.* Edinburgh, 1843.

*The Case of Disbanding the Army.* London, 1698.

*The Celtic Magazine* VIII (1883).

*The Celtic Monthly.* Volume 20 (1912).

*The Character of Pericles.* London, 1745.

Christie, Nimmo. *Lays and Verses.* London, 1896.

Clark, J. C. D. *English Society 1688–1832.* Cambridge, 1985.

*Revolution and Rebellion.* Cambridge, 1986.

Cleery, Thomas R. 'Henry Fielding and the Great Jacobite Paper War of 1747–49'. *Eighteenth Century Life* 5:1, 1–11.

*A Clue to the Comedy of Non-Juror.* London, 1718.

*The Collier of Preston. A Farce.* London, 1716.

*A Congratulatory Letter to John Murray, Esq.* [by Atticus]. London, 1747.

'A Copy of what Dr Archibald Cameron intended to have delivered at His Execution'.

Cowan, Ian B. 'The Inevitability of Union – A Historical Fallacy?'. *Scotia* 5 (1981), 1–8.

Craig, Sir Thomas. *Scotland's Soveraignty Asserted.* Published by George Ridpath. London, 1695.

Crawford, Tom. 'Political and Protest Songs in Eighteenth-Century Scotland II: Songs of the Left', *Scottish Studies* 14 (1970), 105–31.

(ed.) *Love, Labour and Liberty: the eighteenth-century Scottish lyric.* Cheadle Hulme, 1976.

*Society and the Lyric.* Edinburgh, 1979.

Crofton-Croker, T. (ed.) *Popular Songs, Illustrative of the French Invasions of Ireland.* Percy Society Vol. XXI. London, 1845.

Cruickshanks, Eveline. *Political Untouchables: The Tories and the '45.* London, 1979.

'The Convocation of the Stannaries of Cornwall: The Parliament of Tinners 1703–1752'. *Parliaments, Estates and Representation* 6:1 (1986).

Cruickshanks, Eveline and Erskine-Hill, Howard. 'The Waltham Black Act and Jacobitism'. *Journal of British Studies* 24 (1984).

Cullen, L. M. *The Emergence of Modern Ireland 1600–1900*. London, 1981.

Cusare, Marion H. *Narrative Structure in the Novels of Sir Walter Scott*. The Hague; Paris, 1969.

Daiches, David. *The Scottish Enlightenment*. Edinburgh, 1986.

'The Declaration of the Rebels Now in Arms in the West of Scotland'. 1679.

Defoe, Daniel. *Hannibal at the Gates or, the Progress of Jacobitism*. London, 1712.

*Diamond Cut Diamond: The Lamentations of the Nonjuring Clergy &c.* 2nd edn. London, 1724.

Dickinson, H. T. 'The Eighteenth-Century Debate on the Glorious Revolution'. *History* 61 (1976), 28–45.

*Liberty and Property: Political Ideology in Eighteenth Century Britain*. London, 1977.

*A Discourse Concerning the Nature, Power, and Proper Effects of the Present Conventions in Both Kingdoms*. London, 1689.

*A Discourse Concerning the Union*. n.p., n.d. [1707?].

*A Discourse of the Necessity and Seasonableness of an unanimous Address for Dissolving the UNION*. n.p., 1715.

Dixon, Willmott. *The Jacobite Episode in Scottish History and its Relative Literature*. Edinburgh, Glasgow and London, 1874.

Donaldson, William. 'The Glencairn Connection: Robert Burns and Scottish Politics, 1786–1796'. *Studies in Scottish Literature* 16 (1981), 61–79.

Downie, J. A. *Robert Harley and the Press*. Cambridge, 1979.

*Jonathan Swift: Political Writer*. London, Boston, Melbourne and Henley, 1984.

Dugaw, Dianne. *Warrior Women and Popular Balladry 1650–1850*. Cambridge Studies in Eighteenth-Century Literature and Thought. Cambridge, 1989.

*The Eagle and the Robin and An Old Cat's Prophecy*. London, 1709.

'The Eclectic Magazine': 'Scottish Cavaliers and Jacobite Chieftains'. Reprinted from *The Dublin University Magazine* July 1855.

*Epigrams* n.p, n.d.

*Episcopal the Only Apostolical Ordination*. London: G. Strahan, 1713.

Erskine-Hill, Howard. 'Under Which Caesar? Pope in the Journal of Mrs. Charles Caesar 1724–1741'. *Review of English Studies* 33 (1982), 436–44.

*A Form of Order of Thanksgiving and Prayer*. London, 1687.

*A Form of Prayer with Thanksgiving for the Safe Delivery of the Queen*. London, 1688.

Frawley, Shelagh. 'Poetry and Politics: The Case of Charles Churchill'. Unpublished M.Phil. thesis. Oxford, 1980.

Gay, Peter. *Voltaire's Politics: The Poet as Realist*. 2nd edn. New Haven, 1988.

Gerrard, Christine. 'The Patriot Opposition to Sir Robert Walpole: A Study of Politics and Poetry, 1725–1742'. Unpublished D.Phil. thesis, Oxford, 1986.

Gibson, John. *Playing the Scottish Card: The Franco-Jacobite Invasion of 1708*. Edinburgh, 1988.

*The Poetical Works of Oliver Goldsmith, Tobias Smollett, Samuel Johnson, and William Shenstone*. Illustrated by John Gilbert. New edn. London, 1865.

Greig, Gavin. *Folk-Song in Buchan and Folk-Song of the North-East*. Foreword by Kenneth S. Goldtein and Arthur Argo. Hatboro, Pennsylvania, 1963.

*The Greig-Duncan Folk Song Collection.* Volume 3, ed. Patrick Shuldham-Shaw, Emily B. Lyle and Peter A. Hale. Aberdeen, 1983.

Henderson, Hamish. 'Scots Ballad and Folk Song Recordings'. *Scottish Language News* 1:2 (1971), 42–51.

Henderson, Sir Neville. *Crisis and Change.* Brisbane, 1986.

Hogg, James. *Tales and Sketches by the Ettrick Shepherd.* Edinburgh, 1883.
  *The Private Memoirs and Confessions of a Justified Sinner.* Intr. Andre Gide. London, 1947.
  *Memoir of the Author's Life and Familiar Anecdotes of Sir Walter Scott.* Ed. Douglas Mack. Edinburgh and London, 1972.

Hudson, Nicholas. *Samuel Johnson and Eighteenth-Century Thought.* Oxford, 1988.

Hutton, W. H. 'A Glimpse of the Exiled Stewarts'. *Cornhill Magazine*, June 1905.

Ingelow, Jean. 'A Jacobite Laureate' [William Hamilton of Bangour]. *Macmillan's Magazine*, March 1893.

Isaac, D. G. D. 'A Study of Popular Disturbances in Britain 1714–1754'. Unpublished Ph.D. thesis. Edinburgh, 1953.

Jones, George Hilton. *The Main Stream of Jacobitism.* Cambridge, Mass., 1954.

Kenny, Virginia C. *The Country House Ethos in English Literature 1688–1750.* Sussex and New York, 1984.

Kenyon, J. P. *Revolution Principles: The Politics of Party 1689–1720.* Cambridge, 1977.

Kramnick, Isaac. *Bolingbroke and His Circle.* Cambridge, Mass., 1968.

Lang, Andrew. 'Ker of Kersland'. *Blackwood's Magazine*, December 1897, 769–77.
  *Prince Charles Edward Stuart: The Young Chevalier.* London, 1903.

Langford, Paul. *A Polite and Commercial People: England 1727–1783.* The New Oxford History of England, gen. ed. J. M. Roberts. Oxford, 1989.

*The Laws and Acts Made in the First Parliament of Our most High and Dread Sovereign James VII.* Ed. George Viscount Tarbet et al. Edinburgh, 1731.

Lenman, Bruce. *The Jacobite Cause.* National Trust for Scotland. Glasgow, 1986.

*A Letter from a Member of the Parliament of Scotland to his Electors.* n.p., 1702.

*A Letter to a Tory Friend.* London, 1745/46.

Levack, Brian P. *The Formation of the British State: England, Scotland, and the Union 1603–1707.* Oxford, 1987.

Lewis, Mary Ellen B. '"The joy of my heart": Robert Burns as Folklorist'. *Scottish Studies* 20 (1976).

Lindsay, Maurice. *Robert Burns.* 2nd edn. London, 1968.

Linklater, Magnus and Hesketh, Christian. *For King and Conscience: John Graham of Claverhouse, Viscount Dundee.* London, 1989.

Livingstone of Bachuil, Alastair, Aikman, Christian W. H., and Hart, Betty Stuart. *Muster Roll of Prince Charles Edward Stuart's Army 1745–46.* Foreword by Sir Donald Cameron of Lochiel KT. Introduction by Bruce P. Lenman. Aberdeen, 1985 (1984).

Lock, F.P . *The Politics of Gulliver's Travels.* Oxford, 1980.

Logue, Kenneth John. 'Popular Disturbances in Scotland 1780–1815'. Unpublished Ph.D. thesis. Edinburgh, 1977.

Lucas, John. *England and Englishness: Ideas of Nationhood in English Poetry 1688–1900.* London, 1991 (1990).

MacDonald, Keith Norman. *MacDonald Bards from Mediaeval Times*. Edinburgh, 1900.

MacDowell, Margaret. *The Emigrant Experience: Songs of Highland Emigrants in North America*. Toronto, 1982.

McDowell, R. B. *Irish Political Opinion 1750–1800*. London, 1944.

McEwen, John. *Who Owns Scotland*. 2nd edn. Edinburgh, 1981 (1977).

Maclean, Magnus. *The Literature of the Celts*. London, Glasgow and Dublin, 1902.

Macleary, K. *Historical Memoirs of Rob Roy*. Edinburgh, 1881.

McLynn, Frank. 'Voltaire and the Jacobite Rising of 1745'. *Studies in Voltaire and the Eighteenth Century* 185 (1980), 7–20.

  'Jacobitism and the Classical British Empiricists'. *British Journal for Eighteenth-Century Studies* 4 (1981), 155–170.

  *The Jacobite Army in England 1745*. Edinburgh, 1983.

Maguire, W. A. (ed.). *Kings in Conflict: The Revolutionary War in Ireland and its Aftermath*. Belfast, 1990.

Mahl, Mary R. and Keon, Helene (eds.). *The Female Spectator: English Writers Before 1800*. Bloomington and London, 1977; New York, 1977.

Malcolmson, Robert W. *Popular Recreations in English Society 1700–1850*. Cambridge, 1977.

Mathew, David. *Scotland Under Charles I*. London, 1955.

Mathieson, William Law. *The Awakening of Scotland*. Glasgow, 1910.

Mazzeo, Joseph A. 'Cromwell as Davidic King'. *Reason and Imagination*. New York, 1962.

Mercer, Vivian. 'Swift and the Gaelic Tradition'. *Review of English Literature* 3 (1962).

Moore, Donald (ed.). *Wales in the Eighteenth Century*. Swansea, 1976.

Muder, Wolfgang. *Tradition and Innovation in Folk Literature*. New England, 1987.

*The Murmurers: A Poem*. London, 1689.

Nairne, Lady Caroline. *The Songs of Lady Nairne*. London and Edinburgh, 1911.

*A Narrative of the Late Treatment of the Episcopal Ministers*. London, 1708.

Nokes, David. *Raillery and Rage: A Study of Eighteenth-Century Satire*. Brighton, 1987.

Norbrook, David. *Poetry and Politics in the English Renaissance*. London and Boston, 1984.

O Luain, Cathal. *For a Celtic Future*. Dublin, 1983.

O'Rahilly, Cecile (ed.). *Five Seventeenth-Century Political Poems*. Dublin, 1952.

Overton, J. H. *William Law: Nonjuror and Mystic*. London, 1881.

Parsons, Coleman O. '*Waverley*: Jacobite History and the Historical Novel'. *Scotia* 7 (1983).

*The Patch. An Hero-Comical Poem*. By a Gentleman of Oxford. London, 1724.

*The Pious Life and Sufferings of the Reverend Dr Henry Sacheverell*. n.p., 1710.

Pitsligo, Alexander Lord Forbes of. *Essays Moral and Philosophical on Several Subjects*. London, 1734.

Pittock, Murray G. H. 'Sources and Dates for the Jacobite Lyric'. *Archives* 20:89 (April 1993), 25–9.

Plumb, Sir J. H. *The Growth of Political Stability in England 1675–1725*. London, 1967.

*Poem on Her Sacred Majesty Queen Anne*. Edinburgh, 1703.

*The Poetical Works of the Inimitable Don Carlos, Commonly called the Young Chevalier.* With An Introductory LETTER from a Gentleman in *Edinburgh* to his Friend at *London*, giving a very curious Account of this pious Bard's Sentiments about *Religion* and *Morality*. London, 1745.

*Political Ballads of the Seventeenth and Eighteenth Centuries.* Annotated by W. Walker Wilkins. 2 vols. (vol. 2). London, 1860.

*Political Fables with Proper Reflections.* London, 1721.

*Political Poems.* Written by a Student at Oxford. London, 1719.

*The Poems of Alexander Pope.* Volume v: *The Dunciad.* Ed. James Sutherland. London, 1963.

Porter, Roy. *English Society in the Eighteenth Century.* London, 1982.

*Reasons Why the Parliament of Scotland cannot comply with the late K. JAMES'S Proclamation.* London, 1689.

Reynolds, Myra. *The Learned Lady in England 1650–1760.* Vassar Semi-Centennial Studies. Boston and New York, 1920.

*The Rhapsody.* London, 1750.

Riley, P. W. J. *The Union of England and Scotland.* Manchester: Manchester University Press, 1978.

Rogers, Pat. 'The Waltham Blacks and the Black Act'. *The Historical Journal* 17 (1974), 465–86.

*The Royal Blackbird.* Waterford, n.d.

*The Royal Stuart Calendar 1931.* Ed. David Ross Fotheringham.

Ryan, Desmond (ed.). *The 1916 Poets.* An Chomhairle Ealaian series of Irish Authors Number Five. Westport, Connecticut: Greenwood Press Publishers, 1979 (1963).

Sambrook, James. *James Thomson: A Life.* Oxford, 1991.

Saur, K. G. (ed. with Adolf M. Birke and Kurt Kluxen). *England und Hanover: England and Hanover.* Prince Albert Studies Volume 4. Munich and London, 1986.

Schwoerer, Lois G. (ed.). *The Revolution of 1688–1689: Changing Perspectives.* Cambridge, 1992.

*Scotland's Grievance.* Edinburgh, 1746.

Scott, P. H. *1707: The Union of Scotland and England.* Edinburgh, 1979.

*The Scottish Toleration Argued.* London, 1712.

*The Scottish Toleration Truly Stated in a Letter to a Peer.* London, 1712.

Sharpe, J. A. *Crime and the Law in English Satirical Prints 1600–1832.* Cambridge, 1986.

Sherburn, George. *Roehenstart.* Edinburgh & London, 1960.

Shields, Hugh. *A Short Bibliography of Irish Folk Song.* Folk Music Society of Ireland booklet 2 (1985).

Simmons, James C. *The Novelist as Historian: Essays on the The Victorian Historical Novel.* The Hague; Paris, 1973.

Simpson, Margaret Stewart. *The Scottish Songstress: Caroline Baroness Nairne.* Edinburgh and London, 1894.

Southern, A. *Clavers The Despot's Champion.* London, 1889.

Speck, W. A. *Tory and Whig: The Struggle in the Constituencies 1701–1715.* London, 1970.

*Society and Literature in England 1700–60.* Dublin, 1983.

Stafford, John J. *The Pretender or The Rose of Alvey.* London, 1845.

Starr, Nathan Comfort. *King Arthur Today.* University of Florida Press, 1954.

Swire, Otta F. *The Highlands and Their Legends.* Edinburgh and London, 1963.

*The Tale of the Robin-red-breast, A Poem By the AUTHOR of the Black-Bird's Tale.* London, 1710.

Tayler, Alistair and Henrietta. *Jacobites of Aberdeenshire and Banffshire in the Rising of 1715.* Edinburgh and London, 1934.

*1715: The Story of the Rising.* London, 1936.

Tayler, Henrietta (ed.). *The Jacobite Court at Rome in 1719.* Edinburgh: Scottish History Society, Third Series Vol. XXXI, 1938.

Taylor, Beverly and Brewer, Elizabeth. *The Return of King Arthur.* Cambridge, 1983.

Terry, Charles Sandford. *The Jacobites and the Union.* Cambridge 1922.

*The Theatre-Royal Turn'd into a Mountebank's Stage.* By a Non-Non-Juror. London, 1718.

*The Trial and Life of Thomas Cappoch.* 2nd edn. Carlisle, 1839.

*The Trials of James, Duncan, and Robert M'Gregor.* Edinburgh, 1818.

Tunstall, William, Gent. *A Collection of Ballads and some other Occasional Poems.* London, 1727.

Van der Zee, Henri and Barbara. *Revolution in the Family.* London, 1988.

*Verses Occasion'd by the Present Rebellion.* London, 1745.

*Villpone: Or, Remarks on Some Proceedings in Scotland.* n.p., 1707.

*The Vision of Good King Hezekiah.* London, 1710.

Weinbrot, Howard. *Augustan Caesar in 'Augustan' England: The Decline of a Classical Norm.* Princeton, 1978.

Welding, Sir A. *A Cat May look upon a King.* Amsterdam, 1714.

*A Whip for the Weesil.* London, 1690.

Whyte, Lawrence. *Poems on Various Subjects.* Dublin, 1740.

Wilkes, John. *The History of England from the Revolution to the Accession of the Brunswick Line.* Vol. I. London, 1768.

Williams, Gwyn A. *The Welsh in their History.* Beckenham, 1985 (1982).

Wright, William. *Jacobite Curse, or Excommunication of King George and his subjects.* Glasgow, 1714.

## Manuscripts and Broadsides

Aberdeen University Library MS. 2222.

AUL MS 2740/4/18/1 (Pitsligo papers – including 14/15, Memsie and Aucheries copies of apologia for the Rising).

Bodleian MS Eng. misc. c116.

Bodleian MS Eng. Poet. e87 (Western MSS. 46482).

National Library of Scotland ACC 9202.

NLS Adv. MS 19.1.13.

NLS Adv. MS 19.3.44 (Balcarres' Memoirs).

NLS Deposit 221/62 (Maitland's *Aeneid*).

NLS FB. l. 162: 'The Highlander's RIDDLE, Or Who's in the Right: Tell if you can'.

NLS MS 98 (Irish Brigade recruitment in Scotland f. 39).

NLS MS 210 (Charles Kirkpatrick Sharpe ballad collection).

NLS MS 300 ('Rebellion').

NLS MS 1695.

NLS MS 1696.

NLS MS 2092.

NLS MS 3740 (unrest in N. Ireland).

NLS MS 10782.

NLS MS 16971 f. 1 (potentially treasonable conduct of Pelham).

NLS Rosebery Collection: 'Scotch Ballads and Broadsides 1679–1730'. Ry. III.a.10.

NLS Wodrow Collection XIII Quarto 48.

Public Record Office SP 35/22/57.

PRO SP 35/41/86.

PRO SP 35/42/35.

PRO SP 36/79/19.

# Index

CAMBRIDGE STUDIES IN EIGHTEENTH-CENTURY
ENGLISH LITERATURE AND THOUGHT